LETHALITY IN COMBAT

A STUDY OF THE TRUE NATURE OF BATTLE

BIG SKY PUBLISHING
www.bigskypublishing.com.au

Copyright © Tom Lewis 2012

First published 2012

Big Sky Publishing Pty Ltd
PO Box 303, Newport, NSW 2106, Australia
Phone: 1300 364 611
Fax: (61 2) 9918 2396
Email: info@bigskypublishing.com.au
Web: www.bigskypublishing.com.au

Cover design and typesetting: Think Productions

National Library of Australia Cataloguing-in-Publication entry
Author: Lewis, Tom, 1958-

Title: Lethality in combat : a study of the true nature on battle / Tom Lewis.

ISBN: 9781921941511 (hbk)

Notes: Includes bibliographical references and index.

Subjects: Combat--Moral and ethical aspects.
          Shooting, Military.
          Civilian war casualties.

Dewey Number: 355.02
Printed in China through Bookbuilders

LETHALITY IN COMBAT

A STUDY OF THE TRUE NATURE OF BATTLE

BIG SKY PUBLISHING
www.bigskypublishing.com.au

TOM LEWIS

THE AUSTRALIAN ARMY HISTORY COLLECTION

ARMY·HISTORY·UNIT

PROTECTING ARMY HERITAGE
PROMOTING ARMY HISTORY

Winning with Intelligence
Judy Thomas

Duntroon
Darren Moore

The Warrior Poets
Robert Morrison

The History of the Royal Australian Corps of Transport 1973–2000
Albert Palazzo

Defenders of Australia
Albert Palazzo

The Fight Leaders
D. Butler, A. Argent and J. Shelton

Operation Orders
Pat Beale

Little by Little
Michael Tyquin

Red Coats to Cams
Ian Kuring

Bowler of Gallipoli
Frank Glen

Vets at War
Ian M. Parsonson

Only One River to Cross
A.M. Harris

The Fragile Forts
Peter Oppenheim

Hassett: Australian Leader
John Essex-Clark

Persian Expedition
Alan Stewart

The Chiefs of the Australian Army
James Wood

Never Late
Gordon Dickens

To Villers-Bretonneux
Peter Edgar

Madness and the Military
Michael Tyquin

The Battle of Anzac Ridge 25 April 1915
Peter D. Williams

Doves Over the Pacific
Reuben R.E. Bowd

The Lionheart
David Coombes

Battlefield Korea
Maurie Pears

Chemical Warfare in Australia
Geoff Plunkett

A Most Unusual Regiment
M.J. Ryan

Between Victor and Vanquished
Arthur Page

Country Victoria's Own
Neil Leckie

Surgeon and General
Ian Howie-Willis

Willingly into the Fray
Catherine McCullagh

Beyond Adversity
William Park

Crumps and Camouflets
Damien Finlayson

More than Bombs and Bandages
Kirsty Harris

The Last Knight
Robert Lowry

Forgotten Men
Michael Tyquin

Battle Scarred
Craig Deayton

Crossing the Wire
David Coombes

Do Unto Others
Alan H Smith

Letters from Timor
Graeme Ramsden

I Confesss
John Joseph Murray

Fallen Sentinel
Peter Beale

Sir William Glasgow
Peter Edgar

Traning the Bodes
Terry Smith

CONTENTS

Introduction...1

On the veracity of sources 4

Acknowledgements..12

Glossary...13

Part One – Enthusiastic Warriors: the Necessary Face of War....................15

1. The necessary face of war..16

2. Combat euphoria 30

3. Necessary enthusiasm for combat in leadership behaviour 48

4. Revenge as a motivator 64

5. Aggression in flying tactics 74

6. The prevalence of lethal behaviour...86

7. Ultimate discipline in battle 102

8. Desecrating the dead: military necessity or abhorrent behaviour? 112

Part Two – Prisoner-Taking and the Reality of Combat............................135

9. The rules of surrender..136

10. Surrendering to a hot-blooded enemy 150

11. Killing in revenge: understandable behaviour?.....................................172

12. Killing in cold blood for military necessity 183

13. The killing of enemy wounded: an excusable necessity? 201

14. Executions...217

CONTENTS

Part Three – Targeting Civilians: Who is the Enemy?..................................**241**

15. Verification of the enemy..242

16. Targeting civilians for military necessity.....................................259

17. Is that village friendly?...270

18. Conclusions..285

References 287

Endnotes 300

Introduction

War is an ugly thing, but not the ugliest of things. The decayed and degraded state of moral and patriotic feeling which thinks that nothing is worth war is much worse. The person who has nothing for which he is willing to fight, nothing which is more important than his own personal safety, is a miserable creature and has no chance of being free unless made and kept so by the exertions of better men than himself.

John Stuart Mill
English economist and philosopher

This book was written for a number of reasons. The first is that it seeks to illustrate the truth of combat. It sets out to destroy several myths, and to understand the true nature of lethal behaviour in war.

It also seeks to counter an attitude that seems to have developed among some people that lethal behaviour in battle is somehow wrong. Joanna Bourke, for example, in *An Intimate History of Killing*, said that she aimed to 'put killing back into military history'[1], and presents to her readers her disgust that armies and soldiers have undergone a 'monstrous and multifarious celebration of violence'. Of course they did, and they still should – if they want to survive and to win. The whole point of warfare is to be lethal, and that means that training for combat must concentrate on turning people into killers. Indeed, what Bourke condemns as a 'celebration of violence' is to be applauded, for only by being enthusiastic about their task can those placed in the actuality of combat survive.

Studies by SLA Marshall of World War II suggested that troops have an aversion to taking life.[2] As a result, a more positive attitude towards being lethal was introduced in many armed forces, with more aggression worked into initial training; greater dehumanising of the enemy, for better targeting; and greater firepower introduced into the battlefield. Marshall may well be right in that soldiers may begin their combat experience with aversion. But that must be changed, and usually is changed, to make those charged with dealing in death more capable. Successful soldiers in battle are killers, and they must be determined to kill.

Warfare is about exterminating the enemy. It is unpleasant for some, and for others it probably is the ultimate 'high'. Nevertheless, it is sometimes necessary for countries to go to war. And when they do, it is foolish to go into combat with too many restrictions: the idea is to win, with as minimal a cost to your side as possible. But films such as *Platoon* portray the infantry soldier in a negative light: he is sinning; he is doing bad things; he is to be condemned. It has become fashionable to attack those who go too far, such as Lieutenant Calley in Vietnam, without considering what sort of constraints and demands were placed on those soldiers, and what system allowed them to do what are undeniably bad things. The aggression unleashed by modern warriors is debated by people sitting at home, who have the wars of today beamed into their lounge rooms, and who find it easy and fashionable to criticise their own soldiers for firing at retreating Iraqi troops.[3] Political parties and the United Nations insist on placing foolish Rules of Engagement on the soldier in combat.[4] A 'Green' political party announces that it will save money by getting rid of the 'offensive' capabilities of a country's armed force.[5] A soldier is charged with 'kicking an enemy corpse' after combat.[6] Another is branded a murderer on the front page of national newspapers for ensuring that a wounded non-uniformed guerilla is actually dead by shooting him when he stirs.[7] By way of a response, British soldiers on duty in Iraq have cynically suggested they need a solicitor with them before they shoot back at any Iraqi who attacks them.[8]

Bourke presents us with instances such as, 'In 1955 two senior American officers directed that "the killing of an individual enemy with a rifle, grenade, bayonet – yes, even the bare hands – is the mission of the Army"'. Her tone suggests that sort of behaviour is worthy of condemnation, evil, and to be outlawed. This book suggests a dichotomous alternative – that it is correct, to be practised with eagerness, and carried out efficiently. That is what soldiers are for, and that is what they fight for – to survive and to win. Readers must suspend their aversion and horror to examine and understand the true face of battle.

This book looks at infantry fighting, tactical aviation combat, and submarine attacks on shipping, and argues that:

- While warriors may be initially reluctant to engage in taking life, once combat is joined and the first fatality inflicted, they are more lethal than we usually suppose

- Many engage in inflicting death with ferocity, and that indeed to be effective, soldiers need to be 'enthusiastic warriors'

- While revulsion at the trade of the soldier is a common public response to a conflict's first battles, as civilians are targeted, they become more sympathetic to the soldier's creed and necessary behaviour in battle

- Many soldiers fail to accept enemies surrendering, and prisoners are often shot out of hand rather than taken. This is often unavoidable, and sometimes even a military necessity

- The dead enemy are often mistreated, and this may well be normal behaviour

- If combatants can possibly be confused with civilians, then civilians are routinely dispatched

- Such scenarios are part of all tactical combat, and further examples are given from the areas of aviation and submarine warfare

- Such scenarios are part of normal battle, and cannot be discarded without psychological disadvantage to those who avoid the truth of battle

- Given such lethality, the concept of 'rules of war' is questionable

- If these behaviours normally occur, then most warriors engage in war crimes

- If this condition is unavoidable, then the concept of tactical war crimes is flawed.

This book is a request for a change in the conventions and rules of warfare. It is not an encouragement of ferocious combat without some semblance of rules or pity, but to correct what the author perceives as inconsistencies and illogicalities.

Shakespeare gave us the line, 'Cry "Havoc", and let slip the dogs of war'.[9] We need to reevaluate our understanding of what happens when the dogs of war are let off the leash. If we want lethality from our warriors, we will also have to understand the human nature of the warriors that we let go: they will kill with ferocity, and the genie cannot be put back in the bottle.

On the veracity of sources

*Let the Staff write their own books
about the Great War, says I.
The infantry were biased against them.
And their authentic story will
be read with interest.*

Siegfried Sassoon, World War I infantry officer and poet.

This study draws on both published and unpublished accounts of soldiers' experiences in battle. Some may argue that the rationale for proving the thesis is too selective. Indeed, many diaries and letters written by combat personnel have been examined, but only some have been used because they support the thesis.

It might be suggested that the majority of combat soldiers do not react in the manner proposed. However, it must not be forgotten that soldiers have many reasons for censoring their own accounts of their experiences. They may have done something for which they can be held accountable legally, so why would they wish to admit their actions in writing? Any soldier experienced in the ways of military forces knows there are lots of ways to get into trouble, thereby bringing on a grinding and tiresome disciplinary mechanism that can take years rather than months to reach its finale. Military justice is quite inexorable, and anyone who has survived basic training in a military force is extremely wary of invoking its wrath.

Second, military personnel know full well they may be held accountable ethically, by others whose ethics at that time are different. They may not wish to enter into such debate, and may not wish to be judged as unethical. Will a soldier admit to his mother that yesterday he killed three prisoners in cold blood, or that he sprayed a thicket with machine-gun fire, only to find that the shots his unit received had come from two twelve-year old boys, both of whom are now dead? Do fighter pilots routinely point out to those who may praise them that their best tactic is to close to within minimal distance of an unsuspecting enemy, and then shoot him in the back?

Australian soldier Barry Heard, fighting in Vietnam, reflected that little was recorded in his diary of fights between soldiers in his company, the wild sex and drinking on leave; drunken incidents in camp; the hatred they all felt for the enemy – all of it was sanitised, as it was in letters sent home, 'avoiding the harsh realities of death and horror'.[1]

One only has to ponder the findings of historian Stephen Ambrose, who interviewed more than 1000 combat veterans. While only one admitted to having shot a prisoner, over a third said they had seen incidents where American soldiers had shot prisoners who had had their hands up.[2] In other words, behaviour such as that which is recounted here was routine, but it was not admitted to, at least to those outside the soldiers' circle.

Third, those involved in fighting may well have enjoyed what they did – in a variety of ways, from fulfilment to glee, to simply having enjoyed the adrenaline 'high' that combat often produces. For soldiers to admit to civilians that they have had such feelings may well mean that they are excluded, criticised or regarded as abnormal. As soldiers spend – in the main – a small amount of their life as combat troops, and must 'fit in' the rest of the time as quasi-civilians, they necessarily suppress such characteristics, thus making it harder for us to glean their true behaviour.

Soldiers who have returned from combat tend to be reluctant to talk about their experiences. It is often thought this is because their experiences were too traumatic to relate to others. While this can be true, it is more often the case that someone who hadn't experienced combat simply would not understand that completely different world, with a completely different set of rules, into which the combat soldier is plunged.

Reports of combat therefore differ widely. Some read like a 'boys' own adventure': the enemy dies cleanly, prisoners are taken in an orderly fashion, and no one does anything too savage. An excellent example of such a work is Erwin Rommel's account, *Infantry Attacks*, of his commands in World War I. His men behave in just such a fashion, and so too do the enemy. Only one example of nastiness can be found, and that seems to have been edited out, in part at least.

On another occasion, Rommel assures us that, in the latter half of the war when civilites had waned after two years of massive casualties, he prevented his troops – unbelievably! – from firing at enemy troops who broke and ran. [3] This sort of account is one that has had true combat behaviour sanitised from it, for the reasons given above.

Conversely, one can come across accounts that seem too bloodthirsty and sensationalistic. An example is some of the testimonies given to the Vietnam War investigations carried out by the International War Crimes Tribunal. In some of the examples of behaviour given in such cases, it seemed to have suited the political ends for a few of those giving evidence to make it sound as bloody as they could, in order to evoke the maximum amount of condemnation for those who sought to end the war.

In other exaggerated accounts, one side seeks to invoke rage from one's own country in order to invoke support for a conflict. While stories of babies being bayoneted in the early stages of World War I come to mind, variations on such stories are a recurrent motif of conflict that often does not bear closer inspection.

There are other ways an informed examiner can determine the veracity of combat accounts. Reading hundreds of source accounts, one begins to understand which have the flavour of reality, and which do not. Stories of front-line behaviour either have a ring of truth, or they seem lacking in the tiny details of veracity. For example, troopers involved in front-line operations may describe the smallest details of their equipment. Soldiers engaged in covert surveillance operations went to great lengths to ensure their equipment was examined to make sure they did not have any items that would rattle. Many soldiers engaged in patrol operations in Vietnam did not wear underwear – a small touch of reality that allows an account to ring true. Many accounts have the realistic ring of 'SNAFU' (see Glossary), which pervades many military operations: a reader who lacks military experience might think that the lack of body armour[1] for helicopter pilots in Vietnam simply would not have been allowed to happen – but situations such as that occur all the time in military operations. After all, procedures to procure such equipment are being processed by an enormous human undertaking, with all of the frailties of humans and all of their resultant weaknesses.

---

1   Mason, Robert. *Chickenhawk*. Middlesex: Penguin, 1984. The writer makes several references to the lack of chest armour for helicopter crews in one of his first postings. By comparison, another posting saw ready availability.

In summary, an informed reading can detect, or at least have some suspicion as to whether individual accounts are genuine. Where such suspicion exists, these accounts have been rejected and do not appear in this work.

It is also important for the reader to remember, when looking through the behavioural instances which follow, that it is a general rule of armed forces, especially in our technological age, that most members of such forces do not engage in combat. They are instead working in supporting arms such as personnel, logistics, communications, and so on. Even those sections which deliver artillery fire to the enemy are not engaged in the sort of combat that is being discussed here. Sergeant Bob Buick, fighting in the Australian Army in Vietnam, was of the opinion that for every rifleman who engaged the enemy there were five men backing him up in support who would not see combat. And even some front-line soldiers, he noted, would not fire a shot in anger in their whole tour of duty, or even see an enemy soldier, dead or alive.[4] So many readers, even though they may be experienced in the military world, would not have engaged in, or witnessed, the behaviours described in these pages.

The true nature of combat behaviour, therefore, is difficult to discern. The conclusions drawn here may be judged as wrong. However, I stand by them, for although it is difficult to perceive the reality, there is enough here to convince me that I have found the truth.

The more experienced a soldier is in warfare, the more he seems prepared to accept the strange – the story which sounds unbelievable to a civilian; the tale that provokes a response of, 'No, they wouldn't do that'. The research presented here tells a reader that they would – warfare sees all sorts of behaviours that one never sees elsewhere. When I began this research, I would not have believed that a fighter pilot would attempt to cut an enemy pilot, descending under a parachute, in half with his own propeller. I would not have believed that a soldier who turned up drunk, without the company rum ration he had been sent for, minutes before his comrades were to go 'over the top' would have been executed on the spot. I was of the opinion that the infamous Lieutenant Calley, of Vietnam, was a thoroughly unusual officer who behaved in an unforgivable way that defied understanding. He was not: his case is examined in detail, and what is shown is that he was a normal person pushed to the limits of stress, and that he and his men negated that stress in a boiling-over of their situation which is not unusual – My Lai was inevitable, and it was not alone.

War produces all of these behaviours and more. The fighting British brigadier, FP Crozier, who led from the front and seems to owe his survival to a sort of nonchalant yet fierce madness, commented: 'My own experience of war, which is a prolonged one, is that anything may happen in it, from the very highest kinds of chivalry and sacrifice to the very lowest form of barbaric debasement … '[5] Crozier should know: he admits to ordering men shot out of hand for cowardice, and of engaging in extremes of behaviour in battle which raise the eyebrows, all the while arguing that in fact his style was the unadmitted norm.

There is a range of combat behaviours exhibited in this book. Broadly speaking, they can be narrowed into three sections. First, tactical fighting behaviour 'in the field'. Second, attitudes and actions carried out towards prisoners. Third, attitudes and actions carried out towards civilians.

In the analysis of tactical fighting behaviour, I argue that the vast majority of soldiers exhibit the same sort of continuum. When they are first engaged in combat, they transit through a range of emotions, including fear, in various degrees from apprehension to terror. The depth of these feelings is not the same for all: some enjoy combat, although they are in the minority; most are apprehensive about it, and need stimulation to engage further. Soldiers exhibit a varying degree of proficiency and acceptance about combat.

If a soldier progresses beyond this initial experience of combat to fight on another occasion, his feelings are going to be different. The more fighting he engages in, the more time he has to adjust, to analyse his own reactions and performance, and to modify any reaction he perceives as being non-useful to his performance.

The more combat a soldier sees, the more of the range of behaviours discussed in this work he will see, and the more likely he is to engage in them himself. Soldiers learn from others how the business of tactical fighting is carried out, and what is really necessary for survival. Much of this 'on-the-job' education cannot be taught in battle schools. For example, Marine Johnnie Clark describes some of his first fighting in Vietnam. 'The three Marines approached each unmoving body with equal caution, kicking each one hard to get a groan'.[6] They are engaging in this sort of behaviour because they have learnt that apparently dead enemy are not always dead, and can still be dangerous. How can this sort of behaviour be taught in battle school, where there are no 'real' dead bodies? It cannot, although admittedly the cautionary attitudes demonstrated here can be imparted through a lecture. Clark himself later participated in a fierce fight, and then, on taking an enemy trench where a body lay, he 'stomped the man's head, then kicked him in the groin. No groan. Felt stiff.'[7] Clark is engaging in behaviour that will be condemned by many – unsuitable treatment of the enemy – but I argue that this is the central ethos of this work: real combat behaviour is largely unknown to anyone who has not engaged in tactical fighting.

The more intense the combat, the more prevalent this type of behaviour will be. This relates both to the intensity of experience for an individual, and to the intensity of experience for an armed force as whole, or as the armed force's country as a whole. So, for example, in World War II the American Intelligence Officer and PhD-qualified philosopher Glenn Gray observed that the more a soldier had lost to the war – relatives, friends – the more ferocious in his treatment of captured enemy he would be. The war turned into a vendetta, with 'hatred penetrating every fiber of his being.' His reason for living was to seek revenge, preferably a 'tenfold retaliation'.[8] Not every soldier is going to be in this situation, and therefore not all soldiers will behave in this way all of the time. So not all soldiers display the behaviour in which infantry officer (and poet) Siegfried Sassoon indulged when a close comrade in his platoon, Lance-Corporal Kendle, was killed. Sassoon obtained a bag of Mills bombs and went off and attacked a trench of Germans by himself – the enemy soldiers promptly fled. But that was not enough for the normally thoughtful and kindly Sassoon: 'I definitely wanted to kill someone at close quarters.'[9] But not all soldiers experience what Sassoon had been through – the death of a close comrade – and therefore not all soldiers feel the impetus to act in the way Sassoon did.

If a country has suffered, then its soldiers will be markedly more savage in the treatment of the enemy than those of a country which has not suffered as much. The Poles, who suffered terribly under the German advance in World War II, were cruel in revenge. Soldier RJ Weston thought they were the most ferocious and callous soldiers he had met, who 'literally butchered' any Germans they came across. He described their treatment of a captured German: they tied his hands, put a hand grenade with the pin out into his pocket, and told him to run …[10] We could not imagine a British soldier behaving the same way – in the main – but then again, if his family came from Coventry, which was substantially bombed by the Luftwaffe in World War II, then perhaps we might see such savage behaviour from a man who had lost all of his family in those bombings. A New Zealand soldier fighting in World War

II would know that his country was virtually untouched by the war, and so at a general level we would expect that New Zealand soldiers would not behave in the way Polish soldiers did.

Therefore, the treatment of prisoners – the second main focus area of this work – also differs according to the criteria given above. Not all soldiers will be placed in positions where they carry out actions which may seem to some to be doubtful treatment of prisoners. Australian soldier Richard Weston was sanguine about his unit's actions in North Africa, when three British tanks herding a large group of Afrika Korps prisoners to the rear were delayed. The Germans took the opportunity to run. Within seconds all three tanks opened fire with their machine-guns and kept shooting till none was left standing.[11] By comparison, most prisoners do not attempt mass escape – and therefore most soldiers are not involved in having to shoot prisoners. But it does happen, and often enough to be of interest to this work.

Similarly, most soldiers are not involved in combat where an enemy force, when clearly out-manoeuvred, refuses to surrender. So the experience of US infantryman Charles Gadd's unit is unusual. They had surprised many North Vietnamese soldiers swimming a river one night, and the enemy would not surrender, but retreated into the river again, and began to swim back to the other side, taking deep breaths to maximise their time underwater. The Americans called 'Come here' in Vietnamese, and fired warning shots, but the soldiers would not return. When the US forces realised they were going to get away, they opened fire.[12]

The third area of discussion this work is concerned with, the targeting of civilians by soldiers, was usual in some wars – Vietnam, for example – but unusual in others, such as World War I (although it did occur). This again is an area of controversy, but out of the three areas of the study it is the easiest to understand, and to believe that soldiers do behave in the way they did in Vietnam: targeting civilians, both for good military reason and for bad military justification. In any war where non-uniformed personnel may become combat personnel merely by picking up a weapon, soldiers are going to be suspicious, act on reflex, and fire at a person they believe – rightly or wrongly – is now a combatant. And so we come across the instance of the US Army sergeant who related:

> Yesterday I shot and killed a little 8- or 9-year-old girl, with the sweetest, most innocent little face, and the nastiest grenade in her hand, that you ever saw. Myself and six others were walking along, when she ran out

to throw that grenade at us. Of course there is always the old argument that it was either us or her, but what in hell right did I have to kill a little child?[13]

This was an action which was militarily unavoidable. But we also come across the converse: US Army combat advisor Martin Dockery noted of his patrols with the South Vietnamese Army that 'any farmer who ran from us was shot'.[14] It would be doubtful that all of these people are in fact 'fleeing Vietcong', and such behaviour is not argued as being justifiable.

In summary, the book's methodology is to examine accounts of combat, reject them if they seem false, and use them to suit the three main areas of discussion of the work.

The term 'infantry' is used generally and inaccurately in this book. Normally it means the attacking foot-soldiers of an army, who fight with a variety of weapons and who are organised into platoons of roughly 30–50 men. These soldiers are designated as infantry, although that may be tagged with Armoured Infantry, or Mounted Infantry – to designate soldiers carried into battle in armoured vehicles, or helicopters, or Airborne, to distinguish paratroopers.

However, the account also draws on the experiences of those in other areas who fight the personal tactical battle. Therefore it examines accounts from members of armed forces – including navy and air force – who fight in close contact against the enemy, using the traditional weapons of the infantry: rifles, pistols, bayonets, machine-guns and so on. I apologise for including Marines and other specialised forces in this loose description.

The work concentrates on six wars in the main, but I have made reference to others where it suits me. This is not being too selective, I hope, for to properly examine all wars would have been impossible. Nevertheless, in the main the work concentrates on the second Boer conflict, World War I and World War II, Korea, Vietnam and the Falklands. These have been chosen simply for the reason that we may surmise the soldier of the 20th century to be more literate than his counterparts in previous conflicts, and therefore he has left us more to examine.

The work proposes that what is found in the following pages represents the true, and largely unknown, face of battle.

Acknowledgements

The author would like to extend his gratitude to the following people for their assistance in compiling this work.

Craig Tibbitts, the Curator of Official Records, Australian War Memorial; and the librarians of the Australian Defence Force Academy Library.

My editor Peter Dennis, who made many helpful suggestions; Roger Lee of the Australian Army History Unit; and my copy editor, Sean Doyle.

Maurice Ellvey and Alexandra Wyles for their readings of the manuscript in its draft stages.

In alphabetical order, historians Greg Blake, John Bradford, Hal Colebatch and Peter Williams for their critical comment and suggestions.

Chaplains Collin Acton, RAN, Dean Griffiths of the RAAF, and Sergeant Andrew Barham of the Australian Army for their comments.

My wife, Kaylene Anderson, who put up with his impassioned critique of far too many "war films", but who also was prevailed upon to "read this", to understand the nature of this work.

Glossary

ARVN	Army of the Republic of Vietnam – the Southern army.
CAR-15	Colt Automatic Rifle – used in Vietnam by some units.
FO	Forward Observer – calls in artillery or air strikes where necessary.
K-bar	A combat knife used by US forces in Vietnam.
Kit Carson	The term for a Vietnamese scout, usually a Vietcong or North Vietnamese Army (NVA) soldier who had deserted and was fighting for the other side in the Vietnam War. Kit Carson was a famous scout of the American West in the mid-1800s.
MACV	Military Assistance Command, Vietnam.
M-16	The automatic or semi-automatic assault rifle used by US forces in Vietnam.
M60 machine gun	A heavy machine-gun, belt-fed, used by US and Australian forces in Vietnam. Usually supported by a bipod, this weapon delivered heavier and more accurate fire than that dispensed by the M-16, although that was also an automatic weapon.
M79 grenade launchers	A rifle used for firing grenades, much further and more accurately than they could be thrown by hand, in Vietnam.
Marine	The British and the US armed forces have employed Marines for a long time. They typically are infantry forces capable of going to sea and being landed in amphibious assaults.

Glossary

NCO	Non-commissioned officer: corporal, sergeant, etc. Officers' commissions are routinely given by a monarch or president, and cannot be lightly removed, indeed often only by a parliament. NCOs, below the rank of warrant officer, can be dismissed more easily.
POW	Prisoner of War.
PFC	Private First Class, US Army – one rank below SP-4.
Sp-4	Specialist, US Army – one rank below Corporal.
SAS	Special Air Service – multi-disciplinary assault troops.
Second Lieutenant	The lowest officer rank of many armies; the equivalent of a naval Midshipman or an air force Pilot Officer.
SNAFU	World War II acronym – 'Situation Normal, All Fouled (or Fucked) Up'.
VC	Vietcong – irregular and usually non-uniformed forces of North Vietnam.
VC	Victoria Cross – the highest decoration for valour in the face of the enemy, in the armies of the British Commonwealth.
Zippo	The famous US cigarette lighter.

PART ONE

Enthusiastic Warriors: the Necessary Face of War

1
The necessary face of war

For it's Tommy this, an' Tommy that, an' 'Chuck him out, the brute!'
But it's 'Saviour of 'is country' when the guns begin to shoot.

Rudyard Kipling

Necessary efficiency

How savage in combat are infantry? Very much so – enthusiastic and keen, if they want to survive. Infantry survive because of their abilities. These include speed of reaction, appropriateness of reaction – use a grenade on a group as opposed to a rifle – willingness to fire, and acceptance as opposed to revulsion when inflicting violence. Often, they cannot hesitate when in a combat situation. Audie Murphy recalled after the D-Day landings:

> As I round a slight bend in the gully, I run head-on into two Germans. For an instant they recoil in surprise; and that is their mistake. My combat experience has taught me the value of split seconds. Before the Germans can regain their balance, I kill them both with a carbine.[1]

Murphy, the most highly-decorated soldier of America's armies in World War II, was by his own account, and of others, a most efficient dispatcher of the enemy. In one battle, where he and his squad encountered heavy resistance, he stormed two positions, one after the other, and killed at least nine German soldiers.[2] He dispatched, by one estimate, 241[3] of the enemy, and in one engagement led an assault where he personally killed 50 soldiers.[4] There are other, albeit rare, examples from other armies. The Australian soldier Albert Jacka was thought so effective by his brigadier that 'A company under his lead was as good as an extra battalion to me' – testimony to Jacka's extreme aggression in combat and the spirit it imbued in his men.[5] US soldier David Rubitsky was estimated by the US Army to have killed over 500 of the enemy when fighting in New Guinea, and said of himself, 'I was completely an insane man'.[6] Then again, many soldiers don't get to shoot down anyone.

The philosopher and soldier J. Glenn Gray thought of such keen soldiers as 'soldier-killers', possessing a 'consuming lust which swallows up other pleasures'. Such people are denied, said Gray, ' … more normal satisfactions'.[7] This study occasionally glimpses such people, but does not suggest that all combat personnel could or should become such 'ultimate warriors'. Nevertheless, the encouragement of warriors to be lethal is essential.

The dilemma of encouraging lethality, and the ultimate warrior

There is a dilemma in the encouragement of such warriors for most modern societies. In peace they may be controversial figures who are perceived as too aggressive, too serious, and too potentially combative. As war is joined, they may be seen as infringing Rules of Engagement, or coming dangerously close to committing war crimes. As combat becomes heavier and closer, they emerge, like Mr Hyde, to take their place at the focus of battle, where after a time they are rewarded with honours and praise. In a little while they are pointed out as being an example to follow, and their actions are regarded with awe and admiration. When peace is joined, they are praised and feted, but regarded uneasily by some. Many of them are urged to quietly fade away to obscurity. After a while, their behaviour is criticised by a few, and then as peace lengthens, more join in that criticism, forgetting that they and their country may have been well saved by such men from annihilation.

Given that, when expert warriors are needed, a strategic battle needs someone like General Patton, and a tactical engagement needs someone like Audie Murphy, how are armed forces to solve the dichotomy of the necessary warrior in peace and war?

Playing by the rules

Firstly, we should understand that assaulting an enemy in wartime is not always a matter of fighting every day. Infantry combat is not all the stuff of engagement after engagement; terrified infantry crouching in trenches; tanks sweeping in squadrons towards each other; constant brave charges resulting in hand-to-hand combat, and so on. These things happen only occasionally. Movies have deceived the general public because they only present the exciting action scenarios. Anyone who has served in military forces knows of the boredom, incompetence and general SNAFU scenarios of military operations. After all, military operations contain enormous numbers of variables – such as equipment and planning – and all of this utilises humans, with all their usual problems: fear, lethargy, jealously, incompetence, self-serving scheming and more. The military analyst Carl von Clausewitz called this the 'friction of war'. To get an operation mounted consists of manipulating all of this, and lots of waiting time: warfare in the field often consists of very little happening. 'War,' said World War II Marine EB Sledge, 'is mostly waiting'.[8] World War I Australian soldier Albert Jones was surprised at how little there was to do when he arrived in France in March 1916: he noted three months later that 'it's been one long rest since I hit France'. But then again, as a signaller he was experiencing a quiet time, because preparations were being made for the Somme campaign.[9]

For example, Henry Metelmann's account of his World War II service in the Wermacht is remarkable for the amount of time he describes not being in combat, but patrolling, repairing his tank, being transported from place to place, and so on. And wars do not go from peace to savage combat the instant they are declared: the Boer War's beginnings saw a respectful attitude taken on each side, with firing ceasing in order to take wounded away, and shouted 'pleasantries' between opposing positions.[10] World War I saw the interesting spectacle in 1914 in Europe where both sides largely broke off combat for Christmas Day – an attitude that would not be seen again, for, as we shall see, lethality increases in proportion to the damage inflicted on one's side.[11] For the whole day, despite the preliminary exhortations from some officers to stop, along the Line many British and Germans talked, played football, swapped food and drink, and unofficially agreed that the truce would end at midnight.[12] British officer Bruce Bairnsfather swapped buttons from his uniform with a German officer.[13] It was different the next year. George Coppard was on the front line in December 1915 when an officer came to their position; specially commissioned with visiting the troops and telling them there was not to be a repetition of that break in the fighting this year. It was not necessary, thought Coppard:

> Speaking for my companions and myself, I can categorically state that we were in no mood for any joviality with Jerry. In fact, after what we had been through since Loos, we hated his bloody guts. We were bent

on his destruction at each and every opportunity for all the miseries and privations which were our lot. Our greatest wish was to be granted an enemy target worthy of our Vickers gun.[14]

Robert Graves tells of two other occasions when shouted conversations were held between the opposing sides, items exchanged, and so on.[15] There are plenty of peaceful scenes in warfare. Infantry officer Siegfried Sassoon spent many an evening in France musing on the beauty of the dusk:

Wednesday, 6.15pm. On Crawley Ridge. Ormand up here in the redoubt with a few men. I relieve him while he goes down to get his dinner. Very still evening; sun rather hazy. Looking across to Fricourt; trench mortars bursting in the cemetery; dull white smoke floats slowly away over ... green grass with buttercups and saffron weeds ... Sky full of lark songs. Sometimes you can count thirty slowly and hear no sound of a shot; then the muffled pop of a rifle or a slamming 5.9 ... [16]

Tony Ashworth, in *Trench Warfare, 1914–18: the Live and Let Live System*, suggests[17] that there were many 'quiet sectors' on the Western Front where aggressive action was not pursued. This is not surprising, though: in materiel terms the two sides could not fight for every hour of the day. In the European land theatres of WWI, for much of the time both sides refused to withdraw, and occasionally attacked, and so on, for the whole weary campaign. Australian soldier Barry Heard fought in Vietnam, and noted that battle was not as reported in the newspapers, where one engagement followed another. In fact, Heard observed, most of his infantry unit's time was spent on 'exhausting patrols', with an 'odd brief contact' on occasion. [18]

So combat is not characterised by firing at all and every appearance of the enemy. In many wars it is almost a staged scenario: they are mounting an attack, so we must defend. Next week we will assault. If we shell them, they will shell back, so let's not open fire. CS Lewis – later, the famous children's author – observed that this principle was still in effect in 1917 when he joined his infantry unit as a new officer to the War. He was being shown his unit's position, and spotted some Germans in the far distance. On suggesting that a shot be taken with a rifle grenade, his sergeant acquiesced, but added that ' ... once 'ee start doing that kind of thing, 'ee'll get zummit back, zee?'[19]

Courage in quantity is often the element most needed in close quarter combat. The Western Front of WWI saw men tested to their utmost as units fought out the war with enemy formations sometimes only yards away for weeks. Here Private J Hines, A Company, 45th Battalion, sits with his trophies obtained on the morning of the advance of the 4th and 13th Brigades at Polygon Wood, in the Ypres Sector, during the Third Battle of Ypres. AWM E00822

Adherence to unwritten rules is a constant factor in war. Eddie Rickenbacker describes an incident in 1918 where a German sniper in some woods fired on an American burial party and injured one soldier. The rest took their weapons and disappeared in the direction of the marksman, returning a little while later to finish the ceremony. Curious because he had not heard firing, the visiting officer then walked over to where the soldiers had gone, and found ' ... the German sniper who had had the yellowness to fire upon a burial party. The man's head was crushed flat with the butts of the doughboys' guns.'[20] One had to play by the rules, and engage in combat where appropriate. So lethality is not encouraged all of the time. Private George Coppard, fighting in France in WWI, noted that peace was a general enough rule, because ' ... if one side started up any bloody nonsense, then the other would follow suit. And that's how it was for days on end, except for snipers'.[21]

Some units may have been more accommodating than others, and some nationalities too. Arthur Gould Lee cites the time he was flying his Sopwith Pup over the Allied and German lines in World War I, and was puzzled to see grass growing in front of some trenches. He was low enough to be able to identify the uniforms: some of the troops below waved to him, and he identified them as Portuguese. 'On this part of the front both sides had agreed to live and let live'.[22] An Australian battalion assigned to a section of the Lines relieved the British '5th Yorks'. Upon inspecting their position and the enemy to the front, they were astonished to see two Germans in plain view in their sector, obviously an everyday occurrence. One of the Australian officers thought that things were about to change rapidly: 'In a few days ... it will be war to the teeth.'[23]

World War II, thought Infantryman Bill Mauldin, did not have the same level of live-and-let-live attitude; rather, the two sides hurled abuse or sarcastic comments at each other when within shouting distance. Nevertheless, there was still some sense of playing by the rules: he noted that if propaganda leaflets were fired at the enemy, the Americans would stop all firing while they were retrieved.[24] There are countless scenarios, too, some of them outlined elsewhere in this work, where fighting stops to allow wounded to be recovered. Pleasantries may be even exchanged, but after a while, both sides return to their positions and the campaign returns to its daily routine: occasional sniping, infrequent 'hates', determined preparation, and inevitably the concentrated assault. All war has a rhythm.

Combat fulfilment

When extended combat is joined, it is often met with a keen willingness to fight. This is strange for the civilian, but understandable for soldiers. The Royal Navy toast, shared by its Canadian, New Zealand and Australian cousins – as used on a Friday night – is for 'a willing foe and sea room' – somewhat terrible to the outsider, and puzzling as well. However, this might be considered the toast of the warrior: one who has trained hard and long in the profession of arms. Now, those toasting say – if we are given an enemy who is just as willing, and sufficient ocean in order to bring about a battle, we may show our qualities and our mettle. So it is in many armed forces: an understandable desire to prove one's worth. And so in a US movie theatre in North Carolina, when the commencement of the war was announced, all of the Marines present burst into their anthem 'From the Halls of Montezuma'. They threw their hats in the air, and then 'snake danced in the aisles', according to one of their officers, who pondered: 'Do the Japs know what they have started – if they could see the reactions of the Marines?'[25]

Many warriors accept what their job is – exterminating the enemy – and go about it with great efficiency. These are the ones who are the best at what they do. Sergeant J. Fitzpatrick in World War I recalled killing many men: 'I probably shot off going on for a hundred rounds and I reckon at least 80 percent scored hits.'[26] A German warrior was no less capable. He recalled that he ' … turned to the lower trench. It seethed with English. I fired off my cartridges so fiercely I pressed the trigger ten times at least after the last shot. A man next to me threw bombs among them as they scrambled to get away.'[27]

The infantry officer Robert Graves was a soldier who took his job seriously, and he seems to have been necessarily lethal in his behaviour. He reflected that he would not take unnecessary risks, but he had a job to do, and so he shot and bombed as was necessary for a competent infantry officer. He only once refrained from shooting a German when he had the opportunity, when sniping from a good position, when he spotted a German taking a bath in the ' … third line. I disliked the idea of shooting a naked man … ' so he asked his sergeant to do the job.[28] Private First Class George Niland said of the Japanese he was fighting on Okinawa: 'Shooting one of those people was like picking up a piece of popcorn … it meant nothing emotionally.'[29] Australian marksman Roland Griffiths-Marsh noted, when he first shot three, perhaps four Italian soldiers at a distance in North Africa: 'I felt no emotion, only a combination of excitement and great concentration'.[30] Marine officer Nicholas Warr observed the actions of a sniper team in the battle for Hue, Vietnam, and noted the tone of one of the marksmen as ' … no emotion in his voice, no indication of horror, or glory, or anything. He was merely reporting the facts' as he told how he and his comrade had cold-bloodedly shot down four NVA soldiers.[31] In the Falklands, British soldier Dominic Gray bayoneted one of the enemy 'with almost obscene ease … the power surging within me was taking over. I was keen to get on, to take out more positions, to kill more enemy, to carry on without even taking cover'.[32]

Raw courage. In Greece during April 1941 with pieces of unexploded bombs at his feet, a New Zealand soldier stands tall after a successful action. His unit shot down a German plane (left) with Bren guns. New Zealand troops fought with superb courage in the Greek mountain passes. AWM 007636

A memorial was erected after the end of World War II, by grateful locals, to the executive officer of the 589th Field Artillery Battalion of the US Army, a Lieutenant Wood. When his unit was mortared and scattered in the Battle of the Bulge, he took refuge in a wood on the bank of a river. For some weeks, and enlisting the support of other soldiers separated from their units, he attacked nearby German positions. When he was finally cornered and killed, he took seven Germans with him: their bodies were found close around him by local Belgian residents.[33] Wood accepted that his duty was to cause the maximum amount of damage he could to the Germans; despite little support, being outnumbered and ill-equipped, his fight is testimony to soldiers' abilities to fight and win as determined warriors. British soldier Lofty Large, in Korea, was equally determined. While serving as a British infantryman, he closed with an enemy soldier and bayoneted him. He found 'mixed sensations of anger, fear, excitement, exultation' all competing within himself, and also a 'terrible determination' that he would not be beaten.[34] Second Lieutenant Peter Cochrane noted that in one of the first major fights he was involved in during World War II, he was in 'a berserk state of rage at the machine-gunner because he had frightened me so badly', and he killed that enemy soldier.[35] Some 40 years later, Paratrooper Kevin Connery echoed the sentiment within his emotions as he bayoneted an Argentine soldier: 'I was in a rage, doing my job, knowing that if I didn't kill him it would be me dead'.[36] US Marine EB Sledge looked into a bunker where a Japanese soldier had an automatic weapon set up – the resultant burst of fire just missed him as he ducked, and 'my terror subsided into a cold, homicidal rage and a vengeful desire to get even'.[37]

Lofty Large noted that sheer determination was part of the 'Glosters': one man was seen to play dead until an enemy submachine-gunner jumped into his trench, whereupon he 'came back to life', disabled the enemy, and carried on with the enemy weapon. After the battle in which Large and others were finally defeated and taken prisoner, a Chinese officer who surveyed them and the scene of many enemy dead, commented that they were 'Twelve thousand miles from home – and you fight like this. God help anyone who lands in England'.[38] The British SAS were showing the same sort of spirit 30 years later in the Falklands: their commanding officer, Lieutenant-Colonel Mike Rose said that one unit, detached to attack the Argentine aircraft at Port Stanley, were told three times to withdraw, and each time found a 'strangely suspicious reason' to ignore the order.[39] British Army soldier Colonel Tim Jones, who fought in Iraq in 2003 with the Royal Irish Regiment, understood the need for aggression in his soldiers: 'The Irish way is to be in the frontline … Why have an Irish regiment if you don't expect them to behave like paddies? Our military culture in Ireland hasn't changed in a thousand years. They still expect their chieftain to lead from the front.'[40]

The Japanese infantry in general in World War II were excellent fighters – determined, efficient, and extremely bloodthirsty. British General William Slim thought: '… there can be no question of the supreme courage and hardihood of the Japanese soldiers … I know of no army that could have equaled them'.[41] A US Marine report was of the opinion that the Japanese were ' … well trained and disciplined army troops of exceptionally high morale and splendid physical condition'.[42] Any illusions about their abilities and temerity were swept away after a few days of combat. On Okinawa, where the US Marines suffered extremely heavy casualties in taking the island, one platoon leader told new, 'green' replacements in no uncertain manner about the calibre of the enemy they faced:

Pointing his pistol at these bewildered lambs, he concluded, 'And if I hear any bullshit about the Japs being lousy fighters, I'll shoot you. If one of you motherfuckers says they can't shoot straight, I'll put a bullet between your fuckin' eyes before they do.'[43]

Bob Neiman, the Executive Officer of the 1st Tank Battalion of the US Marine Corps, thought of the Japanese as '... tenacious, among the finest fighters in the world, next to the Marine Corps ... well trained, well disciplined, with little regard for their own lives.'[44] Japanese tenacity was often extremely strong, with the infantry holding their positions in the face of odds which would have broken the hearts of many Westerners. One account from a Japanese soldier describes advancing to the Allied positions at night in an effort not to take the ground – the Japanese unit was not strong enough for that – but to get the enemy to retreat enough so that the ammunition, food and equipment they left behind could be taken by the Japanese for their own use. Then they would go back to their own positions. Those who could not contribute through wounds were apologetic:

If he [was] heavily injured he would regret overtaxing his mates. Those men passed away saying, 'Excuse me. I regret dying.' They died apologizing and weeping. The battlefield takes the life of such brave men, and there is no way of helping them. We were short of food, but most distressing was that we did not have bullets. Still, we did not give up ... [45]

In Vietnam, Marine Jeff Kelly remarked on his own wish to get into combat, though he also noted his own remote experience in his first firefight: 'Tiny gray figures ran across a misty field and we knocked them down'.[46] He thought that 'War isn't hell, it's decent', but also noted in later combat experiences his own feelings of fear and grief at the loss of comrades – which also made him more aggressive. Marine Johnnie Clark felt the same way about wanting a confirmed kill. 'We searched for bodies but came up empty. I felt an odd sense of disappointment.' Later, his first confirmed kill was a 14-year-old boy, part of an attacking force that the Americans defeated. Clark told one of his platoon: 'I wanted a confirmed like I always wanted a touchdown and never got it. But that's not the worst of it. I just don't feel as bad about killing a kid as I should.'[47] Australian soldier Barry Heard notes, of his unit's reaction to their first kills in combat in Vietnam: 'We mostly had a sense of success and pride at our proven war-like skills'. Later, he relates how a competition developed between the companies of his battalion to see who could score the most kills.[48] Heard notes his own participation dispassionately, although he also relates his psychiatric problems after the war. It's an interesting comparison: revulsion later at what you have done, but at the time, is not such enthusiasm for combat necessary?

Underlying this reality is also the rule that if you want to be a winner and a survivor in infantry combat, then casual lethality, or everyday aggression, is the essence of the seasoned warrior. Marine company commander Martin Sexton thought that 'Once a person has experienced actual combat and survived, the initial reaction is relief. But the soldier must avoid the trap of being too careful. An offensive can only be successful if it is conducted in an aggressive, unrelenting mode.'[49] Peter Cochrane said that in face-to-face combat, 'animal rage and a determination to survive at the other man's expense were the driving forces'.[50] Philip Caputo, in Vietnam, noted that the instinct for self-preservation turned a soldier into a 'creature who destroys without hesitation or remorse whatever poses even a potential threat to his life'.[51]

Examination of a first-hand account such as *The Storm of Steel* provides plenty of examples. Written by Ernst Junger, who rose from trooper to officer on the Western Front in the German Army, it is matter-of-fact in its accounts:

> … I saw an Englishman walking along over the top behind the third line of the enemy trenches. His khaki uniform showed up distinctly on the horizon. I seized the nearest rifle, sighted it at 600, got the man in the tip of the foresight, and then, aiming a bit in front of his head, I pulled the trigger. He went three steps, and then fell on his back …[52]

Junger describes similar incident after incident throughout his book, interspersed with time behind the Lines, getting shelled, and all of the other scenes familiar to anyone who has studied the Great War. But what is telling is his acceptance of his duty to kill the enemy, and how it was done every day, every hour, somewhere on the Front. His colleague Stephen Westman, serving as an infantryman, thought that it was the same for all nation's soldiers: 'They lose all sense of humane feeling in the fury of battle'. He mused further that all of them were 'on the brink of insanity', that there was no room for sentimentality, and that General Sherman's observation on war was quite true: 'War is cruelty and you cannot refine it'.[53]

The massive Battle of the Somme was so intense in terms of numbers of men employed that one would have expected massive casualties. Significantly for this argument, the attacks by the Allies commencing on 1 July 1916 were marked by ferocious fighting. Martin Middlebrook notes that very few of those who reached the German lines survived to be taken prisoner: 'The British casualty figures were to show that very few of these men surrendered. They fought to the end and met unrecorded deaths in some squalid corner of a German trench'.[54] A pitched battle sees more savagery than the day-to-day sniping of World War I trench life. A raid does too: the more widespread and important the cause, the more lethal are the warriors.

Lieutenant J. Annan, of the 1st/9th Battalion of the Royal Scots, described one assault in 1917 during the Ypres battle:

> We didn't have a single casualty until we got to Minty's Farm. It was a strongpoint, an outpost, fortified by the Germans and bristling with machine-guns, but the Gordons had taken it. They took it with the bayonet, like wild things, and when we got to it the dead were lying all around. Germans, grey against the mud, all mixed up with the dead Gordons lying there in their kilts. But they'd taken it all right.[55]

For professional soldiers there is doubtless some acceptance of the idea that to dispatch the enemy is why you became a warrior, and that ideological imperatives are not so necessary as they might be for the hostilities-only soldier. Major Tom Bridges of the 4th Dragoon Guards was matter-of-fact about his place in the British Army and why he was there: Belgians, French or Germans – his job was combat, summed up by the cavalry's motto of 'We'll do it; what is it?'[56] Sergeant Major Basil Plumley, fighting in Vietnam – the third conflict he had fought in, the others being World War II and Korea – personifies the stoicism and matter-of-fact acceptance of combat that is shown by many a seasoned soldier. The Battle of Ia Drang was a furious engagement where thousands of Vietnamese were pitted against a depleted American battalion. Depicted in the film *We Were Soldiers*, the battle saw intense infantry-to-infantry combat, backed up by artillery attacks on both sides, and air support for the US soldiers. Throughout the battle Sergeant Major Plumley's presence was a calm reassurance that indeed one can cope in a world dominated by unbelievable noise, stress, fear, and demands on one's physical endurance. At one stage combat photographer Joe Galloway was flat on the ground taking cover from fire and he felt a boot in his ribs.

> There, standing tall, was Sergeant Major Basil Plumley. Plumley leaned down and shouted over the noise of the guns: 'You can't take no pictures laying there on the ground, sonny.' He was calm, fearless, and grinning.

I thought: 'He's right. We're all going to die anyway, so I might as well take mine standing up.' I got up and began taking a few photographs.[57]

Where the enemy present themselves as a target, professional soldiers view their job of extermination as routine. A World War I soldier commented on a firing opportunity as

> ... an amazing sight ... several platoons of infantry ... behind them were groups of cavalry ... (and) horse-drawn general service wagons and horse-drawn ambulances ... We opened fire. The Lewis guns got busy and the enemy scattered. They had very little cover and no chance of survival ... After a while nothing was moving ...[58]

Brigadier-General FP Crozier accepted the necessary brutality of combat, and he condemned those officers who did not accept the need for aggression. 'You must have those 'butchers' if a war is to be won or conducted with less distaste than might be otherwise. Delicacy and timidity are not virtues for the field of battle.'[59] World War II 2nd Lieutenant Peter Cochrane noted that his company killed the enemy 'methodically enough; the kick came from success in achieving the object'.[60] In more modern times, sniper Sergeant Jack Coughlin noted of his job, when killing someone, 'I feel nothing at all, other than a bit of professional satisfaction'.[61]

Pinned down by two machine-gun nests in the Vietnam battle for Hue, one Marine corporal calmly realised what was necessary to negate the enemy. He gathered as many grenades from as many wounded and dead Marines as possible, and without telling anyone, embarked on a one-man assault, taking out first one nest, then the other. He was wounded four times in the process.[62]

Bob Oslin, flying helicopter gunships in Vietnam, summed up the attitude of most who engage in combat as acceptance of the facts of the matter:

> When I say that killing was easy, I don't mean to sound flip or trivialize the impact on the psyche of this most horrendous act. My biggest surprise about my war experience was that, under those conditions, it was not more difficult to overcome the civilized veneer. I never served with anyone who seemed to derive pleasure from killing another person, but I also saw little evidence that it was a huge moral issue for most.

Oslin was flying a mission to chase Vietcong who had ambushed and killed some American and ARVN troops. They followed the trails of the VC from the battle into the open area under about two feet of water, and caught about 80 VC in a dozen large sampans with weapons and wounded. The VC started bailing out of the boats and firing at the two helicopters. Oslin recollected that it was the first time he had ever seen his target clearly, and during the attack he expended the helicopter machine-guns' ammunition. The helicopters engaged at about a half-mile and made runs over the VCs' heads. Oslin remembered: 'I estimate that I killed at least a dozen. In hindsight, it was a little like spearing a fish in a barrel, but I had no problem morally or emotionally in killing them.'[63]

In summary, once front-line soldiers understand their job and get down to it, they are everyday dealers in life and death. Acceptance of the fact that 'it is him or me' marks their attitudes from that moment on. That is the true nature of their terrible but necssary occupation.

2
Combat euphoria

*Just wait until you kill one, then you'll know how good
it feels. I hope I get one every day.*

US soldier on Okinawa after shooting his first enemy

Enjoying combat

Some soldiers like combat. Field Marshal Slim, when a junior officer, was clinical in analysing his feelings in shooting a Turk in 1917, noting that he felt a ' ... most intense satisfaction'.[1] Siegfried Sassoon in the same war tells in one battle of how adventurous he was feeling and how he and Lance-Corporal Kendle were 'having great fun together' in a trench fight.[2] World War II battle surgeon Brendan Phibbs described how he saw the celebrations of an infantryman who had carried his rifle for two years and 'today I got this Kraut right in the ringsights',[3] leaving Phibbs in no doubt that he was a 'profoundly happy, fulfilled man'. The surgeon reflected that this was 'savage elation' and that the man was also releasing frustrations at being shot at from long-range. And 2nd Lieutenant Peter Cochrane noted that he is 'still ashamed of the inordinate pleasure I felt at hitting my man with a single round, 1000 yards on the sight'.[4] Watching the firing of the 16-inch guns on a battleship, one WWII veteran thought: 'There is a certain feeling, I don't care who you are, a feeling of exultation about combat'.[5] Australian soldier Andrew Barham thought that his time in combat in the East Timor campaign of the late 1990s was 'the BEST high I've ever had'.[6] Nora Stewart, interviewing Falklands veterans, had an NCO tell her that, 'Lots of chaps resigned after we got back ... They could never recapture those moments in battle. The Falklands was their highest moment in their lives and a peacetime Army would be too boring for them'.[7]

Dave Grossman has analysed the thrill of satisfaction that results from hitting the target. This can translate for some individuals into being able to avoid remorse altogether. [8] Avoiding remorse is to be applauded – not frowned upon, as seems to be the fashion today. In truth, it is a very real and necessary understanding.

Peter Young recalled that in one of the combat actions following D-Day in his Commando company, ' ... everyone was enjoying the battle; rapid advances, short pauses to put down a withering fire ...'[9] In the same campaign, British Army Corporal Harry Bloodworth Smith climbed up the outside of a church tower to get at a sniper. He silently made his way in through one of the windows after seeing the sniper on the other side of the tower with his back to him. Smith crept up behind and bayoneted the man. 'It was interesting. I'd enjoyed doing it, and although it was murder, I'd no regrets.'[10] Brigadier Michael Carver, fighting in WWII, mused on whether he would 'miss the intensity of an active life, lived to the full close of nature ... I was afraid I might.'[11] Soldiering on the Russian front in WWII was horrifying and dreadful, thought Guy Sajer, and he savoured the little leave he could get. But he also noted that, 'It often strikes me with horror that peace is really extremely monotonous'.[12] There are plenty of people like that around, even in more modern battle times, but the acceptance of, and praise for ferocious soldiers is muted in peacetime, and indeed can produce career-threatening action. In 2005:

> A senior US Marine Corps General who said it was 'fun to shoot some people' should have chosen his words more carefully but will not be disciplined, military officials have said. Lieutenant General James Mattis, who led troops in Iraq and Afghanistan, made the comments at a conference on Tuesday in San Diego.
>
> 'Actually it's quite fun to fight them, you know. It's a hell of a hoot. It's fun to shoot some people. I'll be right up front with you, I like brawling,' said Lt Gen Mattis.

And he went on to describe openly and honestly the contempt he felt for the lack of warrior bravery in the people he was fighting. The unusual nature of the soldier's remarks were reflected in the worldwide publicity they received, and for the condemnation from some circles. One commentator noted that 'Gen. Mattis told the truth about a fundamental human activity – war – and was treated as though he had dropped a nuclear weapon on an orphanage'.[13] The US Army, however – perhaps reflecting a trend towards acceptance of the war against terrorism being fought in that year, and the still-recent 11 September 2001 terrorist attacks – was circumspect in its castigation:

> In a statement, General Michael Hagee, commander of the Marine Corps, praised Lt Gen Mattis as 'one of this country's bravest and most experienced military leaders'. 'While I understand that some people may take issue with the comments made by him, I also know he intended to reflect the unfortunate and harsh realities of war,' Gen Hagee said. 'I have counseled him concerning his remarks and he agrees he should have chosen his words more carefully.'[14]

Some soldiers revel in the intense excitement and go looking for trouble. They are unusual enough. The writer CS Lewis noted that, in his service as an infantry officer in World War I, only one man 'really longed for fighting'.[15] Similarly, US paratrooper David Webster observed among his companions only one, Don Hoobler, who he thought ' … actually enjoyed fighting; he got a kick out of war.' Hoobler volunteered for all of the patrols in combat, and avoided work when in garrison.[16] Such warriors are rare, but do exist. Enthusiasm for testing a newly-issued bayonet was the cause of two of Cam Bennett's fellow soldiers disappearing in the direction of the Japanese positions in New Guinea. The two highly experienced combat veterans sneaked up on two enemy sentries, shot one and bayoneted the other. Enraged soldiers from the Japanese position then chased them back to their own Line. The bayonet received a glowing report.[17]

Fulfilment

For many, the emotion is not so much enjoyment as satisfaction at doing a job properly; a sense of fulfilment in utilising their training, and of relief that they were able to do the job. They may have been very fearful that they could not. All of this produces a sense of 'getting the job done', which sounds strange to civilians. Even those new to combat can find it a little unsettling: as Ludovic Kennedy, who had joined the Royal Navy to become a sea-going officer, noted on board *HMS Tartar* (one of the destroyers hunting the German battleship *Tirpitz*): 'To my surprise I found this prospect wonderfully exhilarating, and prayed that the opportunity for it might come'.[18] Australian soldier Ted Mofflin was able to shoot a Turk dead in the landings at Gallipoli with his first round fired in combat, and noted: 'I was that pleased I could have danced on his body'.[19]

Lieutenant Bill Little was in his Sherman tank when the squadron caught up with some German forces on D-Day:

> The excitement was just fantastic, and I talked to my other tank and said 'Let 'em have it'. Well, then, it was just a real bird shoot ... This was the first time we'd actually hit German soldiers and the exhilaration, after all the years of training, the tremendous feeling of lift, of excitement, of exhilaration, it was like the first time you go deer hunting.[20]

George MacDonald Fraser, later a famous author, noticed with interest his own reactions as a World War II infantryman in combat: 'The joy of hitting him was the strongest emotion I felt that day ...'[21] and thought that some men enjoyed it to a degree, and most felt satisfaction in battle. Later he reflected further and thought that killing in combat was 'exciting' and that most soldiers found it so; when 'the blood-lust would take them hot and strong ... the truth is that he gets a kick out of it'.[22] These emotions are often suppressed for a variety of reasons, including Christian teaching, unpleasant memories of violence, the wish not to be thought a psychopath, and a total failure by those outside the military to understand combat. A US soldier on Okinawa exhibited a marked change in his demeanour due to shooting his first Japanese. Another soldier remarked on the change in his attitude, and the man answered: 'Just wait until you kill one, then you'll know how good it feels. I hope I get one every day'.[23] US soldiers on Okinawa succeeded in blocking off some Japanese positions so that there was no escape, and then the heavy weapons company set up their water-cooled machine-guns. According to one witness: ... it seemed like they would never stop shooting. Some of them were laughing and chortling all the while they were killing anything that moved ... I was disgusted with their glee.'[24] US soldiers fighting in 1945 watched one of their snipers hit a German up ahead in an exposed position. The wounded soldier tried to crawl back into cover, and the sniper hit him twice more, each time to the 'whoops and shouts' of his comrades.[25]

PFC John Bishop wrote of his first combat in Korea: ' ... up on a mountain, we spotted a gook FO. About twenty of us shot the shit out of him. It made me feel good because I was in on my first kill.'[26] Vietnam Marine Johnnie Clark was in his first combat under mortar fire, and remembers he was face down waiting for 'the pain' when he heard the command for his M-60 to go forward: 'Guns up!' His section leader yelled and ran forward and 'His shout went through me like a shot of adrenaline. Suddenly I wasn't terrified any more ... an odd sense of exhilaration, almost pleasure, pounded through my system ...'[27]

Vietnam Marine Jeff Kelly was part of a situation where advancing enemy forces in open ground were an easy target for the Americans, and ' ... men were taking the time to adjust shooting slings on their arms' and 'the competition for confirms was fierce'. Then an officer 'ruined everything' by calling in an artillery strike, provoking a disgruntled response from the men: "Fucking officers always gotta hog everything for themselves,' they said, staring directly at him.'[28] The soldiers were engaging in what they had been trained and encouraged to do; human beings had become mere targets, and the men were probably enjoying themselves. This is anathema to many, but it is part of the truth of close combat. Philip Caputo experienced frustration for weeks and months on end in Vietnam, with the enemy engaging from a distance. So when a full engagement was made it was with 'the manic ecstasy of contact'; he analysed his own feelings and felt happy.[29]

What needs underlining in this discussion, however, is that infantry have to be aggressive in combat if they wish to win. Given too, that their survival depends on them firing before the enemy does, an effective infantryman is necessarily quick on the trigger. German senior NCO Oberfeldwebel Hans Erich Braun, beating a fighting retreat with his unit back across Europe, said: 'Often, we were accused of fighting fanatically, but we had long since learned the lesson, that one thing alone counts in war: to fire first, by a fraction of a second, and kill; or otherwise, be killed oneself'.[30] Sergeant Gariepy of the Canadian Army agreed: 'It was necessary to appear ruthless in every action, each incident a case of 'his life or mine".[31]

This fierceness is reflected in the almost omnipresent aggressiveness developed in training soldiers. British soldiers sailing south for the Falklands were proudly and fiercely aggressive. To the tune of the Cliff Richard hit, 'Summer Holiday', members of 42nd Commando sang[32] (with some translation alongside):

We're all going to the Malvinas,	– the Argentine name for the islands
We're all going to kill a Spic or two,	
We're all going on a pusser's holiday, For a month or two ...	– slang term for navy people and equipment
We're going to kill the wops with phosphorous	– phosporous grenade
We'll get them with our GPMG's	– General Purpose Machine-Gun
They'd better not try to take cover, 'Cos they're ain't no fucking trees.	

T-shirts proclaimed the intentions of the wearer: 'Falk off, Galtieri' sent a message to the Argentine leader. Others simply proclaimed the lethality of the British: 'Start Crying for Us, Argentina, we're Coming to Bomb the Shit out of you' recalled the famous rock-opera song, and the shirts proclaiming 'X Troop, Plastic Killers' spoke of the effectiveness of the plastic bullet.[33] Doubtless a goodly section of the British population would be horrified at such apparel, and would urge that soldiers not be allowed to say such things and wear such clothes. They would be wrong.

All tactical warriors must be encouraged to be lethal – indeed, it should be integral part of their training. Getting US Marines to chant slogans in recruit training is developing the necessary aggression, as is the emphasis on bayonet fighting and general lethality at close quarters. This is not commanders' foolishness, as historian Joanne Bourke suggests:

According to a huge range of military professionals, even in the age of gas and tanks and aeroplanes and nuclear warheads, wars could only be won by infantrymen, skilled in the use of bayonet and rifle.[34]

Just so. Despite any technology, a war is won only by aggression. It is over only when the infantry go in and hold ground. Despite the huge armies of Britain, the US and Russia in WWII, the war in Europe was only over when some infantrymen broke through the Berlin bunker's defences and established that Hitler was dead. The desperate fighting that is part of a last stand often results in hand-to-hand combat, where bayonets are used, and the acceptance of such savagery as necessary may well be the difference between winning and losing. The war in the Gulf in 2003 was only over when Saddam's palaces were captured and the very heart of Baghdad was taken – by infantry. Until that happened, Iraqi Information Minister Mohammed Saeed al-Sahaf was able to keep up a constant stream of misinformation, and at least credibility in the eyes of Allied detractors.

Even modern warfare needs infantry, something that often seems overlooked by those who maintain that air power can solve all military problems, that 'high-tech' can give you all the answers. As sniper Sergeant Jack Coughlin observed, when the necessity of sniper teams was being overlooked in the US Army: 'Tangled urban environments sharply inhibit the advantages of our smart bombs, overhead imagery, and standoff robotics, and jet fighter bombers, and aircraft carriers cannot hold territory.'[35]

Burial of Argentine dead at Darwin. Acceptance that war kills people, and that a soldier has to kill, is a difficult but necessary part for a soldier to succeed and survive. The acceptance of this is often hidden from those who do not understand. IWM 8301-32 FKD 997

In fact, it is testimony to many a military commander's ethical sense of proportion that infantry are used in these situations. The Falklands were won by both seapower and infantry, not by British submarines firing ICBMs at Argentina. Would critics of military aggression rather a superior enemy simply stood off at a distance and levelled the opponent's entire country to radioactive slag?

Nevertheless, it is important in combat to use the necessary force to acquire the position at the least cost to your side. During the push towards Germany, a group of SS troops were holding out in a shoe factory. The American forces facing them, after taking some casualties, fired immense numbers of rocket batteries and high amounts of explosive at the factory, and those Germans that were left surrendered.[36] The point is to take minimal casualties yourself – and that means focused lethality. Much has been written on ethics in war: how to maintain a degree of civility while at the same time needing a degree of savagery. One of the much-discussed principles of fighting a 'Just War', with a proportional use of force, might well be deployed here in an attack on what might seem to many to be unnecessary force on the part of the infantry in descriptions such as those cited above. It is encompassed by the Latin phrase *jus in bello* – what is right to do in war. In essence, this states that 'the means adopted in fighting the war must not be so harmful and destructive as to outweigh the good to be achieved'.[37] Critics might therefore argue that the use of rockets in the shoe-factory scenario is disproportional. In reply, although a theorist might argue that if the end result was 63 Germans and 62 Allies dead, and then it was the correct path to follow, the reality of the situation is such that no army in such a situation will hesitate to use superior firepower. And it was indeed proportional enough: some of the Germans survived.

So the use of the bayonet and the training with such aggression is an integral and necessary part of any efficient force. The British Air Force had in fact stopped such training by 1982 when the Falklands war began. Guy Bransby was an officer serving with the RAF Regiment of ground-attack airmen at the time: he presumed that 'some high-ranking theorist had no doubt decided that we were all far too technological by then for such primitive behaviour.'[38] Modern Western society has slowly but surely misunderstood the reality of combat ... here is the revelation of its reality. Bayonets were indeed used[39] in the Falklands, and Nora Stewart's study of unit cohesion in that campaign notes, with perception, that:

> Here on a modern high-technology battlefield with satellite communication to faraway capital cities, napalm, space-age weapons

that destroyed bunkers in a moment, night-vision goggles, jets and submarines, here, in half light, in trenches and foxholes, men lunged at each other with bayonets in the same dreadful manner that combatants in long forgotten wars over countless generations had done so many horrifying times before.[40]

To not understand this is to not understand the true nature of combat. And so FP Crozier, as second in command of the Royal Irish Fusiliers in 1914, related of their training that 'we foster, inculcate, teach and build up the blood lust for the discomfiture of the enemy, without which no war is possible'.[41] The advice of the United States Marine Corps' Small Wars Manual in 1940 is just as relevant to day as it was then: men armed with rifles should be imbued with "the spirit of the bayonet' – the desire to close with the enemy in personal combat and destroy him'.[42]

The place of women in combat

Many forces, especially in the modern Western world, have experimented with using women in combat, particularly as feminism developed in the 20th century and women claimed the right to not be excluded from 'male' occupations. There have been successes and failures, scandals and satisfying careers, and much re-adjustment – organisational, attitudinal and even physical – to allow women to take their place in uniform. The organisational aspect has seen training courses instituted to counsel both sexes as to appropriate behaviour. Men have either adjusted their attitude or left their armed force, unable to change to suit the new structure. The physical aspect has seen changes in warship design, for example, to give both men and women the appropriate privacy; and in aircraft cockpits, so ejection seats now suit the different physical structure of women.[43]

Many armed forces would, if polls were taken of such things, probably agree that the introduction of women into uniform has been a positive change. In volunteer forces, it widens the recruiting base by 50 per cent, for one thing. And women have been found to be just as capable as men in many roles. One of the most efficient snipers in history is the Russian World War II woman soldier, Lyudmila Pavlichenko, who killed over 300 of the enemy.[44]

However, in tactical physical combat, women have not been tested in large numbers, although women have fought in the Israeli Army and in the Vietcong forces. Indeed, this work quotes the famous Australian woman soldier, Nancy

Wake, a little later in this chapter – and she was more than effectively lethal. But many combat forces still bar women from these areas, with the infantry in particular being a challenging area, for women have flown effectively in aircraft – they did so in World War II in the Russian air force – and various forces have enrolled them into artillery and armour, and various types of warships.

If aggression is to be encouraged, and is the mark of the successful combat soldier – engaged in hand-to-hand fighting – then women may lack this necessary ingredient to be successful. Of course, this is a highly politicised question. If, as Steven Pinker has argued in *The Blank Slate*, women are by nature less aggressive than men, then they necessarily may be excluded. However, an alternative argument is that aggressive behaviour is learned, and that women can make effective combat soldiers. The possibility has been explored with much vigour in the 1998 film *G.I. Jane*, which certainly advances the image of a highly effective soldier in the character embodied by Demi Moore. Another depiction may be found in *Alien*, in the depiction of two female space Marines, who also present as highly efficient soldiers.

The question may be left open, but if it is the case that females are less aggressive than men, this needs to be countenanced in the composition of forces.

The 'Berserker'

The Vikings had this term for a warrior who apparently went ferociously mad in battle. Many a soldier has surrendered to feelings of bloodlust when the fighting starts, or when he is convinced it is necessary. Of course, an effective soldier also must not let such feelings blind him to the larger tactical picture.

Ernst Junger described such emotions when he was part of an advance from his World War I trench:

> The turmoil of our feelings was called forth by rage, alcohol, and the thirst for blood as we stepped out … In my right hand I gripped my revolver, in my left a bamboo riding cane. I was boiling with a fury now utterly inconceivable to me. The overwhelming desire to kill winged my feet. Rage squeezed bitter tears from my eyes.[45]

Such intense feelings seem unusual. One can read account after account of front-line fighting and not see savagery. Lord Moran served with the 1st Royal Fusiliers in World War I and noted that, in the 30 months he was with them, he never saw one man lose his temper with the enemy.[46] But sanitised accounts are what constitute many such stories. They do not present the true face of battle for many reasons: civilians will not understand the need for such savagery, and will condemn the writer; the writer does not want to be rejected from the rest of the human race; the writer wants to save the reader from disgust and pain …

For example, Sergeant Charles Martin was present when a captured German officer was treated for leg wounds. When the Allied troops began advancing again, the German pulled out a concealed pistol and shot at the backs of those who had helped him. He killed one man, and was somewhat beaten up in the ensuing fracas, with a broken arm resulting, before he was carried off on a sheet of corrugated iron with a note for the MPs. Martin rather phlegmatically pondered that perhaps the officer thought he would meet the fate of those captured on the Russian front: he was being taken off to be shot.[47] It would be most interesting to interview Martin and see if this story was really true, or whether the officer was in fact shot out of hand.

On another occasion Martin tells us of a Gestapo officer who had surrendered. He managed to draw a concealed pistol and shoot twice at Martin, inflicting a minor wound, and receiving two shots in return, ' … one in each shoulder. He was lucky I hadn't lost my temper!'[48] This is a little doubtful, and perhaps Martin is sparing us from the ultimate fate of the would-be assassin; or perhaps he deliberately inflicted such wounds in revenge …

The omission of such actions from combat accounts, to spare the feelings of those at home, or to avoid admission of actions that should not have been taken, is common. The truth often isn't wanted in letters home, as Martin Dockery found out at an early age. When he graduated from the US Army's parachute school prior to going to Vietnam, he enlightened his mother and sisters as to the gory death of an accident victim with the words of one of the school's songs of black humour, 'Blood on the Risers'. The reaction was such that 'the letters I wrote my parents from Vietnam were devoid of hardship, danger and combat.'[49] Also, as mentioned, Australian soldier Barry Heard noted, of his time in Vietnam, that he recorded little in his diary of fights between soldiers in his company, the wild sex and drinking on leave, drunken incidents in camp, the hatred they all felt for the enemy – all of it was sanitised, as it was in letters sent home, 'avoiding the harsh realities of death and horror'.[50]

Erwin Rommel's sanitised first-hand account, for example, of his fighting in World War I – in *Infantry Attacks* – shows at least one such edit, with Rommel deleting from one edition the charge that the French deliberately killed some Germans lying wounded by the side of a road. The book reads like a report of proceedings at company level: the Germans advance, some French fight them, a few on each side die, prisoners are taken, and then on to the next action.[51] And anyone reading *Commando Attack* by Gordon Holman would be forgiven for thinking that British chaps were all brave, decent, cheerful troops who never did anything wrong – the main reason for the overall tone probably being that the book was published during World War II, perhaps as propaganda to boost morale at home.

It is a similar case with Bruce Bairnsfather's *Bullets and Billets*, published in 1916. While the work does have some honest descriptions of trench warfare, the British soldiers are painted as almost universally cheerful and positive, and very few actions are described which bring the condemnation of those 'at home', who simply did not understand the necessities of combat. In fact, the official histories of combat units routinely leave out such matters. As quoted previously, Siegfried Sassoon, infantry officer and poet of World War I, commented dryly, 'Let the Staff write their own books about the Great War, says I. The infantry were biased against them. And their authentic story will be read with interest.'[52]

It is possible to read two accounts of the same campaign and see how it is portrayed in different lights. Russell Davis's *Marine at War* is centred around some of the same Pacific campaigns described in EB Sledge's *With the Old Breed*. That the two men fought in the same companies is apparent: they both describe, for example, the same officer, a 'Lieutenant Mac', although Sledge sees him as incompetent, whereas Davis does not.[53] But Davis's account lacks Sledge's stories of dispatching enemy wounded, souveniring body parts from the Japanese, and other near-'war crimes'. It is obvious both cannot be giving us a 100 per cent factual account.

The Biggles books, once extremely popular stories of World War I and II flying and fighting, portray in the main 'decent' behaviour, as do the military novels of Ronald Welch. Admittedly, these two authors' many works are written for 'young adults', but, like a lot of books and films, they leave out the true behaviour of the battlefield. Watch a film such as *A Bridge too Far*, for example, and it becomes apparent that what we are seeing of infantry combat cannot possibly be true. Soldiers advance in house-clearing operations and fire one shot at an enemy, who falls dead or wounded. The victorious soldier moves on, never hesitating to ensure that his opponent is no longer a threat. This is patent rubbish, for as we shall see, wounded soldiers are a considerable threat: the normal, sensible behaviour is to fire two shots to the head of the opponent.

The true behaviour of infantry in combat is that they dispatch the enemy with routine duty, accepting the grim nature of their task, and engaging in it with efficiency if they want to survive. Some are simply good at their job because they see the truth of it: kill or be killed. Other have hatred in their hearts.

EJ Rule served in the Australian infantry for the entire duration of World War I, and he noted that '(Bill) Dawe was the only man I ever met who had a personal hatred of the enemy. Unlike the rest of us, who viewed an enemy across the sights of a rifle as one would a log of wood, he cleaned and sharpened his bayonet prior to going into battle with a sort of religious satisfaction.'[54] A British soldier on the Somme said he and his comrades were ' … filled with the most terrible hate' which was born out of fear, and he described how they shot Germans who were getting up out their trenches with their hands up or running back to their reserve trenches.'[55]

Enthusiasm marks many efficient fighters. Cam Bennett, an officer in the Australian Army, said that he and the rest of his command 'cowered low and were terrified' during Stuka raids in the retreat in Greece by Allied forces. However, he saw one of his men, Jock McNair, fire a magazine from his Bren gun at each of seven planes as they came in.[56] The World War II Australian Nancy Wake, who was parachuted into France to work with the Resistance, was still accepting of her lethality sixty years after the war ended. She was made a Companion of the Order of Australia, and commented when asked by the media about her wartime experiences: 'I killed a lot of Germans, and I am only sorry I didn't kill more.'[57] We might well reflect on Wake: the sex, and indeed the physical appearance of an effective killer is immaterial. CW Waters, an Australian soldier of World War II, commented on ' … a little schoolteacher, thick-rimmed glasses, a pansy-looking little fellow. I often used to wonder what the hell's this? And he shot three legionnaires just like I'd shoot rabbits, and never took the grin off his face. Cool as a cucumber'.[58] Siegfried Sassoon, despite his writings and a professed and published abhorrence of the Great War, was a capable warrior in the eyes of fellow poet Robert Graves: ' … I had never seen such a fire-eater as he – the number of Germans whom I killed or caused to be killed could hardly be compared with his wholesale slaughter.'[59]

After a while, most long-term soldiers settle down to their job, and even dismiss the humane side of it altogether. Australian infantryman Roland Griffiths-Marsh saw constant combat in several theatres through World War II. By his own account he was fearful, and at one stage tried to get out of being sent back into the war, but failed. Nevertheless, he found himself, in 1945, commanding Javanese warriors with a capable collection of automatic weapons, and thinking ' … how pleasant it would be to ambush a large force of enemy on the trek to Iburu'.[60]

Sergeant William Manchester was a Marine in World War II. He led a platoon of tactical Intelligence fellow soldiers: map-readers; photo interpreters, and so on. He was quite honest about his own fears and how determined he and his 'Raggedy-Ass Marines' – as he called them – were to survive, and how accepting of their roles fellow Marines were. He remarked on the resolve of the Raiders battalions, who carried out stealthy patrols far forward of the main battle sites. He thought them 'born killers'. They would penetrate deep behind Japanese lines at night, looking for two Japanese in a foxhole together. Then they would 'cut the throat of one and leave the other to find the corpse in the morning' – a savage psychological blow that must have caused many fearful nights in the Japanese areas.[61] He relates the tale of Private First Class John Ahrens, found after one of the battles for Guadalcanal, shot twice and bayoneted three times. Around him lay the dead bodies of one Japanese officer, a sergeant and 13 infantrymen.[62] Soldiers turn into efficient killers. In the European theatre an officer of the German army – suitably named Rockhammer – wrote home to his wife during the Battle of the Bulge in joyful tones about the development which will 'throw these arrogant big-mouthed apes into the sea.' Rockhammer described for the lady a combat action he had just been in, where 60 tank guns and 120 machine-guns had been turned against an 'endless column' of retreating Americans: it was 'a glorious bloodbath'.[63]

The World War II psychologist Samuel Stouffer and his associates found that in the three combat divisions they surveyed that had been fighting in the Pacific, 38 per cent of the respondents said that thoughts of hatred of the enemy helped them a lot.[64] Perhaps the extremism of enthusiastic warriors is still hidden in the mists of combat experience – not admitted to, but resolutely there.

The work *Men Against Fire* is held up as an important study of men in war, and it is best known for its (perhaps flawed) finding[65] that men in combat rarely fired their weapons. But occasionally its author, SLA Marshall, came across the converse: that men, once they have been blooded, become crazed killers. In one World War II incident, an infantry commanding officer

> … lost almost an hour, alternately bullying and pleading with them before they would go forward. At last they charged the enemy, closing within hand-grappling distance. The slaughter began with grenade, bayonet and bullet. Some of the patrol were killed and some wounded. But all now acted as if oblivious to danger. The slaughter once started could not be stopped. [The officer] tried to regain control but his men paid no heed. Having slaughtered every German in sight, they ran on into the barns of the French farmhouses where they killed the hogs, cows and sheep. The orgy ended when the last beast was dead.[66]

World War II battle surgeon Brendan Phibbs was part of a desperate infantry defence of a position against advancing Germans armour and infantry when at the last minute the American armour arrived in support. The soldiers took heart and went forward with the exulted cries of warriors who sensed victory:

> American war cries, violent short sounds ring back:
>
> 'Okay, you guys, now okay!!!
>
> AwRIGHT!!
>
> Comeoncomeoncomeon!!!
>
> GET them fuckers, comeoncomeoncomeon!!!'[67]

Infantryman Bill Mauldin observed of his time in World War II that there were occasional combat enthusiasts: he knew one who liked to go on patrol alone, and who once killed 'eight krauts with one clip from his M-1 rifle'. Another type hated Germans. Mauldin thought that the 'army couldn't get along without soldiers like that', but they were in the minority – most were afraid, but accepted their duty, and in the main served because they didn't want to let their buddies down.[68] The enthusiastic killer is not common, but he does exist, and just as well too. Commando Peter Young noted that some of the British Army's snipers 'enjoyed' their work, and he describes several in the company he commanded who entreated him to let them loose.[69] Attacking St Nazaire in the famous World War II raid, Royal Navy Stoker LH Ball kept up a spirited attack from Motor Launch 262, as it came under heavy fire from the Germans. His shipmate Ted Burt noted: 'I never saw a man, who laughed in action as he did.' [70]

Max Hastings tells us of the 'young fanatics of the Waffen SS' who liked combat for its own sake, even though they were losing. One captain of the 1st SS Panzer said that his command lived 'entirely for the next clash ... there was a tremendous sense of "being", an exhilarating feeling that every nerve in the body was alive to the fight'.[71] Marine EB Sledge felt, as his Higgins boat took him towards Peleliu Island, with an enormous bombardment going on in front of the massed assault craft, that 'Everything my life had been before and has been after pales in the light of that awesome moment when my amtrac started in amid a thunderous bombardment towards the flaming, smoke-shrouded beach for the assault ...'[72] That didn't mean Sledge liked combat, but it did have that indefinable attractive quality. Sergeant Andrew Barham reflected, of his experiences in East Timor, that combat ' ... is the ultimate high. Every sense is finely tuned and you are very aware of your surroundings.'[73] For Marines fighting in the Falklands, the war was a good thing, because ' ... until you can get one of these little wars and you can prove that you are a blooming good soldier ... it's a waste of time'.[74]

Some soldiers are just well suited to tactical engagements. Australian Army Lieutenant Colonel CGW Anderson, fighting against the Japanese, led his command in four days of continuous action during the Battle of Muar. They destroyed 10 Japanese tanks – they had none of their own – and four guns in an attack Anderson led personally. TC 'Diver' Derrick, a sergeant of the same Army, won the Distinguished Conduct Medal in North Africa for an attack in which he advanced standing in his Bren gun carrier, firing his automatic weapon against all comers until the opposition were vanquished. He followed this in New Guinea in 1943 in an attack which won him the Victoria Cross. Sergeant Derrick's section had been beaten back but he asked for one last try. Advancing alone, Derrick destroyed an enemy post with grenades, and then, with men from his section following on, took another nine positions in a similar manner. One of his companions said later: 'He was a born soldier (a warrior really), left nothing to chance in training and was the ideal fighting soldier.'[75]

Lieutenant Commander Dudley 'Mush' Morton, of the US Navy, was well known for his aggressive approach to warfare. His submarine *Wahoo* had posters throughout bearing his motto, 'Shoot the Sunza Bitches', and it flew a flag with the motto too.[76] He refused to dive once when under attack by a Japanese destroyer, firing torpedoes until he had expended his last: the enemy ship was cut in half even as it fired its depth charges at close range. Morton let the crew take turns at the periscope to see the victims – 'those slant-eyed devils in the rigging' – struggling in the water.[77]

The men of His Majesty's submarine Truant celebrate their aggression on its return to Britain after an absence of two and half years. The skull and crossbones flag indicates her success of over 20 Axis ships sunk or damaged, four stars indicating successful gun actions while 16 white bars stand for ships torpedoed. The boat was commanded by Lieutenant Commander HAV Haggard, DSO, DSC, RN. AWM 128465

Although it probably a psychological necessity for a 'red mist' to descend to cope with the demands of combat, preferred is the calm model, exemplified by men such as Audie Murphy. He was promoted, in his CO's words, for 'coolness and alertness under fire';[78] on one occasion he made jokes down the telephone while assaulting a superior number of Germans. It needs emphasising, though, that there are not enough Murphies or Jackas in most forces. As Captain William Knowlton of the 7th Armoured Division thought: 'A few guys carry your attack, and the rest of the people sort of participate and arrive on the objective shortly after everybody else.'[79]

Perhaps some races make better warriors than others? David Hackworth, fighting in Korea, saw the enthusiasm for combat exhibited by the Hawaiians in the US Army: 'the wildest, bravest and most undisciplined fighters on the block'.[80] The Gurka soldiers of the British Army were observed by their foreign companions to be ferocious warriors. They had a battlecry which was shouted:

'Ayo Gurkhali!' ('The Gurkas are coming!') Their *kukris* – long knives – were their preferred close-quarter weapon, a slash from which could decapitate their enemy. Lieutenant Michael Marshall of the 4/5th Royal Gurka Rifles noted of the Gurka soldier generally: 'When killing the enemy he is elated ...'[81]

Australian soldier Richard Weston was told by one of the New Zealand Maori soldiers fighting on Crete of an incident where, while the German paratroopers were still in the air, the New Zealanders spent all of their ammunition shooting at them, and had none left to defend themselves. The Germans were between them and the ships. So the Maoris ' ... fixed bayonets and did their war dance, the Haka. Because of the resulting battle rage he remembers very little of what happened next, but they made it to the ships and there were no Germans left behind them. His cousin and many Maoris were killed, and he lost the antique sacred tribal *tiki*.' Royal Marine Edward Hill, fighting in the same area, described the Maoris as 'classic warriors of the type that would rather use knives than automatic weapons', and he describes how they would do their war dance before each advance, standing on top of the trenches all the while.[82]

Weston describes another war dance that the Maoris were persuaded to do for the Australians:

This Haka is not to be taken lightly. It's serious business. They scared the daylights out of us. It took a long time for them to calm down. Later that night Tui and I became blood brothers. I was on leave from front-line Alamein, and when it was time to return, all the Maoris wanted to come. Their blood was up they said. But Tui vetoed that and said only he was coming. But at the first check-point the MPs sent him back.[83]

Such enthusiasm for combat could therefore be described as a racial characteristic.

3

Necessary enthusiasm for combat in leadership behaviour

Do you want to live forever?

Lieutenant Colonel AC Newman,
leading a detachment during the shore component of the St Nazaire raid

Enthusiasm for combat is a necessary prerequisite for many a military leader, and their good example can make all the difference. US Navy Admiral William F. Halsey exhibited it on the strategic level in his characteristically blunt way to any Navy personnel landing at Tulagi in the Solomon Islands. A large sign proclaimed: 'KILL JAPS. KILL JAPS. KILL MORE JAPS. You will help to kill the yellow bastards if you do your job well.'[1]

This book is more concerned, though, with the tactical level. An engagement described to infantry surgeon Brendan Phibbs was proof enough that one aggressive officer could save the day for your side. Pinned down, awaiting mortar fire with dread, a platoon was urged into combat by a lieutenant. He first called down artillery on the enemy position, and then berated the men into following him while the enemy was thus occupied: 'If they can't see you, they can't hit you; those guns are to shoot with you know. You shouldn't be lying' on them; you can't fuck them,' and he walks along the platoon kickin' asses and pretty soon we're all standing' up bangin' away ...'

The officer gets rifle grenadiers and bazooka teams firing, and then runs ahead of the men. They follow, and then he

> ... gives a scream like a wild fuckin' Indian and we all start yelling' like maniacs and runnin' after him ... we were all different inside. Them Krauts must have thought they were up against some kind of murderin' lunatics, 'cause I never saw so many white faces under them big helmets

and handkerchiefs wavin' ... [2]

An officer in the South Nottingham Hussars, who were waiting to go forward into an attack in North Africa, was asked by one of his men if he was scared. 'I'm as scared as you are,' he said, 'but, being an officer, I have to hide my feelings.'[3] Another officer, a lieutenant leading his British platoon during Operation Market Garden, commanded his men to charge, and leapt forward, but none followed. He turned back and exhorted them to follow, and still none moved. Finally ' ... he said furiously: 'If you don't charge, you bastards, I'll shoot you!' and at that they moved.[4]

US Paratrooper Richard Winters was a well-known officer by the time the war was over. He exhibited excellent leadership throughout his training and in combat. After the D-Day landings, his men were attacking one night, but the advance was not going well. Eventually, exhausted, without preparatory fire on their target, the troops were lying on the ground and then were ordered to assault. Winters, running, led the way, but a machine-gun opened up on the men and the company was split, with most taking cover on either side of the road. Winters yelled at them to move, but they did not, so he resorted to running across the road from side to side, under fire, kicking their backsides, yelling and screaming, something that was very out of character for him, for he was a well-liked and respected officer who led by example. Eventually they followed him – and the action saved the flank of that section of the army.[5] Stephen Ambrose, who interviewed many men of Winters's association, came to the conclusion that Winters provided 'not only brains but personal leadership. "Follow me", was his code. He personally killed more Germans and took more risks than anyone else.'[6]

World War II Commando officer George Knowland was leading 24 men who were besieged by 'platoon after platoon' of Japanese in the Far East in the final stages of the war. He led personally in a vicious fight for the high ground the Commandos had taken:

He himself was everywhere, hurling grenades, manning a Bren, encouraging his hard-pressed soldiers. He was last seen engaging a horde of Japs with a 2-inch mortar, firing it right in their teeth against a tree. His first bomb slew six men. Then the Japs surged forward.[7]

Royal Marine Commandos march towards Port Stanley in the Falklands. High morale, pride in their fighting abilities, and esprit de corps were some of the qualities that carried the professional British Army to victory in the Falklands. Many of their conscript enemy, by contrast, waited gloomily for their fate. IWM 8307-07 FKD 2028

Knowland died in this part of the assault, but the stand he took and his leadership meant that the position was held. Some of the American generals fighting in the Pacific certainly believed in setting a direct example. General Simon Buckner, head of the 10th Army, appeared at the front occasionally, and on at least one occasion spent some 'ten to fifteen minutes' sniping at the enemy. General Claude Easley, the General of the 96th Division, also was known to visit the front lines for the same reason.[8]

Commando officer Lieutenant Colonel AC Newman, of Essex Regiment and 2 Commando, was leading a detachment during the shore component of the St. Nazaire raid. Newman's men had had several setbacks, and then 'His blood was up. He was damned well going for it bald-headed now. Observing one man struggling, he shouted at him angrily: 'Do you want to live forever?' The effect of this startling challenge ... was magical, and (soon) ... they had all become charged with the same burning ardour.' Newman was awarded the Victoria Cross for his valour in the raid.[9] A Victoria Cross was awarded to Colonel H. Jones of the 2nd Parachute Regiment in the Falklands for similar reasons. His unit was delayed by the enemy in front of them, and finally the Colonel, urging on his men, went forward with a sub-machine-gun, and was shot down by an outflanked Argentine position. There has been some comment on the wisdom[1] of being so far forward, but as one of his men said: 'Hero or lunatic, he was a leader of men'.[10] The same might be said of Lieutenant-Colonel JHC Pearson, leading Canadian forces in the storming of a bridge in 1944. His men, demoralised by the experiences of the previous day, were refusing to advance. Pearson got out of his armoured carrier and walked forward, with a walking stick and a red rose in his hat. He was shot down, but his men went forward, led by his example.[11]

Philip Caputo was taking his platoon further into jungle in Vietnam, chasing some Vietcong they had fought. Eventually, with the trail growing cold, he had to make the decision to move on or not, with one of his men looking at him with the expression that Caputo thought every infantry officer has seen: 'What are you going to do now, mister officer?'[12] Caputo went on, admitting to himself that although he was afraid, he also wanted to get into the fight to prove himself, and that the Marines had also pushed such aggression into him. Later, in an action he was leading, the Marines took

---

1   Fitz-Gibbon, Spencer. *Not Mentioned in Despatches*. Cambridge: The Lutterworth Press, 1995. Fitz-Gibbon spends considerable time on the different accounts of Colonel Jones' death.

on some Vietcong and beat them thoroughly, with the soldiers going into a 'frenzy' and wanting to cross the river – across which they had exchanged fire – to finish off the enemy. Caputo could 'feel the whole line wanting to charge across the river … and smash the life out of anything that stood in its way … Wanted to level the village and kill the rest of the Viet Cong in close combat. I wanted us to tear their guts out with bayonets.'[13] Caputo was on such a 'high' that he later walked up and down in a clearing, shouting insults at the enemy and trying to draw their fire so their positions would be exposed. On another occasion he lost control of his men – not to be recommended, but at least exhibiting a fighting spirit. As part of an extended operation to take a certain hill, two companies met heavy resistance and called in air support. The fighting got heavier and louder and closer. Then it happened:

> The platoon exploded. It was a collective emotional detonation of men who had been pushed to the extremity of endurance. I lost control of them and even of myself. Desperate to get to the hill, we rampaged through the rest of the village, whooping like savages, torching thatch huts, tossing grenades into cement houses we could not burn … We were past feeling anything for ourselves, let alone for others. We shut our ears to the cries and pleas of the villagers.[14]

The effective non-commissioned leader is also a necessary enthusiastic leader in the infantry. In many ways it is the personnel on the ground leading the actual fighting who are more important than the strategic commanders, the generals. As General Sherman said, 'We have some good corporals and good sergeants and some good lieutenants and captains, and those are far more important than good generals.'[15] In World War II the top sergeant of a Russian platoon – attached to the Americans in the last two years of the war – led a charge into a building where snipers had held up the advance, storming the place with extreme aggression rather than careful tactics. US battle surgeon Phibbs, observing the action, noted that, 'One genuinely savage man can move mountains, or mounds of enemy … there really aren't many of that kind around.'[16] The coolness of his sergeant stopped Australian infantryman Roland Griffiths-Marsh from failing in the battlefield early in his career: 'The sergeant's deep, confident words, "Take it easy. Don't move.", brought me back to sanity.'[17] Such examples are still exhibited in more recent wars. In the Falklands Corporal Stewart McLaughlin encouraged his section forward when it mattered. A private following McLaughlin recalled that he himself was trying to dig into the rocks he was lying on, as the unit was under very heavy fire, when:

Suddenly, ahead of us, there was Scouse, standing up on a rock, tracer everywhere, shouting: 'Come on lads. I'm fucking bulletproof, follow me!' And we did. We followed him. On that mountain he was an inspiration to us all. He found his hour.[18]

Lieutenant Bob Dougherty, fighting in World War II New Guinea, exhibited this sort of coolness under fire.[19] Despite being outnumbered four to one, he assessed the situation as being suitable for an attack, during which a bullet hit his rifle butt, carving out a gouge six inches long. According to another officer: 'Dougherty was the coolest man I've ever seen in my life. He just sort of looked at it and said, 'Ah, look at that!' He put in a most remarkable attack …'[20] Lieutenant William Hawkins's technique in the Pacific Islands for taking Japanese pillboxes was to stand up and fire directly into the rifle slits, and then toss in grenades: in his final combat he took four such posts before a shell took his life.[21] Hawkins Field on Tarawa Island is named for him.

What is meant by 'looking the part of a leader' is behaving in such a way that people can be inspired. But it is also something more. It means to look resolute and act with resolution – as did Horatio Nelson in his battles. To lead by example. To not show physical cowardice. The great soldier and writer von Clausewitz said: 'War is the province of danger, and therefore courage above all things is the first quality of a warrior'. In *Leaders and Battles*, WJ Wood defined 'physical courage' as involving ' the exposure of the body to the threat of wounds or death'.[22] One of the most famous generals of World War II, Montgomery, as Wood later notes, added to that ' … moral courage: " … that resolution and that determination which will enable him to stand firm when the issue hangs in the balance" '.[23] Another notable British General, Wavell, agrees: he calls it 'robustness', and notes: 'The general is dealing with men's lives, and must have a certain mental robustness to stand the strain of this responsibility'.[24] It might include 'panache', which the military novelist Ronald Welch once usefully described as: ' … the almost untranslatable expression of dash, of valour, the ability to do things with an air of reckless courage and inspiring leadership'.[25]

Of course, there is a fine line between the exhibition of bravery and willingness to engage and suddenly becoming that most inefficient of officers – a dead one. But often the officer must be the first to expose himself to fire. Donald Macdonald, fighting against the Boers, noted that 'When an officer rises to advance with his resolute 'Come on, men', he is the first one seen, and becomes a target for a score of rifles.'[26] Richard Holmes noted in *Acts of War* that 'blood is the price of epaulettes', and of chevrons too. He notes the often disproportionate price paid by leaders – 27 per cent of officers killed on the Western Front as compared to 12 per cent of the men – but concludes that 'in the last analysis it is determined and charismatic leadership, and the selflessness and dedication that it represents, that helps to pull men through the rigours of battle'.[27] EB Sledge, fighting in the Pacific in World War II, noted the death rate of new officers in practical terms:

> During the course of the long fighting on Okinawa, unlike at Peleliu, we got numerous replacement lieutenants. They were wounded or killed with such regularity that we rarely knew anything about them other than a code name and saw them on their feet only once or twice. We expected heavy losses of enlisted men in combat, but our officers got hit so soon and so often that it seemed to me the position of a second lieutenant in a rifle company had been made obsolete by modern warfare.[28]

Stephen Westman was commissioned after serving in the German Army in the European theatre of World War I. He accepted the promotion with a wry sense of humour, noting that the move was known as an 'Express Ticket to Eternity' due to the reduced life expectancy.[29] Officers like Frank Reasoner, who won the Congressional Medal of Honor in Vietnam, are always necessary leaders by example. Reasoner, leading a Marine company, had run into two machine-gun nests. In the ensuing fight, he charged one single-handed, knocking it out, and then attacked the other while trying to retrieve one of his wounded men. He has had a military training camp and a ship named after him.[30]

Incompetent officers exhibiting unnecessary bravery are a liability, but they usually don't last long. William Manchester's platoon was pinned down behind a seawall when the Marines were making an amphibious landing on a Pacific island. The Japanese knew they were there and occasionally raked the top of the wall with machine-gun fire. More Marines were being landed, and eventually an officer crawled his way to them. Manchester knew him: they had been to officer school together (Manchester had decided 'officering' was not for him, and had gone back to being a sergeant). Now this former colleague, a second lieutenant, exhorted them to advance. Manchester advised against it: they were a much-needed intelligence platoon; the machine-gun fire was too heavy and too accurate, and anyway, eventually the Japanese position would be flanked and their gunners would have to withdraw. He pointed out that the platoon was highly experienced – more so than the officer – and capable, but they were not foolish and could realise the tactical situation just as well as anyone, and would refuse the order. The lieutenant would have none of it, and accused Manchester of cowardice. Then he climbed up on the wall, straightened and called, 'Follow me'. No-one did, and the officer was riddled with machine-gun fire a second later.[31]

The enthusiastic tactical combat warrior, therefore, is rare, but the species should be encouraged and, when found, prized and praised. For some infantrymen, their calling is combat, and they are naturally enough fulfilled when they find their niche. Albert Jacka, the Australian infantryman who fought in World War I and was eventually commissioned, was described by one of his comrades as ' ... in love with his company. Not many of us looked forward to fighting, but we all knew Jacka's ambitions. He was longing for the day when he would lead D Company into battle.'[32] In a previous engagement, Jacka had earned a Military Cross (he already had the Victoria Cross), taking seven wounds in a savage fight with revolver, rifle and bayonet, and killing at least five Germans.[33]

Audie Murphy described it as 'Audacity ... which is often mistaken for courage or foolishness. It is neither. Audacity is a tactical weapon. Nine times out of ten it will throw the enemy off-balance and confuse him. However much one sees of audacious deeds, nobody really expects them.' He coupled that with another maxim: never retreat, because it was demoralising, dangerous, and meant having to take the same ground again.[34]

James R. McDonough arrived in Vietnam as a new lieutenant in the US Army's 173rd Airborne Brigade. While awaiting transport, he noticed an obviously experienced officer of the same brigade, and approached him to ask for advice.

As my words registered he sprang away from the beam and stood close to me, staring into my face. His smell, his look of horror, and the tension startled me. As his face contorted into speech, I realized that madness, not maturity, marked the man.

His lips twisted into a grimace and the gleeful evil in his eyes rocked my senses. 'It's wonderful,' he said. 'Nothing like it in the world. You'll get more than your share of killing. The bodies are everywhere, and in no time at all you'll have a collection of ears that will make those rear echelon mother fuckers green with envy.'

I could not believe it. He went on, but I lost track of what he was saying. He was practically drooling, as if savouring every recollection ...[35]

Studio portrait of Captain Albert Jacka, VC, MC and Bar, of the Australian forces in WWI. Brave, resourceful, and determined, he characterises the best – and most desirable – spirit of the warrior: aggression. AWM A02868

Describing his best soldier, James McDonough noted that Private Killigan was 'a deadly shot and ferocious in a fight, and he never showed the slightest bit of concern for his own safety'. After his second tour of Vietnam, he was discharged, and when entering a recruiting station to sign up again, was met with some college youths who tried to persuade him otherwise. "Don't let them draft you!' a young girl had pleaded. 'Draft me?' was his derisive reply. 'Lady, I'm asking for it. I want to go kill some of those bastards'.[36] McDonough had another savage soldier in his platoon: a former Vietcong who had defected to fight with the Americans; those defectors were known as 'Kit Carsons' to the Americans, and as 'Bushmen Scouts' in the Australian forces'.[37] He received five Silver Stars, had cut forty-five notches into the butt of his M-16 to signify the kills he had made, and was extremely aggressive in firefights.

Are some races more warriors than others? This photograph from 1941 is entitled: "Alexandria. The Maoris frightened blazes outa the Hun with their bayonet charges...this one "got his man" and also a decent souvenir, a German Iron Cross." AWM 007783

In World War I Robert Graves had a 63-year-old soldier serve under him. The man, Private James Burford, first came to Graves's attention by asking his platoon commander what the safety-catch on his .303 Lee-Enfield was, as the last rifle he had fired, the obsolete Lee-Metford, didn't have one. Burford had spent most of his life soldiering here and there, as well as working in other roles. He was not alone in his enthusiasm to join up: Graves describes many middle-aged men, and many under 18 as well, who he observed in his time in the Army.[38]

Soldiers who stayed on for further combat tours in Vietnam were not as rare as might be thought. Marine Rocky Jay said of such men in his Vietnam service: 'I was amazed at the guys that had been there since '67 or '68. They were independent and had a seabag full of Purple Hearts, but they didn't want to go home. They loved being the hunter.'[39] First Lieutenant James Simmen wrote to his brother and commented, 'You'd be surprised how similar killing is to hunting ... I get all excited when I see a VC, just like when I see a deer.' He noted the strange world in which he was operating: 'If I killed a man in the U.S., everyone would stare. Last night I killed and everyone has been patting me on the back, including the battalion commander'.[40] One Special Forces sergeant did three tours, was wounded three times, but still planned on returning. He was given a social club to run while recovering from his latest wound, and back in the States his wife and three children ate their dinner in front of the display case containing his decorations and commendations.[41] A door gunner, 17 months in-country, kept a score of enemy he killed: 150 and 'fifty caribou', presumably water buffalo. [42]

To celebrate such warriors in the twenty-first century would be rejected by many today – especially in the Western societies, where many sociologists and anthropologists want the human psyche to be moulded within certain parameters of decorum. But social niceties and dictated patterns of behaviour count for little in the world of tactical battle, where the musings of millennia on the human condition disappear in the face of the bayonet.

Some of the training US Vietnam soldiers received doubtless contributed towards their aggression. Marines were made to chant slogans about killing the enemy; they were constantly reminded to be aggressive warriors, and for Vietnam, according to some accounts, they were told they could be as aggressive as they liked towards the enemy:

> ... throughout the entire training they emphasized the animalness of the Vietnamese. They were subhuman, we were told. We could (do) anything we wanted to them when we got there ... Every effort was made to glorify the extermination and torture of these lowly Vietnamese ... [43]

The men of the commando/reconnaissance platoon Tiger Force – drawn from the US Army's 101st Airborne – were known for their aggression. The journalist Ward Just, who visited them, opined: 'They liked the adventure, and the weapons. One of them regularly sent the ears of dead Viet Cong to his wife, through the army postal system.'[44] Just was introduced to the new leader of the platoon, Captain Lewis Higinbotham, by then-Major David Hackworth: ' "You'll like Higinbotham," Hackworth said. "He's a good killer'. Hackworth then briefed the troops: "Goddamnit I want forty hard-chargin fuckin' dicks. And if anybody ain't a hard-chargin fuckin' dick I want him out." … I unconsciously wrote the words in my notebook.'[45]

Becoming brutal is perhaps psychologically more necessary than might be thought. J. Glenn Gray was a trained philosopher who fought in World War II – his induction notice arrived in the same mail as his doctorate from Columbia University. He reflected on his thoughts in action and how he felt about them afterwards in *The Warriors*, published in 1959 and then slowly achieving fame – much-deserved, in my view.

Gray noted his own thoughts as battle approached. He found that his 'Interests and refinements' were disappearing, to be replaced, as was the case with his fellow soldiers, with ' … natural urges – eating, drinking, and lusting for women'.[46] Soldiers may say that they are not changing, and may write home to this effect, arguing that they are the same as they always were. But they are deluding themselves, because each is becoming, Gray thought, ' … a fighting man, a *Homo furens*', realising that this was essential, as nearby were the enemy, who would gladly kill you if they could. As such, 'man as warrior' is able to 'subordinate other aspects of the personality, repress civilian habits of mind' and become a true warrior.[47] Gray pondered further that war had three primary attractions: as a spectacle, as comradeship, and as 'delight in destruction'. He experienced all three, and thought it part of being a human. Marine Officer Philip Caputo, fighting in Vietnam, volunteered after staff work to go back to a Line company, feeling useless and guilty for having others take risks for him, but also admitting that there 'was a magnetism about combat. You seemed to live more intensely under fire.'[48]

It is important to the theme of this work to note that curbing lethal behaviour can be destructive to one's own side. Placing restraints on the aggressiveness of the warrior can lead to casualties, and placing restraints on one side that do not apply to the other can be dangerous. Marine Jeff Kelly, working as a Forward Observer, was involved in a situation in November 1968 when the forces fighting in the south of Vietnam were denied the ability to fire back in the Demilitarised Zone. The enemy did not observe the spirit or letter of the Zone, and when the American forces began taking rocket fire, the usual air support was denied because, as the air-support centre advised, ' … the target is over the red line. We must wait on clearance from higher authority. Do you copy?' The Americans lost 10 dead, and scores wounded, all while ' … we have the firepower circling overhead, watching them kill our guys, and do nothing'.[49]

The type of training infantry receives means they call down massive firepower on a target; indeed, their job is delivering maximum destruction – not the minimum force necessary. Basically, armies function at platoon level: a group of soldiers of (depending on the army and the attrition rate) between 20 and 50 men, led by a second lieutenant. If they receive fire, be it from sniper, infantry fire, or whatever, they automatically deploy into what is called a skirmish line. Their heavy automatic weapons – in Vietnam, crew-served, belt-fed machine-guns called M60s – would be deployed to the flanks with the command 'Guns Up!' These guns are on the flanks because the machine-gun is an enfilade weapon, meaning it is mounted on a tripod and fires from the flanks in a cone of fire. The platoon leader will be by this time in the centre and slightly behind the skirmish line with his radio operator. Nearby will be the platoon's 'portable artillery', its mortars, which deliver small bombs in a high arcing descent. It is important to note that the platoon at this point is not advancing, because if they did they may well be destroyed. What they are doing is maintaining the contact and delivering high explosive onto the target with their mortars, and delivering streams of bullets from the crew-served weapons and the riflemen's individual weapons.

Meanwhile, the platoon leader is calling for more firepower. This can be from artillery, which may be several kilometres behind him, but with pre-planned maps accurate fire is quite possible. The first round will be 'Willie Pete' – white phosphorous, for marking – then, with a little adjustment if needed, the command 'Fire for effect' is given over the radio. Or he may call down aircraft to rocket and bomb the enemy. Blasting them like this is preferable to finding out the hard way that you have not done enough blasting. As one World War II veteran put it: 'The longer troops remain in battle, the more they want to be supported by artillery and air … if we can do it with the air, let's not spill the blood'.[50] The US Army in World War II, as described by historian Samuel Eliot Morison, advanced 'only after everything visible in front had been pounded down'.[51]

In other words, the job of infantry taking fire is not to charge in, firing away. That gets your men killed. Hopefully, in every soldier's head is the sentiment best expressed by General Patton when he said, 'Your job is not to die for your country. Your job is to make some poor bastard die for his.' Call down firepower on that person or persons who are targeting you. Indeed, soldiers know well the folly of not doing this. And that firepower in modern wars is massive. At the battle of Ia Drang – the first major battle between the US forces and the Vietnamese – in an engagement which lasted 53 hours, there were more than 18,000 rounds of field artillery alone fired by the Americans. The engagement tellingly went heavily against the Vietnam forces: they lost 834 dead by body count, with an additional 1215 estimated due to artillery, air attacks and aerial rockets. The US forces lost 79 killed in action, with 121 wounded.[52] In the comparatively smaller battle of Long Tan, the Allied side fired around 3000 rounds of artillery in an engagement lasting from mid-afternoon until evening.[53]

Another example from Vietnam is significant, given the typical scenario above. Marine Officer Nicholas Warr fought in the 1968 battle for Hue, where the American Marines were fighting in the city. In one attack that became a battle lasting several days, the Marines were ordered to assault without the normal preparatory fire, because the areas they were fighting in were considered 'sacred ground.'[54] They lost many lives as a result of this decision. In fact, if they had gone in with as much force as they normally did, it is reasonable to suggest that fewer lives, on both sides, would have been lost. Using the maximum force available, within logical[2] limits, is the best way to fight a battle. Several days and many lives later, the command changed its mind, and, as Warr relates, most of the buildings were smashed: 'So much for trying to protect this valuable real estate'.[55] In World War II parachutist Daniel Webster was part of the US forces' attack on Nunen when his unit requested a tank commander knock down a nearby church steeple, where it was suspected an enemy observer was targeting mortar fire on them. The request was refused, because the tank commander had orders not to destroy too much property in a friendly country. Webster observed that wars are won by 'fighting 100 percent with every weapon at your command'.[56] C Company of the

---

2   For example, it is not suggested that using a nuclear weapon to solve a small tactical situation is suitable. Nor would it have been logical and ethically reasonable for the British to level the Argentine capital with one to win back the Falklands …

2nd Battalion of the Parachute Regiment tried an advance across open ground in the Battle of Goose Green in the Falklands War. As one historian noted dryly: 'It was a gamble that did not pay off', for the Argentines opened up on the British with everything available.[57] What should have been done, of course, was to assault the Argentine position with preparatory fire ...

To return to the enthusiastic warrior, Franklin Miller served one tour in Vietnam as a draftee and then signed up to come back. He joined the Special Forces, and enjoyed his Vietnam experience because of the power it gave him:

> That's one reason I enjoyed 'Nam so much. Over there you could be a bad motherfucker. Back in the States you couldn't. Could you run around in the woods kicking ass back in the U.S.A.? Could you legally carry fully automatic weapons down Main Street?[58]

However, Miller also stated that he didn't necessarily enjoy killing, just that it was sometimes necessary.[59]

Judging the number of enemy killed in Vietnam and the level of lethality is extremely difficult to do. In many accounts of combat, the well-known 'body count' was falsified, as there was pressure from above to achieve a high count – indeed, officers were rewarded with positive reports if they succeeded. So the count was routinely mis-stated:

> During the night in radio conversation after the battle lulled, there was a wager made by 1 of the company commanders, the A Company commander to the C Company commander, as to who would find the most bodies out in front of their positions, a case of beer, as a matter of fact. The next morning they went out to police up the bodies. The A Company commander had 8 and the C Company commander had 5, for a total of 13, as I recall. The asst div commander landed his helicopter, surveyed the situation. It was clear to him there were 13 bodies in front of the position. He proclaimed by some strange way that I will never be able to figure out that there were 197 bodies, and that is what was printed in the paper the next day.[60]

US soldier Charles Gadd saw the same distortions at work, and describes one incident where three VC kept their weapons in a shallow part of a river. A local village boy led an American patrol to them. The weapons were brought into the patrol's headquarters with a story about how they had been captured from three of the enemy, and the three enemy 'dead' were routinely added to the count.[61] The concept was in use early in the war, and by the ARVN too. US Army combat adviser Martin Dockery noted that everyone who the South Vietnamese battalion he was attached to shot 'was considered a Viet Cong' and added to their body count, which every commander would increase as it made its way back to division headquarters.[62]

In conclusion, we can see that some soldiers are drawn to combat. Warfare has different attractions for different people. Some human beings are imbued with a warrior spirit, and indeed we may conclude that it is present, to a degree, in all soldiers. It is certainly not the case, though, with all who take part in combat. But it certainly is the case that combat enthusiasm is a essential part of being an effective force. Such understanding needs to be reflected not only in the training of the modern soldier, but also in societal treatment of that individual.

Revenge as a motivator

… I definitely wanted to kill someone at close quarters.

Infantry officer and poet Siegfried Sassoon after
Lance-Corporal Kendle in his platoon was killed.

We have seen that there are different types of combat motivators. Another, apart from satisfaction in doing one's job properly and the pure excitement of warfare, is the desire for revenge. A dilemma for commanders is when the act of taking revenge is excusable, and therefore its breach of the Geneva Convention is understandable, rendering that part of the Convention questionable.

It does not take too much personal loss to turn men into savage, vengeful warriors. Actual or supposed breaking of 'the rules' – official or unofficial – can be enough to tip the balance from necessary lethality towards extreme ferocity. The British war policy of taking Boer civilians into captivity was supposed to undermine morale, according to one Boer soldier, but he thought it actually strengthened the resolve of his side, and prolonged the war by 'a year or more'.[1] The finding of a Boer atrocity – burying a British corporal alive, according to a witness, and it was certainly the case that one leg was protruding from the grave – made 'all those who saw his lonely grave and heard the story' vow they would avenge him.[2] The town of Ladysmith was besieged for a lengthy period by the Boers, and they shelled the buildings from a distance on a regular basis. The hospital was marked by a well-known tower, and many of the British defenders thought that it was deliberately targeted. This aroused much thirst for revenge: ''It's pure brutality,' I heard one of the Carbineers say, with clenched fists, 'and may God Almighty help the first Boer who asks me for quarter'.[3]

Royal Marines of Naval Party 8901 with hands and weapons raised, surrender to Argentine Special Forces at Government House in Port Stanley during the invasion of the Falkland Islands. IWM 9903-12 FKD 3020

Some national parties to a war may be more lethal than their foreign counterparts. Donald Macdonald, fighting against the Boers, thought his adversary was a resourceful and brave fighter who had a fair code of conduct. But he also thought some of the Dutch – the 'unspeakably bearish Dopper' – would do anything to an Englishman, and he gave examples of sheltering behind a wounded English soldier, or killing wounded.[4] JHM Abbott, fighting with the Australian troops in South Africa, agreed with the Boer soldier's qualities, but also thought that to them an Englishman ranked lower than a 'Kaffir', and they would 'quite permissibly extend the harshest treatment' to their enemy.[5]

The use of 'illegal' ammunition in the Boer War was a sore point on both sides. There are suggestions the Boers used soft-nosed bullets, cut with a cross in order to spread upon impact, but there is dispute as to both whether the British did too and who did so first.[6] Of course, such a practice may well not be official, just something carried out by soldiers on their own. So when World War I Private George Coppard's unit found clips of German soft-nosed bullets on one occasion, they took 'grim satisfaction' in firing them back using captured Mauser rifles.[7] Frank Richards, on the same side in the same war, said that they could tell if a bullet which hit one of their men had been an 'expanding bullet', because of the nature of the wound. If this happened, Richards explained, they retaliated by cutting off their own bullet tips to flatten them, but he conceded that 'it would be very difficult to decide which side used those bullets first'.[8] Similarly, bullets which had been allegedly drilled out to have a hollow point were found by British troops overrunning Argentine supply positions in the Falklands.[9]

The use of saw-back bayonets, particularly by combat engineer units, has also been the subject of vitriolic debate. Harsh treatment was often meted out to those found carrying them, in many wars, despite the fact that this type of bayonet was designed to be a useful tool in the field for cutting wood and the like.

World War I infantry sergeant Thomas Marks was convalescing with a French family who had befriended him after he was injured in a gas attack. He got to know them well, dining at their house frequently, and concluded that while the British simply killed the Germans because it was their job, the French looked upon them as 'Huns and Vandals', and killed them as vermin who were not fit to live.[10] Similarly, British Army Corporal Harry Bloodworth Smith noted that it was bred into him that the Germans were inhuman.[11] But this wasn't the view held by all. Corporal WHA Groom, who survived three years of the war as an infantryman, thought that people at home, manipulated by propaganda, hated the Germans more than did the 'old' front-line soldiers, who were always ready to give a prisoner a cigarette and reassure him'.[12]

In World War II, Intelligence Officer Glenn Gray noted, in his detached, philosophical way, that the more a soldier had lost to the war – relatives, friends – the more ferocious in his treatment of captured enemy he would be. The war turned into a vendetta, with 'hatred penetrating every fiber of his being.' His reason for living was to seek revenge, preferably a 'tenfold retaliation'.[13] The Poles, who suffered terribly under the German advance in World War II, were cruel in revenge. RJ Weston thought they were the most ferocious and callous' soldiers he had met, who 'literally butchered' any Germans they came across. He described their treatment of a captured German: they tied his hands, put a hand grenade with the pin out into his pocket, and told him to run ... [14] One World War II veteran commented on his feelings of hatred for the Germans at the end of the war. 'My own viewpoint was, that the war for me had been a complete failure because there were 60 million square-headed bastards still living'.[15]

At an individual level, as mentioned, Siegfried Sassoon wrote of his feelings when Lance-Corporal Kendle in his platoon was killed. Sassoon got himself a bag of Mills bombs and went off and attacked a trench of Germans by himself. The enemy soldiers promptly fled, but that was not enough for the normally thoughtful and kindly Sassoon: 'I definitely wanted to kill someone at close quarters.'[16] Frank Richards spent two days sniping after a friend was killed, and concluded: 'I was very fortunate on two days and felt that I had amply revenged Stevens'.[17] Corporal John Lucy had lost a brother a few days before he described this attack by the Germans in 1914 France, and his jubilation at revenge:

We let them have it. We blasted and blew them to death. They fell in scores, in hundreds, the marching column wilting under our rapid fire. The groups melted away, and no man was able to stand in our sight within five minutes. The few survivors panicked, and tried to keep their feet in retreat. We shot them down through the back. A red five minutes ... We had cancelled out our shell-tortured day with a vengeance.[18]

Daniel Webster, parachuting into France on D-Day, experienced feelings of curiosity as to why someone would want to kill him when he came under fire for the first time. A little while later, when he saw fellow parachutists coming down and being attacked by ground fire, he could only watch with 'mounting anger and hate', and thought of the enemy, 'I wanted to kill them all.'[19] Later, after some leave, he wrote to his parents and advised: 'I hope to go back soon ... for I owe the Germans several bullets and as many hand grenades as I can throw.' This was retaliation for the Germans cutting the throats of fellow parachutists caught in their harness, and other acts considered unacceptable.[20] US infantryman Bruce Zorns recalls his unit hearing about the massacre of around 100 US soldiers by the SS in a location to the north of them. Zorns notes that, from then on, 'we fought with a determination we had not before'.[21]

After the fight for Sugar Loaf Mountain on Okinawa, Private First Class Malcolm Lear surveyed the enemy dead littering the ground in their thousands and thought it ' ... in his bitterness towards the enemy 'the prettiest sight in the world''.[22] In that battle Corporal O'Connor, a Marine who had lost a lot of friends killed and wounded the previous day, acquired for himself a bag of grenades and started off towards the Japanese positions alone. He grenaded individual positions until they were all gone, backing up his attack with his pistol. His company commander was so astonished at this that, when O'Connor returned, he sent him off for psychological testing.[23]

The Goettge patrol incident on Guadalcanal was a prime motivator for the American Marines fighting later on Peleliu Island, as EB Sledge relates. A captured Japanese soldier had claimed some of his starving comrades would surrender. A patrol of 25, including a surgeon and a linguist, went out – all were ambushed as they came ashore on a landing craft. Three escaped. The 'Goettge patrol' incident, as it came to be known, was the cause for 'a passionate hatred' in all Marines, according to one of them, EB Sledge.[24] He thought this hatred made them reluctant to take prisoners. William Manchester sheds more light on it: apparently an English-speaking Japanese prisoner was taken. Interrogated with alcohol, he reluctantly – or so the Americans thought – revealed that hundreds of Japanese soldiers, starving, were ready to quit near the Matankau region of the island. Surveillance of the area revealed a white flag flying, and the party was dispatched to accept the surrender. But it was a trap, and the Americans were met with a hot reception. Only three escaped, and told of those Marines taken alive being beheaded immediately afterwards.[25] The taking of Peleliu Island indicates the consequences of that: Sledge suggests 10, 900 died, with 302 prisoners, but of the latter only seven were soldiers and 12 sailors – the rest 'laborers of other oriental extractions'.

The Japanese routinely had a 'take no prisoners' policy, according to some accounts. In one engagement the Japanese infantry won the day and took ground which their enemies had previously held. There they found some of their own dead who had met their ends at the hands of the defenders. Because of the respectful treatment of the body of a Japanese officer – he had been wrapped, together with his sword, in a blanket – the victorious Japanese commander gave orders that the Allied wounded should be treated and enemy prisoners should not be killed – implying, of course, that routinely the converse was the case. The writer, Captain Shosaku Kameyama, commented, 'After fierce battles where many comrades were killed, men were excited and felt strong hatred against the enemy soldiers and were provoked to kill even helpless prisoners.'[26]

The British Army in training in Britain, 1944. Private A Campin with fixed bayonet practises assault. Today, some critics of warfare and warriors have called for the bayonet to be abolished. IWM TR 1596

The Russian soldier Timoshenko thought 'a soldier who hates the enemy is a good soldier', and he entered Germany 'with the sense of a long, bloody score to pay off', for his friends, even his teachers, had been killed by the Germans in their occupation of his home district.[27] One Russian historian wrote that 'hatred for the enemy had become the most important emotion for our men. Almost every Soviet soldier possessed some personal reason to seek vengeance.'[28] It would not be a surprise to hear that the Russians might have had a battle-cry similar to the British in the Boer War – 'Remember Majuba!' – and it would have been 'Remember Leningrad!', where they lost 900, 000 or so of their people. But there were instances of prisoners surviving the Russians. Henry Metelmann fell into Russian hands briefly. He was interrogated – he spoke Russian – without much rancour, and then put to work on domestic duties. When the Russian unit suffered a reverse shortly afterwards, he was able to drift off and find his own side again.[29]

We may well wonder whether war might be shorter and millions of lives saved if these countries' armies had not behaved in this way. Knowing that there was no possibility of survival if one was captured must have caused many a desperate action to continue in hopeless situations, whereas in a 'normal' battle, surrender in such cases would have been feasible. Nevertheless, it paints a picture of part of the reality of prisoner-taking on the battlefield, and doubtless the revenge equation remains the same today, as we shall see.

In Vietnam, Warrant Officer Richard Elliot of the US Army's 1st Cavalry Division was involved in a particularly long and arduous fight, during which his helicopter was shot down and many Americans were killed and wounded. In a letter he wrote home afterwards, he said:

Dad, now more than ever I am determined to do everything possible to wipe these rotten bastards off the face of the earth. I have a long time here, and heaven help anyone of them, man, woman, or child, that crosses my path. Total and complete destruction is the only way to treat these animals.[30]

Marine Officer Nicholas Warr had a Lance Corporal Ed Estes in his platoon. Estes changed, with the death of four of his comrades to mines, to a hater of the Vietnamese, because the local villagers had not warned the Americans of the laying of the mines. He took out a patrol in revenge, which did not in fact kill any locals, for ' ... the villagers were not stupid, having lived and survived in a battle zone for most or all of their lives; they all took off, and they stayed as far away from the Marine patrol as possible.'[31] But Estes, said Warr, changed in a day to a 'Zippo warrior', and he and the patrol burnt down several huts. Warr himself noted later his own reaction to seeing the bodies of four NVA who had been killed by Marine snipers as 'gleeful vengeance for the deaths of Morgan and Estes and all the others who had lost their lives in the streets of Hue.'[32] Second Lieutenant Bob Oslin, flying helicopters for the US Army, thought: 'Killing was easy for almost everyone ... after you saw a friend wounded, you stopped considering the other guy as a human.'[33] Revenge was the motivation for the execution of 21 enemy captured by US soldiers in mid-1966. The North Vietnamese had spent the night torturing their six US captives within earshot of their comrades, and then killed their victims, who were found dead with their genitalia in their mouths. When the US forces took the position the next day, they executed all the prisoners they took.[34]

In World War II, 2nd Lieutenant Peter Cochrane took part in a heated action against Italian mountain troops, and his company took many casualties. By the time his platoon was down to three privates and himself, they were 'angrily looking for someone else to shoot or bayonet'.[35] But the feelings of anger about seeing your friends shot was not everlasting for most. As one veteran put it: 'After the first battle, the fellows were real mad, seeing all their buddies killed. But the reaction of being mad wore off after a while'.[36] After a bad mauling by the German 12th SS Panzer group after D-Day, the Canadian units which had taken a beating were filled with a spirit of revenge. ' ... everyone was rather vindictive, and silently swearing revenge'.[37] Urged on by stories of atrocities, there was actually an order issued not to take prisoners, although it got its writer into some trouble and did not stand for long. However, the Canadians were 'fighting mad', and one of them, Sergeant Gariepy, reflected that this was a good thing for new people, who often hesitated before shooting – 'this is a normal reaction for the first time,' thought the sergeant. 'After that, it's easy'.[38]

Seeing their comrades fall was the prime motivator behind bloodthirstiness in battle, thought Donald Macdonald, going in with the British infantry in the Boer war:

The hour of pity and forgiveness is not yet. The dominant note is pure savagery, the overmastering emotion – Destruction ... All day men have seen their comrades dying around about them ... they are panting for close quarters, for the wild, indescribable bayonet melee – most of all for revenge. They cannot be turned loose at such a moment and play the saint.[39]

EB Sledge and some companions found the bodies of three American Marines who had died on Peleliu; they had been dismembered. Sledge recalled: 'My emotions solidified into rage and a hatred for the Japanese beyond anything I have ever experienced. From that moment on I never felt the least pity or compassion for them …'[40] The incredible stresses of combat against the Japanese created such feelings in the Marines fighting them that there were some terrible responses in combat. Following a fierce fight where friends had been lost:

> A grimy Marine with a dazed expression stood over the Japanese. With a foot planted firmly on the ground on each side of the enemy officer's body, the Marine held his rifle by the forestock with both hands and slowly and mechanically moved it up and down like a plunger. I winced each time it came down with a sickening sound into the gory mass … we gently took him by the arm. One of his uninjured buddies set aside the gore-smeared rifle. 'Let's get you outa here, Cobber.'

The writer, EB Sledge, commented: 'Replete with violence, shock, blood, gore and suffering, this was the type of incident that should be witnessed by anyone who has any delusions about the glory of war. It was as savage and as brutal as though the enemy and we were civilised barbarians rather than civilised men'.[41] A further point is that such accounts as those we have seen above may well bring expressions of revulsion and requests for disciplinary action in some of these cases. But who, faced with the same situation, might not honestly admit that they too would act in this way?

In Vietnam, William Merritt served with a soldier who lost a friend to weapons fired from a nearby village. The soldier, when on sentry duty using an M-60, removed the tracer rounds from the ammunition belts and, during the 'Mad Minute' – when an entire detachment would fire their weapons for practice – targeted the village, the absence of tracer meaning others could not see where his rounds were going.[42]

Philip Caputo, serving as a Marine officer, carefully analysed his own reasons for staying in the Vietnam theatre of combat. He was fighting a terrible war, having served in combat front-line operations, and then as a staff officer, where he titled himself 'Officer in Charge of the Dead', identifying their own killed soldiers and keeping a statistical analysis of the enemy killed, wounded, prisoners and so on. He returned to front-line combat and stayed fighting because 'I burned with a hatred for the Viet Cong and … a desire for retribution. I did not hate the enemy for their politics, but for murdering

Simpson, for executing that boy whose body had been found in the river, for blasting the life out of Walt Levy'.[43]

Determined warriors loyal to a cause. Two blindfolded Viet Cong, after capture during a 1968 firefight in the Vietnam war. AWM CAM/68/0144/VN

The Marines with whom Johnnie Clark was fighting took casualties every day to mines, but could not make contact with NVA soldiers. Clark noted that 'the hatred builds when there's no fighting back … craving for revenge infected us like a virus and built steadily with each new casualty. I wanted to kill as many as possible. I looked forward to it with lust.'[44]

And in every war the situation is the same. Fighting on the Argentine side, soldier Felix Barreto noted that he was 'overcome with hatred for the British' because they had, he heard, made prisoners walk through minefields to clear them.[45]

We will see in another chapter how revenge is also a motivator not to take prisoners. But we have seen here that it is a powerful force in creating effective troops. It is a very natural human impulse, and one that should not be easily disregarded. Any tactical commander who does not account for it, look for behaviour motivated by revenge, understand it and cope with it in his troops, does not yet understand the true nature of combat.

5

Aggression in flying tactics

We are nothing but hired assassins.

Canadian World War I ace, Billy Bishop.

The methodology of fighter aircraft tactical combat was born in World War I, and developed rapidly over the four years of war. Aircraft were originally used for reconnaissance and artillery spotting, but quickly became fighters and bombers. Pilots began aerial combat by taking rifle shots at each other, and machine-guns were soon mounted on aircraft, to be manned by observer-gunners. Some of the greatest developments were the use of the aircraft itself to aim a forward-firing machine-gun, and of interrupter gear to enable such weapons to fire through the propeller. Tactics evolved rapidly in the face of regular and lethal improvements to each side's flying. Formation flying evolved, as did concepts of layers of scouts to protect those below, and radical innovation was the norm: one, two or three sets of wings; rotary or in-line engines; the 'pusher' or the tractor engine arrangement – all were tested in war.[1]

Attacking from behind, by surprise, soon became the normal practice of many pilots. Thus many inexperienced fliers died, probably without even knowing they were under attack. Neither side used parachutes (until a few German pilots acquired them at the end of the war[1]), although balloon observers did, and an aircraft catching fire in combat was common, with the subsequent death plunge known as a 'flamer'. (As an aside, balloon observation was not new: by this time, it had been used in wars for over 100 years for general observation and to spot artillery fall of shot. If soldiers knew what they were doing, the balloon and its observer became a target.)

---

1 Useful descriptions of the tactics of war in the air can be gained from books such as Lee's *No Parachute*, and from the excellent fictional but well-researched novels of Derek Robertson.

By the end of the war, aircraft and their operators had evolved into several specialised areas. Reconnaissance for artillery spotting and intelligence gathering was an important complement to army operations. Bombing of the enemy's installations had become a specialised art. German bombers had attacked London, and defences had evolved as a result. Naval aviation had seen fighters operated from ships, with the development of the slide catapult and the flight-deck concept slowly being advanced. The fighter pilot had become a specialised operator of a unique craft of the air. Strategic aviation concepts had evolved: achieving air superiority over a battlefield, and eventually air supremacy; gaining intelligence; and using bombers to impose materiel loss. The role of the fighter aircraft as an essential part of the tri-service nature of war had been born.

Basic World War I flying tactics

Flying Officer RS Wortley explained the basic World War I German attacks in a letter to a friend:

> The tactics of the pilots seldom varied. They would climb to a height of about 10, 000 feet whence they would swoop, hawklike, upon our machines as they passed below them, firing continuously as they dived … The Fokkers hunted in pairs, sometimes, even three of them would fly together.[2]

A book by the well-known flier Eddie Rickenbacker, the top American ace of World War I, is full of references to the standard tactical approach of shooting your enemy from behind before he saw you, preferably with the sun at your back to ensure any searching pilots were blind to the approaching killer. 'None of them had seen my approach. At fifty yards I pressed my triggers and played my bullets straight into the pilot's seat.'[3]

On another occasion:

> I was not observed by the enemy until it was too late for him to escape. I had him exactly in my sights when I pulled both triggers for a long burst. He made a sudden attempt to pull away, but my bullets were already ripping through his fusilage (sic) and he must have been killed instantly. His machine fell wildly away and crashed just south of Etain.[4]

Thus the basic fighter attacking tactic became one of achieving surprise, and closing to within short and therefore effective range. What, in later years, might be termed a 'snapshot' was always to be taken advantage of:

Suddenly a D-V passed across my front from the west, about 200 feet below. As it slid by, I saw the pilot looking out of the further side of his cockpit at the smoke of battle below. He hadn't seen me. I swung steeply down onto his tail, and caught him up so quickly he seemed to be coming towards me. At twenty yards' range I pressed the triggers. The tracers flashed into his back.[5]

World War II flying

The tactics of air combat were developed further in World War II. Erich Hartmann, with 353 confirmed victories, is one of the highest-scoring 'aces' of all time. His tactics included ensuring 'the windscreen is filled with the enemy', and to always use the element of surprise. 'Never get into a turning battle with an enemy who knows you are there' was one of his maxims.[6] British ace Douglas Bader, famous for his artificial legs and his refusal to quit combat, exhorted: 'He who has the sun creates surprise. He who has the height controls the battle. He who gets in close shoots them down'.[7]

Walter Krupinski, another high-scoring German World War II flier, also preferred to get close and to attack from behind the enemy 'so he can't see you until it's too late'.[8] Major Gilbert O'Brien, a World War II fighter pilot, noted: 'I was in range astern and closed on the Zeke to about fifty yards before firing. The first few shots burst on the right elevator. I fired until flames shot out from all parts of his plane. The enemy pilot appeared skilled and eager for combat but I don't believe he saw me …'[9] And if you were lucky enough to take on opponents who possessed less capable machines, it was simply their misfortune and they were simply killed more quickly, as the ground observer noted on seeing a Hurricane fight above Derna shoot down three Italian biplane (CR42) fighters 'in about the time it would take to say one, two, three.'[10]

Chivalrous moments

The concept quickly arose of these aviators being the 'new knights of the sky'. The concept of the 'ace' – one who had scored over five victories – arose in France, and quickly spread.[11] In Germany, Baron Manfred von Richthofen – popularly known as 'The Red Baron' – was the celebrated leader of those fliers who became heroes to the nation: lionised at functions; celebrated in the newspapers; even becoming the subject of postcard collectors. Max Immelmann – the inventor of the famous evasive turn – was invited to dine with royalty, and noted that, with the publicity, 'My mail swelled to fifty letters a day'.[12]

Die Jagdstaffel des Freiherrn von Richthofen, im Apparat sitzend Rittmeister Freiherr von Richthofen.

Zensiert
Paul Hoffmann & Co.
Berlin-Schöneberg.

Flying officers attached to Rittmeister Manfred Freiherr Von Richthofen's squadron, Jasta 11. Richthofen is seated in the Albatros aircraft. Much romanticised, the "Red Baron" of WWI was in reality a cold-blooded determined killer – qualities still necessary in military aviators assigned to kill the enemy. AWM C05002

The Allied nations pursued similar tactics. Prime Minister Lloyd George proclaimed: 'They are the knighthood of this war, without fear and without reproach; and they recall the legendary days of chivalry, not merely by the daring of their exploits, but by the nobility of their spirit.'[13]

The flier Cecil Lewis recalled, when on leave:

> Too soon I was back in town again, spending my bank balance in riotous living. To belong to the R.F.C. [Royal Flying Corps] in those days was to be singled out among the rest of the khaki-clad world by reasons of the striking double-breasted tunic, the Wings, the little forage cap set over one ear, but more than this by the glamour surrounding the 'birdmen.' Flying was still something of a miracle. We who practiced it were thought very brave, very daring, very gallant: we belonged to a world apart. In certain respects it was true, and though I do not think we traded on this adulation, we could not be but conscious of it.[14]

There was a massive outpouring of grief in America when their first flier fell in combat. The death of Victor Chapman brought forth eulogies such as that of the *Boston Transcript*, which proclaimed: 'the loss of a man who had all the noble and chivalrous instincts in such overwhelming proportions that it was literally impossible for him to act like the average person. It was as though Prince Rupert or Richard Plantagenet himself had stepped down from history.' One of his friends perpetuated the new idyllic picture: 'He died the most glorious death, and at the most glorious time of life to die …'[15]

In the British forces, the concept was more muted: for example, the label of 'ace' was never used officially. Instead, the pilots were celebrated in accounts such as 'With the Australian Flying Corps in France', where the 'Elsternwick Boy Hero' was lauded – albeit with 'hot air' and 'bombast', according to the victim.[16] The fliers were given plenty of decorations: Military Crosses and Victoria Crosses were awarded. These propaganda efforts distracted people at home from the bad news of a stalemated war, and gave them heroic figures upon which to focus. The image of the fliers was perpetuated in books, films and newspapers. The notion of chivalry was therefore fostered, as in this example:

> … he got the machine under control and looked around for the bomber. It was steering an erratic course for the ground, obviously in difficulties. He dived after it and noticed that the rear gunner's cockpit was empty. 'I've hit the pilot and the observer is trying to get the machine down,' he decided instantly, and closer view confirmed his suspicions …'I hope he manages it,' thought Biggles anxiously, and held his hand up to show they had nothing to fear from him …[17]

Although, as will be seen, the concept was more honoured for propaganda reasons than observed in reality, the image is a persistent one. *Dawn Patrol*, starring Errol Flynn, was a movie which featured aircrew wearing scarves on top of their helmets, an echo of the plumes on knights' helmet. This film probably did more to influence the image of the knight of the sky than any other: pilots are universally resolute and good-looking; the enemy drops insults on one's aerodrome (a pair of Army boots are dropped on an enemy aerodrome in retaliation – this happened in reality[2] but not after 10 bombing passes!); and on the hero's last flight, bested in aerial combat, he waves goodbye to the victor, who salutes him.

---

2   Cobby, Group Captain AH. *High Adventure*. Melbourne: Robertson and Mullens, 1942. The dropping of boots and the sending of other derisory messages was employed several times when the Germans would not stay and fight but rather had a strategy of avoiding combat. (98-99)

World War II posters of pilots reflected the knight's helmet, with the visor pushed up. Profiles were ones of resolution and pride. A modern recruiting poster for the American forces feature the equivalent of the knightly steed, the modern jet fighter. His parents reflect the stereotypical ideal family, and thus reinforce the societal values for which he fights.

The Blue Max was an interesting development in the evolution of this portrayal. The central character – Bruno Stachel, played by George Peppard – is a former infantry soldier who transfers from the German Army to the cloistered officers' messes of its fighter squadrons. He sets his heart on winning the coveted 'Blue Max' – the popular name for the Pour Le Merite – a decoration given to those pilots who had downed twenty of the enemy. But Bruno's methods set him apart immediately, for he tries to shoot down – despite his squadron commander's directive not to – a two-seater in which the observer is trying to land the machine over the pilot's wounded shoulder, an echo of the Biggles scenario above. Bruno makes the kill, and is somewhat ostracised by his fellow officers as a result, partly because of his attitude to war and partly because he is not of 'Prussian officer corps' background.

By the film's end we see the two sides of the equation, and they are skillfully played out. Should we side with the squadron commander, who wants to fight the war for the values of Germany, with honour and chivalry? Or should we be like Bruno, who is a cold-blooded killer?

How true was this in reality?

Certainly some pilots arrived with the perception – doubtless fostered by what they had read and heard – that the combat in which they were to be engaged had some chivalrous or sporting notions to it. Longstreet describes an occasion in World War I with the 'Mad Major', an eccentric individual who was actually Captain AAB Thompson of the RFC's 16th Squadron. He lived apart from the rest of his Squadron, and spent his leisure time reading the classics – it was said that he was once a schoolmaster. On one occasion he was said to have let an enemy escape: ' … on the tail of an enemy flying an Albatross, [he] moved into firing range but just slid past the enemy giving a happy wave.'[18] This was early in the war, and there are a few such instances to be found in the records. The French ace Guynemer is said to have let Ernst Udet, a German ace, live when his guns were jammed and the hapless pilot was hammering at the breeches of the weapons.[19]

However, moments of chivalry were rare – and even if they were presented, could be a trap for unwary players. Nungesser, the French ace, was once challenged to a solo duel by a message dropped at his aerodrome. It was addressed to 'My worthy opponent, Monsieur Skull and Bones' – a reference to Nungesser's personal device painted on his plane. Upon arriving at the appointed time and place, the Frenchman was jumped by six Albatrosses hiding in clouds. The ace took them on, though, and shot down two, with the remaining four fleeing the field of combat.[20]

The Canadian ace 'Billy' Bishop romanticised his profession a little, describing it on one occasion as ' … a wonderful game. To bring down a machine did not seem to me to be killing a man; it was just like destroying a mechanical target … '[21] Norman MacMillan noted that, in 1916–17, 'contemporary references' evolved to 'knights of the air' and 'the chivalry of air combat'. He thought that 'sometimes there was evidence of chivalry, but more often there was just the sheer bloody murder of the head-hunter'.[22]

Sometimes the 'rules of chivalry' were considered and rejected. Eddie Rickenbacker relates an account where a fellow pilot was attempting to shoot down a two-seater engaged in photographic reconnaissance. The observer-gunner ran out of ammunition and, as the Allied pilot approached on another pass, was seen to be standing up in the cockpit with folded arms, awaiting his death. The Allied pilot was ' … so impressed with the bravery of the action that he felt he could not continue the combat against an unarmed enemy'.[23] But then he acknowledged that the German plane obtained pictures which might mean 'the deaths of hundreds of our boys'. He shoots, and kills both of the enemy airmen.

Arthur Gould Lee, a British flier, recounts the dropping of messages to the enemy, and even, on the death of one respected German flier – Boelcke – a wreath, commenting that: 'This mutual consideration is one of the few decent things in this mutual killing business'.[24] Sometimes there was a moment when two enemy fighters might coincidentally arrive at a moment of peace. The British ace Albert Ball recounted a time when he tried to shoot down a German two-seater with his usual attack of firing from under the enemy's tail. However, on this occasion his adversary was too skilled, and with a sideslip each time Ball tried it, gave his observer a sufficient opportunity to fire. For half an hour the two machines fought, until they both ran out of ammunition, and then, as Ball said in a letter home: 'There was nothing to be done after that, so we both burst out laughing. We couldn't help it – it was so ridiculous. We flew side by side laughing at each other for a few seconds, and then we waved adieu to each other and went off. He was a real sport that Hun'.[3]

Paul Richey, in World War II, describes his feeling of relief at seeing an enemy pilot's escape from a fiery death:

> … a mass of bits flew off him – pieces of engine cowling and lumps of his glasshouse [hood] – and as I passed just over the top of him, still in a left-hand turn, I watched with a kind of fascinated horror as he went into a spin, smoke pouring out of him, I remember saying 'My God, how ghastly!' as his tail suddenly swiveled sideways and tore off, white flames streamed over his fuselage. Then I saw a little white parachute open beside it. Good![25]

In the film *Aces High* the squadron commander (played by Malcolm McDowell) forces down an enemy aircraft and then finds the German pilot, by now a prisoner, and brings him back to the mess for dinner. The same scenario occurs in the 1938 film *Dawn Patrol*. Unrealistic, perhaps, but the World War II German ace Johannes Steinhoff was described as 'another member of the old school'. He once downed an enemy flier and then brought him to his own tent and entertained him, merely accepting his parole that his guest would not try and escape.[26] Fighter pilot Paul Richey records his No. 1 Squadron doing just that with a German pilot they shot down in France in 1940.[27] And so that scenario in the films was true enough.

By World War II, feelings were more hard-headed, but there were still traces of at least some consideration for the enemy, if not chivalry. The German ace Galand, for example, was known as a 'chivalrous soldier' who believed passionately in fair play, which governed his actions towards his foes in the air.[28] During the Battle of Britain, Flight Lieutenant Frank Carey participated in an attack over the North Sea on a Heinkel 111 which, after being hit, caught fire. Carey's flight commander 'immediately ordered us to stop attacking it', and the enemy aircraft turned towards Britain and was escorted towards land. But soon a Hurricane from another squadron came upon the scenario and immediately attacked the Heinkel, which crashed into the sea with no survivors.[29]

---

3   Bowyer, Chaz. *Albert Ball, VC*. London: William Kimber, 1977. (97) Incidentally, Ball's assessment was mistaken – he had killed the observer and wounded the pilot.

A portrait of Lieutenant Audie Murphy with the Medal of Honor hanging around his neck.
His photos seem to suggest a polite, homely US boy, but Murphy was one of the fiercest warriors
of WWII. http://www.audiemurphy.com/photo mil 022.htm

The reality of aerial combat

Did all of the World War I aerial fighters try to kill their enemy? Dave Grossman, who wrote on the psychological aspects of combat lethality, suggests not: he is of the opinion that the fliers ' … in relatively slow-moving aircraft, could see enemy pilots, and thus large numbers of them failed to fight aggressively.'[30] But this is not borne out by first-hand accounts such as Rickenbacker's: by way of contrast, he notes as unusual behaviour one pilot who his Squadron could not persuade to fight aggressively. This officer fled the scene, and this was sufficiently unusual for Rickenbacker to note as being different. AH Cobby noted: 'I think I only met one coward during the whole of my flying experience at the War and he was to be pitied'.[31]

Notions of chivalry were either rapidly changed or dispelled. Lieutenant William Fry, for example, joined the British 11th Squadron in July 1916, and met the well-known ace Albert Ball. He noted: 'There was in his attitude none of that sporting element which to a certain extent formed the basis of many scout pilots' approach to air fighting'.[32] In reality, of course, as the Canadian ace Billy Bishop commented, ' … we are nothing but hired assassins'.[33]

Most pilots – by their own accounts and often by others – seemed determined to attack the enemy as aggressively as they could. Arthur Gould Lee shot down his fair share of enemy aircraft, but admitted: 'I'm just not keen on getting flamers'.[34] James McCudden, VC, notes in his autobiographical account of his war years an occasion when he:

> … missed that Hun because I did not at that time possess that little extra determination that makes one get one sight on a Hun and makes one's mind decide that one is going to get him or know the reason why … [35]

Mick Mannock, the British fighter ace, was well known for his savagery towards the enemy. One of his squadron noted: 'He told us if we ever let a German get away alive that we could have killed, he'd shoot us himself.'[36] Another pilot said:

> The Hun crashed, but not badly, and most people would have been content with this, but not Mick Mannock, who dived half a dozen times at the machine, spraying bullets at the pilot and observer, who were still showing signs of life. I witnessed this business, and flew alongside of Mick, yelling at the top of my voice (which was rather

useless) and warning him to stop. On being questioned as to his wild behaviour, after we had landed, he heatedly replied: 'The swines are better dead – no prisoners.'

Billy Bishop is reported to have said: 'You have no idea of how bloodthirsty I've become and how much pleasure I get in killing Huns'.[37] Even those who were clearly more humane settled down to the grim business of dispatching the enemy. Arthur Gould Lee recalled: 'Being so close when I fired, and seeing him collapse, made him another human being, not just a target in an aeroplane. But I can't say it worries me unduly – after all, he started it'.[38] Aircrew routinely emptied their guns into the trenches at the end of a patrol; and *Cavalry of the Clouds* describes an incident where an enemy train was bombed, at first targeting the locomotive itself and then, four times over, targeting the troops trying to escape from the carriages.[39]

Rickenbacker's autobiographical account contains some light-hearted references to the killing he was engaged in. He describes the aerial machine-gunning of a line of artillery as '... the most amusing little party I had ever attended'.[40] But he was also capable of remorse, describing the pilot of the first enemy machine he sent down in flames as a 'poor devil'.[41]

The Frenchman René Fonck was one of the highest-scoring aces of World War I. The editor of the autobiographical account[42] of his World War I exploits credits him with '75 confirmed victories', and acknowledges Fonck's own tally of 127. The flier was an enthusiastic executioner: his first shared victory, with him flying as a pilot, saw his observer shoot an ' ... enemy observer at point-blank range. It was for me a veritable ecstasy and a particular consolation to see the plane plunging rapidly ...'[43] On occasion, Fonck writes of his respect for a brave enemy, but he also sometimes rages at them as cowards, describes them as 'beautiful prey', suppresses a 'desire momentarily to spare him', and describes a fight where he shot down two aircraft, one after the other, as a 'picnic'.[44] In another incident he admits: 'I always felt a little compassion for my victims, despite the slightly animalistic satisfaction of having saved my own skin and the patriotic joy of victory'.[45]

This is an excellent summary of how many a pilot must feel. Fonck is honest enough to admit feeling positive about his actions, but they are tinged with a slight feeling of sadness. It is at once the warrior admitting that he must do his job without deviation, and at the same time feeling a little remorse about taking human life. It is notable, and a key to this discussion, that Fonck survived the war and was able to write his account, and in later years did not relent from his stance. He was a warrior; he excelled at killing, and there is an end to it.

6

The prevalence of lethal behaviour

We don't want this sort of soldier in peacetime.

Returned Falklands Paratrooper Tony Gregory.

Are those engaged in close-range combat really intentionally lethal? Some suggest otherwise. Dave Grossman, in his work *On Killing*, proposes that many troops avoid taking on the enemy for various reasons, one of them being a natural repugnance for taking life. He posits that infantry, for example, often fire high, or simply do not fire at all in combat. He cites 12,000 loaded weapons found after the Battle of Gettysburg, for example, as proof that soldiers went through the drill of loading, but did not actually fire, becoming 'conscientious objectors'.

But surely to survive in close-up combat you need to be aggressive, and that means attack. As infantryman Bill Mauldin put it in World War II:

> … you don't fight a kraut by Marquis of Queensbury rules. You shoot him in the back, you blow him apart with mines, you kill or maim him the quickest and most effective way you can with the least danger to yourself. He does the same to you. He tricks you and cheats you, and if you don't beat him at his own game you don't live … [1]

Instead, I suggest here that troops quickly realise the truth of Mauldin's words – it's him or me. There are many reasons why Grossman's view is wrong. First, the finding of loaded weapons at Gettysburg cannot necessarily be conclusive. A muzzle-loaded long arm goes through a lengthy process of loading, retaining the ramrod, bringing up to the aim, and firing – the weapon's owner may well be shot in the process. How many rounds had been fired there is not known.

What actually happens when troops are defeated is not that they are necessarily engaged in a firefight: they break and run more for psychological reasons than any other. Typically they see the troops on their flank flee and, deciding the battle is lost, make haste to depart. It would be normal for their weapons to be loaded at this moment, but then they are shot down by the victors while retreating. Perhaps 50 per cent of casualties at Gettysburg were caused by artillery. Typically, infantry were standing around getting shot at from long range by artillery and could not reply. If they are in formation – that is, under orders near the battleline – then their weapons are loaded. Every man killed or wounded drops his weapon.

Battles are won more by the psychological effects of weapons than by their physical impacts: a defeated army very rarely suffers even 50 per cent of its number in killed and wounded, and indeed can rarely endure losses of over 25 per cent before acknowledging defeat. The psychological effects are a direct result of the physical ones – it is primarily the sight of comrades being wounded and killed that demoralises an attack and causes it to fail.

So, for example, in Pickett's Charge on the third day of the Battle of Gettysburg, the attacking Confederates had only suffered about 25 per cent casualties when their assault broke. In other words, although three-quarters of the troops were capable of fighting, they stopped doing so.

Grossman cites, through various wars, the thousands of rounds fired in terms of people hit, as further evidence of man's unwillingness to take life. 'In World War II, 75 to 80 per cent of riflemen did not fire their weapons at an exposed enemy, even to save their lives and the lives of their friends'.[2]

I take some issue with this, although it must be concluded that there is much food for thought in Grossman's work, and he makes some conclusions that seem well supported. For example, he suggests that killing decreases in repugnance with physical distance from the subject, so that the firing of a missile, the dropping of a bomb, or the long-distance shots of a sniper are all less repulsive than say, the use of a knife against a human target. Quite so. One World War II veteran flier observed: 'The further you are from the target, the less likely you are to have an understanding of the devilry your weapons are causing.'[3] Another World War II soldier commented: 'We're all unable to imagine what people are feeling a few hundred yards away – it's very much a lack of imagination, one of the greatest human weaknesses I think.'[4]

Some of Grossman's suggestions, though, seem too far-fetched. For example, he argues that the classic use of a knife from behind a target is the result of a rejection of seeing the victim's face – although it would seem much more sensible to attack a sentry from behind. Grossman's allegation of soldiers deliberately firing high is dubious, for a number of reasons. My estimation of most soldiers' firearms ability is not high. I have seen hundreds of trainees attempt to pass their firearms qualifications with assault rifle and pistol, and their abilities decry the movies. It is not unusual to see people miss a man-sized target from 10 metres with their first few shots with a pistol. Many fail the fairly simple requirement of being able to hit a man-sized target a certain number of times with a rifle, and need further coaching in order to gain the minimum standard. This benchmark is not a high one: the shooter must only gain a competency of basic accuracy – that is, hitting the target about 60–70 per cent of the time.

Competency with a handgun is even harder. Most armed forces' trainees are too used to seeing this sort of weapon used in the movies or on television, when an actor, who has had plenty of time to practise, is firing blank charges of lesser recoil in a calm and scripted environment. This is against a target which does not even have to be hit – the special effects people simply can ensure it looks as if it has.

Contrast that in reality with a loud explosion going off at the end of your outstretched arm, with a short-barrelled weapon with primitive sights; a weapon which bucks and incites hand tremors, which must now be mastered to fire again. This is why it is not uncommon for trainees to miss a human-sized target a few metres away. A telling story by Robert Graves illustrates what terrible shots most people are with handguns. A group of experienced World War I infantry officers, billeted in an abandoned French house, decided to use a glass case filled with artificial fruit and flowers for target practice. They fired five shots each at it at a range of fifty yards, and all missed. They reduced the range to twenty yards, and one of them succeeded in hitting the post they had mounted it on. Finally one of them shot it up at close range.[5] This is a telling example – these officers had seen much practice and combat itself, yet they were still terrible shots.

In essence, competency with even comparatively effective modern firearms is not easily gained. How much less capable must soldiers have been in the past, with fixed sights, muzzle-loaded weapons, recoil that was onerous, and variable charges and projectiles. The fact that a soldier is not very good at inflicting death does not mean that he is not trying to inflict it.

At the risk of a generalisation, it seems to be the case that many firearm-carrying soldiers – musketeers and riflemen – had, since the weapon was introduced, little experience with their weapons before battle. Unlike the bowmen of medieval battlefields such as Agincourt and Crecy, highly practiced in their weapon from hunting and compulsory weekly practice, they were not masters of their weapon; quite the reverse. In World War I, most soldiers – excluding the peacetime professionals – had little experience with their primary weapon.

There are indeed enough exceptions to cause an argument: the professional armies of Wellington, for example, had years of experience of combat against the French and Spanish, and Napoleon's men were similar veterans. The armies of the South in the American Civil War were comparatively highly skilled with their weapons by comparison with the North, particularly as the men from the South were usually experienced field hunters. But in World War I and II, many citizen-soldiers, to use Ambrose's phrase, were lacking in extensive weapons experience.

That is not to say there were not some superb shots around: the British professional army which went into battle in 1914 was legendary in their mastery of that magnificent weapon, the Lee-Enfield .303. Infantryman Thomas Marks noted that 'most of us' could shoot 15 rounds a minute 'without much difficulty' with their .303s.[6] Frank Richards and his friends managed 25 a minute on occasion.[7] Australian infantryman Roland Griffiths-Marsh in the next war would have agreed: on several occasions he describes himself and his comrades as delivering '15 aimed rounds in the minute' with the same weapon.[8] The British rifleman of the Zulu Wars, firing a single-shot weapon, could manage 12 shots a minute for a while.[9] Marines training in the United States in World War II received lengthy and exhaustive firearms training, including a week of dry-firing with recoil simulation and the finer techniques of shooting before they fired a shot on the range. Then they had a week of live firing, with anyone who didn't qualify at least at the 'marksman' standard being told they would not be allowed to go overseas.[10] However, this certainly contrasted with the training many US soldiers were receiving at the end of the war, when the massive armies of America were demanding more and more soldiers. One officer of the 101st Airborne commented in 1945 that the officers they were now receiving had been merely taught to say 'Follow me', and then shipped overseas, as the quickest way to get replacements to the battlefield.[11]

Black and white photograph (from colour originals) taken by an Argentine soldier of the occupation of the Falklands in 1982, showing Argentine troops in Port Stanley, their billets and digging in the mountains. The sentry's lonely duty focuses – if he is alert and wants to live – on the necessity of being quickly and efficiently lethal as necessary. IWM 8505-12 FKD 225

First, the hurriedly-trained citizen-soldier amateurs of the massed armies of the 20th century's two World Wars were, in the main, not of a high standard. Royal Marine Edward Hill, deployed to fight in the attack on Crete in World War II, noted before the landing that: 'I had only actually fired five rounds on the rifle range.'[12] Lieutenant-Colonel Cedric Isaachsen noted, of some new arrivals in New Guinea for the World War II Australian Army, that they ' … had never fired a Bren gun or a Tommy gun – never thrown a grenade … '[13] In fact, the work from which that comment is taken devotes an entire chapter called 'Intensively Trained', to showing that the vast majority of these troops were exactly not that.

Second, the rifleman in battle is not the rifleman of the butts. In the latter role he has a comfortable position, a clear target, and measured precision to adhere to in the ritualised firing practice. In the field he may have no rest at all: he might be firing standing for a few seconds, or lying awkwardly, or even moving. His target might be poorly lit, or visible for only a brief moment. As an example of this, 'Lofty' Large related his Korea experience of trying to hit 10 walking enemy troops, 'about 350 metres' from his position, with his Lee-Enfield .303. About five of the British troops fired at their leisure at these enemy, and did not get one hit. One old soldier, who had not fired, observed that their shooting had actually been getting worse as they shot.[14] World War II soldier Corporal Vernon Scannell reflected on the various battles he had been involved in: 'When you consider the amount of stuff coming over in terms of the actual shells and mortars, bombs and small arms and the rest of it, when you consider the expenditure of weaponry – how few were hit'.[15]

Infantryman Charles Gadd relates how one of his companions in the US Army in Vietnam, on point for his platoon, met almost face to face two NVA soldiers on a trail with their weapons slung. They were so close, the US soldier said afterwards, that he could have shaken hands with them, which of course he did not; rather, he emptied an entire magazine from his M-16 at them – and failed to hit either in their immediate flight.[16] On another occasion two American platoons mistakenly targeted each other at night. At around 200 metres' distance, the two forces engaged with M-16s, M79 grenade launchers and M60 machine-guns until the mistake was discovered. No-one was killed, although several soldiers were wounded.[17]

Third, fire from machine-guns must account for many millions of rounds expended since automatic weapons first began to be seen on the battlefield in quantity, from World War I. The machine-gunner is an enfilade weapon, and is best used on the flanks in sweeping arcs mounted on a tripod. Thus many, many rounds are expended. It is also a suppression weapon which can be used very effectively to keep the enemy's heads down on that hill on the flank of your assault. While there may be no one on that hill you are going to be happy to spend plenty of rounds just to be sure.

Firing into cover 'just in case' is common enough with all sorts of weapons, and accounts for much expenditure of ammunition. First Sergeant Pasquale Fusco of the US Army, fighting against the Japanese on Makin, said that if they did not see any Japanese snipers, they still 'fired occasional shots into trees that looked likely'.[18] Philip Caputo's platoon, when advancing on the enemy in Vietnam, did the same: 'we fire without aiming into a field of elephant grass'.[19] An American major, observed some Canadians meeting up with him and his column advancing in 1945, looked up from his map and casually sprayed some tree-tops with his Tommy gun, observing 'Snipers', before returning to the discussion.[20]

Fighting in the battle of Ia Drang, the American infantry came under extremely heavy fire from advancing NVA members. It was so heavy that Sergeant John Setelin commented that if you looked up and out of your position you got shot in the head, and if you stood up to move forward you got shot in the feet. As a result, many US soldiers simply remained in cover and fired that way: as one recalled, you 'stuck your weapon up, pulled the trigger, and emptied the magazine'.[21] One US combat adviser observed that, when attacked, the ARVN routinely took cover and then fired their weapons in the general vicinity of the enemy. If one soldier fired when taking fire, then 'all those around him would shoot in the same direction.'[22] Soldiers in general just direct lots of rounds in the overall direction of the enemy. In World War I, British officer Bruce Bairnsfather observed routinely that in the trenches a rifle shot at night might be followed by a retaliatory shell or shot from the other side; more soldiers would join in, and then firing would break out between both sides all along a section of the Line. Then it died away. 'Total result of one of these firework displays: several thousand rounds of ammunition squibbed off, hundreds of star shells wasted, and no casualties.'[23]

Vietnam infantryman Charles Gadd's platoon took automatic fire from the opposite bank of a canal; they all fired back for a 'mad minute of firing … but no one knew what he was shooting at'. [24] Even quick rifle fire, Thomas Marks noted in World War I, usually stopped an attack from developing against you.[25] Similarly, as Charles B. MacDonald noted when leading his infantry company in World War II, at night troops in some situations fired their weapons, simply in the hope that they might hit an approaching enemy.[26] A combat team might fire to get the enemy to shoot back, so the latter's position could be identified[27] – a common technique known as 'reconnaissance by fire'.[28] This was usefully employed in the battle of Ia Drang, where the Americans decided near the end of the 53-hour engagement that the enemy were too quiet. By pre-arrangement, at 6.55 am every soldier opened fire on whatever he thought was a target. Immediately, about 30–50 of the enemy responded and were cut down, as were several snipers concealed in trees. [29]

The amount of ordnance expended can also relate to the strategic need, and to the composition of one's own forces. The assault on Europe from 1944 by the Allies was marked by knowledge that Germany could not escape the trap they were in, and therefore materiel was the key to the game, not expending infantry lives where one could avoid it. This cautious approach is not always the best: General Patton's speed in attack is often more preferable to General Hodges's caution. But the knowledge was there that the Allies were, as Professor Sir Michael Howard, military historian and combat veteran, later put it, ' … fighting the best professionals in the business.' The German Army, still dangerous and possessed of immense tactical skill, fought hard for every inch of ground, and was superb in counter-attack. So the Allies used their superior artillery and airpower before committing their infantry. Howard said: 'We blasted our way into Europe with a minimum of finesse and a maximum of high explosive.'[30] Canadian soldiers meeting up with Americans in 1945 discussed their approaches towards advancing. One of the Canadians commented that the Americans 'admitted their policy was to blast the objective with airplanes and artillery, and if even so much as a single Spandau replied, to blast it again, before going in.'[31]

Further, the rifleman's ability is lessened by the knowledge that his target may well be firing back, accompanied by several of his friends. Placing yourself calmly in a position where you can see the enemy, and can steadily shoot him, is made much less easy once you realise he is going to have that opportunity to target you. Rather, a quick snap shot or two in the hope of hitting him might be preferable, or some rounds sprayed over the top of a barrier in the general direction of the enemy. Firing back is a good idea: it will alarm the enemy, spoil his aim and manoeuvre, and generally make life difficult for him. Indeed, soldiers who do not fire at the enemy are rare enough to warrant comment in first-hand accounts. Lieutenant Simon Buckner, fighting his way forward with his company on a Pacific island, saw one devout Jewish soldier deliberately firing high while under fire. Making his way to the soldier, the officer demanded to know why he was doing so, and in the midst of the explanation the soldier was hit – in the canteen, and then again twice more, miraculously perhaps, in other equipment without being injured. 'Lieutenant, you're right. They are trying to kill me!' exclaimed the religious one, and joined the battle.[32] Experienced soldiers realise that one must be lethal, and that new recruits must be urged to be lethal, for good reason. A pocket book for troops, published in 1941 for the Australian Army, urges:

> Shoot to kill. If you do not, to-morrow morning, some of those men will sit behind fresh machine-guns. Their bullets will flay your flanks, kill good soldiers, perhaps kill you. Remember that panic is soon overcome. Remember that only a dead or captured enemy can do you no further harm. I have seen futile pity weaken our hands. As an enemy party breaks away in ludicrous desperation men will say: 'let the poor bastards go.' He who lets an enemy escape may be the means of the death of his best friend.[33]

Lastly, firing one's own weapon is a psychological support, in that you feel you are doing your best to defend yourself. The knowledge that you are indeed powerfully armed and just might kill the attacker before he does the same to you must be a strong imperative to indeed seek maximum lethality. Soldier Thomas Marks, fighting in World War I, thought firing in general was useful as a psychological effect even if it didn't cause too many casualties amongst the enemy.[34] Similarly, Private George Coppard in the same conflict noted: 'Bust-ups with the Prussians would start on the slightest pretext, and although a lot of ammunition may have been wasted, it was good for morale and made the noise of war. It did one good to have a bang in Jerry's direction, if only with a rifle.'[35]

Fear as a motivator should not be underestimated, as Guy Sajer thought in World War II after some years of combat as an infantryman in the Wermacht:

> … most of us were resigned to death – a resignation which often created the most glorious heroes of the war. Simple cowards or pacifists, who had been opposed to Hitler from the start, often saved their lives and the lives of many others in a delirium of terror provoked by the accident of an overwhelming situation … We fought from simple fear, which was our

motivating power. The idea of death, even when we accepted it, made us howl with powerless rage. We fought for reasons which are perhaps shameful, but are, in the end, stronger than any doctrine. We fought for ourselves, so that we wouldn't die in holes filled with mud and snow; we fought like rats, which do not hesitate to spring with all their teeth bared when cornered ... [36]

Sajer's story illustrates very well the concept of utilising maximum firepower. The retreating German army poured everything they had into the oncoming Russians, and one only has to travel through accounts like Sajer's to realise that there would not have been one Wermacht member aiming low. So thousands of rounds being expended for little casualties is the norm, and proves little of intent to kill. The retreat of an American column during the Battle of the Bulge is a useful example. With a variety of vehicles, only a few armoured, a garrison retreated through a 'gauntlet of Germans on both sides of the road' who 'fired repeatedly', yet only one American was wounded and none killed.[37]

Even if lethality in combat is not embraced with fervour by the soldier, after the first death it becomes easier. In combat, most fighters drop their civilities, and are more lethal than we generally think.

Grossman argues[38] that modern soldiers are more lethal now than ever before, primarily because of their more effective training. This lethality is obtained through desensitisation: thinking the unthinkable (conditioning), doing the unthinkable, and then denying the unthinkable (engaging denial defence mechanisms). While this is true enough, I argue in addition that the warrior has always been much more lethal than we thought. This is true throughout the ages: the British infantrymen who killed or wounded around five Zulus each at Rorke's Drift[39] are the same as the soldiers who sprayed automatic fire in Vietnam. Grossman is wrong if he proposes that infantry were not always determined to kill.

So, what is the answer to the question originally posed: how are armed forces to solve the dichotomy of the necessary warrior in peace and war? By acceptance that, like it or not, warfare is part of the human condition. This is a sad thought, and means that not for a moment must we cease puzzling over how to change this grim facet of the nature of man. But, as one commentator has pointed out, warfare is with us almost always: by the calculation he quotes, in 3241 years of recorded history, only 268 have not seen war.[40] Some writers have argued that warfare is not part of the human condition. Santiago Genoves, for example, points to studies that suggest societies exist, or did exist, that know, or knew, nothing of war, such as the Eskimos or the Australian Aborigines. [41] I know nothing of the first, but a little of the latter groups' history, and suggest that in fact Australian Aboriginal tribes went to war against each other just as enthusiastically as did the warring groups of ancient Britain. Genoves goes on to propose that warfare is in fact a modern concept, 'less than ten thousand years old', therefore implying that what was learned can in fact be unlearned. [42] Although this is verging dangerously close to anthropology, I would suggest instead that humanity's mere existence as the top predator in the food chain of the planet is proof enough that we are in fact a dangerous, aggressive and clever species that has war as part of its essential make-up.

So the dichotomy of retaining and training warriors in peace and war is solved by accepting soldiers as being necessary and indeed essential for societies to survive, by training for pervasive lethality in peacetime, and by their society accepting the grim reality of what combat is about. This is not a pleasant thought: to propose that we recruit, foster, train and deploy armed forces which should be as lethal as possible. But it is a little like the sentiments expressed in the Kipling poem 'Tommy'. In peacetime, we prefer not to think of the reality of what soldiers do.

But it was always thus. Brigadier-General FP Crozier argued passionately in his 1937 book *The Men I Killed* for an understanding of the need for ferocity in war, but also that there is this dichotomy for armed forces in peacetime. Crozier, illustrating his theme with accounts from his World War I experiences, thought that 'The man who shines at war is usually at a loss in times of peace, particularly in the regular army.'[43]

The British soldiers returning from the Falklands saw this happen, as it does in all wars. Their treatment and their comments underline the essential hypocrisy of many civilians and indeed many service personnel who fail to see, or deliberately ignore, the reality of fighting forces – they are there to destroy a country's enemies, and they need training, equipping and acceptance for that role. Listen to the bitterness of those interviewed by Vincent Bramley for his work *Two Sides of Hell*:

'We don't want this sort of soldier in peacetime' said returned Falklands Paratrooper Tony Gregory. 'They have been trying for years to destroy the Paras ... We are the best at clearing up the dirt for the shiny-arses, but afterwards the government and the MoD always nip in quickly to stab us in the back. Morale was sinking as the new thinking and attitude towards us took over.[44]

Dominic Gray said:

The new CO seemed to have a thing about us Falklands guys. I don't know if it was just him or if he was having his strings pulled by some arsehole above, in the Ministry of Defence … he never stopped any guys leaving, just stamped their records without so much as a thank you … For years the shiny-arses in the Ministry of Defence had starved us of the proper equipment we needed for our role. Time and time again we held together and did our job despite them, but as soon as a war appeared we had all the kit delivered within hours, equipment the hypocritical bastards had been telling us for years was impossible.[45]

Kevin Connery thought: ' … I could see straight away the Army did not want experienced troops … Within a year about sixty per cent of the guys who had served in the Falklands had gone from the battalion.' He joined the Foreign Legion, who, he said, ' … liked my professional outlook'.[46]

Denzil Connick, after returning to Britain, felt that the new CO of his battalion – who had not fought in the Falklands – ' … wanted rid of the Falkland men who remained. Morale was not good, in my opinion. It got worse when the lads going on courses found the instructors were insisting on teaching out-of-date tactics … '[47]

But in a time of hostilities, acceptance of the need for soldiers to be as aggressive as possible grows in proportion to civilian losses. In forces deployed to be peacemakers or peacekeepers, we impose strict Rules of Engagement, and we prosecute those who break them. But when our cities are bombed, and our own loved ones killed, and the possibility emerges of the war becoming, as General Von Ludendorff put it, a 'total war', then we want our soldiers to become more lethal. We begin to accept more enemy dead. In World War I, the Bishop of London applauded the captain of a fishing boat who refused to take on board the survivors of a crashed Zeppelin encountered in the North Sea.[48] As the reality of the true nature of the scale of the conflict grew in World War II, people became enthusiastic about the enemy's cities being hit. As a tribute to their survival post-war, the British put up a statue to RAF Air Marshal 'Bomber' Harris, who orchestrated the strategic bombing raids by the British against

Germany. Eventually, the attitude of the majority of citizens in danger is that the more lethal their forces are, the better. We want George Patton, Audie Murphy, Albert Jacka *et al* to come to our aid. And so our country is saved.

Many accounts of lengthy wars bear this hallmark – the prevalence and acceptance of maximum lethality increases in proportion with the losses taken and the intensity of the situation. Frank Richards's account of several years of World War I illustrates this, with the scenario of a British soldier in 1914 jumping onto the parapet of his trench with his hands up, and pointing to a wounded German who was trying to crawl to the British lines. Richards was not fired on, and went forward and carried in the enemy soldier, to the cheers of the German trenches.[49] That would not have happened in 1918.

Robert Graves saw this tendency at work in World War I. He had returned to the front line once more after being wounded, and perceived that the soldier's initial education had changed:

> *Infantry Training, 1914*, laid it down politely that the soldier's ultimate aim was to put out of action or render ineffective the armed forces of the enemy. The War Office no longer considered this statement direct enough for a war of attrition. Troops learned instead that they must HATE the Germans, and KILL as many of them as possible. In bayonet-practice, the men had to make horrible grimaces and utter blood-curdling yells as they charged. The instructors' faces were set in a permanent ghastly grin. 'Hurt him, now! In at the belly! Tear his guts out!' they would scream, as the men charged the dummies. 'Now that upper swing at his privates with the butt. Ruin his chances for life! No more little Fritzes![50]

Then – peace breaks out. After a few marches and medal-pinnings, we want to put the warriors back in their box. We insist that the savage warriors become tame again. We eventually modify our training in ferocity to become less lethal. We discard the bayonet and satisfy Joanna Bourke and her ilk and swear that 'we ain't gonna study war no more'. Eventually Bourke and her cohorts produce texts which condemn the 'monstrous and multifarious celebrations of violence'. If there is one aspect of Bourke's work I agree with, it is that she at least produced a work which aimed 'to put the killing back into military history'.[51] For we must celebrate the warrior if we want our warriors to win. Condemning the essential matter of warfare – killing the enemy – as behaviour worthy of society's negative sanctions will result, inevitably, in the soldiers of your country's enemies marching through your capital city in triumph, and then truly will such a peace-loving society be able to declare that they will have no part of war – for they will be extinct.

We impress upon our fighters the restrictions of civilians; make them behave as such – even after combat experience – and after the parades and the medals, insist they are run down like so many clockwork soldiers, and begin to tell them that they are civilians again, and not warriors at all. And then – at its most revolting – is the reverse of deification: these members of our society are in fact dangerous, worthless, expensive and unnecessary. Bomber Harris's statue is defaced, accusations of war crimes are made against warriors who saved their society, and soldiers are warned not to be too aggressive in their training. And of course, swear many pacifists, we will never commit them to combat again. We want a peace dividend: we can therefore sell off capabilities; buy new equipment fitted 'for but not with' (meaning equipment's ancillary items – on a ship, for example, these might include decoy devices such as chaff launchers: a basic fitting is included in the ship's construction, but the device itself is not installed, to save money); put up with gaps in defence planning, and above all insist that our soldiers are just public servants in uniform, to be treated the same as other workers, and indeed subject to the same rules – as if combat is an office exercise.

This is essentially a modern view. For thousands of years the warrior has been celebrated for what he is, and for what he does. He defends his family and his country, or he takes land from others too weak to defend it, and who are despised for their weakness. A study of soldiery shows us that from ancient times this has been the case.

The link might well be made between the 19th century, where the need for warfare was perhaps more understood, and ancient Roman times. Lord Macauley's poem outlines the stand of a hero, Horatius, against his society's enemies, the Estruscans, who were attacking Rome.

> Then out spake brave Horatius,
> The Captain of the Gate:
> 'To every man upon this earth
> Death cometh soon or late.
> And how can man die better
> Than facing fearful odds,
> For the ashes of his fathers,
> And the temples of his gods.'[52]

"Bomber" Harris – applauded in war; derided by some in peace, is here seen (left) debriefing an aircrew. In 1943, when this photograph was taken, very few British people would have questioned his ordering of the ferocious bombing that eventually helped destroy the German forces. Years into peace, many critics of his actions emerged. Would those same critics condemn such a warrior of their country four years into another world war? IWM CH 9683

And with two true companions, Horatius holds a narrow bridge, thus giving the Romans time to defend themselves better. We should celebrate those like Horatius, who defend what we hold dear. We should acknowledge the difficulties of their duties, and realise that it is part of the human condition to fight wars and therefore to have warriors, who are therefore necessary for our survival and should be celebrated as saviours. The philosopher Socrates was a Hoplite who fought in battle, and was distinguished by his bravery. He and his comrades thought that war was exciting, manly and honourable. Alexander the Great was given that title because of his capacities in battle and in conquest. Henry VIII celebrated the soldier's arts, and his daughter Elizabeth I told her troops that she had the heart and stomach of a soldier. There was no great revulsion at what soldiers stood for, and for what they did, before the late 20th century.

The modern Western view of combat many hold as being unnecessary and extreme is foolish, deceptive and dangerous. No nation of the past thought that its armed forces were unnecessary, so why should we do so now? There is a dilemma in understanding battle for the modern reader. It is that an understanding of the true nature of war produces revulsion and horror, given the sensibilities of the modern world: that life is deserved, that it is valued above all, and that society is there to guarantee it. How therefore can we praise the converse: the warrior whose aim is death?

The examples given so far, however, reveal the need for warriors to be lethal, and if we want them to survive and win, then we must encourage their lethality. They are not about minimum force, but maximum. They are not about enduring a certain amount of risk, but of doing all they can to reduce that risk. We must acknowledge their horrible task, embrace them for the brave warriors that they are, and understand this is the necessary face of war. To not do so is hypocritical, for how can we at once celebrate life but not laud those who guard us? This is the nature of combat.

7
Ultimate discipline in battle

*I had to shoot a man of my own
company to get the rest out of the trench.*

World War I infantry officer and poet, Robert Graves

Enforcing battle discipline

Combat efficiency has often been encouraged by ultimate discipline being enforced by members of an armed force on their own members. British officer Siegfried Sassoon in World War I noted that the noticeboard in his officers' mess carried routine notices which included the gloomy news of whose units had been posted back into the Line, and also the names of soldiers who had been shot for cowardice.[1] Fellow officer and poet Robert Graves was lucky to swap a place on a court-martial board with another officer, and he notes somewhat caustically that the practice was discussed in the British Parliament in May 1915, with the Minister responsible declaring that no executions for cowardice or desertion had taken place. However, Graves himself had sighted a file listing 'something like twenty' such cases.[2]

Indeed, the Imperial War Museum's Keeper of Education and Publications noted in 1969 that, on average, one British soldier was shot by firing squad for every week of the war.[3] Private George Coppard, in June 1915, was on parade when his CO announced that 'nearly a score of Tommies ... had been sentenced to death' for a variety of reasons, including desertion, mutiny, leaving the trenches without permission, cowardice and sleeping while on sentry duty. The soldiers' names, ranks, units and offences were read out, and then the words 'and the sentence was duly carried out', together with the date and time of the execution.[4] Coppard relates his belief, developed later in the war, that because of the political row the execution of soldiers in such cases was causing, an unofficial policy developed of placing such men in the first wave of an assault, where 'it was left to the Almighty to decide his fate'[5] – although unofficial actions like this are hard to prove. But it was certainly the case, according to Brigadier-General FP Crozier, that soldiers were often so drunk when they were led out to execution that they could hardly stand – it was the one act of kindness their comrades could do for them. Crozier says he ordered this himself for one of his troops, who had deserted and been recaptured.[6]

Lieutenant Colonel Graham Seton Hutchinson commanded his machine-gunners to fire on British troops when they attempted to surrender in 1918, to stop the spread of 'dry rot' through the army.[7] He explained: 'If there does not exist on the spot a leader of sufficient courage and initiative to check it by a word, it must be necessary to check it by shooting'.[8] Sergeant John Halpin, captured by Turkish troops in 1918, saw a Turkish officer order his men forward to stop a counterattack. Some of the men were driven forward with kicks, and one who would not move was shot by the officer with his pistol.[9]

There is something in this. Especially with soldiers who have not seen combat before, there is a great danger that they might freeze on the weapon, or fire a shot and then clamp down on the trigger, or that they might panic and not realise that their magazine is empty. If one is allowed to run, then others will follow.

This is bad enough in the ranks of the privates, but what if an officer tries to get away – his unit will doubtless disintegrate. In the Line, Sassoon once came across one of his own battalion's officers making his way to the rear with what seemed a feeble excuse. Sassoon drew his pistol and threatened to shoot him if he didn't turn around.[10] Robert Graves told a captain about his experiences in forcing his men onward: 'I had to shoot a man of my own company to get the rest out of the trench'.[11] Some Australians broke and ran from their positions during action in 1917 in Europe; they were remonstrated with, and one soldier said: 'I saw Lieutenant Bruton in the end with his revolver drawn and preventing the men from going further back … '[12]

This may have been more widespread that realised in World War I. Brigadier-General FP Crozier wrote a frank account of the situation in his aptly-named book, *The Men I Killed*, published in 1937. He confesses that he made it usual practice to have placed men in his battalion who were prepared to 'act often in complete violation of all decency, chivalry, and custom, in order that the line might be saved.' These men, probably company commanders – although Crozier is circumspect about such detail – would threaten to shoot those who abandoned their positions, and would carry out the action if necessary. Crozier himself says he shot an infantry officer who ran away, and turned his men's machine-guns and rifles on some Portuguese troops who were abandoning their position on the Line. And, he says, the measures worked. He argues that they were necessary for the safety of all, and that ' … history does not record it; regular armies disown it … It is not and cannot ever be taught'.[13] Such instances seem rare, but occasionally surface in history's annals. French artillery was directed against their own troops in 1917, according to German surgeon Stephen Westman, when an advance was halted by a massive enemy bombardment.[14]

Crozier goes on to argue that the practice is necessarily subsumed, and cannot be one for which a soldier is decorated – for who can imagine a citation that reads that by shooting an officer, an NCO, and two privates of his battalion he restored the situation?[15] He argues that such sanctions are not always applied, and indeed are not always commonly found, although he does suggest that three-quarters of lost objectives might have been taken if such measures were adopted. He explains at length that training in ferocity, leadership by officers, and if necessary the use of lethal punishment was understood by those who succeeded. General Monash understood it, according to Crozier.

Sometimes the necessity of such measures is underlined by the seriousness of the tactical situation. George Coppard noted, while waiting to advance in a World War I night attack, that his officers had been given orders to shoot anyone caught smoking, because the light would give away the position of the massing troops.[16] Frank Richards relates an incident early on in the war when Indian troops would not put their heads up to aim their rifles, but just fired over the top of the parapet. The British Regulars had to 'threaten to shoot or bayonet the lot of them' if they did not defend the position properly.[17] In another World War I incident, just as a German attack was beginning, an Allied soldier in an ambulance began shouting in panic, 'Get out! Get out! We're all going to be killed'. To stop the panic spreading, he was brained with a shovel by a sergeant.[18] One rather strange officer was posted to Frank Richards's unit: on patrols he would loudly curse the Germans in their own language, thus drawing fire. After six weeks he was shot from behind, probably by the sergeant who was with him at the time.[19]

If this was the true situation in World War I, does this not suggest that the practice is also common in other wars? An *Australian Military Handbook*, published in 1941, urges officers to use lethal force if necessary, in no uncertain terms: 'If any one of any rank makes a move to surrender, shoot him and carry on. If a bunch of men have surrendered, open fire on their guards and give them a chance to get away. If their guards are mixed up with them open fire just the same.' In advice to all ranks, it urges that if panic is 'being communicated to others, then it is your obvious duty to shoot to kill.' [20]

EB Sledge, fighting on Peleliu Island, tells of a night-time incident where one of the Marines began crying out, raving that the Japanese had got him. Reassurance by his comrades, a punch to the jaw, and morphia were all tried – to no avail – and finally a command was given to hit him with 'the flat of an entrenching shovel'. That worked, but in the morning he was found dead. Nothing official was done about the incident. [21]

US Army soldier Willy Slovik was executed in World War II for refusing to fight, and his name was invoked by leaders in the field to get their men to fight: 'They just shot that guy, they'll shoot you.' [22] In fact, executions in the US Army were limited to just this one: 21,049 American military personnel were convicted of desertion, and 49 were sentenced to death, but all of the others were commuted. [23]

Combat fatigue as an excuse for avoiding fighting was not given much respect in the German Army of World War II: Max Hastings notes that ' ... suspected Wermacht malingers were shot'. And it was no excuse at all for the German forces in Russia. [24] Henry Metelmann noted that, in the retreat from Russia, the penalty for a self-inflicted injury was death, and 'all injured going back to the Lazaretts had to have a special report by their commanding officers as to the genuineness of their injuries.' [25] The German defence of Konigsberg in 1945 was characterised by the execution of 80 soldiers for cowardice. Their bodies were exhibited at the north railway station bearing signs: 'They were cowards, but they still died.' [26] An American soldier, Sergeant Patton, said the Germans manning the position in the field which held them up were 'bastards': 'They had two AA guns,' he said. 'Some of them wanted to surrender, but every time a Kraut would jump out of his hole to surrender, some other Kraut s.o.b. would shoot him right in the back. Counting the ones they killed and the ones we got too, there're nineteen dead'. [27]

Acceptance of the need to be a determination warrior. These US Marine Raiders had earned the bloody reputation of being skillful jungle fighters. They are gathered in front of a Japanese dugout on Bougainville, Solomon Islands, which they helped to take, in January 1944.NNSP 80-G-205686.

The use of penal battalions for those convicted of offences was a feature of the Russian armies of World War II. These were given sparse support, and the death rate was high. Major Yury Ryakhovsky watched one go into an attack 'shoulder to shoulder, with a rifle between three men', the weapon being taken by the unarmed when the armed member fell.[28] One writer notes that over 250 Russian generals were either sent to the penal battalions or executed for failure in World War II.[29]

Russian soldiers who gave themselves a self-inflicted wound could expect short shrift. They were forced to dig their own grave, the regiment stood around them in three sides of a square, and they were shot, the command being 'For our motherland … At the enemy … Fire!' Their graves were labelled as belonging to cowards.[30] By comparison, such cases in the British forces were treated, then often court-martialled and imprisoned.

Although incidents of 'fragging' – whereby troops killed their own officers in Vietnam – have been documented before, occasionally a superior might be killed by his own side for military necessity. Robert Graves tells of two men of his own unit who were court-martialled and executed for shooting one of their own side.[31] FP Crozier tells of a bullying NCO who was blown up by a grenade put down his trousers.[32] Henry Metelmann, fighting with the Wermacht on the Russian front, experienced battles in which an incompetent, if brave, officer led his section into several hopeless attacks in which the Germans suffered many unnecessary losses. Metelmann saw him shot from the left-hand side of his own position, although the Russians were to their front. Later, it was reasonably obvious who had done it, but no charges were ever laid, no-one complained, and the probable sniper was quietly thanked.[33] CJ Selby, fighting in the Australian Army, recalled one OC (Officer Commanding) who had too much of a penchant for discipline as opposed to 'bullshit'. 'We drew that line after a few weeks in Palestine, when our OC was *told* that he had to treat us as *men*, or the first bullet fired by us in anger would be up his arse. He was fantastic after that … '[34]

In some cases, extreme violence is necessary against one's own side for survival. Pressed hard by the advancing Russians, the retreating Germans of Henry Metelmann's Panzer division were joined by two truckloads of SS when they came across a recently-built German storage depot all by itself in the tundra. The depot was manned by sentries and commanded by a supply-branch major who refused to open the gates and release the food to the half-starved soldiers, citing the need for official forms. Good-natured ribbing turned to argument and, when the major, furious at having his authority disputed by the group, announced that the argument was finished, he was suddenly shot by an SS sergeant. The guards quickly saw the logic of the argument and the food was taken.[35] But the boot was on the other foot for two members of Guy Sajer's detachment, part of a massive fleeing but fighting army pursued by the Russians in 1945. Sajer's friends, about 12 of them, found a crashed supply truck full of food, and took as much as they could carry. Two of them were caught by the military police and summarily hanged, their bodies adorned with notices which read, 'I am a thief and a traitor to my country'.[36]

British gunner Edward Telling was evacuated from Crete, and eventually, aboard a ship, was sent to one of the holds along with many others. He tells of a sailor with a tommy-gun who was then posted at the top of the hold steps, who told the soldiers below: 'Anyone that tries to get out, gets the lot'. This was, Telling reasoned, to prevent panic and attempts to get out which would imperil the defence of the ship if dive-bombed.[37] During the evacuation of Dunkirk, Sergeant Leonard Howard of the Royal Engineers saw a coxswain threaten to shoot a man who was trying to get into an already overcrowded boat. The offender ignored the threat, and was shot. Captain Anthony Rhodes, also of the Engineers, saw a naval officer threaten to shoot a man who had run up to the head of a queue formed for disembarkation; on this occasion the threat worked.[38]

There is a simple need for discipline in a place where recourse to paper rules probably will not work. In their diaries, soldiers sometimes caustically note words to the effect that discipline is of a certain type in the 'front lines' or combat sections of a force. Many a soldier has committed offences and got away with them, partly because of their triviality – drunkenness at the wrong time, disrespect, and so on – but in the main because on the front line men were measured by one thing only: combat efficiency. Many a soldier has quipped, 'What are they going to do – send me to Vietnam?' or its equivalent theatre.

The type of crimes to which ultimate discipline is turned are therefore of the most serious sort: combat inefficiency which can bring disaster to the whole team. If this man is allowed to do this, we all die, runs the logic. Therefore … someone is shot. I suggest that ultimate combat discipline is widespread in warfare, and because it is often necessary and understood by combat troops, such behaviour tends to go unreported. Because, as is the theme with much of this book, who else will understand, and who else would therefore tolerate it? It is rare indeed to find a soldier who admits that such measures were, and are, necessary, because he knows full well – like the soldier who says he enjoys combat – that such statements will bring the wrath of many who, unfortunately (and especially in these days of intrusive and powerful media), will be able to command attention because of the scandalous nature of the story.

US soldier Roland Lea had problems with a new replacement assigned to him on Okinawa. Twice in the same night, with the replacement supposed to be taking his turn on night watch in their shared foxhole, Lea awoke to find the sentry asleep. The second time Lea forced him out of the position, with 'the steel tip of my knife in his butt'. The new soldier was not seen again.[39] Then again, such stories grow in the telling. Stephen Ambrose's interviews for *Band of Brothers* saw a 'rumour mill' swirl around one Lieutenant Speirs: he was said to have shot a trooper dead who had disobeyed an order about drinking, and also to have machine-gunned a group of German prisoners.[40]

Robert Graves cites the case of the storeman who was to bring up a three-gallon jar of rum for the usual dose before the infantry advanced for an action in World War I. He came up drunk, collapsed and dropped the open jar on the ground where the remainder bubbled away. The company captain said nothing, but ' … this was a crime that deserved the death penalty. He put one foot on the storeman's neck, the other in the small of his back, and trod him into the mud. Then he gave the order "Company forward!" The company advanced with a clatter of steel, and that was the last I ever heard of the storeman.'[41] This might be seen as most extreme, but it was a well-known part of 'going over the top' in the Western armies to have had a tot of rum before advancing.

World War II Guards Officer Philip Brutton was quite prepared to shoot one of his own men who began to object to being told to go forward into a difficult situation: 'My Tommy gun was slung over my right shoulder, naturally cocked and fully loaded. I brought it up slightly to shoot him on the spot. He saw the movement and froze. I then thought better of it. The others would be demoralised.'[42] The soldier, nevertheless, obeyed, and that is the important thing. Audie Murphy related an account of World War II Germans putting captured American soldiers – a sergeant and a lieutenant – on the front of one of their advancing tanks. The defending soldiers attacked the tank nonetheless, and the lieutenant was killed.[43]

In Vietnam, Lieutenant McDonough had one of his soldiers, whose marijuana he had confiscated and burnt, fire a Light Anti-Tank Weapon, or LAW, at him from behind before the platoon set off on patrol. McDonough's response was to force his own M-16 up underneath the soldier's chin with the safety off until the man was standing on tip-toe, and keep him there for some time …[44] The historian Robert Sterling Rush notes, in the 1965 edition of the US Army manual *Military Leadership*, that reference is made to shooting your own men as a means of control: 'If all else fails, shooting at those that are fleeing'.[45]

Marine Michael Cousino remembers having considerable problems with the discipline of the South Vietnamese irregular troops – known as PF, or Popular Forces – he was working with. He finally enlisted the help of a regular South Vietnamese soldier to interpret his disquiet and pull them into line:

One night this interpreter discovered a PF asleep on perimeter watch – so he cut his throat. Then he woke up all the PFs, took them to the body, and told them he'd cut the throat of any PF he found sleeping on perimeter watch. We never had another PF fall asleep on us after that.[46]

The strange dichotomy of war and peace. Japanese flight crews cheer on one of their aircraft – and its determined killers aboard – as it roars off the deck of their aircraft carrier. Eventually, in peacetime, the ferocity of the warrior is shunned by many civilians. (Captured Japanese photograph; taken aboard a Japanese carrier before the attack on Pearl Harbor, Hawaii, December 7, 1941) NNSP 80-G-30549

During the battle of Long Tan in Vietnam, Neil Weeks was commanding a platoon. When they stormed an enemy position, he found one of the enemy, dead, who had 'apparently been garrotted. He had obviously been yelling out and giving away his position and his mates had decided to shut him up.[47]

The Argentine Army also seems to have practised executions of their own troops as a disciplinary measure in the Falklands War. One account concerned a Corporal Alvarez, who woke his unit companions screaming that he had appendicitis. When a doctor was found he was examined and declared fit for duty in no uncertain terms. 'He's got fuck all. He just wants to go to Stanley. A coward.' One of the soldiers put the barrel of his rifle against the corporal's forehead and squeezed the trigger – the weapon misfired and the corporal ran off.[48] Another account depicts a British soldier who jabbed a captured Argentine with his bayonet when the prisoner would not leave his trench. Investigation revealed that the soldier had been shot by someone on his own side so he could not desert from the position.[49]

In conclusion, we can see that lethality is sometimes needed – for good military reason – against members of one's own side. In many of the cases given above, there was little alternative to ultimate discipline. The dilemma that modern military forces face is how to define such situations. Do they say that this type of battle problem may arise, and if it does, then be prepared to do what is necessary to save the command or the moment? If they do, then doubtless, one day, such instructions will be discoveed, and critics will argue that such behaviour is anachronistic, intolerable, and must result in immediate changing of the rules, and of course the court-martialling of many.

Or do modern military forces say that this sort of behaviour must now not be allowed to occur, and that there are never any circumstances where modern military forces must utilise ultimate battle discipline? Then, as platoon commander, what are you going to do when the supply-branch major refuses to open the gates, or the Marine begins crying out that the Japanese have got him, thus drawing fire down on all?

Or of course, we may suggest that such behaviour never happens.

Desecrating the dead – military necessity or abhorrent behaviour?

*Sam pulled out his K-bar. It looked sharper than any knife
I'd ever seen. He ripped the dead man's shirt open
and began carving 'A 1/5' across his chest.*

**Marine Johnnie Clark describes action
by one of his platoon comrades after a fight in Vietnam.**

For hundreds, if not thousands of years of recorded military history, ritualistic treatment of a defeated enemy's body has been the norm. I am careful here not to use the modern word 'mistreatment' – that would imply already that the action is wrong. Perhaps, of course, by the ethics of modern Western societies, it is indeed wrong. But this is a comparatively new concept, and probably one only in the modern West. Even today the 'adjustment' of defeated enemy dead may well be common in some societies – do today's African tribesmen engage in ritualistic behaviour with their defeated enemy, and do societies in parts of Asia, where the modern Western media do not carry cameras, still behave this way?

Soldiers have, for millennia, physically manhandled the bodies of their dead enemies. In *The Iliad*, Achilles desecrated Hector's body for several days, dragging it behind his chariot around the site of his dead companion Patrocles's tomb.[1] Indians of the American West practised scalp-taking, as did some white bounty-hunters.[1] The Sea Dyaks of Borneo took heads as recently as World War II, and one might reflect uneasily on this if their enemy today.[2]

---

1   *Flashman and the Redskins*, by George MacDonald Fraser, while fiction, presents an excellent analysis of the factual history behind this practice, and gives an impressive list of sources to support its veracity.

Adjustment of dead enemy may well be normal behaviour. Further, it might well be necessary normal behaviour. For the soldier to survive psychologically, he may have to indulge in ritualistic behaviour which allows one to cope with what one has done. An alternative modern view, as put by the US Army, says that the practice ' ... has been prohibited by civilised nations as a violation of the Law of Land Warfare', but notes is still 'approved' of in some parts of the world. The practice 'must be prohibited', it goes on to say, as it 'tends to provoke reprisals, alienate world and home front opinion' and contributes to guilt and post-traumatic symptoms.[3] But how prevalent is such behaviour and – more importantly – is effective behaviour in combat promoted or lessened by such practice? What constitutes such abuse, and what should a modern military leader do if such behaviour occurs?

One minor form of what might seem abuse is in fact an infantry habit of ensuring a downed enemy is indeed dead, and not shamming death, ready to attack when the victor's back is turned. Rifleman Arthur Viera survived such a check in Vietnam in the battle of Ia Drang. A North Vietnamese soldier came up to Viera, who recalls: 'I kept my eyes open and stared at a small tree. I knew that dead men had their eyes open.' The enemy soldier took Viera's watch and pistol and moved on.[4] Marine Johnnie Clark describes a typical such scene in Vietnam. 'The three Marines approached each unmoving body with equal caution, kicking each one hard to get a groan'.[5] Clark himself later participated in a fierce fight, and then, on taking an enemy trench where a body lay, he 'stomped the man's head, then kicked him in the groin. No groan. Felt stiff.'[6] (In another chapter, we will see a variation of this in the treatment of enemy wounded.)

This may be interpreted by some as unsatisfactory behaviour. In 2003, an Australian soldier was charged with misconduct for kicking a corpse while on duty in East Timor in 1999. The incident occurred after a skirmish between a Special Air Service patrol and a pro-Indonesia militia. The soldier was eventually found not guilty, with the Foreign Minister of East Timor, Jose Ramos Horta, meanwhile contacting an Australian newspaper to plead for leniency for the soldier:[7]

> Mr Ramos Horta rang the *Herald* to plead for the soldiers involved, saying that while he commended the Defence Force for its integrity in wanting to uphold a strict code of conduct, 'I and most of my compatriots have not lost much sleep over how a criminal militia element was neutralised in 1999.'[8]

Special Orders to Nᵒ 1 Section 13/3/18

(1) This position will be held, and the section will remain here until relieved

(2) The enemy cannot be allowed to interfere with this programme

(3) If the section cannot remain here alive, it will remain here dead, but in any case it will remain here

(4) Should any man, through shell shock or other cause, attempt to surrender, he will remain here dead.

(5) Should all guns be blown out, the section will use Mills grenades and other novelties

(6) Finally, the position as stated, will be held

JP Bethune Lt
O/c Nᵒ 1 Section

The spirit of the bayonet - the famous order issued by Lieutenant Frank P Bethune MC of No 1 Section, 3rd Machine Gun Company on 13th March, 1918, when the Section was ordered to occupy a defensive position near Messines in France. The Section survived 18 days in the position. AWMA05248

It appears that Ramos Horta accepts the reality of tactical combat where others do not. The soldier eventually received an apology over the charge, which was dropped.

Further desecration takes a number of forms. It can involve casual abuse, such as kicking – not to ensure safety as outlined above – and manipulation of the downed victim, including photographing him as a ceremonial action of victory. Indeed, the old – and perhaps fictional – symbol of the skull and crossbones on the pirate flag is a rearrangement of body parts that has become an accepted, even humorous symbol of death.

A second form of desecration is mutilation – the leaving of 'trophy markers', such as playing cards, or marking a body in some way. Finally, souveniring of body parts often occurs. A lesser form of this involves taking souvenirs from the enemy.

Casual abuse and mockery

Getting used to dead bodies can be difficult, and soldiers have coped with this in a number of ways. Mere inspection is one way of doing it: Seigfried Sassoon, for example, thought it a good idea to take a newly posted-in officer on a tour of a battlefield where dead Germans were lying.[9] An alternative, employed by US Paratrooper Major Robert Strayer in training his men, was to get them to crawl under machine-gun fire through ground littered with the intestines of freshly slaughtered hogs. None of the men ever forgot it, and they became some of the most efficient of the paratroopers of World War II.[10]

Mockery of the enemy dead is another method of getting used to a taboo subject. As American troops moved up one of the many hills on Okinawa, they came across a defeated Japanese charge, with around 150 enemy dead littering the ground. 'A GI stooped down to one, jammed a cigarette into his mouth and muttered, "Have a cigarette, you yellow son of a bitch. Sorry I don't have time to light it for you".'[11] The abuse can be more brutal. Wermacht soldier Guy Sajer's comrade, in a night position where there were dead Russians, commented with interest on how beards grew after death, and another laughed at a headless body he was dragging out of their house.'[12] Gary McKay, an Australian veteran of Vietnam, recalls a buried body with an arm that was set with rigor mortis protruding near the entrance to his unit's position. It was used as the support for a biscuit tin lid that announced the unit's motto to any visitors.[13] Johnnie Clark, fighting in the same war, saw one of his comrades find 'a spare leg' after a battle; he thought it quite funny, and tried to make a 'three-legged corpse' out of one of the enemy.[14] Robert Mason, serving as a helicopter pilot, saw a squadron band manipulate an enemy skull to sing along with them in a bar.[15]

Casual abuse also gets troops used to dead bodies. In Vietnam one unnamed soldier was posted as an inexperienced machine-gunner to a unit in the field. He asserts that some of the members of the unit found him some dead Vietcong and had him lug them off the trail and kick the bodies, to get him used to seeing dead enemy and not panic when he saw more in combat.[16] War correspondent Michael Herr saw men from a unit which had survived an assault abuse the enemy dead: 'Close but no cigar,' the captain said, and then a few of his men went out there and kicked them all in the head, thirty-seven of them'. They also fired ammunition on full automatic into the bodies.[17] Infantryman Charles Gadd found kicking a corpse unusual – he comments on it happening once after a fight, but by a self-pronounced 'tough guy', who kicked a decomposing body, with disgusting results.[18]

Getting used to dead bodies in this way is perhaps useful: it dehumanises the enemy and makes them psychologically easier to kill. This too is the reason each side uses nicknames for their enemy, as sniper Gunnery Sergeant Jack Coughlin noted of his time in Somalia, where they called the 'ragtag militia "Skinnies" and "Sammies" … we didn't want to think of them as real people, for that might make us hesitate for a fatal moment.'[19]

It is notable that mistreatment of one's own side is much less common. My research has found little, and usually the complete opposite: respect, reverence and removal for burial. Mistreatment of one's own side can be damaging in a way that mistreatment of the other side is not. Marine officer Philip Caputo was in charge of recovering the US KIA in Vietnam and of keeping tally of the enemy killed; he became so disturbed by the experience that he saw himself, in the mirror, as a 'walking dead person', and often saw others in mid-conversation as the same.[20] The presence of the dead of your own side is at first usually a subject for shock, then acceptance. Sometimes a little casual humour can be found. R. Derby Holmes, noted of his work on a burial party in World War I: 'The indifference with which the men soon came to regard this burial fatigue was amazing'. He recalled an argument as to whether a British corpse should be equipped with a stray German leg to remedy the lack of two, to alleviate the 'fair crime sendin' im hover the river wif only one.'[21] Robert Graves commented on some of his men passing a well-known corpse in their section of the Line in World War I. An arm stuck out into the trench, and men shook hands with the dead man, often quipping: 'Put it there, Billy boy'.[22] Captain Ambrose Cull, commanding Australian troops in the same theatre, noted one of his own soldiers placing a tin of bully beef in the hand of an arm that protruded from a shell-hole, saying, 'Get up, you loafer – we're doing your work'. Cull thought it 'the big bluff', and that 'the man who can be coarsely light-hearted, either in assault or endurance, is at the moment a greater moral asset than the quiet thinkers … '[23]

Grim humour directed towards enemy dead is a more common means of coping with the stresses of combat. British soldier Frank Richards, fighting in France in World War I, describes how a dead German officer was arranged in a macabre pose for the benefit of a visiting staff colonel – the rear echelon planning staff were universally hated, and this was designed to taunt the visitor. The dead German was posed on a trench firestep, with a lit candle in one hand and a Bible in the other; and just before the staff officer arrived, a lit cigarette was placed in the German's mouth: ' … the staff officer didn't stay long'.[24] A trench inspection saw an officer comment on a dead German limb protruding from an earthern wall, and detail a man to remove it. As digging out the dead German would have meant dismantling the entire wall, the limb was chopped off with several blows from a shovel. The officer noted the comment the shovel-wielder made to a comrade: 'And what the bloody hell will I hang my equipment on now?'[25]

After the battle of Long Tan in Vietnam, the victorious Australians were burying the enemy dead. One corpse had a hand that protruded from the grave; after a few more hours, it had gained a sign which read, 'The Claw'.[26] Another Australian soldier picked up a severed arm and inquired of his comrades as to whether it would look good hanging in their mess.[27] A photograph of an enemy skull wearing an Australian Army hat caused controversy when published years later. The hat's owner, Lieutenant Colonel Charles Mollison, noted that it was one way of trying to cope with killing people.[28] In the Falklands War, a sergeant who had reminded his men that he wanted a few souvenirs to take home experienced the black humour of his men: an Argentine foot, complete with boot, was deposited in his pack.[29]

The photographic age has brought a new facet to the practice. A World War II Australian serviceman's paybook is found to contain two photos of dead Japanese soldiers.[30] Celebration of one's victories in Vietnam by taking photographs was apparently not unusual. Marine Jeff Kelly noted how his unit celebrated a victory: by 'decorating the bodies with cigarettes placed between dead lips and fingers', of which pictures were taken.[31] A few years into the war, correspondent Michael Herr related an incident where a Marine showed a group of war correspondents waiting to go forward a pocket photo album of pictures of dead enemy. But the startling thing about this anecdote is Herr's casual comment that 'There were hundreds of these albums in Vietnam, thousands', and they all contained shots of enemy dead, mostly desecrated. Herr's account confirms that such practices are routine.[32] In the Falklands, paratrooper Ken Lukowiak participated in photo sessions where the British victors posed with the vanquished bodies of their enemy. Such photos, it appears from his account, were common, and the resultant prints were displayed in the soldiers' mess back in Britain.[33] We may safely presume that, with the growth of digital-camera technology and miniaturisation, this is even more prevalent. Indeed, souvenir photos taken in Iraq in 2004 were produced as evidence in the trial of Marine Officer Lieutenant Ilario Pantano, charged – and later acquitted – of premeditated murder in the killing of two enemy.[34]

Mutilation of the enemy

Mutilation can occur as a type of psychological warfare, in which one side 'leaves their mark' to tell anyone on the other side 'we were here', 'we are savage' and, by extension, 'this will happen to you too.' Marine Johnnie Clark saw this type of casual everyday practice in a platoon comrade's actions after a fight:

> Sam pulled out his K-bar. It looked sharper than any knife I'd ever seen. He ripped the dead man's shirt open and began carving 'A 1/5' across his chest. I could hear Sudsy sputtering out coordinates over the radio. It lent a perfect background to Sam's bizarre ritual. Sam pulled an ace of spades card out of the black band that he wore around his helmet. He took a small metal clip off one of his bandoliers of M79 rounds and tacked the ace of spades into the forehead of the dead officer.[35]

Clark's unit later tacked cards on to 21 enemy soldiers they had killed.[36] Showing you have triumphed is a widespread practice. After a fight, noted US Army combat advieor Martin Dockery, the ARVN routinely and proudly displayed dead enemy bodies.[37]

Humiliating the dead enemy is equivalent to the victorious cry of triumph. Driver Ewart of the Australian Army was part of an exploration of a German position captured on the Western Front. Eight dead Germans were found, along with a dead woman. Ewart wrote, 'My God it made my blood boil what I saw', and he kicked one of the dead Germans.[38] Wermacht infantryman Guy Sajer saw the Russian Army's tanks deliberately run over dead Germans: ' ... the treads worked over the hole for a long time, and ... as they manipulated their machine the Russian crew kept shouting, "Kaputt, soldat Germanski! Kaputt!" '[39] Marine Eugene Sledge describes finding three decapitated bodies, with severed hands, heads and other parts. He admitted that his fellow soldiers would go through the packs of those enemy they had downed, and that some took teeth, but 'I never saw a Marine commit the kind of barbaric mutilation the Japanese committed if they had access to our dead'.[40]

In Vietnam, Marine officer Nicholas Warr saw an American tank deliberately run over a dead enemy soldier: Warr considered both sides of the argument for taking such action, and coped with it by compartmentalising it into 'some dim corner of my mind'.[41] Famous US soldier David Hackworth noted the practice of marking the enemy dead occurring in 1969. 'Squad leader Sullivan says, "One night we killed five VC in an ambush. In the morning before we moved out, I saw our boys cutting off ears and tacking Recondo pins in dead gooks' eyes." '[42] Mistreatment of the dead was used as a psychological weapon: an American commander had 'twenty or thirty' dead VC flown in a sling up to a village that had harboured the enemy, and dropped the bodies into the middle of the settlement from 200 feet.[43] A Vietcong attack on an American position, and the subsequent torture and mutilation of those US soldiers captured, resulted in the summary execution of all the Vietcong the Americans captured the next morning – they had had to listen to the cries of their comrades all night, and were in no mood to take prisoners.[44]

Modern times see the same sort of behaviour. Sergeant Andrew Barham was on a patrol in East Timor which found a dead body. It had been badly mutilated and disembowelled. Whether it was from the Indonesian militia or was that of a dead Timorese was unclear, but it was thought that the mutilation was revenge by one side or the other.[45]

Souveniring as trophy-taking

Soldiers always take souvenirs off their victims. The famous World War I air ace, Baron von Richthofen, took a keen interest in those he'd downed as his score mounted.[46] Each was recorded with a small silver cup which were displayed in rows in his quarters. The recovered machine-gun of one aircraft[47] was hung above a door in the family home – despite his mother's protests – and he kept a photograph of the mutilated body of one of his victims, often displaying it to others. Some of the American crew of the World War I Q-ship *HMS Baralong* took blood-stained clothing from German seamen, killed in their fight with *U-27*, back to New Orleans with them after the action, and proudly displayed it in bars.[48] The taking of rifles from the battlefield during a truce at Gallipoli nearly ended the mutual burying of the dead; the Australians fired off machine-guns, and the souveniring Turks came in for some discipline from one of their officers.[49] Sergeant John Halpin was captured by four Turks in 1918: they took his boots, haversack, waterbottle, a religious medal, and his trousers, leaving with him with nothing but his underwear and helmet.[50] One modern combat veteran confirmed it: 'Soldiers always take souvenirs whenever they can – they're told not to, but they all do it'.[51]

George Coppard amassed nearly twenty pounds weight of souvenirs in his time in France in World War I: he eventually abandoned his collection due to the burden. It included German fuse tops, bits of shrapnel and a saw-tooth bayonet. Soon afterwards, he had added a Luger pistol, a pair of watches, some German photographs, and a collection of German badges, which he pinned to a belt he wore, eventually selling the belt for five francs – a move he regretted, as it might have bought 'a tidy sum' in later years.[52] British officer Bruce Bairnsfather took with him on his first leave from the Front a pair of clogs he had found, several clips of German ammunition, four heavy cast-iron German shell cases; several fuse tops, and a collection of spent German bullets dug out of walls.[53]

Souveniring in this manner is a means of celebrating one's courage and skill, and it also 'crows' over a downed enemy. The US soldier and philosopher Glenn Gray thought that a man scooping up a part of the battlefield was ' … a promise that he might survive'.[54] Taking souvenirs was standard practice for infantry in all of the wars discussed here, and while references to the practice are common in all stories of infantry life, it was mainly confined to captured helmets and other pieces of equipment, especially firearms. Robert Graves was superstitious about taking souvenirs, but eventually he succumbed to a large chalk carving, which he arranged to have shipped to Britain.[55]

Lance Sergeant Ian Sinclair, fighting with the British Army in Tobruk, got himself 'a dagger with a beautifully ornamented coat of arms on the handle', but was really on the lookout for a Beretta automatic.[56] Anything with a swastika on it was highly regarded in the European theatre: daggers, flags, and so on. One US soldier managed to get a motorcycle and sidecar onto a transport back to Britain just after D-Day; he and a comrade happily went riding to Scotland on it for their leave.[57]

In the Pacific, US Marine EB Sledge was still recovering from the terrifying shock of his first combat when two of his comrades arrived and, more experienced than he was in the ways of war, reproached him for not looting the two dead Japanese in the position. They quickly gathered up a pistol and two flags, secured inside the helmets of the enemy, and departed, with the advice that Sledge should not 'take any wooden nickels', meaning he should souvenir too, but go for the original field equipment, not fakes sold by enterprising soldiers. The casual attitude suggests normal, everyday behaviour, and indeed it was: Sledge himself became an ardent collector.[58] In June 1945 in southern Okinawa, the US soldiers and Marines were victorious in an action where Japanese bodies were searched after the fighting: 'four to six watches' were found on each Japanese forearm, taken from Marines' bodies the previous day.[59] War correspondent Edgar Jones suggested that making 'table ornaments' out of Japanese skulls was common.[60]

US Infantryman Charles Gadd was on the lookout, throughout his year in front-line Vietnam, for a 'non-automatic' weapon he could register in the States. He finally ended up with a World War II K-44 Russian carbine.[61] Australian soldier Barry Heard relates how, after the first combat actions in Vietnam, his Australian unit coped with their anxieties:

> The uniforms of dead Viet Cong soldiers, and parts of their battle webbing and other regalia, were strewn on the ground. Originally, we had sent them in from the jungle. The garments and equipment had been with Intelligence, were of no further use, and were now available as souvenirs. They were quickly snapped up. Enemy weapons from successful contacts were already hanging in the boozer. There were a lot of blokes sorting through the enemy gear; in fact, I would say there was a clamber for them. Somehow, we were changing. We were a team, we were winning and, in killing terms, we were held up as a very successful company. We had overcome our initial fears about killing, and about dealing with dead bodies. The taboo subject of 'slaughtering' other humans was dismissed, and replaced with a culture of bragging and self-belief.[62]

Once Port Stanley in the Falklands was taken, it became a 'looter's delight' for the victorious British: two journalists who were there said that even a Pucara fixed-wing aircraft was souvenired and taken back to Britain on a container ship.[63] In Iraq, according to Australian Sergeant Andrew Barham, the local population in many areas profited from the foreign soldiers' desire for souvenirs by collecting Iraqi Army items and selling them at bazaars. Firearms were forbidden, but uniforms, bayonets, medals and photographs were very popular, commanding high prices.[64]

Sometimes, of course, paying too much attention to souvenirs and not one's primary task of remaining alive could be fatal: the history of a battalion of Welsh Fusiliers relates casually the shooting of one man who went after the wristwatch of a dead German lying outside the trenches.[65] British soldier Frank Richards and his friends crawled out into No Man's Land in World War I to go through the packs of fallen German soldiers.[66] He relates the story of how three soldiers had been trying to unscrew the nosecap of an undetonated German shell which they had found – there was a great demand for nosecaps from the rear lines, and the three were in the habit of selling such items. On this occasion they were unsuccessful and threw it down in disgust – it exploded and killed all three of them.[67] Major Roy Murray, of the US Rangers, lamented that the American World War II soldier was not easily convinced that sometimes souvenirs were boobytrapped – 'he has to lose his arm before he realises this is not the way to go'.[68]

Soldiers in the rear echelons annoyed those on the front lines by venturing too close to a combat area for souvenirs. Souvenirs were also the target of those in the rear lines who did not have such opportunities. EB Sledge tells of a major in the Seventh Marines who resorted to placing any such looters caught in the act into the front lines for a period.[69]

Seigfried Sassoon had to draw his pistol on two soldiers who were disputing the ownership of a pair of German field glasses, and gives several examples of souvenir hunting – helmets were popular.[70] Captured enemy were routinely 'ratted'; that is, searched for trophies (but not personal items like photos) such as uniform badges, and also for anything useful. US soldiers called the process 'field-stripping'.[71] US soldier Richard M. Prendergast was captured by Germans in Europe, and he and his comrades had taken off them their wristwatches, fountain pens, and any cigarettes they possessed. The Germans would have taken all of their personal sidearms too, except the Americans had destroyed them, which angered their captors. Prendergast was amused that they wanted the .45 pistols the Americans used, because the Walthers and Lugers of the Wermacht were regarded as better weapons by the US soldiers.[72] Parachute infantryman

Daniel Webster and his comrades relieved the surrendering Germans in 1945 of their 'watches, pistols and binoculars' before sending them to the rear. However, when his unit saw two 'outsiders' rob an old man at pistol point of his money, they booed and hissed. Webster thought there was 'an inverse ratio between courage and looting.[73]

The victor of a fight was entitled to first pick of his vanquished enemy's property. In Vietnam, Johnnie Clark was told, in one of his first fights, that the pistol of a dead VC was his by right, as Clark had fired the M-60 machine-gun that had killed him.[74] Australian infantryman Roland Griffiths-Marsh received an order in the field to send back 'all Japanese swords and flags' to his commander, so that they could be distributed among rear-echelon troops.[75]

Japanese officers' swords were much sought after by troops in the Pacific, although fake versions of these and other items were often sold to unsuspecting Americans by wily Australians. Cam Bennett tells a great story of the 'factories' that were set up for this. Sword blades were produced from car springs. Hilts, scabbards and even blade etchings were included in the racket, and the final product was sold off at a high price to the US soldiers. The Americans were also fair game for fake flags.[76] Then again, some of those Americans on the front line may have themselves produced fake souvenirs. Marine Russell Davis tells of a unit who not only carried in souvenirs on the stretchers which took the wounded off the battlefield, but of a few soldiers who proclaimed, 'My Rising Sun flags are better than the ones the Japs make. My Micronesian war clubs are better than you get on the islands …'[77]

In more recent times, British soldiers in the Falklands demonstrated the same sort of behaviour. Some members of 2 Para took the surrender of a helicopter and its crew. 'They were wearing shades, smart flying jackets and pearl-handled pistols – real John Wayne stuff. Within minutes the Paras had left them nearly naked. Even their boots were taken. Everyone took Argie boots: they were far superior to ours'.[78]

Body-part souveniring

Taking body parts is an extension of taking equipment as a souvenir. It is a warrior celebrating his triumph, and taking proof of it. In this manner, World War II infantryman George MacDonald Fraser observed one of his friends decorate his jeep with a skull for a while, before he was told to remove it by an officer.[79] In 1944, Sub-Lieutenant Marsden Hordern arrived to join his Australian Navy Fairmile vessel, to find the ship's company had decorated the crosstrees with a Japanese skull. Hordern, shocked, later saw, on New Guinea trails, other skulls marking points in the road – apparently common practice, and again underlining the triumph of the victors.[80] Australian infantryman Roland Griffiths-Marsh had to cope with the Dyak habit of taking heads when he commanded native warriors ambushing the Japanese in 1945:

> Ah Toh and I screamed to stop firing. My soldiers obeyed, and then with a hideous series of howls drew their parangs. From my vantage point up on the root of a mangrove, I saw a monstrous scene enacted. A few feet in front of me was a seething mass of alternately rising and falling parangs ...[81]

It is perhaps best to draw a veil here, for shortly afterwards Griffiths-Marsh had to congratulate his native warriors on seven new trophies. The case illustrates one of the themes of this work: what was he to do in such a situation? Forbidding the practice of millennia would have done nothing but, at worst, cause the Dyaks to stop fighting for the Allies, or, at best, sown resentment, confusion and mistrust.

Elsewhere in the Pacific, US Marines, outraged at the mutilation of those captured by the Japanese, took ears off the enemy they killed.[82] (The practice was not illegal at the time, and only became so in 1949.)[2] According to one Marine sergeant, it was common: 'Some collected ears; some gold teeth. We had one guy who was collecting skulls, which didn't go over too well with the brass'.[83] Implicit in that comment, of course, is that 'the brass' was comfortable with ear- and teeth-collecting ...

Incidentally, Japanese soldiers routinely took body parts of their own comrades for return to the Home Islands of Japan, as part of their religious beliefs that the spirit would not rest unless part of the body, at least, was interred at home. So they removed fingers, to be one day returned to the fallen soldier's family. Staff Sergeant Yasumasa Nishiji, of the 20th Independent Engineering

---

2   Article 15. At all times, and particularly after an engagement, Parties to the conflict shall, without delay, take all possible measures to search for and collect the wounded and sick, to protect them against pillage and ill-treatment, to ensure their adequate care, and to search for the dead and prevent their being despoiled. UN Convention (I) for the Amelioration of the Condition of the Wounded and Sick in Armed Forces in the Field. Signed at Geneva, 12 August 1949. http://www.hrweb.org/legal/geneva1.html February 2005.

Regiment, describes such an act. 'Before we buried him next to others of our unit, I managed to cut off one of his fingers to send to his family. It was not at all easy and bloodless pieces of flesh fell off.'[3]

Tim O'Brien describes the practice of taking ears in Vietnam. A Green Beret officer known as 'Mad Mark' habitually engaged in this behaviour.[84] A soldier Philip Caputo took for an Australian commando visited Caputo's Marine unit in April 1965, and shocked the American by displaying two ears, taken earlier that day, strung on a wire.[85] Alan Camden, in Mark Lane's controversial book *Conversations with Americans*, described it as a not unusual practice in his unit, and commented: 'Over there the best soldiers are the ones with the most ears.'[86] However, we might also note that the practice may have become a little mythologised: in October 1967, the CBS evening news had shown a young American soldier engaging in this habit. The incident was investigated and the cameraman concerned was revealed to have 'dared' the soldier to do this, and provided the knife. The two men concerned were tried, convicted and punished.[87]

As is the case with mutilation, soldiers practising this 'in-house' behaviour are celebrating their success and the downfall of the enemy. It can reach bizarre levels. Captain Robert B Johnson noted:

In 1965, I was taking a class in West Point on land warfare, even [sic] by a major who had returned from Vietnam after being wounded, and he showed us the slides and told us in a joking way how American pilots and other pilots in Vietnam would send each other parts of VC bodies – heads, angers [sic] and ears – as jokes, wrapped as Christmas presents.[88]

By showing off the proof of one's kills, one was proclaiming prowess – a particularly useful technique for impressing soldiers who had not seen combat. Private Jones of the US Army collected 39 pairs of ears and strung them round his helmet, and was in the habit of performing a black man's 'shucking and jiving' dance for new arrivals in Vietnam.[89] The Korean troops deployed to Vietnam also took the heads of those Vietcong they killed, according to US helicopter pilot Robert Mason.[90]

---

3   Tamayama, Kazuo and John Nunneley. *Tales by Japanese Soldiers*. London: Cassell, 1992. (210) This work, a series of accounts from soldiers of all kinds and ranks within the Japanese Army, gives several other such instances; see pp. 141, 163, 176.

Taking a hand and drying it was deemed too much by the World War II Marines of EB Sledge's unit, when a comrade proudly displayed such a trophy. Citing the CO's disapproval – although no-one apparently made a protest about the taking of teeth – and the smell of the offending item, the soldier was persuaded to throw the hand away.[91] Vietnam, the 'television war', probably saw no more occurrences of this behaviour than did other conflicts. However, the penetration of the war by the media – the dichotomy of its support, while also seeking revelations – and the literacy of many of the soldiers serving there might well mean we know more of such actions than in previous conflicts. There are many. Marine Johnnie M. Clark arrived in Vietnam, and when he got to his platoon, which was in a forward position, noticed one of the soldiers had an ear attached to the outside of his helmet. When Clark remarked on it, the Marine said that he'd had several others, but they wouldn't keep.[92] Infantryman Charles Locke advised the War Crimes investigation that, after executing a captured prisoner: 'Well, his ear was cut off and that was presented to the LT [Lieutenant] as sort of a war gift.'[93] And there is a suggestion that the men of Charlie Company, the perpetrators of My Lai, engaged in such practices on a patrol: 'Harry Stanley saw them come back ' … with an ear. Medina was happy; it was his first kill.'[94]

An unnamed Vietnam soldier said that he kept ears on a 'green, nylon string' around his neck, but they would only keep for around three days.[95] Correspondent Michael Herr encountered a 'reedy little man who grinned all the time but hardly spoke', who showed him a bag of what Herr at first thought was dried fruit. He thought taking relics off the enemy was a 'transfer of power'. Serving in the US Army in Vietnam, Peter Hefron had not been long in-country when he saw a photograph of a Vietnamese head in the newspaper of the base where he was working. It was not long after My Lai became public and Hefron, a public relations officer, queried the sensibility of this to a superior officer.[96]

Less well known but doubtless as common was the mutilation of dead Americans and their allies in Vietnam. Marine officer William Van Zanten was engaged in a lengthy firefight, with several American wounded out in front of their position who they found very difficult to recover. Several times the enemy overran the forward sections of the American positions, and therefore were close to the US wounded. After the VC were eventually repulsed, the Marine Gunnery Sergeant was found decapitated: his body was booby-trapped and both his arms and legs had been removed with some sort of machete. His head lay nearby.[97]

Home Guard bayonet instructor Corporal Charles Batchelor shows the necessary aggression as he thrusts his bayonet firmly into a hanging sack (representing the enemy) during a 1942 Home Guard training exercise in an English village. "No more little Fritzes", was a popular war-cry of the instructors. If the enemy is not dehumanised, how can you kill him? IWM D 9265

One British soldier in the Falklands – perhaps in jest – showed journalists a pickle jar and proclaimed it was for ears, but 'not just any ears. I want Argie ears. They'll keep nicely in here.'[98]

Souveniring body parts for monetary gain

In the Boer War, the fingers of dead British soldiers were hacked off to get their rings.[99] This was a practice in World War I, too, although unusual perhaps then. For example, the complete informal history of the 2nd Battalion, His Majesty's 23rd Foot, the Royal Welsh Fusiliers, is filled with anecdotes of soldiers going after watches, pistols, helmets and so on, but has only one account of a German officer's finger being cut off so his wedding ring could be taken.[100] US Paratrooper Joseph Liebgott proudly displayed a ring to a comrade – he'd cut the finger off a German to get it.[101] Such behaviour in the European theatre seems to be lesser in nature than in the Pacific during World War II. Robert Leckie fought with the First Marines at Guadalcanal, and often saw one of his comrades at work after a battle, removing any gold teeth from the Japanese dead with pliers.[102] The soldier did this so often that he was known as 'Souvenirs', and he habitually toted with him a bag of his prizes. Australian soldier Ken Davies saw an American 'busily extracting gold teeth with a pair of pliers' in the aftermath of the defence of Milne Bay in August 1942.[4]

US soldier EB Sledge witnessed this routinely, and even described the best way it could be done with a bayonet, although he also thought it was a way of getting back at the Japanese.[103] Sledge was warned off taking teeth, when just about to do so, by the company medic, and later he was glad that he had retained at least some of his sensitivities.[104] But it was as routine as the taking of other souvenirs by the Marines. He tells the gruesome tale of an argument over one incident: the Japanese was still alive, and the gold-seeking Marine was shouted at by his comrades to at least put the enemy soldier 'out of his misery'.[105] An American Marine named Tex was an industrious taker of teeth in the aftermath of the ferocious battles on Okinawa: one of his comrades came across him one day and estimated he had 'half a tobacco sack full' at that stage.[106]

---

4   Baker, Clive and Greg Knight. *Milne Bay 1942*. NSW: Baker-Knight Publications, 1991.
    (233) A bracketed comment from the authors of this anecdote-laden work comments that
    'Research shows that some Australians and Americans did engage in this unsavoury practice'.

On the Russian front, Guy Sajer's war was one of much ferocity, but he notes only a single such case: presumably gold teeth had little value in a steppe where there was nothing to buy and only food was vital.[107] Does the practice happen in today's wars? British soldier Ken Lucowiak describes a soldier who took to the Falklands battlefields a 'laughing bag' – a small electronic device which had a button which, when pressed, caused it to emit cackling laughter. This soldier occasionally pressed the button in combat. The soldier – an experienced private in his thirties – carried two pairs of pliers as well. When Lukowiak asked him what they were for, he answered: 'To acquire gold.'[108]

Souveniring as proof of enemy killed

Souveniring can indeed be done – if not ordered – to prove that an enemy has been killed. The Boer War saw an incident of a Canadian taking scalps to prove he had, alone, shot down three of a party of five enemy gunners.[109] Sometimes a body part is taken to prove that a target has been taken or met. Cam Bennett, commanding a company in New Guinea, resorted at one stage to the time-honoured practice of holding a competition to keep up the men's enthusiasm for combat. He promised a bottle of beer, brought up especially to the front areas where there was no possibility of alcohol, to the soldier who shot the unit's one hundredth Japanese. The prize was claimed by a sergeant, but Bennett disputed the claim, whereupon the soldier

> … smiled at me. 'Have a look at this then, Sir,' he said. 'Would I tell you a lie?' He reached into his pocket, brought out a handful of little yellow fingers and, having shown them to me and the assembled group, let them slowly slip one by one to the ground.[110]

Captain Fred Laughlin, US Army, said that when he was a first lieutenant he learnt that

> It is very important to verify some member of the body [sic], particularly the ears. The ears seemed to be the favourite in order to report validly a BC. This was not promulgated officially. It could not be, of course, but this was taught in the school …'[111]

Mike Beamon, a Navy SEAL Scout, saw Provincial Reconnaissance Units paid bounties for bringing back weapons and ears from their missions in late 1968.[112] Lieutenant Robert D. Parrish told his Vietnamese troops that they needed to bring in proof of kills, and the next day was handed six ears.[113]

In the East Timor UN-backed campaign of 1999 and beyond, a New Zealand soldier was mutilated. This may have been done to show proof of a kill – the soldier's ears were taken.[5]

Joanna Bourke, in *An Intimate History of Killing,* catalogues even more examples.[114] She sees it as 'proof that a man had seen active combat' and lists cases with the tone that imbues her work: one of disapproval. Broadly speaking, it may be argued that it is only a 20th- and 21st-century phenomenon for some people to look down on the practice of engaging in human-to-human fighting. More specifically, Bourke fails to take account of the motives for such trophy-taking.

First, participating in combat is stressful. Some combatants, as other parts of this work establish, can take pleasure in it. Many do not. But whether they gain pleasure or have negative reactions does not minimise the fact that combat is stressful, fearsome, physically and mentally demanding, terrifying and exhilarating all together. One needs to cope with the stress, and warriors have done it, probably from time immemorial, by taking trophies and by being irreverent about the dead that surround them. It is important to note that this only applies to the enemy dead, not your own.

Loyalty to the group

In a combat group that kills successfully, it is probably more difficult not to imitate the leader than to follow, for by doing the same thing one is demonstrating one's loyalty to the combat group upon which one depends.

This is of paramount importance. That loyalty, as Lawrence LeShan point outs in a collection of thoughts from combat veterans, is a most powerful driving force.[115] 'We were closer to each other than we were to our wives' was one significant comment. Historian Stephen Ambrose noted that virtually without exception those he interviewed said that their closest friends, 'the men from whom they have no secrets, the men with whom they would gladly share their last piece of bread', were their combat comrades.[116] Australian soldier NX31016 was eloquent on the subject: 'Your mate was your tender companion,

---

5   AFP. 'NZ military say soldier killed in Timor had throat cut, ears removed.' http://www.etan. org/et2000c/november/ 12-18/17nz.htm 26 April 2005. Australian soldier Sergeant Andrew Barham advised in an interview that it was said by some soldiers in Timor that the ears may have been removed to provide proof for a reward.

the rough-house drunken bum you went on a spree with, the bloke you could depend on in life or approaching death, who would never let you down …'[117] US Paratrooper Don Malarkey wrote of his World War II experiences: 'There is not a day that has passed since that I do not thank Adolf Hitler for allowing me to be associated with the most talented and inspiring group of men that I have ever known'.[118] Soldier Daniel Webster could have been withdrawn from his unit on several grounds: experience, parental influence at home, promotion, or his two combat wounds. Yet on one journey by truck, surrounded by his comrades, he had returned, he said, to a 'bright home full of love'.[119]

Despite the stresses and horrors of close-quarter combat, soldiers will often return to it rather than let their comrades down. Poet and infantry officer Seigfried Sassoon went back to the horrors of World War I trench warfare because he could not live with the thought of his comrades being there without him: ' … he couldn't bear to think of poor Old Joe lying out at night in shell-holes and getting shelled'. His poem 'When I'm asleep, dreaming and lulled and warm' is about the ghosts of soldiers he had known reproaching him, in his dream, for his absence.[120] World War II Marine EB Sledge, at first puzzled by why former members of his unit would want to return to the horrors and dangers of fighting, concluded that it was because no-one else would ' … understand what we had experienced, what in our minds seemed to set us apart forever from anyone who hadn't been in combat.'[121] In Vietnam, wounded by a white phosphorous grenade which burnt sections out of his arm, Sergeant John Setelin received first aid and was due to be helicoptered out of the battle of Ia Drang. He changed his mind, took the sling off, and went back into battle, explaining: 'I couldn't in good faith get on a chopper and fly out of there and leave those guys behind.'[122]

The closer to combat one is with one's comrades, the more one bonds. Wermacht soldier Guy Sajer transferred from transport to infantry, and while he noted that the decision almost cost him and a like-minded comrade their lives, he did not regret belonging to a combat unit. 'We discovered a sense of comradeship which I have never found again, inexplicable and steady, through thick and thin.' [123] US paratrooper Leo Boyle was wounded in combat in World War II and never returned to his unit; he commented: 'I never became fully resigned to the separation from the life as a 'trooper' – separated from my buddies, and never jumping again.'[124] Marine Officer Philip Caputo felt that the US Marines in Vietnam fought as hard as they did rather than be a deserter who 'ran out on his friends'.[125]

Shared fears make for self-stabilisation. World War I soldier George Coppard thought that 'the daily comradeship of my pals, whether in or out of the Line, gave me strength.'[126] In World War II New Guinea, Corporal Lofty Cox told his mate that, after seven straight days of fighting and being shelled, the only thing that stopped him jumping out of his position and running was that he had 'a bloke like you alongside me', only to be told in reply that his mate felt exactly the same.[127] So the last thing a soldier will do is inform authority about his battle-partner's behaviour, leading us to surmise that such behaviours as are discussed in this work may very well be widespread (because unreported).

The worst thing one can do as an infantry soldier – or as anyone engaged in close-quarter combat – is to let down one's friends. World War II battle surgeon Brendan Phibbs took part in an assault by his infantry company in the Battle of the Bulge which was not supported very well by the two companies on either side, and noted the pained giving and taking of the comments that followed its bloody aftermath. ' "Where were you guys, for chrissakes? We needed you on our right." [It is] exquisitely painful when a wounded man points a bloody hand at a friend from another company, [and] mutters, "Where the fuck was you, Tom?" '[128]

Second, desecration of the enemy is a dehumanising factor, and so another stress minimiser. Richard Holmes has noted, ' … without the depersonalisation of the enemy during training, battle would become impossible to sustain,' and he notes that there is a conundrum between encouraging this – which, if taken to excess, results in any restraints being swept aside – and the converse, which would mean soldiers could not fight against those who shared their 'common humanity'.[129] If one does not perceive the enemy as oneself, or like oneself, but rather as sub-human, then the killing does become easier. In one respite from furious action, US soldier EB Sledge saw a fellow fighter flipping pebbles into what remained of the top of a Japanese soldier's head, and thought, 'there was nothing malicious in his action.' Another soldier spent quite a few lackadaisical shots firing off the genitalia of a dead enemy.[130] As the philosopher-warrior Glenn Gray noted of his combat experience, there was a necessity to dehumanise your opponents and to have an 'image of the enemy sufficiently evil to inspire hatred and repugnance'.[131] It might sound unpleasant, and it might be the stuff of modern military crimes, yet it has always happened this way and probably always will.

If such behaviour is going to occur, where does a platoon leader or company commander step in to prevent it, and where does he charge his soldier with an offence? Probably lesser forms of such actions – photography, disrespectful behaviour, and so on – are the stuff of routine verbal admonishment. To go beyond this may result in public condemnation and loss of support from home – the average member of the public would feel that body-part souvenirs, for example, are not appropriate for members of a liberal democracy. Nevertheless, what is posited here is that no matter what training and warnings a force may give, such attitudes towards the enemy are probably impossible to eradicate. In the Falklands War a British corporal, Stewart McLaughlin, was killed in action, and his ammunition pouches were inspected for supplies shortly afterwards: a collection of ears was found.[132] It is suggested that such actions are routine, established, and impossible to stop.

So how are we to summarise such behaviour? Firstly, it has been established here that such behaviour is widespread. It occurs in all battles and in all societies, suggesting that it is probably psychologically ingrained.

Second, it is probably extremely difficult to stop such behaviour: as we have seen, once it starts, it spreads, and it does so primarily as an affirmation of combat group allegiance.

Thirdly, if such behaviour has a value in tactical terms, should it be at least ignored?

Therein, of course, lies the dilemma. If it profits us militarily, should we change our society's laws to match our military behaviour and our military needs? One of the themes of this book is that combat behaviour is often inextricably linked to the needs of efficient combat. However, it is doubtful whether a modern liberal democracy would tolerate such battlefield conduct.

If this is the case, then the existence of such habits might well need to be acknowledged, and rigorously prepared for via intensive training. This may well include intelligent discussion down to at least non-commissioned rank, for NCOs are the controllers of so much at the tactical level. To curtail the habits of many societies and many centuries would be difficult indeed.

PART TWO

Prisoner-Taking and the Reality of Combat

9
The rules of surrender

Too late, chum.

**Traditional British World War II soldier's comment
to anyone who did not surrender promptly enough.**

The illogicality of not taking prisoners in warfare has been commented upon
by several authors. The warrior-writer Sun Tzu noted: 'When you surround an
army, leave an outlet free', because soldiers who knew there was no possibility
of escape would fight all the harder. Sam Grossman and others have pointed
out that, in the main, a 'take no prisoners' policy would result in your own
side's people who were captured being killed out of hand by the enemy.[1] British
historian Max Hastings noted what happened as the Russian armies invaded
Germany, killing all before them in scenes of barbarity:

> The Russians paid an immediate price for their savagery … Seeing what
> had happened in East Prussia, Germans realised there was no purpose
> in trying to survive a Soviet victory. They had no alternative but to fight
> to the end. The consequence of the victors offering the vanquished only
> death or unimaginable suffering, was the huge losses that Stalin's armies
> subsequently suffered before Berlin finally fell.[2]

So taking prisoners is militarily sensible and logical. But in all wars, taking
captives has presented problems. Legally, the situation is laid out in terms which
seem understandable and simple enough. 'Persons taking no active part in the
hostilities, including members of armed forces who have laid down their arms
and those placed hors de combat by sickness, wounds, detention, or any other
cause, shall in all circumstances be treated humanely … '[3] But, as Vietnam
Marine Philip Caputo put it: ' … the world of laws … [was] so easy to obey

when you eat well, sleep well, and do not have to face the daily menace of death'.[4] In reality, the taking of captives is difficult.

First, the taking of prisoners requires a detraction from the business of taking a military objective. The capture of prisoners requires soldiers to stop pursuing their aim, and instead divert their attention to another priority: securing the new captive, searching for weapons, corralling and in some cases protecting him from either side's anger, and then separating the prisoner from the combat situation. This can require considerable resources. The millions of Russian prisoners taken by the Germans during World War II would have required thousands of men to feed, house and guard them – a valuable loss of personnel for a country fighting for its life. The German Army, retreating in front of the Russians after their failed attempt to take the country, still won the occasional action, and an army in desperate straits, without supplies, was thus burdened with an enormous problem. Guy Sajer's division took 1100 prisoners; they turned many loose, but hundreds came along with them on their retreat, with the Germans even sharing some food with them, and Sajer musing on whether they would have to shoot them later.[5]

In many cases, such diversion from the aim can be dangerous. The new focus means less effort directed towards securing that aim – which may mean failure. The prisoners are still members of an enemy force, and depending on formalities such as paroles being given, prisoners being bound so they cannot take up arms, and so on, they may still be a threat. At the battle of Agincourt, between English and French forces in 1415, large numbers of French prisoners were taken and directed to the rear of the English position. When the battle looked momentarily like going against the English, whether an order was given or an initiative taken – there is some confusion – the reality was that the captives were massacred in case they turned against their captors from their advantageous position.

Prisoners can be a genuine danger, even in small numbers. World War II Panzer driver Henry Metelmann witnessed a Russian lieutenant, taken captive with hundreds of his fellow soldiers, kill a German general. Obviously not searched properly, the lieutenant saw the general and other high-ranking officers stroll over to see the many captives after the Germans had won the day. Presumably figuring that the exchange was worth it for the motherland, the Russian officer pulled out a concealed pistol and shot the general at close range. He was clubbed to the ground with a rifle butt by a nearby guard and finished off a few minutes later, but a valuable victory for his side was complete.[6]

A snapshot taken by a British officer showing German and British troops fraternising on the Western Front during the Christmas truce of 1914 in World War I. By the time the next Christmas came, there was no desire on either side to show friendship – or mercy – to the enemy. Both sides hated each other too much by then. IWM Q 11718

Here the suggestion is made that infantry engaged in combat take fewer prisoners than might be popularly thought, and that in battle prisoners are routinely dispatched. This analysis is further divided into three sections: the killing of prisoners 'in hot blood', as a military necessity, and by execution.

The rules of surrender

It is not suggested that, in all combat scenarios, possible prisoners are always killed; rather, that it happens frequently. Typically, Private W. Morgan recalled taking the surrender of a German soldier during the Battle of Ypres:

When we got to Frezenburg the boys went with their bombs at these pillboxes and we went for the trenches. I saw a lot of the lads using the bayonet, but I didn't have to use mine, though the place was packed with Germans in shell-holes and trenches. I got to the top of a trench and there was one Boche just in front, looking up at me. I can see him now. He had glasses on, and I pointed my rifle and bayonet at him and he just said, 'Oh, no, no, no, no.' And he put his hands up.[7]

Sometimes the capture is quite kindly. Corporal Lee, in the same battle, shot and wounded with machine-gun fire a 'Bavarian sergeant' and then accepted his surrender. He helped bandage the wound, and gave him some chocolate. The two talked, and exchanged details, and after the war became firm friends.[8] Private J. Parkinson related how he had manned his machine-gun and held up a World War I German advance for some time when

I was loading another belt into the gun when I felt a bump in the back. I turned round and there was a German officer with a revolver in my back. 'Come along, Tommy. You've done enough.' ... I know what I would have done if I had been held up by a machine-gunner and had that revolver in my hand. I'd have finished him off.[9]

John Keegan points out that 'surrendering was a ticklish business in trench warfare'. The prisoners had no special value, they had to be managed, and soldiers on 'hair-trigger reactions' would shoot rather than risk being shot at. That was what Argentine soldier Oscar Carrizo experienced when he crawled quietly out of a Falklands foxhole and tried to present himself to two British soldiers standing nearby: one of them reacted to the movement and shot him in the head, but not fatally.[10] In another incident in the same war an Argentine failed to put his hands up and just kept repeating to the four British soldiers confronting him, the words *Por Favor* ('Please'). He was wearing a poncho and when, after the third command, his hands were seen moving underneath the garment, all four soldiers immediately fired.[11]

If the initial distrust can be overcome, then the enemy may become what the captors are – human beings – and trust can be established, good feelings displayed. Glenn Gray was an Intelligence Officer in World War II, and recounts the experience of newly-captured German prisoners being regarded with mistrust by their American captors, who had weapons trained on them, as they were no doubt 'treacherous and fanatical storm troopers'.[12] Then one of the Germans was heard humming, and he was joined by three others who apparently had previously formed a singing quartet. Within a few minutes communication was being struck up and a friendly atmosphere prevailed. In the fierce fighting after D-Day, a soldier of the German Army and a soldier of the Canadian Army – the former taken prisoner by the latter – felt the hot blood of the encounter they had just survived rapidly defuse by finding they were both Polish: ' … they got talking together and forgot the war and became buddies', in the words of one of the Canadians.[13]

If you surrendered, you had to do it properly. Trooper Frederick Tucker, fighting in the Boer War, said that the Boers used treachery in displaying a white flag and then firing. He noted that the action was soon concluded and 'soon everything was quiet', with no further information given about prisoners.[14] George Clarke Musgrave, fighting at the Battle of Elandslaagte, saw white flags hoisted when the Boer position was about to be overrun, then a Red Cross flag, and the orders were given to cease fire. Then, to the victors' fury, they saw the Boers run to their horses in the rear and ride off.[15] The same writer describes a similar incident a little while later, and another occurred where the Red Cross flag was displayed by the British but the medical soldiers were shot down by the enemy. In a further example, the Boers used a white flag to stop the British firing, but in actuality were bringing up soldiers crawling through long grass. On another occasion a Red Cross-flagged ambulance was used to bring up a Maxim gun.[16] Such actions, of course, can well lead to the white flag being disregarded in future, and an increased level of ferocity on both sides. Trooper Donald Macdonald, in the same conflict, saw a lancer lift his spear-point rather than kill a Boer who screamed for mercy, but, turning, he saw the man he had spared reach for his thrown-down Mauser. The lancer turned back and killed him.[17] Corporal Abbott, in his account of Australians in action, said of white flags that ' … they had three of them over Du Ploy's chimneys when they fired on the English scouts'. He also describes another action where one 'Hans Larsen and his son' were shelled because they had fired from a kraal over which a white flag flew.[18]

It is the same in all battles: the rules of surrender must be adhered to or dire consequences will follow. In World War I, a Turkish sniper ' … put up his hands but still held his rifle and fired point blank. Instantly, the Australian swung his rifle and struck the head of the Turk. There was no need for a second blow … '[19] Australian troops at Passchendaele stormed a two-storey pillbox: the survivors in the lower section had begun surrendering when a shot was fired from the upper, killing one of the Australians. All of the Germans were immediately shot.[20] A well-known incident in World War I saw Germans advancing towards the positions of the British ' "B" Company of the Queen's', as Private George Coppard described it. Around 18 March 1917, three hundred Germans apparently advanced with their hands up but, upon reaching the British wire, pulled grenades from their pockets and flung these into their opponents' trenches. 'From then on', said Coppard, 'the advance of a crowd of Jerries with their hands up would be the signal to open fire'.[21] Captain Ambrose Cull tells of a similar incident in the early days of the European campaign, when three Germans surrendered in a dugout and then, as they came out with their hands up, two of them suddenly reached for revolvers and opened fire, hitting one of the Australian troopers – whose sergeant responded with three shots of his own, killing the Germans. Then the Australians opened up on every other one of the enemy in the trench, killing around 60 of them.[22]

An Australian military pocket book, published in 1941, and written by a major with World War I experience, outlined situations like this with bluntness:

Germans fired their machine-guns from the pill-boxes of Flanders, reaping a harvest of our men at the last moment. Then, they often put their hands up and 'kameraded'. Our men, maddened by the loss of mates, frequently slaughtered them to the last man. I quite agree with that action. Let the enemy know that your coming means death to him, unless he surrenders early. This knowledge will cause him to break when attack becomes threatening. And this breaking will save half your men who would otherwise be knocked out in the close fighting. Always kill an enemy who fights till you get close. He seeks an unfair advantage by trying to save his life at the last moment. When the enemy learns the price you exact for prolonged resistance, unless he be very brave, he will either run or surrender early ... Not for a moment, however, would I suggest that prisoners should be wiped out indiscriminately. No great victory was ever won except by the surrender of large bodies of enemy ... The time to kill is when they are by the smoking weapons they have used too long. Otherwise it is not proper to slaughter them.[23]

Once surrendered ...

When does a prisoner become a combatant again, and what happens to their status if they do? In the Battle of Bardia a large number of Italian troops had surrendered, when six Italian tanks appeared. The six soldiers guarding around 500 of the enemy had no anti-tank weapons, and took cover. One of them was captured and sent off by the triumphant tankers to the local HQ to request surrender. This was refused, and the tanks were attacked by a small force sent out to deal with them. They departed, and one of the attackers 'fired a few bursts into the clustered Italians, who re-surrendered'.[24] A similar situation was seen after the D-Day landings, when some German prisoners had been taken by American paratroopers. Then an enemy machine-gun opened up on the Americans, and the surrendered Germans attacked their captors. One of the US soldiers shot them all dead.[25] It is clear that in such situations confusion reigns, and the chance of firing on a non-combatant – and committing a technical crime – is high. But what other recourse is there?

Sergeant John Halpin, captured by the Turks in 1918, was under escort when other British captives began calculating that there were 15 Turks and 25 prisoners. Plans began to be made by some, others urged caution, and then one of the captives began urging the prisoners to attack. Their guards grew suspicious, rifle bolts were cocked, and as the movement to revolt grew into commands, they shot the chief instigator.[26] It is hard to know what else they could have done. Soldier Richard Weston was present when three British tanks herding a large group of Afrika Korps prisoners to the rear were delayed. The Germans took the opportunity to make a break for it. Within seconds all three tanks opened fire with their machine-guns, and kept shooting till none were left standing.[27]

R. Derby Holmes, fighting in 1918, had a German officer who had surrendered along with his troops stop marching to the rear and refuse to move. When menaced with a bayonet, the German drew a concealed pistol and fired at one of his captors, hitting him, but not well enough to prevent his own immediate dispatch via rifle.[28] Surrendering properly also means having the courage to make the visible signs rather than hiding. An advancing British unit in the Falklands noted that many of the Argentine soldiers did not do this. A company commander noted: 'What surprised me was the number of Argentinean soldiers who were just not fighting. Some of them were just lying supine in the bottom of their trench with their sleeping bags pulled over their heads; others pretending they were asleep … '[29]

Those on the run are not immune from being targeted. EB Sledge's unit of Marines fired at some Japanese walking and running away from the American position on Peleliu island. Some of them were swimming away in the sea. Urged on by their NCOs, the Marines fired until they had killed all of the Japanese.[30] When a Japanese bunker was cleared, several enemy soldiers raced out and were ruthlessly shot down. Sledge commented: 'We felt not pity for them but exulted over their fate. We had been shot at and shelled too much and had lost too many friends to have compassion for the enemy when we had him cornered'.[31] In the heat of battle after D-Day, a fight with grenades, machine-guns and rifles between some Americans and Germans saw three German infantry start to run: they were all shot down and one who was wounded and fell, calling 'Help! Help!', was machine-gunned.[32]

Confusion in the fog of war leads to accidents. Peter Young, fighting in a World War II Commando unit, was in command of troops who took surrender from around 10 Italians one night. Then one of the British troops thought the Italians were attacking him and fired, which led to more shots; whether the Italians were killed is not clear.[33] Around 60 German captives were killed in an action after D-Day by the US 11th Armored Division because the American soldiers, who were new to combat, mistakenly believed they were not to take prisoners.[34] Some of the advancing Canadians, following the D-Day landings, noted how difficult it was to take prisoners:

First, they had to brave their own troops, then to face the opposing force, not always clear on their intentions. They come forward aligned down the muzzles of enemy guns, and a single shot fired by one man can cause thousands of others to follow suit. This was not yet 'savagery' or 'revenge', it was 'SNAFU', or organised confusion. Nevertheless, men going forward to surrender were shot down.[35]

Accidents happen routinely. In World War II, an advancing tank saw four Germans coming out of a wood, so the tank's gunner opened up with a machine-gun and shot two. Unfortunately, they were being escorted at gunpoint by an infantryman behind them, who had been wounded in the arm by the fire and was now loudly complaining about his prisoners being shot at. Major H. Wake, who recorded the incident, noted that it was a good idea to remove prisoners' helmets and get them to keep their hands up all the time when being escorted.[36] Eight German infantry were surrendering to a US corporal in 1945 when ' … I saw the leader suddenly realise he still had a pistol in his shoulder holster. He reached into his jacket with two fingers to pull it out and throw it away. One of our guys yelled, 'Watch it! He's got a gun!' and came running up shooting and there were eight Krauts on the ground shot up … '[37] Similarly, three Germans were surrendering to some Americans in late 1944 when one of their sergeants reached into his coat, as did another, causing one of their captors to cut down all three with a burst from his submachine-gun.[38] In the Falklands War a running fight to take an Argentine position saw one officer comment:

> A lot of individual actions were fought at very close quarters, from trench to trench, with a grenade going in, a machine-gunner raking it, then moving on. And I think consequently the number of Argentinean casualties reflected this very aggressive tactic; and I think unfortunately a lot of Argentinean soldiers were either killed or wounded in this manner purely because you can't determine at night whether a bloke is surrendering, or is going to fight …[39]

In the Falklands, a small temporary ceasefire occurred for a discussion to take place between two members of the 2nd Parachute Regiment and an Argentine officer, Lieutenant Gomez Centurion, as to whether the latter would surrender his position. There was some misunderstanding, both sides fired on each other, and the two British soldiers, Lieutenant Jim Barry and his escort Corporal Sullivan, were killed.[40] Confusion still surrounds the supposed surrender: misunderstanding about who was supposed to surrender to whom, and some stray firing, were probably the cause of the several British soldiers dying and the fierce resumption of battle that ensued.[41]

Just as certain formalities on the battlefield were sacrosanct, so too was what you did with the prisoners once taken. Wounded prisoners in the Boer War were well treated, with one Boer soldier noting that there was never any hesitation in abandoning a wounded man because it was a certainty that he would be well cared for.[42] He captured a wounded Cockney soldier on one occasion, and the two talked at length, partly about the British soldier's photograph of his family. Those were often left alone: EJ Rule noted on one occasion in 1918 that when his men saw 'Huns carrying out their wounded', they did not fire on them.[43] This nicety, however, as we will see, was not a general rule. FP Crozier tells of a time in World War I when 400 German prisoners were employed in carrying British wounded through a shell-swept area, with many of the Germans being killed. Crozier thought such use of prisoners to be quite fair.[44]

Surrendering had to follow a shared, unwritten code. Middlebrook notes: 'The actual moment of capture could be very dangerous, especially if a British position had put up a good fight and caused many casualties among the German attackers, but such moments of anger usually passed quickly … '[45] The traditional comment for anyone who did not surrender promptly enough was 'Too late, chum!' as they were shot.[46] If the proper gestures of surrender were not made, prospective prisoners were routinely killed. Soldiers from the Canadian Army overcame a German 88mm gun emplacement. 'I moved up to the gun emplacement and mercilessly shot all the gun crew of fourteen men who were cowering in the trench'.[47] There was no mention of whether they had their hands up. Soldier Richard Weston was part of the Australian defence of Tobruk in 1941. In one action where the Allies and Germans were disputing a section of the front line: 'A Perth boy with a Tommy-gun was forcing some Germans to surrender when a German officer poked a Luger in his back. The boy slowly raised his hands above his head, still holding the Tommy-gun, pointed it downwards towards the German and pulled the trigger. He kept firing until the German was about cut in two'.[48]

The Western Desert of 1941. A New Zealand Bren gun carrier follows German prisoners walking across the barren landscape, being taken in during the Allied offensive. What happens if the prisoners break and run – and is it a war crime to shoot them down if they do? AWM 010842/29

Prisoners in the European theatre of WWII were often well treated, particularly in comparison to the Pacific war. Here a New Zealand doctor treats a German soldier. AWM 010853

For those who abused the proper process of surrender, the results were swift and savage. One cannot fire until the last second and then expect to suddenly have surrender accepted. In the World War II Battle of Bardia, one Italian paid the price for not observing the rules of surrender. Two officers were watching the surrender of enemy troops when one

> ... bobbed up from one of the pits, put a rifle to his shoulder and shot Green through the chest. He then dropped his rifle, put up his hands and climbed out of the post, smiling broadly. An angry Australian threw him back into the post and emptied his Bren gun into him. At the same time

146

others demanded of Macfarlane that they should be allowed to bayonet all the other prisoners, but Macfarlane – now the only officer in the company – forbade them to take revenge, and was obeyed.[49]

Somewhat later, the same officer's troops were fighting other Italians, and 'At one stone wall the Italians threw grenades until the last yard, then flung up their hands; and one threw a grenade from among his surrendering comrades and killed an Australian.' A Bren gun was fired into the others, killing twenty (according to one observer).[50] Australian infantryman Roland Griffiths-Marsh noted, of fighting the Italians in North Africa, that there were several 'confirmed' incidents of white flags being shown and then soldiers shooting at the oncoming Australians or throwing grenades.[51] In Vietnam, the Americans scattered leaflets to persuade a Vietcong soldier to become a 'Chieu Hoi': an enemy soldier who would now fight for the Southern cause. But this would not be honoured after an ARVN patrol took sniper rounds or a group exchange of fire. US Army combat adviser Martin Dockery saw 'Viet Cong, some wounded, who were shot trying to surrender while grasping their leaflets and shouting "Chieu Hoi" … '[52]

Prisoner-taking – special rules for special forces?

Soldiers who differ from the normally recognised formations of armed forces often receive harsher treatment in capture than do their comrades. Churchill famously declared in World War I that submariners should be given harsh treatment. U-boat crews should not have the usual rights accorded to them: 'Survivors should be taken prisoner or shot – whatever is the most convenient'.[53] The use of strange weapons was enough to label a force as different. Infantry captain Robert Graves, fighting in World War I, tells of a type of canister filled with explosive and shrapnel that was fired by the Germans from close range. Attacked by this for some time, the British eventually found the cannon and crew that fired it. Graves noted dispassionately: 'The crew offered to surrender, but our men had sworn for months to get them'.[54] The Germans in the Battle of the Bulge had organised a large detachment of soldiers under Lieutenant Colonel Otto Skorzeny who wore US uniforms and used US vehicles and equipment, and whose main job was sabotage. The US forces who captured 18 of them shot them all.[55] Germans trying to escape from France after D-Day were shot out of hand by French Resistance members if they were found in civilian clothes, related soldier Glen McBride.[56]

Specialised members of armed forces often get dealt with more harshly than normal by the enemy. Presumably, regular soldiers feel somewhat aggrieved at those who fight with different tactics. So a German sniper found in a hollowed-out haystack by members of the Welsh Fusiliers in World War I was 'finished there and then'.[57] Max Hastings notes that, on both sides, snipers in World War II were frequently shot out of hand if captured, simply because the killing was too personal.[58] Roland Griffiths-Marsh, an experienced Australian soldier who, halfway through his World War II service, trained as a sniper, noted that it was normally the case that 'snipers and flame-throwing operators received short shrift if captured'.[59] The flame-throwing Marines fighting on Okinawa were targets for special attention by the Japanese, who knew very well what that equipment was designed to do: finish them off in the caves from which thousands of them were emerging to fight.[60]

Similarly treated were any parachuting members of what one writer calls the 'French SAS', who landed after D-Day and assisted local Resistance cells. Even though they fought in uniform, the Germans arrested and later shot, or simply shot out of hand those they found.[61] Roger Ford tells us that a German order had been issued to shoot all 'commandos' or hand them over to the SD (Sicherheitsdienst, or Security Police of the SS) for 'disposal'. The cause for this was the execution of three German soldiers during a raid on the island of Sark,[62] giving weight to the argument for treating prisoners well, for the converse leads to reprisals. Eight SAS Other Ranks were later shot, as a group, by the SS. Five of the Jedburgh three-man teams – comprising a British or American officer, a French officer and a radio operator – were shot, one of them after having been reported as a POW; the other four were also killed, when they could have been taken prisoner.[63] Anthony Scariano, one of the parachuting OSS members of what would today be called 'Special Forces', tells of a party of 13 officers and men who had been dropped onto Elba on a sabotage mission. They were captured by a surprise movement of German troops into the area and, despite being in uniform, were tied up, blindfolded, lined up, shot and dumped into a common grave.[64] An Australian military pocket manual, published in 1941, suggested that 'parachute troops should be given no option to surrender', because 'There will be few volunteers if this treatment of them becomes general'.[65]

From 1942, with the 'Top-Secret Commando Order', Hitler ordered that all commandos 'armed or unarmed, in battle or in flight, are to be slaughtered to the last man' for their acts of sabotage. Fifteen US Commandos were shot under this order in March 1944 in Italy after being captured in a behind-the-lines operation. Their uniforms did not save them, and they were executed without trial by firing squad. Under the Kommissar Befehl order, all Russian political officers and members of the Communist Party were to be shot: Wermacht soldier Henry Metelmann, on guard duties after recovering from a wound, saw this routinely done in a camp on the Russian Front.[66] In January 1945, 15 members of a combined British–American mission, including a war correspondent from the Associated Press, parachuted into Slovakia, were captured, and all executed. Such actions, even if carried out in the name of revenge, fit into the category of atrocities and war crimes.[67]

Paratrooper David Webster's unit was told, before their jump behind the German forward positions on D-Day, that Hitler had ordered all Allied parachutists were to be treated as spies and killed on the spot of capture. So 'Don't forget that word *kill* … you know what to do with the Germans.'[68]

Special forces, it can be seen, are often treated differently. That does not mean they should be so treated. But the scenarios described here, in the first of several chapters on prisoner-taking, have shown that there are both formal and informal rules in this aspect of warfare. Even so, prisoner-taking is difficult. We are about to see that it is more complex and more confusing than at first thought – and that some of the rules governing the capture of enemy personnel are both difficult to adhere to and illogical.

'10
Surrendering to a hot-blooded enemy

Bayonet the bastard!

Comment from Australians at Gallipoli when passing a Turkish prisoner.

In the heat of combat, it is common for soldiers not to accept surrender. Sometimes this may be due to the combatant being 'fired up' to fight and therefore not attuned to anything but killing the enemy. Sometimes there will be feelings of anger and hatred which have been aroused for a variety of reasons: fear, seeing one's comrades killed alongside one, and/or a vicarious anger aroused by what one has seen of the enemy's actions in general.

Richard Holmes cites an Australian World War I soldier's account of Germans trying to surrender:

Strike me pink the squareheads are dead mongrels. They will keep firing until you are two yds. off them & then drop their rifles & ask for mercy. They get it too right where the chicken gets the axe.[1]

The Australians may have been ferocious from the start. A Turkish prisoner was taken in the Gallipoli landings, and the Anzac soldiers 'ratted' him – the term for checking out a prisoner or position for loot – and then: ' … yelled out. "Prisoner here!" The only advice they got from men passing was "Bayonet the bastard!" ' Instead, they cut his buttons off and had him taken down to the beach. Others were not so lucky. Six Turkish soldiers, caught brewing coffee in a hut, were bayoneted by attacking Australians who overran their position. [2]

Sixty Turks were shot trying to surrender in Shrapnel Gully during the Gallipoli landings, throwing their rifles down to no avail. Another hundred or so who were captured on a section of the battlefield known as The Chessboard were treated the same way.[1] A British officer wrote to his sister after Gallipoli, and commented: 'we took 300 prisoners and could have taken 3000 but we preferred shooting them'.[3] Hard feelings were strong on both sides in this initial landing period, and few prisoners were taken by the Turks, either.

However, later in the Gallipoli conflict, feelings may have been kinder: Corporal John Gallishaw fought there for some time and was of the opinion that the Turk ' ... respected the Red Cross and never ill-treated our wounded'.[4] But EJ Rule thought otherwise: his unit captured a Turkish soldier who, although treated kindly, was 'trembling like a leaf' because 'he fully expected to meet the fate met by most of our boys, who were unfortunate enough to fall into Turkish hands.'[5] The perception of what would happen to one if surrendering counted for a lot. R. Derby Holmes noted at High Wood that, 'Almost inevitably the Boche prisoners were expecting harsh treatment', and that some German soldiers had been told by their officers they would be skinned alive if they surrendered to the English.[6] Conversely, Erwin Rommel's platoon took some time to coax possible French prisoners out of hiding early in World War I: the enemy soldiers had been told that capture would mean that they would be beheaded.[7]

After the Second Battle of Ypres, in June 1915, Private Charles Tames managed to get a letter past the censor system which described taking part in the final charge, when 'a great number' of Germans came out of their trenches and ' ... asked for mercy, needless to say they were shot right off ...'[2] Corporal WHA Groom said of his time in Europe, where he saw three years of the war as an infantryman, that by 1917 troops were often told on parade 'the only good German is a dead one – kill the Boche – we don't want prisoners'. Later at Passchendaele he saw some British soldiers shooting at Germans who had their hands up – again, he notes that parades had been told that the British were short of food and that prisoners would have to be fed.[8]

EJ Rule noted an occasion when a 'Captain V' told a patrol not to being back prisoners: they were not popular with senior command because they 'ate a hole in the rations'.[9]

1   Winter, Denis. *25 April 1915*. Queensland: University of Queensland Press, 1994. (175)
    Winter is citing Bean, the official historian for World War I, who was actually there at the time.
2   Brown, Malcolm. *The Imperial War Museum Book of the Western Front*. London: Sidgwick & Jackson in association with the Imperial War Museum, 1993. (177) Brown views the account with some suspicion.

Ernst Junger recounts an episode towards the end of the war where he participated in a successful German advance, and where

> ... the defenders advanced by hundreds with their hands held high. No quarter was given ... An orderly of Gipkens' shot a good dozen or more of them with his 32 repeater ... the defending force, after driving their bullets into the attacking one at five paces' distance, must take the consequences. A man cannot change his feelings again during the last rush with a veil of blood before his eyes. He does not want to take prisoners but to kill.[10]

On another occasion he witnessed the same from the other side: ' ... two gigantic Englishmen were using their bayonets in a length of trench from which hands were held up imploring mercy'.[11]

It may well be the case that the more ferocious the battle, the fewer prisoners are taken. On the opening day of the Somme, an enormous number of casualties were experienced as the Allied commanders attempted to break through the German lines. The figures vary, but many historians have noted figures up to 60,000 under British command, with 20,000 of those killed. As the first days of Gallipoli were marked by massacres, so too may have been the Somme. After a while the fighting settles down to a long, slow slog – patrols, raiding – and so prisoners are taken in greater numbers. Second Lieutenant Philip Caputo noticed this in his first days in Vietnam. Watching and listening to an enemy position being pounded by 155-millimetre shells, he pitied the soldiers on the other side.[12]

Aerial combat and surrendering

A previous chapter established that effective tactical combat in the air requires particularly aggressive pilots. How do they deal with the rules of letting a surrendering enemy live? Longstreet suggests that, later in his career, von Richthofen was a savage killer: ' ... machine-gunning enemy fliers as they dangled helpless in parachutes, gunning them on the ground as they escaped or crawled from burning, crashed planes.'[13] (We must presume the parachutists were balloon observers, as Allied aircraft personnel in World War I were not equipped with parachutes.)

Towards the end of the war, however, von Richthofen may have become more kind-hearted: perhaps this was provoked by his lengthy stay in hospital, the result of a hard crash landing. Longstreet suggest that, in von Richthofen's final months, he sent his sixty-fourth victim, who was in hospital, a box of cigars; and his last and eightieth victim, who survived the crash of his plane, was waved at by the Baron as he swooped low overhead.[3] But another account says that the Red Baron was an inexorable killer. A new flight commander of a British squadron ' … says that von Richthofen may have the reputation of being a good sport but that he showed him no mercy – shot his engine up and then followed him down while he was trying to land and shot him three times'.[14]

Unfortunately, most people get their understanding of combat behaviour from sanitised books and films, and for various reasons – ignorance, potential audience, unwillingness to shock – they are well removed from the truth. WE Johns, the famous writer of the Biggles books, paints such a picture, admittedly for a 'young adult' audience:

> … he got the machine under control and looked around for the bomber. It was steering an erratic course for the ground, obviously in difficulties. He dived after it and noticed that the rear gunner's cockpit was empty. 'I've hit the pilot and the observer is trying to get he machine down,' he decided instantly, and closer view confirmed his suspicions … 'I hope he manages it,' thought Biggles anxiously, and held his hand up to show they had nothing to fear from him …[15]

As previously noted, the concept quickly arose in World War I of these new aviators being the 'knights of the sky'. The concept of the 'ace' – one who had scored over five victories – arose in France and quickly spread.[16] In Germany, von Richthofen was the celebrated leader of fliers who became heroes to the nation: lionised at functions, celebrated in the newspapers, even becoming the subject of postcard collectors. As mentioned previously, Max Immelmann dined with royalty, and noted: 'My mail swelled to fifty letters a day'.[17]

The Allied nations pursued similar tactics. Prime Minister Lloyd George proclaimed: 'They are the knighthood of this war, without fear and without reproach; and they recall the legendary days of chivalry, not merely by the daring of their exploits, but by the nobility of their spirit.'[18]

---

3 Longstreet. (341) Peter Kilduff quotes from records in *The Red Baron* to confirm the survival of the two aircrew. (183)

In truth, many pilots were extremely lethal, and carried out actions that would not have been glorified at home and that might have even seen them condemned. Rather than letting an observer land a machine – as in the Biggles scenario – Wesley Archer remembered: 'We came down full engine on and could see obs. reaching over into the pilot's cockpit, apparently trying to pull him off the stick, so he must have been hit, as he was slumped forward. We were diving at terrific speed and I pressed the triggers ...'[4] Another account relates how a squadron member was killed. 'He was in a fight with a Fokker and he had to land. He landed all right and got out of his plane. The Hun dove on him and shot him as he was standing by his plane'.[20] Similarly, AH Cobby shot down one of his opponents and then ' ... went down and dived three times at the machine and fired about four hundred rounds into it, but the pilot did not move after crashing'.[21]

Winged Victory, although fiction, was written by a World War I pilot – VM Yeates – and is in fact a disguised version of the author's time in fighters. It is a starkly realistic portrayal of life in a combat squadron: the descriptions of everyday life include accounts of the lavatory routines, the visits to prostitutes, and the horrors of aerial war in a way that gives a bluntly honest depiction. Writing to a friend who he had served with and who was encouraging his writing, Yeates said:

> You say I mustn't let things happen as in life. I MUST. Art is selection, not alteration ... Mirror up to nature. There is no meaning whatever in events that are not as-in-life ... I read an awful book the other day called *The Camels are Coming;* it was about Camels in the war and it was super-bunk.[5]

Winged Victory did not sell well upon release in 1934, perhaps striking the wrong tone for the times. But Yeates's friend was able to note in a subsequent edition, and with some satisfaction, that during World War II volumes were being sold for five pounds a copy among combat fliers, and that pilots had told him ' ... it was the only book about war-flying which "wasn't flannel" '.[22]

---

4   Archer, Wesley D. *Death in the Air*. London: Greenhill Books, 1985. (102) This book, purportedly a diary, was published in 1933 with photos taken by a World War I aviator. In later years, it turned out the diary was in fact written well after the war, and the photographs were fakes.
5   This was one of WE Johns's famous 'boys' novels' of World War I flying. Johns was a fighter pilot himself, and he does describe tactical combat very well. In defence of his sanitised accounts, he was writing for a juvenile audience, and therefore the grimmer aspects of combat were often omitted or glossed over. Nevertheless, there are several instances in *The Camels are Coming* and in his other novels where the author might be accused of making air-fighting more glamorous and chivalrous than it really was.

Much of this was perhaps due to Yeates's cold-blooded accounts of battle:

> It wasn't too glorious for six Camels to set about two separate two-seaters; indeed it was, like most of the war, mere blackguardism; but two-seaters with their spottings for artillery, their photographings, their reconnaissances; their bombings were the real danger: German scouts were of no direct importance in military operations.[23]

At least the aircrew were somewhat divorced from the action, and that made it easier to take life. Yeates described ground strafing:

> You pointed your aeroplane towards the ground and pressed a lever on the joystick for a second or two, that was all. It wasn't like going up to a man and sticking a bayonet into his neck or guts and giving it a twist; nothing like that: you pressed a lever.[24]

Aerial attacks on crowds of people on the ground were extremely devastating. In World War II, Glen McBride saw what Typhoon ground-attack machines equipped with rockets had done at Falaise after D-Day, when they assaulted the retreating Germans, resulting in 'thousands of dead'.[25] Most pilots got the point – you were there to destroy the enemy – and most did. Yeates described the relentless pursuit and killing of a squadron member:

> … he was split off from the flight and chased down. Apparently he was wounded but got across the lines before he crashed. A Hun followed him right down and put a final burst into the crash in case he wasn't dead.

> Everyone in sight on the ground shot at the Hun, but he got away.

World War II saw more instances of fierce, intentional lethality amongst fliers. Major Gilbert O'Brien, a World War II fighter pilot, recalled while escorting bombers:

> Many B-17 crewmen had bailed out and at least three Me-109s were gunning our bomber crewmen while they were hanging in parachutes. This angered me beyond words. I got behind one of these Germans, pulled up at extremely close range and fired a short burst. The German pilot, hit and bleeding profusely, bailed out almost instantly … I immediately executed a wingover, fully intending to shoot the German pilot in his parachute, but … his chute never opened.[26]

Billy Drake, a British Hurricane pilot, was shot down by German aircraft attacking from behind. He bailed out with some difficulty – the aircraft was on fire – and says: 'As I recall, the German was still shooting at me in the air' as he hung under his parachute.[27]

Bobby Gibbes bailed out of his stricken Kittyhawk in World War II, but

> ... hesitated before pulling the ripcord of his parachute because [of] his fear of being strafed on the way down ... there had been precedents. In October the previous year, one of No. 3 Squadron's pilots had been attacked by four 109s and his harness shot off in midair. Consequently, the pilot fell 4000 feet to his death without a parachute.[28]

Nicky Barr bailed out of his Hurricane in Africa, but admitted he ' ... couldn't be sure a German pilot would not use him for target practice'.[29] Gunner William Harding observed a duel between a German and a British fighter in 1940; the Messerschmitt won and the British pilot 'parachuted out, swinging from side to side, and the German fighter flew around, firing bursts at him'.[30]

R. Bruce Porter's friend, Sam Logan, bailed out of his Corsair and was then attacked by a Japanese Zero, whose pilot at first tried to machine-gun him, and then, out of ammunition, tried to hit him with the propeller in two separate passes. Logan escaped at first by manipulating his parachute shroud lines wildly, but then the Zero hit him and his right foot was cut off. The aircraft came around again but this time was attacked by a New Zealand aircraft, at which point the Japanese machine left. Logan plummeted into the sea, managed to get into his life raft and was recovered some hours later.[31] Historian Eric Bergerud found plenty of evidence of such attitudes when researching the Pacific War. It was standard practices, if parachuting from an American aircraft, to assume that the Japanese would attack you under your 'chute. Rule No. 4 of a list of tactical techniques suggested: 'If you have to bail out while the enemy is in the vicinity, wait as long as possible before opening your chute, because if a Jap sees you, he will machine-gun you.'[32] One aviator, Robert DeHaven, summarised the overall feelings well: 'I saw the strafing of an American pilot in a parachute. We retaliated and the result was a mind-numbing involvement in the Pacific that I don't think existed in Europe.' Another commented on the necessity of killing the pilots: 'If they got on the ground, they were going to be up tomorrow ... None of our pilots reached the ground alive if the Japs could kill 'em. We didn't give any quarter and they didn't either.'[33]

CHAPTER 10

An Australian plane targeted a Japanese aviator under his parachute in World War II in the Pacific theatre. The *USS Russell's* medical doctor witnessed the combat and saw a parachute separate from a stricken aircraft. Then:

> The parachute was about five hundred feet in the air and several hundred yards in front of our bow, when a plane darted from the clouds followed a moment later by another. The wing markings were clear, Aussies. One of the planes dove toward the descending chute. Tracer bullets erupted from its nose. In a moment both planes were gone, in the direction of the beach.[34]

The aviator was recovered by the ship, still alive, but he died a little later.

A Gazelle helicopter was brought down in the Falklands by Argentine ground fire. It made a fair crash landing in the water near the shore, but then the crew had to face being machine-gunned by Argentine soldiers firing from the shore. They were ordered to stop in a shouted order from one of their officers, but did not hear him. The same officer explained later that they were conscripts who had not been trained in relation to the protocols of the Geneva Convention.[35] Then again, the Argentine pilot of a Pucara aircraft downed in the battle for Goose Green was the target of some British soldiers as he descended to earth under his parachute.[36]

In summary, the possible taking of prisoners in another context – that of tactical aerial warfare – sees a slightly different scenario. It is routine, unless the enemy aviator is guaranteed to be a prisoner when he hits the ground, to be targeted even when helpless, because his combatant status is going to be re-conferred within hours of landing, as soon as he receives another aircraft. So, where necessary, in yet another theatre of war the rules and conventions previously thought normal are in fact normally broken.

Infantry prisoner-taking in World War II

World War II saw the same sorts of accounts on the ground. Fighting in Italy, Sergeant Audie Murphy led a night patrol to take prisoners. They found a hut in the German sector and called on those inside to give themselves up. The Germans would not come out, so Murphy's men threw in grenades, killing all inside except one, who they captured.[37] But when the Germans were defending positions that were obviously going to fall, on occasion they surrendered readily. Canadian infantryman Charles Martin noted that, in the Calais region, they

157

surrendered in the hundreds.[38] Despite exhortations from commanders that 'I don't want to see you take too many PWs' and 'If the defenders want to die for Hitler, we'll oblige them', in the Battle for Hurtgen Forest there was a constant stream of prisoners being processed – including 155 in one night.[39] Second Lieutenant Peter Cochrane took part in ferocious actions against Italian mountain troops and was one of many Allied casualties. He noted that, in contrast to the savagery of combat, once a prisoner, 'Nothing could have been kinder than the Italians' behaviour to [the] wounded …'[40]

So prisoner-taking and surrenders were common in the European theatre, at least in the west, but the dispatching of prisoners, generally to suit circumstances, also occurred frequently. Significantly, the writer Stephen Ambrose noted that he had interviewed more than 1000 combat veterans, and that while only one admitted to having shot a prisoner, over a third said they had seen incidents where American soldiers had shot prisoners who had had their hands up. [41]

Ambrose notes that there was only one official order given about not taking prisoners: the order given at Headquarters, 328th Infantry Regiment, which stated that 'No SS troops or paratroopers will be taken prisoner but will be shot on sight'.[42] This was apparently in retaliation for the 'Malmedy massacre' of 80 POWs by the command of Jochen Peiper, a senior Waffen SS officer. Many SS were shot as a result. US soldier Walter Rosenblum was advancing in Patton's army when they ended up having a savage fight with SS troops in a square of Munich. The SS troops were lined up against a wall and shot by Americans with submachine-guns.[43] The Russian Front saw a similar order given by the German command: any captured Soviet political commissars were to be executed.[44]

The situation in the Pacific was different …

The Japanese Army fighting in the Pacific in World War II presents a perhaps unique example of refusal to become prisoners. It would seem to be the case that, historically, armies both give and take surrender. It is logical to take it from a command perspective, because it achieves the aim of defeating the enemy: the more surrendered soldiers they have, the less they can fight. But the Japanese were different. The Japanese Army would, in the main, refuse to surrender. Major General J. Lawton Collins noted:

> The Japanese on both offensive and defense die determinedly rather than give up. Many cases are recorded of men so weak with hunger and disease that they could not stand who stayed by their weapons pulling

the trigger as long as there was life. Surrenders by able-bodied, well Japanese were negligible ... [45]

A significant pair of photographs in Eric Bergerud's comprehensive account of the theatre – *Touched with Fire: The land warfare in the South Pacific* – shows a Japanese soldier in the sea.[46] The caption explains that he was one of four who would not surrender to some Australian troops, and the soldiers therefore shot them. The Japanese holds a grenade to his head, and then, the caption explains, he set it off. There was a lot of this sort of suicide. British Commando Peter Young was leading some men trying to take a prisoner; they came across a wounded Japanese, who simply blew himself up with a grenade rather than be taken.[47] General William Slim tells of a Japanese Army unit trying to withdraw over a river while being pressed hard by Allied troops. Eventually, with most of their force cut down, the remaining Japanese formed up in ranks and, rather than come forward and surrender, instead 'marched steadily into the river and drowned.'[48] An account from a Japanese soldier describes how those too badly wounded to fight were treated: 'It became a routine that a soldier who was emaciated and crippled, with no hope of recovery, was given a grenade and persuaded, without words, to sort himself out.'[49]

Engineer Officer Bob MacArthur watched Japanese kill themselves. 'It was the damnedest thing. I watched them up on a ridge, taking their grenades – they had a button that detonated them – bang them on their helmets and hold them to their chest while they went off. I couldn't fathom it.'[50] Corporal James Day said that in his entire Pacific War, his platoon took only one prisoner: ' ... they just wouldn't surrender'.[51] On Okinawa, a decision was made by the Japanese commander after some days of fierce fighting. He withdrew his force to an escarpment where they would fight to the death. A Japanese soldier observed around 3-400 wounded attempt to come along with the main body of the troops, some of them double amputees, 'pleading to be taken along'. Many of those too seriously wounded to be moved stayed behind, equipped with cyanide or grenades, so they could take their own lives but also take some of the enemy with them.[52] The savagery of the fighting on that island is illustrated by the fact that no American soldier was taken prisoner there, and the US forces showed a similar inclination, one soldier later saying that they didn't take any captives until after 18 June 1945, when the Japanese started to surrender. In all, 7401 were captured, but 110,071 died.[53]

Australian Army Colonel Cummings was present when two wounded prisoners who had been captured for intelligence purposes were being rowed in a small boat out to a lugger. Suddenly, the two attacked their captors and then capsized the boat, drowning themselves in the process.[54] In the actions around Milne Bay in September 1942, Japanese positions were called upon to surrender, the result was, according to Warrant Officer David Marsh, that 'they immediately opened fire on us'. In another case, native police, who had joined the Australian forces, received the same greeting when trying to capture three downed pilots. Observing that the enemy was armed by this time only with revolvers, they waited until they had counted six shots from each, and then closed in for the kill.[55]

No prisoners. The body of a Japanese soldier who had committed suicide, using a grenade against his stomach, after unsuccessfully attempting to destroy a Solomon Islands-based 25 pounder gun position of the 5th Battery, 2nd Field Regiment, Royal Australian Artillery. The Japanese of WWII were perhaps the most determined army in history, with "no surrender" as their maxim. AWM 079991

The Japanese Army had a bad reputation for treachery and cruelty. Australian servicemen learnt early in the New Guinea campaigns that the Japanese treated prisoners badly: Signalman George Barker said, of two comrades, that they had been 'tied and bayoneted'.[56] Captain Charles Bicks found several men, including some of his own battalion, who had been captured and then executed, their hands tied behind their backs.[57] A later report by Sir William Webb, the Chief Justice of the Supreme Court of Queensland, found that between 26 August and 6 September 1942, at least 24 Australian soldiers were executed.[58] The Americans encountered the same sort of actions. Nine American Marines left behind after a submarine-borne raid on Gilbert Island were executed soon after their capture.[59] An American patrol on Saipan found five of their comrades dead, their legs bound with wire, and bullet holes in the back of their heads.[60]

One Marine noted that prisoner-killing was confirmed very early on in the war, when a Japanese bivouac was taken and pictures of mutilated Marines were found. The Marines began taking ears off dead Japanese in retaliation.[61] Bergerud comments: 'The hatred of the ground soldier toward the Japanese was on a completely different level from that found among sailors on warships or airmen … a sense of restraint existed in Europe that was absent in the Pacific.'[62] Not all of this was due to every soldier seeing atrocities. In fact, psychologists surveying three divisions of US troops in the Pacific found that only 13 per cent reported personally sighting such actions – the same rate as in the European theatre – but 45 per cent said they had heard stories of them, as opposed to 24 per cent in Europe.[63]

The attacking armies reacted by becoming more ferocious in their assaults. Australian Imperial Force infantryman Ben Love passed through a Japanese encampment the US forces had taken at night ' … twenty-three days ago. They caught the Nips asleep – killed over 100 of them.'[64] It is worth noting that infantry combat did not then, and does not now, giving the enemy a 'sporting chance': enemy found asleep were routinely dispatched. Captain 'Chips' Heron, MC was leading a patrol of British Commandos at Pauktaw against the Japanese when they came across 10 of them, six of whom he killed, including one officer, saying afterwards: 'The fellow had his back to us, sir! Thought I ought to shout 'Oi', or something.'[65] Similarly, Private Bill McGee of the Australian Army commented in a matter-of-fact way on finding a Japanese asleep in a hut: ' … he didn't last long'.[66] Marine EB Sledge, training in World War II, was told by his hand-to-hand combat instructor: 'Don't hesitate to fight the Japs dirty. Most

Americans, from the time they are kids, are taught not to hit below the belt. It's not sportsmanlike. Well, nobody had taught the Japs that, and war ain't sport. Kick him in the balls before he kicks you in yours.'[67] If a soldier runs away, he is still a target. Years later, in Vietnam: 'Forty yards away a young North Vietnamese soldier popped up from behind a tree. He started his limping run back the way he had come. I fired two rounds. He crumpled.'[68]

Surrendering at sea

The war at sea saw the same ferocity. By virtue of a treaty Japan had signed, passengers and crew of ships under submarine attack in World War II should have been safe.[6] As Lord Russell of Liverpool explains[69] in his seminal work, *The Knights of Bushido*, the personnel of torpedoed ships were not even to be placed in ships' boats unless those small craft were assured of safety by sea conditions, proximity to land or another vessel. However, an order issued by the Japanese in 1943 stated: 'Do not stop at the sinking of enemy ships and cargoes. At the same time carry out the complete destruction of the crews of the enemy's ships ...'[70] Russell lists nine instances during the war where merchant ships were torpedoed. Then the submarine surfaced, a few prisoners were taken for interrogation, and then the lifeboats and rafts were destroyed and the remaining survivors murdered. The ships were the *SS Daisy Moller, SS British Chivalry, MV Sutlej, SS Ascot, MV Behar, SS Nancy Moller, SS Tjisalak, SS Jean Nicolet* and the *SS John A Johnson*. They were of British, American and Dutch flags.

On 26 January 1943, the US Navy submarine *Wahoo*, commanded by Dudley Morton, torpedoed and sank three Japanese ships, one of them a troop transport which was also carrying many Indian prisoners. After surfacing, the submarine closed the lifeboats. One report says that the submarine was attacked by machine-gun fire. Using the deck gun and machine-guns, the submarine crew killed hundreds of those in the water. One of the US crew commented to another ' ... if those troops get rescued, we're going to lose a lot of American

---

6 The Treaty for the Limitation and Reduction of Naval Armament, often known as the London Treaty, was signed in 1930 by United Kingdom, Japan, France, Italy and the United States. Part IV Article 22, states: 'a warship, whether surface vessel or submarine, may not sink or render incapable of navigation a merchant vessel without having first placed passengers, crew and ship's papers in a place of safety. For this purpose the ship's boats are not regarded as a place of safety unless the safety of the passengers and crew is assured, in the existing sea and weather conditions, by the proximity of land, or the presence of another vessel which is in a position to take them on board.' *Wikipedia Encyclopedia*. http://en.wikipedia.org/wiki/London_Naval_Treaty 14 November 2005.

boys' lives digging them out of foxholes and shooting them out of palm trees'.[71] It seems the US crew did not know there were Indian prisoners on board the ship, and therefore many of them were killed too. The men of the submarine *Barb* had the same attitude when they used their four-inch gun on what they thought was a derelict Japanese patrol boat, only to see 'about eight or nine Japs' come running out onto the deck. But 'our four-inch crew, being very bloodthirsty at that time, landed a shot right in their midst, which blew them all apart'.[72]

In the European theatre, submarine warfare saw similar incidents. The German submarine *U-37* torpedoed the 5242-ton *Severn Leigh* in 1940. The submarine then surfaced and used her machine-guns to kill 18 of the survivors, the submarine commander later saying that he thought he was being attacked by them. *U-852*, commanded by Kapitanleutnant Heinz Eck, shot up the survivors from the freighter *Peleus* with machine-guns and grenades after the ship had been torpedoed. He and two of his officers were executed after the war, and another two imprisoned, in the only case of capital punishment being awarded for such crimes by submariners. Some of this sort of action may well have been the result of the infamous Donitz Order, the subject of much debate after the War, by which the German naval leader supposedly ordered against picking up survivors – although there is considerable room for doubt.[73]

Such actions in submarine warfare may well have included the Allied side in the Atlantic. British naval officer, broadcaster and writer Ludovic Kennedy tells of a British submarine, the crew of which had killed seven survivors of a Greek schooner. The men were trying to escape in a rubber dinghy after their vessel was set for scuttling by the submariners. Kennedy does not name the boat's captain or the vessel, but he did research the incident, and found the submarine's report of proceedings confirmed the action, and even listed another, where a small ship flying 'the Nazi flag' had been sunk by a surface gun action, with machine-guns used 'to destroy the boats and personnel'.[74]

The anger troops have for the enemy means that maximum danger exists immediately after capture. In Vietnam, rifleman John Muir said, of his squad's first prisoner: ' ... they really wanted someone to take it out on. Here was somebody they could lay hands on. It took a lot of effort on the part of the NCOs and officers to keep this guy from getting banged around a lot.'[75] Sp-4 Kenneth W. Bagby was involved in a firefight in November 1965 where his unit took casualties. When they captured two Vietcong fighters, he ' ... was going to kill both of them but Sergeant Riley stopped me.'[76]

Japanese refusal to surrender

Sometimes, despite the best of motives, surrender was simply not countenanced by the enemy. A World War II chaplain tried to get some Japanese to surrender:

He yelled into the bunker, which was inhabited by several enemy, 'Come out and be saved.' He was met by a hail of rifle fire. He dumped in a couple of hand grenades. Debris came out the slit. Then he took his pistol and fired all six rounds through the slit. From that point on he was known as 'Come out and be saved.'[77]

As an aside, we might note the chaplain in Vietnam who, somewhat differently to the rest of his calling, carried a CAR-15 assault rifle.[78] His explanation for this unusual accompaniment was that had seen a North Vietnamese kill two wounded soldiers, and that if he had been armed he would have been able to stop it. Where and when and in what circumstances, we might wonder, does one take up arms ...

The incoming forces fighting the Japanese in World War II quickly adopted new tactics in the face of the level of resistance. Japanese in a captured hospital were given no chance to surrender because some held grenades under their blankets.[79] On Tinian Island, where it was thought that there were Japanese soldiers in caves, they were, in some areas, targeted with loudspeaker broadcasts urging them to surrender. Individual caves were given a call from outside by Marines, and if there was no response, the cave was sealed.[80] In New Guinea in January 1943, despite being in hopeless positions, the Japanese troops ' ... actually charged forward to a defiant, faster finish'.[81] Their Australian enemy's ruthlessness was perhaps motivated by the finding of mutilated bodies in October 1942: two Army soldiers were so reported, and there were instances of Japanese cannibalism to further motivate the Allies.[82] The practice was caused by desperation in men at the end of an ineffective supply system: combat soldiers were, in some circumstances, existing on less than 500 calories a day.

Paul Ham notes several incidents of the Japanese eating Australian flesh in Kokoda – and other cases – and says it was widespread.[83] Ulrich Strauss, who studied the Japanese concept of surrender, concludes that it was caused by extreme conditions in the field.[84] An Australian soldier answering a questionnaire under the initials of 'HMW' said he saw 'two cases of cannibalism by the Japanese in the area, one involving the body of a Jap, and Australian bodies in the other case'.[85] Australian naval officer Marsden Hordern said, of his time in New Guinea, that he had heard second-hand stories of the practice, but then met an Australian soldier who told of one of his mates shot in a forward position; when the body was reached half an hour later, it had been substantially stripped of flesh.[86] He also tells of the trial after the war of a Japanese lieutenant who admitted to cannibalism and asked to be shot as a penalty. American soldier Peter Bezich, fighting in New Guinea, said he came across two instances of it, with the Japanese taking meat from their own dead.[87] But there could also be confusion: two natives from the Rabaul area, who the Japanese had been using as carriers, admitted to Australia soldiers that a recent incident where a cannibalistically-mutilated soldier had been found had in fact been caused by themselves.[88]

The battles of Milne Bay and Rabaul had seen numerous instances of Japanese atrocities carried out against Australian prisoners, and these too hardened the attitudes of the soldiers.[7] The attitude may well have been policy: Brigadier Arnold Potts wrote to his wife, saying: ' ... in the future any Jap we meet may kiss himself goodbye on both cheeks. No we didn't take any prisoners ...' Similarly, Sergeant Robert Johns thought that there were 'few opportunities' – he had taken only two captives in his entire war against the Japanese.[89] Peter Young organised a five-pound reward for a prisoner-taking, such was the difficulty of taking one alive: when a captured Japanese soldier recovered consciousness, he struggled so much that he swallowed his gag. Young later walked across the scene where a fierce battle had raged and the Japanese had lost. He commented that 'I could hardly move a step without treading on a dead Jap', and that the dead had mostly taken two or three wounds each: 'they had to be very thoroughly slain'.[90]

American soldier Louis Maravelas said, of the Japanese he fought:

... they were simply stupid. They sacrificed their own men needlessly, for no purpose at all. During a battle along the Matanikau three or four were straggling towards us as though they were going to surrender. There must have been a dozen of us with a bead on them. Sure enough, one bent over and there was a carbine or submachine- gun slung on his back that a comrade tried to grab. We shot them down instantly ... They did this type of thing so many times. It got to the point where we took no prisoners. It wasn't a written order, but a way to survive. No one should take a chance to take a guy prisoner who might kill him.[91]

---

7   Ham, Paul. *Kokoda*. Sydney: HarperCollins, 2004. (331) The Webb Report cited many horrific stories.

Fanatical loyalty eventually defeated by logistics, bravery and determination. Japanese Prisoners of War on Guam, with bowed heads after hearing Emperor Hirohito make the announcement of Japan's unconditional surrender, August 15, 1945.NNSP 80-G-490320

Japanese feelings on surrender were further illustrated by the actions of the soldiers defending an atoll 120 km south-east of Tarawa. Their commander, addressing them with sword in one hand and pistol in the other, accidentally shot himself in the head. And so, as Derrick Wright tells us, 'The distraught troops, unable to make any decisions without their commander, had dug their own graves and killed themselves …'[92]

At sea, the attitude was the same. *Wahoo* was 'mooned' by Japanese survivors in the water – they exposed their backsides to the surfaced submarine, insulting their victor. The Commanding Officer of the USN submarine *Flasher* tried to entice aboard a dozen survivors of a small freighter which they had sunk – only two took up the offer, with the rest refusing to move from the upturned keel of their vessel. The two who came aboard turned out to be captured Chinese, who the Japanese had been using as servants.[93] When the *USS Tinosa* came across 17 Japanese military members 'in a variety of uniforms' in a lifeboat, they all refused to board the submarine, lying face down in the open boat, some eventually being taken by force for intelligence purposes, and the rest abandoned.[94]

On Iwo Jima, the Japanese General Kuribayashi was sent a message, carried by two Japanese prisoners, advising that ' … his position was now hopeless and he could surrender with honour'.[95] The note reached him, as had another previously, and Radio Tokyo by then was broadcasting that the island was fully penetrated by US Marines. Nevertheless, he refused to surrender. A Japanese officer in New Guinea, with his position overrun, challenged the advancing Australian troops wearing a parade uniform and carrying a drawn sword. He ' … went whoosh with his sword, and he carved all the bits of the side of the palm fronds,' inviting the soldiers to take him, one presumes, with their bayonets. He was given a count of ten to surrender, and then shot.'[96]

Japanese soldiers in hopeless tactical situations always showed the same spirit. Lieutenant Doug McClean observed: 'They seemed to want to die and we were delighted to oblige them. They didn't give in, they didn't surrender and therefore there is no point in saying we showed them mercy'.[97] LM Opie thought 'they were ready to die; when we overran their positions, their personal papers had been laid on the edge of their weapon pits'.[98] Towards the end of the war, Cam Bennett, leading a company of the Australian Army, noted that in the rare event of taking a prisoner, it was difficult to get him to the rear alive: ' … it was essential to send some of them back with a good reliable NCO or they would be shot by their guards while attempting to escape (so the guards said).'[99]

A Japanese assault was repulsed in late 1942 in New Guinea by an Australian force which had been underestimated in numbers. The Japanese retreated, and the Australian followed. While a sizeable portion got away, a large number were run to earth near the village of Gorari. The Australian forces surrounded the area, and after some exchanges of fire and a few intermittent night incidents, the two sides settled down to an uneasy calm. At dawn the Australians went in at the charge, surprising many Japanese having breakfast. All were killed, with many Japanese fighting hard. A total of 580 bodies of the enemy were later counted.[100] Later, at Gona, Japanese troops whose positions were taken after artillery fire were shot down 'as they fled along the beach or swam wildly out to sea'.[101] Every Japanese defending there died – around 1000 of them.[102]

The scale of the deaths was truly shocking. The island of Tarawa, 4.5 km long by 1 km wide, saw over 1000 American lives lost,[103] and only 17 Japanese out of a garrison of 4836 captured.[104] During the assaults on Kwajalein Atoll in 1944, only 35 members of the 5000-strong Japanese garrison surrendered – the rest fought to their deaths.[105] Robert Leckie went in with the First Marines at the island of Peleliu, with 1500 men in his battalion; they were down to 28 effective soldiers when the final assault was made.[106] Perhaps the most well-known defence took place at Saipan, where around 28,500 Japanese died, with the Americans taking 16,631 casualties, out of which 3471 perished.[107] In New Guinea, 95 per cent of the 200,000 Japanese troops sent there died.[108] And many Japanese held on on individual islands until well after the war, with surrenders being recorded through the 1940s, '50s, '60s and finally in 1972, when, on 24 January, Sergeant Shoichi Yokoi was 'captured' by two fishermen, 27 years after hostilities ended![109]

This is not to say that the Japanese were routinely dispatched if killing them could be avoided. The Pacific War was ruthless on both sides. Officer Dick Thom recalls his regiment taking only one prisoner, and US soldier Tom Walker had the same total for his unit.[110] But Eric Bergerud notes: 'If the circumstances were right, military honour and basic humanity on the part of many American and Australian infantry prevented the war from descending into the realm of simple slaughter'.[111] The Australian official history notes an example on 21 October 1943, when a Japanese sergeant who spoke English surrendered to 24th Battalion. He encouraged four more Japanese soldiers, who quickly surrendered. Of interest was the sergeant's story: his command's weaker members had been allowed to discard their ancillary equipment but had been made to retain one grenade to take their own lives, rather than be captured by the Australians, who – they had been told – would torture them.[112]

Death before Dishonour might not have been their motto, but the Japanese Army of WWII were ordered not to surrender, and so they obeyed. Here Australian service personnel, Corporal JJ Mavin and Flying Officer AT Jordan, examine a Japanese sword taken from an enemy officer, who had committed suicide by blowing himself up with a hand grenade. AWM OG1694

In a later comment, Bergerud states that the 'Allies collected over 80,000 prisoners in the Pacific War.'[113] (This is in contrast to Bourke's claim[8] that, by July 1944, only 1990 Japanese prisoners had been captured *in total* – her emphasis. The *Pacific War Encyclopedia* notes that, until the collapse of the Japanese resistance, only 11,600 Japanese military were taken.[114]) And while surrender was mostly not an option for the Japanese, there were occasions when they broke and ran – at least, in the case of the Army, in one Marine's opinion. But he also stated that their Marine Corps was as tough as America's own: 'Their Marines were well equipped, and would fight to the bitter end. The Japanese Army broke under pressure, but not their Marines – when we met head on it became like running into a brick wall, neither side gave an inch.'[115] They were indeed tough troops. The Marines who Robert Leckie fought with in the final year of the war took on the Japanese when they were probably at their most determined. Even when it was obvious that a unit was broken, its soldiers would still not surrender, so the Americans exterminated them. Robert Leckie's Marine comrades found that 'They all resisted, and they were all destroyed, bayoneted for the most part ...'[116]

Even by the final few months of the war, the shattered Japanese armies possessed soldiers who were not surrendering quietly, even when it was apparent to the lowliest infantryman that the cause was lost. British soldier George MacDonald Fraser found this out when he was attacked by a soldier ' ... who came howling out of a thicket near the Sittang, full of spite and fury, in that first week of August. He was half-starved and near-naked, and his only weapon was a bamboo stake, but he was in no mood to surrender.'[117] But some were taken, expecting the worst. Japanese soldiers at Sattelberg in 1943 were told that the Allies would eat them or torture them if they were taken prisoner. Often 'prisoners seemed surprised at the fair treatment accorded to them, and soon were keen to give information ... they would ask to see the interpreter again and tell him everything'.[118] In fact, the Japanese seemed completely unprepared for interrogation, simply because it had not been foreseen that they would be captured alive. British Commando Peter Young noted of one captured: 'Like all Japanese prisoners he knew nothing of security and would answer any questions to the best of his ability. They just did not expect to be captured; it was against honour.'[119]

---

8   Bourke, Joanna. *An Intimate History of Killing.* (184) Bourke also accuses the Allied troops of having a 'propensity ... to kill anyone who attempted to surrender'. As Bergerud and others show, this is not the case.

We can see that, in most wars, surrender is difficult in the midst of combat. While it does happen, such events are almost discrete in themselves, in that they comprise a unique set of circumstances where the captor and captive are involved in a one-on-one scenario where the two of them must set the rules – with disastrous consequences for one side if many variable factors are not understood. Having said that, the situation in World War II with the Japanese is unique, at least in this study.

In conclusion, we can gather that, routinely in hot-blooded combat, the line between death at the enemy's hands and being able to surrender is extremely fine. Living on the edge of their reflexes, people in combat are not machines but human beings, subject to their feelings and prone to error. It is unfair to judge them by standards set by others who do not understand the true nature of combat.

11
Killing in revenge – understandable behaviour?

… the more I knocked down the easier it became,
the easier the feeling was. I was paying them back.

Sergeant John Meredith, commenting on his thinking
when avenging his fallen comrades in the Falklands War.

The knowledge that there is a whole set of military laws waiting to entrap debate on this point might be seen as a discussion inhibitor. This is not necessarily so, for military law, like civilian law, is subject to precedent, and variation of level of guilt according to the situation. So, just as a civilian who kills vengefully but 'unlawfully' may, in certain circumstances, be given some consideration, so too might there be some understanding extended to a soldier who exacts lethal revenge. There are plenty of examples of such cases.

Revenge was on the minds of the British soldiers attacking at the battle of Pieter's Hill in the Boer War. With cries of 'Remember Majuba!' the British infantry stormed the hill, supported by their artillery. In the words of Trooper Frederick Tucker, ' … we were revenging Majuba. White flags meant nothing to us …' While this action took place on 27 February 1900, the action they were avenging had taken place in 1881, with much[1] aggression, and resulted in a defeat for the British in what many call the first Boer War. British aggression at Pieter's Hill may well have been heightened by an order given by their general, Sir Redvers Buller, stating that any use of a white flag meant nothing unless it was accompanied by the enemy halting, throwing down their arms and putting their hands up.[1]

---

1   According to George Clarke Musgrave's *In South Africa with Buller*, the Boers had fired on unarmed personnel in an ammunition train, locked up 300 women and children in terrible conditions, and executed prisoners and civilians. (See pp: 24-26.)

In the Boer War, eventually both sides hated each other, and wanted revenge too much to be overly concerned about prisoners. Here graffiti scrawled by both sides who in turn occupied a house proclaims their hatred. The Boer says 'Don't forget Majuba, Boys'. The British proclaims 'No fear, Boojers, no fear'. (Majuba was a disastrous British defeat in the earlier Boer War of 1881). IWM 7210-03

On another occasion, British soldiers took some Boers prisoner after a British officer had been mistreated, with some confusion as to whether they were combatants, until ' … a fellow called Fraser said, "Well, Boers or not, here goes for that old ----" and shot one dead, which opened the ball, of course.'[2] The same writer – Murray Cosby Jackson – was of the opinion that the Boers always shot any 'Kaffirs' they caught, and also any white men operating as scouts at night, for not 'playing fair'. Mistreatment of one 'Scout Simon' – a black – took place, according to JFC Fuller, whose party came across the tortured body. Fuller thought the Boers, 'according to their code, had every right to shoot him; but the way they did it was unnecessarily Trojan'.[3] Jackson heard of one occasion when the black soldiers had their revenge: four or five Boers surrendered to them without seeing they were not white, but it was too late, for the blacks took their rifles and shot them all.

Perhaps the most famous incident of prisoners being executed in revenge in the Boer War is the case of Lieutenants Harry 'Breaker' Morant, Peter J Handcock and George R Witton of the Bushveld Carbineers. The details of the court-martial are lengthy and complicated but, in essence, a party of Boers had been attacked, and one of them was found in possession clothing belonging to a Captain Hunt, who had been tortured. The prisoner was then shot by firing squad. Other allegations were that a party of probably eight more Boers was also executed; and furthermore, that Lieutenant Handcock had pursued and shot a German civilian missionary, Daniel Heese. Morant admitted the eight had indeed been executed and said that he had orders from Captain Hunt not to take prisoners. Furthermore, it was claimed, this was official policy throughout the army.[4]

The finale of the action is well known. Morant and Handcock were executed, and Witton sentenced to penal servitude. The survivor wrote a book – *Scapegoats of the Empire* – and maintained through his life that Handcock had indeed shot Heese. The story still attracts vigorous discussion. The existence of the official policy line of 'Take no Prisoners' was suggested as having been proved in 2002 by historian Nick Bleszynski, author of *Shoot Straight, You Bastards!*, who claimed that evidence for this can be found 'in the diary of Provost Marshal Poore, who admitted that the orders existed'.[5]

There are many incidents of revenge in accounts of World War I fighting. Corporal WHA Groom saw a British soldier shoot a German soldier who had his hands up, saying 'That's for my brother.'[6] In 1915 in the European theatre, A. Ashurt Moris took vengeance on a soldier trying to surrender:

At this point, I saw a Hun, fairly young, running down the trench, hands in air, looking terrified, yelling for mercy. I promptly shot him. It was a heavenly sight to see him fall forward. A Lincoln officer was furious with me, but the scores we owe wash out anything else.[7]

Royal Welch Fusilier, Private Frank Richards, saw a man in his regiment take six prisoners away and then return, having killed them with 'two bombs'. Richards noted that the soldier was very distressed over the loss of a comrade.[8] While such examples seem like fairly casual revenge, the more the enemy removes constraints, so too does the other side follow. The sailors of the British Q-ship *HMS Baralong* viewed the bodies of those recovered from the torpedoed civilian liner *Lusitania*, an experience which ' ... engendered in most of them a deep hatred and lust for the blood of U-boatmen'. This may well have been a contributing factor in the savage sinking of *U-27*, and shooting in the water of several of the crew, some time later, while others who had climbed aboard the *Baralong* were hunted down by Marines with cries of 'Lusitania!'[9] EJ Rule noted, of his infantry operations in World War I France, that when the Allies took the town of Bapaume, the retreating Germans had mined many buildings – the resultant explosions took several lives. The 'chiefs' became so incensed at this that an order was issued to put German prisoners into any sections that looked doubtful, so if the building suffered an explosion, the Germans would 'get a dose of their own medicine.'[10]

The thirst for revenge is a powerful motivator. The taking of the Alamo fort in the declared state of Texas in 1836 was coupled with the death of all inside at the hands of the victorious – and overwhelming – Mexican Army. Cries of 'Remember the Alamo!' were such a motivator for Sam Houston's vengeful army that when they brought General Santa Anna's force to a fight, they won the day in only 18 minutes!

The problem with revenge situations is that, central to the theme of this book, such incidents do occur and probably cannot be stopped. This is simply because the feelings of the people who carry out reprisal killings are easily understood by those nearby in the same combat unit – and they are the ones who would have to act as witnesses against them and, in most cases, even initiate the charges. As more comrades are killed, so the feelings of empathy heighten. World War I Infantry captain Robert Graves was discussing the subject with fellow front-line officers who had been picked to be instructors because of their lengthy combat experience. He noted that 'Nearly every instructor in the mess could quote specific instances of prisoners having been murdered on the way back. The commonest motives were, it seems, revenge for the death of friends and relatives … ' although there were also other reasons. The escort would usually report that the prisoner had been hit by a shell. Graves noted that they had every reason to believe the same happened on the other side.[11]

The closer a comrade was before death, the more inclined towards instant revenge are his friends. Richard Holmes cites the World War II case of an orderly who saw his beloved commander die after being shot in the spleen. He ' … snatched up a submachine-gun and unforgiveably massacred a line of unarmed Japanese soldiers who had just surrendered'.[12] Captured SS snipers were being escorted by some soldiers during fighting near Falaise in World War II. Another German stood up in ditch nearby and attacked with an automatic rifle, inflicting serious head injuries on one of the guards. The guard's companion 'went crazy with the bayonet among the prisoners'.[13] Fighting in northern France saw the usual pattern of advance, involving ' … snipers would pick off two, three or four men of an advancing platoon, then as they came to close quarters, stand up and surrender. The men whose friends had just been shot by him did not always feel inclined to let the killing stop at that point.'[14]

In New Guinea, Australian soldier VX66349 noted his distress when 'a patrol of ours found one of our mates, who had been missing. He'd been tied to a tree by the Japs, with a length of bamboo forced into his backside.' The soldier died a little while later, and VX66349 concluded: 'I went a little insane for a while, and when we'd cornered some Japs later on, the things we did to them now seem horrifying – but I guess that's war.'[15]

Intense fear, adrenaline and fury at being taken by surprise can mean lethal results for a surrendered soldier near anyone who has, seconds previously, stopped fighting. Wehrmacht soldier Guy Sajer was on the Russian Front when the German front line was penetrated at night by Russians, who knifed soldiers in their foxholes. Sajer saw one who was rescued just seconds from death by a group of German soldiers, who rushed up and struck down the Russian trying to knife him from behind, while his comrade was held at gunpoint with his hands up. The German sprang out of the hole in a fury, shouting, 'Where is he … where's the other one?', and 'In a few bounding steps he reached the two men and their prisoner. Before anyone could do anything, he had run his knife into the belly of the petrified Russian.'[16] These are the sort of accounts in which extremely difficult decisions must be taken by anyone nearby, whether superior in rank or not: should that soldier be reported, should he be arrested on the spot, or should his behaviour be ignored? Indeed, experienced soldiers know that it is not wise to interfere in such a situation, for a hot-blooded, vengeful soldier is quite likely to turn on anyone who stops him, regardless of who they are.[2]

Marine Officer Nicholas Warr had survived several days of extremely unpleasant fighting in Hue in 1968 when a Vietnamese soldier was captured by his platoon. Warr – who by now was so shattered that he refers to himself as 'the automaton' – gives us some insight into what happens sometimes when one has both a prisoner *and* a clear memory of what has been happening to you and your command:

> From the look on his face, this NVA soldier was apparently relieved to be out of the fighting … he had a big smile on his face. He was holding his hands up in the universal gesture of surrender and was babbling nonstop in Vietnamese …

---

2   Military historian Peter Williams noted this from one veteran, who said, 'Rank!! Ten times more important on the parade ground. The smart officer knows this!' As reported to the author, July 2005.

As Latimer continued his dialog and the NVA soldier continued his grinning babbling, time again warped inside my mind. The human being inside me was filled with the images of death and the shattered bodies of young Marines who had lost their lives … I couldn't balance those images with the image before me of this grinning NVA soldier. His entire body language made it clear that he had totally surrendered his fate into our hands. He was smiling up at me as though he was saying, 'It's all over for me now; I'm out of the war. The rules say that you have to take care of me now.' The automaton could not control an overwhelming rage created by the sight of this surrendering enemy, this piece of slime who had probably killed Estes or Morgan, or who had blown Sergeant Mullan's head off.[17]

Warr walked up to the prisoner, grabbed him around the neck, and began to throttle him. They ended up on the floor, and it took four Marines to drag Warr off him. Nothing further was said about the incident – and why would it, as everyone there probably understood. A prisoner who US Army combat adviser Martin Dockery was shepherding back for interrogation, was shot alongside him by an ARVN soldier who had crept up from behind with a pistol. The soldier was not overtly disciplined because his unit had taken losses.[18] During the Falklands battle for Goose Green, Sergeant John Meredith saw three of his comrades killed while they were trying to arrange a surrender. In the assault that followed, his thoughts were grim: 'The thing was to kill them as fast as we could. It was just whack, whack, and the more I knocked down the easier it became, the easier the feeling was. I was paying them back.'[19]

So we may well conclude, as a battle develops and becomes more lethal and more savage, that fewer prisoners are routinely taken than should be the case. Furthermore, the process whereby such actions – under most forces' Rules of Engagement – should be reported will increasingly be ignored, as the empathy of those in command for their soldiers grows in proportion to the latter's suffering. And as we have seen, revenge is the primary motivator for those involved in combat.

So, understandably, during the Battle for Hurtgen Forest, one company commander became enraged that his unit was constantly taking fire from nearby snipers that he ordered his men 'not to take any more prisoners'. Some were still taken, though 'perhaps not as many as before'.[20] Similar feelings of frustration, and the desire to get some measure of revenge on the overall situation, was perhaps on the minds of a German patrol which found two wounded British commandos in the aftermath of the St Nazaire raid. They shot the private, but took the accompanying officer prisoner after seeing his rank badges.[21] Australian infantryman Roland Griffiths-Marsh was given the task of escorting a downed Stuka pilot to a headquarters. When he got there, he was told by an officer to shoot him, because the HQ was moving and because the German was a 'murderer' – the Stukas had been attacking refugees. Griffiths-Marsh took him away, but released him.[22]

After Pearl Harbor, the desire for revenge would have been a powerful driver. A torpedoed Japanese destroyer photographed through the periscope of either USS Wahoo or USS Nautilus, June 1942. NNSP 80-G-418331

Feelings ran high in the botched Operation Market Garden in 1944, with desperate assaults on both sides to gain crucial ascendancy. In an attack across the Waal River, the Allied troops took heavy losses, and so any Germans who ' … belatedly sought to surrender were cut down ruthlessly by paratroopers enraged by their terrible losses.'[23] Indeed, the loss rate was over 50 per cent – unusually and terribly high. It is not surprising that soldiers take revenge in such circumstances.

Cold-blooded revenge killings are less understandable and excusable. Sepp Dietrich was once Hitler's driver and bodyguard. In World War II, he rose progressively through the ranks to command a regiment in 1940, then a brigade, and then a division. When in Russia, according to one American writer, he learned that six of his troopers had been murdered by the Russians, he ordered that all Russians captured over the next three days be shot. More than 4000 were so executed.[3] In May 1944, Hitler ordered captured airmen who had machine-gunned passenger trains or civilians or German planes which had made emergency landings to be shot without trial. And so in September of that year, 47 officers from American, British and Dutch air forces were murdered at Mauthausen concentration camp.

In the field, where adrenaline and emotions run high, to see one's friends die and then be expected to take surrender is difficult indeed. Commando Peter Young was leading a company in a raid against the Germans when they were subject to grenades thrown at close range by a sailor in a building. The explosions badly wounded the two orderlies of the commandoes' colonel, and immediately after this the German sailor came out with his hands up. Then, ' ... seeing the look in Mills's eyes, he had cried: "Nein, nein!" "Ja, ja," said Mills, and shot him. "Yeah, well, Mills, you shouldn't ha' done that," was all John said.'[24] A German sergeant who had charge of a group of more than 20 captured Americans detached eight of them to dig graves for three dead Germans, and then shot all eight, killing seven of them and wounding the eighth, who survived to denounce him.[25]

The Korean conflict saw vindictiveness embarked upon early by the Northern forces, and this was met with equal ferocity. David Hackworth dug up a buried Allied prisoner by mistake and found he had been executed: the soldier had been shot in the back of the head, and his hands were still tied with wire. Three more were discovered in the same area, and Hackworth noted that it did 'little for morale but a lot for fighting spirit'.[26] The Americans repaid the savage executions, the nature and evidence of which became more

---

3   MacDonald, Charles B. *A Time for Trumpets: The untold story of the Battle of the Bulge.* New York: Morrow, 1984. (160) Further details on this incident have not been researched; however, numerous references to Dietrich's career note that he was much criticised on the Russian Front for his troops' treatment of prisoners, although he was also noted for his concern for his own men. Dietrich was implicated in the Malmedy Massacre, and tried for it after the war, and although he was found to have complicity and sentenced to a jail term, many Allied soldiers came forward in his defence.

prevalent as the war went on. Hackworth, as a sergeant, came upon one of his privates eating some rations, with prisoners dead at his feet, 'each from a single bullet in the back of the head'.[27] Hackworth was angry, and asked why they'd been killed, receiving the answer that they had 'tried to escape'. The private's brother had been killed only a few days before.

The savagery of a bayonet death inflicted on one of their members

> ... pissed the Rangers off. It got to all of us. The word went out: no prisoners ... what followed that day, walking through the valley, was not a sweep but a bloodbath ... Many played possum, lying motionless on the ground, pretending they were dead; when this was discovered, every single 'corpse' got a slug in the head – if blood pumped out you knew you'd gotten a live one.[28]

PFC Floyd Akins's patrol found a Korean 'refugee' who was in a column holding a hand grenade. His sergeant told him to shoot the prisoner; Akins took him around a bend in the road, but found he could not do it, and released the man. Several days later, his squad found the bodies of 26 executed GIs, all bound with wire. He told an officer he was now ready to fight to the death against the enemy.[29] The rationale of the US Marines who executed an old man they had found carrying machine-gun ammunition belts under his clothes is more understandable in this light.[30]

The same feelings are evident in many Vietnam accounts. Some months after the death of one of their comrades in what they concluded was a command-detonated mine explosion (whereby a hidden wire leads to a concealed observer, who triggers the blast at the most opportune moment and then escapes), Marine Jeff Kelly and Forward Observer Lieutenant Dyer brooded over his death. What they wanted for it was 'payback'.[31] Second Lieutenant Phil Caputo, in his first major combat, heard that a Marine in his unit shot a wounded prisoner in the head, after the 'mood of the company turned savage' due to the mud, heat, leeches, thorns and overall danger. Caputo thought at the time that it was 'a perfectly natural thing to do'.[32] Several months later, after a long period of frustrated piecemeal combat, with the unit taking persistent losses, restraint had weakened. Five Marines were discovered, their hands still tied, having been shot in the back of the head. One of the US 28-man patrols was ambushed and took heavy casualties, with the Vietcong dispatching all wounded – two survived after burrowing under their comrades' bodies. And so Caputo noted: 'We paid the enemy back, sometimes with interest.' The number of captured VC who survived dropped markedly.[33]

Quynh Dao, a member of the Australia–Vietnam Human Rights Committee and a former refugee, gives an interesting example of how the media can turn a case of what seems like casual revenge killing into a political controversy. He notes:

> The Western media turned what was a military success on the part of the non-communist forces in the south to a political victory for the communists. The Tet Offensive of 1968 was an unmitigated disaster for Hanoi. Yet it was pictures of US carnage that were publicised to a war-weary audience.
>
> The media also relayed ad nauseam the picture of a South Vietnamese soldier shooting a Vietcong, in civilian clothing. The message was loud and clear – this is the kind of atrocity that the South Vietnamese army did to their own people, with the backing of the US. The Western media did not report the massacre of 4000 unarmed civil servants and civilians in the city of Hue, committed by the communists.
>
> Nguyen Ngoc Loan, the South Vietnamese officer in the picture, passed away in 1998. Neil Davis, the Australian war correspondent killed on assignment in Thailand, set out the background to the killing when interviewed for David Bradbury's 1980 documentary *Frontline*. The Vietcong shot by Loan had, not long before this picture was taken, led a team of communist terrorists who killed the family of a South Vietnamese officer, including his 80-year-old mother, his wife and his children. How often is his background explained?[34]

This is an interesting example of the revenge equation's capacity to be interpreted in a dichotomous way. If one saw that incident, as most did, as a soldier executing what looks to be a non-combatant, then one condemns the soldier. But with the context explained, the average viewer may well not condemn – and may even feel sympathy for, or perhaps empathy with – the soldier.

How far and for how long such behaviour is tolerated is of course most difficult to debate. If the incident for which revenge is taken happened 10 minutes ago, is the soldier excused? If it happened years before, is a detachment of soldiers excused for their actions? This is a significant point: actions in the Kosovo war were purportedly taken in revenge for military campaigns carried out 800 years previously. The thoughts of Wehrmacht infantryman Guy Sajer are, once again, worth pondering: 'War always reaches the depths of horror because of idiots who perpetuate terror from generation to generation under the pretext of vengeance'.[35] Quite so. But what would anyone do in the situation well portrayed some 20 minutes into *Saving Private Ryan*? The Americans, storming with difficulty and suffering many casualties, finally take the pillboxes which have been raining death and destruction, by machine-gun fire, upon so many of the Americans' fellow soldiers. Two Germans emerge, hands held high – and are instantly shot. Almost anyone in that situation would normally, naturally, and understandably take that course of action. If that is the case, how have these soldiers done wrong?

Such an understanding is of paramount importance in this study. Once again, it is shown that the actions taken in revenge are the stuff of Everyman: how many people, placed in that situation, could honestly say they would not do the same. And so once again, we are faced with a dilemma.

Do we condemn troops for doing what anyone would have done? If we do, we are hypocritical.

Do we say that such behaviour is allowable? If we do, where do we stop? What are the 'right set' of qualifications for taking understandable revenge? Is it acceptable for a brother, but not for a cousin? Is it acceptable for the death of six comrades, but not for five?

Perhaps the answer, as with most dilemmas, lies somewhere in the middle, with the art of compromise. If brought to court, mitigating circumstances should be taken into account. But of course, underlying all of this is the uneasy realisation for any reader that, as discussed in previous chapters, such combat behaviour is probably not going to be publicised. Is this once again the true face of battle?

'12
Killing in cold blood for military necessity

… if they're going to slow you down, kill them.

US Army Colonel Rogers to his men before a patrol in Vietnam.

There are plenty of examples to support the proposal that, routinely in battle, possible prisoners are instead dispatched. In many cases, although the heat of battle has died down, and there are no particularly aggressive feelings on either side, to hold prisoners or to split one's force escorting them to the rear of one's lines would dangerously weaken your own side.

When the enemy refuses to surrender

Sometimes refusal to surrender is, of course, sheer pride in one's own unit – an acknowledgment that you and those around you would rather die than surrender. The Old Guard at Waterloo, despite tremendous losses, refused to give in – their General Cambronne proclaimed, 'The Guard dies but never surrenders.'[1] Instances from the wars under study here can also be found. A Canadian cavalry brigade destroyed a Bavarian force in 1918 near Moreuil – 'Not one single man surrendered', and one, bayoneted in the throat, refused a command to lie still for a stretcher-bearer. He seized a rifle, proclaiming, 'No, no. I will not die a prisoner', before collapsing.[2] Peter Young's British Commando unit came across a German Artillery Observer who refused to surrender: the account ends in four ominous dots …[3] In the case of the famous 1942 raid on St Nazaire, in which the explosive-laden destroyer *HMS Campbeltown* was used to blow up the German-held dry dock, several caches of explosives were timed to go off after the initial assault. Interrogated on the deck of the wrecked ship, two Commando officers kept silent about the deadly cargo below them – and were killed when the ship exploded.[4]

We have already seen what the situation was with the Japanese: surrender was so rare as to be unusual. EB Sledge tells of an occasion when an officer and an NCO gave themselves up on Okinawa – the officer spoke perfect English, and had been educated in the USA, which may have been one of the reasons for surrender, in that he understood the Americans. But in all of Sledge's honest account of several battles in the Pacific, that is the only case of submission he cites.[5] Marine Henry Lopez noted that, in training, 'We had been told that the Japs would not surrender, which very few did, and to kill them before they killed you, that they would die rather than surrender, so long as they could take you along with them.'[6] It is also well known that the Japanese in World War II formed special squads of pilots who deliberately committed suicide with the *kamikaze* aircraft, and of lesser-known *kaitens*, or suicide submarines.[1]

In fact, the very concept of never surrendering was official policy. The Japanese Army's Field Service Code, or *Senjinkun*, was released with an Imperial sanction on 7 January 1941. This decreed that it was impermissible for Japanese soldiers to become prisoners of war. The *Senjinkun* was widely publicised, and confirmed an attitude that indeed was already understood and followed.[7]

What was known as the 'Japanese Spirit' was indoctrinated in Japan and universally followed. One prisoner of war summed it up as ' … the strength of mind to carry on with added determination when difficulties arise.' He commented further that 'to give in when beaten is the spirit of the Americans and British, and not that of Japanese, who will fight all the harder when defeat stares them in the face.'[8] General Slim noted: 'If five hundred Japanese were ordered to hold a position, we had to kill four hundred and ninety-five before it was ours – and then the last five killed themselves.'[9]

Russian refusal to surrender in World War II is also well known, although often this was driven by political commissars or the orders of cold-blooded generals, like Zhukov. But in addition, the Russians were tough soldiers and often simply refused to surrender. Henry Metelmann's unit called on two left in a position to give up, but ' … they refused and kept shooting. So in the end one of the Panzers had to get right into their foxhole …'[10] Guy Sajer's unit cornered some Russians partisans in a factory and gave them the option: 'Surrender,

---

1   See pp. 102-113 of Paul Kemp's *Underwater Warriors* for a description. In fact, the *kaitens* were designed around the idea that the operator would escape in the last few seconds before these manned torpedoes hit their target; but as Kemp says, no-one took this seriously – the operator stayed until the end.

or we'll shoot you down like rats.' There was no answer.' The Germans began firing up into the rafters and through the complex, and killed them all.[11] Later, Sajer's detachment was in such a precarious situation that, as the Russian tanks advanced, he implored a comrade to shoot him; the friend asked the same from him. Then the tanks appeared, and Sajer, at least, survived.[12]

Many German soldiers were similarly fanatical about fighting to the end. Sergeant Gariepy of the Canadian Army mused on the lack of surrender from the elements of the Wehrmacht in front of the advance after D-Day. 'Why would a man run back, instead of coming forward to give himself up? Discipline in the German Army must be formidable.'[13] One American medic, advancing with infantry in the last days of the war, tried to approach a wounded paratrooper, who immediately picked up a hand grenade. The medic, expecting to be assaulted, threw himself down, but the German simply detonated the grenade under his own chin.[14] Some of this was doubtless fanatical loyalty: the SS motto of (roughly) 'My Honour is my Loyalty' was taken extremely seriously by that section of the German Army, and all German soldiers had sworn a personal oath of loyalty to the Fuehrer, which included the line 'I will render unconditional obedience to Adolf Hitler ...'[15] In January 1945, six captured Germans gave two men of Easy Company of the 101st Airborne a lesson in that obedience. Six SS officers were captured by surprise in an assault on the village of Rachamps. Second later, when a shell exploded nearby, one of the Germans pulled a knife from his boot and slashed it across an American's throat; the other US soldier machinegunned all six.[16] Therefore, when Field Marshall Model proclaimed that 'None of us gives up a square foot of Germans soil while still alive', such edicts were taken most seriously and amplified further down the line. Himmler too proclaimed: 'Certain unreliable elements seem to believe that the war will be over for them as soon as they surrender to the enemy. ... Every deserter ... will find his just punishment. Furthermore, his ignominious behaviour will entail the most severe consequences for his family ... They will be summarily shot.'[17] This was indeed so: Henry Metelmann, retreating in his Panzer from Russia, had some of his mates tell him they had seen a German colonel hanging from a beam in a nearby village. He had been adorned with a sign bearing the words *Ein Feigling vor dem Feind*: 'A coward in the face of the enemy'.[18] With such 'encouragement', it is not hard to see why the German armies fought hard in retreat.

Defeatism was always treated severely. In 1938 it had been put down most strongly by Field Marshal Keitel, who declared that he 'will not tolerate any officer in OKW indulging in criticism, unsteady thoughts and defeatism.'[2] Three General Staff officers were shot near the end of the war for such talk, and as HR Trevor-Roper puts it, even with doom closing in from three directions, 'With slogans of victory on their lips, everyone was preparing for defeat'.[19] Infantryman Daniel Webster was sanguine about it: fighting his way across Europe, he observed of the last stands, 'how seldom they were executed'.[20] And Hitler was cold-blooded about expecting the armed forces to fight to the end. For example, when one army was cut off in January 1945 by the advancing Russians, the German leader refused, in a heated argument with General Guderian, to withdraw them:

> 'It's simply our duty to save these people, and we still have time to remove them!' Guderian cried out in a challenging voice.

> Infuriated, Hitler retorted: 'You are going to fight out there. We cannot give up these areas!'

> Guderian held firm: 'But it's useless to sacrifice men in this senseless way,' he shouted. 'It's high time! We must evacuate these soldiers at once!'[21]

But Hitler would not withdraw. His attitude and philosophy was 'Victory or Death', a strategic Pyrrhic foolishness that would see the decimation of thousands, if not millions, of his own troops.[3] It was not only seasoned troops who were expected to go down fighting with no surrender. One local *gauleiter* (a regional head of the Nazi Party) issued a proclamation for the enemy to be met ' ... with our fanatical resistance ... the voices of hundreds of thousands who have died on the battlefield for the honour and freedom of the Fatherland ... cry out to us'.[22] By the time Germany reached its end, its older men had been called up: civilians of up to 60 were digging defences, and the youth was caught up in the Hitler Youth movement, training in basic infantry tactics in order to be part of the defence. Then again, not all Germans were foolish enough not to see the writing on the wall – or hear the thunder of artillery in the distance, to be more precise – and although they mouthed the words, their hearts were

---

2   Shirer, William L. *The Rise and Fall of the Third Reich: A history of Nazi Germany*. London: Secker & Warburg, 1960. (379) OKW was the High Command of the German armed forces, and Keitel its chief.

3   For a psychological examination of Hitler's compulsion towards dichotomous strategic planning, see Norman Dixon's *On the Psychology of Military Incompetence*, pp. 318-323.

not in the struggle. Henry Metelmann, recovering from a wound, was placed in the defence of Berlin against Patton's army in the final days of the war. His equipment was a 1917 rifle with a broken sight, and he was part of a motley collection of soldiers who were marched to the front, with a constant eye out for marauding Allied aircraft, for by now the Luftwaffe had all but been banished from the skies. An experienced soldier of the Eastern Front could see quite well what was going to happen to such forces, without armour and artillery and aircraft. His officer proclaimed ' ... with a serious face, "There will be no retreat to Speyer!" "Jawohl, Herr Hauptmann, no retreat to Speyer!" We looked at each other and I think we both "understood".'23

We must ask ourselves if the actions taken to wipe out such fighters, who refuse to surrender, is unreasonable, for it is a recurring feature of combat across many wars. In 1966, a Vietcong unit, besieged in bunkers along a river, would not fight and would not surrender – they were dispatched with grenades.24 Infantryman Charles Gadd's unit surprised many North Vietnamese soldiers swimming a river one night, and the enemy would not surrender, but retreated into the river again, and began to swim back to the other side, taking deep breaths to maximise their time underwater. The Americans called 'Come here!' in Vietnamese and fired warning shots, but the soldiers would not return. When the US forces realised they were going to get away, they opened fire. Gadd mused afterwards that, 'I tried to convince myself that we had done the right thing, but the thought of killing those helpless soldiers would haunt me for years to come.'25

In many situations where one's own force could be imperilled by the still-dangerous mob of prisoners just taken, they were indeed regarded as dangerous, a factor which probably hastened much 'continuation of the combat'. The Australian soldier Albert Jacka was part of a small force in an overrun trench in the European theatre in World War I; they emerged from their position and took on any necessary Germans nearby as they sought safer positions. Some of their own side, taken prisoner, saw them in the distance and, realising hope was not far away, 'grabbed the rifles from their captors and turned the tables on them'.26 In a short engagement afterwards, Jacka stormed a trench with four Germans in it who were firing at him, inflicting several wounds. He kept going, however, and eventually the Germans ' ... flung down their rifles and put up their hands.' However, he shot three and bayoneted the fourth, explaining: 'I had to do it – they would have killed me the moment I turned my back.'27 In a different theatre but in the same war, in February

1916, the captain of the fishing boat *King Stephen* refused to take on board the survivors of a crashed Zeppelin in the North Sea. Fearing his men would be overpowered, he left the 22 Germans to die, an action for which the Bishop of London publicly applauded him.[28] But it is also a question of degree – what is a reasonable expectation of being overwhelmed? An Australian soldier, fighting in World War II at the Battle of El Alamein, saw a group of around six Germans surrender at the end of the battle, but a Bren gunner didn't trust them 'not to play tricks like throwing grenades, so he mowed them down to be on the safe side'.[29]

Loyalty can mean no surrender, and therefore a more intense level of fighting from both sides. With a torn picture of his fuehrer Adolph Hitler beside his clenched fist, a dead general of the Volkssturm – the people's army – lies on the floor of city hall, Leipzig, Germany. He committed suicide rather than face US Army troops who captured the city in April 1945. NNSP 208-YE-148

This is one facet of the argument; another relates to resources at hand at the time. In this case, the processing of prisoners is simply impossible. In April 1917, Gordon Highlander John Eugene Crombie was ordered to bayonet surrendering Germans in a captured trench because it was 'expedient from a military point of view in that the officers of the assault refused to spare soldiers to escort those captured'.[30] World War I infantryman Thomas Marks took part in an attack where the word was passed to the units involved that prisoners were not to be taken, due to the heavy losses his division had taken and there not being enough personnel to escort any captives to the rear. Marks was then involved in an attack on two machine-guns in which his section took the German position, with the eight Germans there surrendering to the five British. Despite their protestations of 'Kamerad', the defeated soldiers were shot at close range by rifle fire. The section then took a deep dugout where Germans took refuge; they were at first subdued with a grenade, and the survivors exhorted to come out. When they did, one by one, they were shot, and eventually, hearing the shots, the remaining Germans refused to emerge, and were finished off with more grenades.[31]

Wehrmacht infantryman Guy Sajer's unit was joined by detachments of *Hitlerjugend* (Hitler Youth) just before an assault on a Russian position. There was discussion as to the tactical nature of the attack, with the inexperienced new troops seeking information about how the Soviet soldiers fought. 'Fire on anything Russian without the least hesitation' was one succinct piece of advice. The Germans were going to try for surprise, so that meant no firing, and all enemy would be dispatched by other means for as long as possible. One of the *Hitlerjugend* soldiers asked about prisoners, and was told they would not be able to handle prisoners in such a situation.[32]

In a similar circumstance during the Falklands War, Lieutenant Mark Cox was leading a small platoon of men forward against the Argentines and took fire from them, sustaining several dead and wounded. The British threw grenades into the rocks where the Argentines were in position, and then charged in to find three wounded enemy. Private Kevin Connery took the initiative and shouted, 'We can't leave live enemy in front of us', and then dispatched all three with a burst of automatic fire.[33] A similar incident saw four Argentines surprised by a pair of British soldiers, who shot one; the other three immediately surrendered. One of the Argentines then produced a US passport from his pocket, but after some debate amongst the British, including with some nearby soldiers, all three prisoners were shot. This incident made the press, and there was rather more vigorous discussion as to whether this meant mercenaries were present than whether the enemy soldiers should have been killed.[34] But the two incidents are largely an illustration of the same reality of forward combat: to weaken your own force by taking prisoners to the rear may well be dangerous. To send them unescorted to the rear is also asking for trouble: who wants disgruntled enemy behind one's position …

Germans soldiers assaulting a Russian town in World War II were 'so exhausted we only stood up when our fire had subdued the isolated and hopeless resistance from some entrenched hole'.[35] Even though Russians surrendered, the Germans shot them down, and in the surrounding context Sajer paints, one can see why:

> We were mad with harassment and exhaustion, running on our nerves, which were stretched to the utmost, and which alone made it possible to respond to the endless succession of crises and alerts. We were forbidden to take prisoners until our return trip. We knew the Russians didn't take any, and although we longed for sleep we knew that we had to stay awake as long as there were any Bolsheviks in our sector. It was either them or us – which is why my friend Hans and I threw grenades into the bread house, at some Russians who were trying to wave a white flag.

Prisoners are hard work: the World War II philosopher/soldier Glenn Gray was present on an occasion when one soldier complained about the work prisoners were causing the unit. Another soldier said, 'I am doing my best, sir, I started with six!', and got laughter as a response – presumably he had dispatched any troublesome ones already.[36] Captain Henley, fighting in the Battle of Hurtgen Forest, noted 'six less to feed' when a German artillery round killed six prisoners who were being taken to the rear for interrogation.[37]

The same battle saw another soldier comment:

> Sometimes you take five or six prisoners and there is what they call a ring of steel behind you with artillery firing in behind you and the Germans were just there to keep you from getting reinforcements or ammunition … What are you going to do with prisoners? If you try to take them back you're taking your life in hand twice. Once going through the terrain to get them back. If you get through it safely that time and don't get killed then you still have to go back up front after you get rid of them. So a lot of them never reached the rear that way.[38]

Daniel Webster, fighting with the 101st Airborne, was part of a force that held several streets of a town, with Germans in front of them across a small river.

Eventually the Americans tried an assault across the river. A wounded prisoner was taken, and then the assault went wrong, and the prisoner was abandoned – to die, it was thought. However, some hours later, his cries could be heard, and it was feared he would be taken back by the Germans and reveal the American positions and strength. Several attempts were made in the night to reach him and dispatch him, and he even survived several thrown grenades before one finished him. A savage example of the reality of the tactical situation, but what else was to be done?[39] Major FP Crozier and his orderly were on an investigative patrol in No Man's Land in World War I when they were surprised by a German sentry and realised they had gone too far. Crozier fired at the man with his revolver and missed, but his orderly didn't. Another German behind the sentry tried to surrender but, realising the 'hornets' nest' behind him, Crozier shot him and the two hurried off.[40] It is difficult to see an alternative, but have they committed a crime?

Parachutist David Webster's unit participated in a surprise night assault a few days after their D-Day landing. They were exhorted to use their knifes and bayonets, then grenades where necessary, but not to take prisoners because ' … we can't be dragging a lot of prisoners around with us at night'.[41] US Army General Maxwell Taylor apparently told US paratroopers before their jump on D-Day not to take prisoners, a command passed down by his officers, who told their men, upon getting into their aircraft: 'No prisoners. We are not taking any prisoners.'[42] This may well have been due to the nature of this attack: it depended on speed and surprise, and it was essential to get enough men ashore fast and to push the Germans back far enough to allow a beach-head, otherwise the precarious foothold in Europe may well have been lost.

Dispatching aviators for military necessity

In aerial combat, persons who might well have become prisoners are often dispatched for military necessity.

Derek Robinson presents a compelling case for killing unarmed observers in his (fictional but well researched) account of World War I aviation combat, *Goshawk Squadron*. The balloon observers were used to spot the fall of artillery shot so as to make it more accurate. With their balloon tethered over their own side of the Lines, they ascended until a good view could be had of the opposing enemy entrenchments, and then proceeded to call the fall of shot down a telephone line to the ground positions. The accuracy of the enemy's direct artillery fire was enhanced to a remarkable degree. Consequently, the balloons were often attacked by enemy aviation, and therefore heavily defended by anti-aircraft fire.

The Germans also had a trick of loading some with explosives, to remotely kill any marauding pilot.[43] In this account, some relatively new pilots have been sent balloon-busting by their squadron commander:

'You did a piss-poor job on those balloons,' Woolley told him. 'I came over there fifteen minutes ago and they had two of the buggers up again, and the Boche artillery was pounding shit out of our lines.'

… 'I did get one,' Lambert protested miserably. 'They moved their rotten sausages during the night, they saw us coming, they pulled them down. You couldn't …' Woodruffe struck a light, but Lambert's eyes didn't see it, and the flame burned itself out. 'We lost old Kimberley, as it was,' he said.

'What did they lose?'

'I got one—'

'Did you get the observers?'

Lambert took in a long shuddering breath. 'They damn near went up with the balloon,' he said. 'They jumped, and I thought their parachutes were going to catch fire.' He discovered the cigarette in his hand and examined it as if it were a mistake.

'You didn't kill them?' Woolley stared bleakly, like a butcher with an incompetent errand-boy.

'No, I got the balloons, I didn't …' Lambert shrugged. 'I didn't … I got the balloon, that was … I got the goddam balloon, didn't I?' he demanded angrily.

'*I got the goddam balloon!*' Woolley parodied in a shrill voice. 'Go back and get the goddam observers. You shoot down the gas bag, dummy, to make them jump so you can machine-gun them while they go down! By Christ! You think you pop balloons for sport?'

'You should have told me,' Lambert muttered.

'Told you? Should have told you we go up to kill men and not pop balloons? I should have told you the Huns have balloons the way you have the runs, but they are short of skilled observers?'[44]

But was such behaviour the norm? RJ Brownell, writing about his own flying experiences in World War I, said that it was 'not done' to fire at observers who had parachuted from balloons: 'I also had a go at a balloon and frightened the chap who hopped out in his parachute. Undoubtedly he thought I was going to shoot him (Not done of course!). I fired all my ammunition into the balloon …' [45] However, we might reflect on this a little: the parachuting observer was a small, hard-to-hit target, and once the enemy aircraft was spotted, it was given a ferocious welcome. It would be highly dangerous to come around again to shoot the observer without what little benefit of surprise the attacker had. Although the observer might have been a useful target, he was more one of luck than opportunity. The fact remains that they were a valuable asset doing a job which, when done properly, resulted in the deaths of many in the trenches to artillery fire: the cause of the majority of deaths in World War I. Brownell was an exception, however – the observer was indeed usually a primary target. Sgt. Edwin Gerth, of the 51st Artillery, noted in his diary:

> Saw a German plane come right over our heads and go thru a machine-gun barrage and shoot down an observation balloon nearby. When the balloon was in flames, he circled around and emptied his machine-gun into the parachute which was drifting slowly to the ground with the observer. Don't know if observer was killed or not. Boche plane got away. [46]

EJ Rule, an Australian infantry officer, observed a German aircraft attack an Allied balloon, which was hit, and the pilot then came back to attack the observers. He hit one: 'we could plainly see the tracer bullets hitting one of the men'. [47] Thomas Penrose Marks, fighting in the infantry lines and overlooked by German artillery observation, said: 'How we wish that our airmen would attack those balloons and send them down in flames! If they did so it would save many lives.' [48] One historian, compiling a history of the balloon at war, notes that observers under parachutes were considered a legitimate target, 'certainly by the latter half of the war'. He cites the case of a British Sopwith Camel, piloted by a Lieutenant Goode on the Italian Front, firing two bursts into an observer under a parachute; he also says there is 'irrefutable evidence that both French and British army commanders gave orders to shoot at balloon observers'. [49]

By his own account, Billy Bishop shot at the observers: 'I had seen no one leap from the observer's basket hanging underneath, so I fired a short burst into it just to liven up anybody who happened to be sitting there.' [50] AH Cobby, by comparison, noted on one occasion that one of his partners 'must have shot one of the observers when he was going down in his parachute, and severed the cord in some way or another as he parted company with his "chute".' [51] Spotting for the artillery was also carried out by two-seater aircraft equipped with radios and cameras: photography was an emerging useful indicator of enemy presence and damage. A fictional account written by a World War I pilot featured a chapter entitled 'The Little Butcher', in which a pilot goes up and kills an aircraft's observer-gunner and then shoots down the two-seater, which can't fight back. Two visitors to the aerodrome are shocked at his matter-of-fact attitude:

> ' … hold on a minute,' said the C.O. 'Have you any idea on why he is so keen on killing Huns?'
>
> 'Lord knows', said one, and 'Pure bloodthirstiness,' the other.
>
> 'I'll tell you,' said the C.O. 'It is because he was once in the infantry, as I was; and because he knows, as I do, what it means to the line to have an artillery observing machine over directing shells … every Hun crashed means so many more lives saved on the ground, every Hun that gets away alive will be the death of some of you …'[52]

Even in Napoleon's time, artillery was becoming the pre-eminent weapon of war. 'Only with cannon can one wage war', he said, and 'Great battles are won with artillery.'[53] There are a number of different sources available which discuss the statistical cause of fatalities in war. The artillery used at the battle of Crecy in 1346 caused no casualties at all, although its psychological impact may be worth considering as a force multiplier. But the art of using the great guns steadily improved, until in the Napoleonic Wars ' … properly handled and massed artillery could ruin good infantry in a relatively short space of time'.[54] The science of it gradually improved in the age of the Industrial Revolution, until – like the devilish work of the Engineers – the Artillery corps of various armies became a fearsome weapon inflicting most of the casualties experienced on the battlefield.

John Terraine's excellent book, *The Smoke and the Fire*, discusses many of the myths of World War I, including the suggestion that the greatest weapon available was the machine-gun, or that the tank was not used properly. He refers to the war as 'the first of the two great artillery wars' and suggests a figure of 58.51 per cent of deaths as being caused by 'shells and bombs'.[55] James Dunnigan's *How to Make War* ominously refers to artillery as 'The Killer': he makes the point that it is very difficult to combat, and suggests that in World War II it accounted for 58 per cent of deaths, with 75 per cent of those occuring in open plains and deserts.[56] So, killing observers spotting for the artillery in warfare is militarily very useful.

The killing of unarmed observers was also practised in the Falklands War in 1982:

> The Argentine Air Force initiated the pre-conflict air action with C-130 reconnaissance flights over the islands in March 1982. Later the Argentines used not only C-130's but B-707's, Lear Jets, Fokker F-27's and P-2 Neptunes all in a reconnaissance role unsuitable to the design of the aircraft. They also had S-2 aircraft, more combatable [sic] with this mission, but they were not used extensively because of unreliable radar. 'Reconnaissance aircraft' were assigned to Air Exploration and Reconnaissance Group-1, significant because it was formed in April, after the British Task Force was already enroute to the South Atlantic. The work of the group continued throughout the war both in reconnaissance and pathfinding roles. One C-130 and one Lear Jet were lost to Sea Harrier fire while attempting to survey the British fleet. Several B-707's used in a deep reconnaissance role were also intercepted but not fired upon by Sea Harriers as the British ships transited the Atlantic.[57]

The British force also targeted an unarmed Hercules transport aircraft bringing in supplies at night, attacking it with a missile and cannon fire. The missile hit one wing between the engines and, knowing of the fire-suppression system on board, the British pilot, Lieutenant Commander 'Sharkey' Ward, closed and attacked the aircraft further with his guns. The aircraft crashed into the sea and there were no survivors.[58]

Shortcomings of the 'Rules of War'

If the concept in war is to kill the enemy, how far does one go to carry this out? This area is, of course, covered by the so-called 'Rules of War' –first formalised in 1864 and revised many times since in the form of the Geneva Conventions, and so on.[59] We might observe in passing, however, that although such concepts are often invoked, they are, as Shakespeare put it, more honoured in the breach than the observance. For example, the 1949 Geneva Conventions specifies[60] that prisoners of war should be paid a daily allowance.

The regulations respecting the laws and customs of war on land, laid down in the Hague on 18 October 1907, specified that it is forbidden 'To kill or wound an enemy who, having laid down his arms, or having no longer means of defence, has surrendered at discretion.'[61] We might consider that a flier who, having run out of ammunition, no longer has a means of defence. However, has he surrendered? And even if he has, what if the opponent has no means of accepting that surrender – being, for example, over hostile territory, where the surrendering flier has no means of landing and giving himself and his aircraft up for capture?

The attacking of aviators under parachutes was first proposed as being forbidden by a committee of jurists in 1923 at The Hague, but the deliberations were not adopted. (The proposal was: 'When an aircraft has been disabled, the occupants when endeavoring to escape by means of a parachute must not be attacked in the course of their descent.'[62])

Are such attacks forbidden today? The wording of the relevant part of the Geneva Conventions does seem to proscribe them, with Article 42 stating, 'Occupants of aircraft. No person parachuting from an aircraft in distress shall be made the object of attack during his descent.'[63]

Enthusiasm for combat often marks out the successful warrior – a difficult concept for those who have not experienced war, and an attitude often guarded once home. German troops in Russia, 1941. NNSP 242-GAP-286B-4

There are possibilities here for ethical consideration. We might fall back on the argument that if a flier did indeed surrender – perhaps by gestures in World War I – and the opponent nevertheless ignored this and killed him anyway, would that constitute an unethical act? One aspect of Ethical Theory suggests we examine what the 'reasonable man' says. In British legal and ethical debates of the 19th century, the legendary 'man on the Clapham omnibus' was the epitome of such debate. He was not to be confused with the rational man. He was not expected to use too much reason and indeed his judgement may be based on feeling. But if 12 men or women were gathered at random from the street and given the above scenarios, would they all still think prisoners should always be regarded as sacrosanct?[64]

However, that is a rather relative argument: what 12 reasonable people might say about a military action would probably differ markedly at the beginning of a war, in times of combat, and at its conclusion. For example, many people may well have said before World War II commenced that it was wrong to assassinate Adolf Hitler. In 1943 they probably would have said it was right. By late 1944 they would have said it was definitely right and, three years after hostilities ceased in 1945, these same people may well be pondering the morality of the whole concept again. As JL Mackie points out: 'There are no objective values.'[65] Morals are largely a product of discrete cultures, so what is right for the Chinese may very well be wrong for the French. If we argue that morals are actually objective, we are saying that there are actions which are wrong for *all* societies at *all* times, and we will have a long argument to establish what they are.

So it is instructive to look at the paragraph from the Biggles book quoted earlier. The practice of shooting down a disarmed and helpless flier might not have sat too well with the prevailing British ethics at the time of publication – in the early 1930s. Yet killing fliers in such situations was – we have proved – certainly done in World War I. This shows not only that ethics are subjective, but also that they differ between sub-groups within society. What Johns and his friends did in their squadrons might well have been challenged in fashionable drawing rooms.

In general, the ethical considerations behind the taking of life fall into a utilitarian[4] area. As Richard Norman puts it: 'In most cases the killing of a person will mean the loss of happiness which that person could have experienced, and

---

4   The ethical arguments generally centre around the works of John Stuart Mill, who claims that the 'right' action to take is that which brings the greatest happiness to the greatest number of people. Utilitarianism can be attacked, however, in some circumstances: in deciding who, of the 10 survivors of an air crash, should be put into the five-person life-raft, we might well see a graduate teacher take precedence over a 10-year-old girl, for example.

will mean terrible suffering for others, and this will outweigh any benefits which someone else might think to derive from the killing.'[66] However, war presents different concerns – for the taking of life which normally would be condemned can be shown to have different considerations in war. In these circumstances, the survival of a pilot under a parachute might well be acted against: that pilot, if he survives, could bring more death and suffering to our side. However, if our side is not acting in a 'just war'[5], then the concerns are different. Given these scenarios, we might well says that the killing of an Allied pilot in World War II by an Axis aviator is unethical, while the killing of an Axis member by an Allied aviator is not – for, as the famous historian AJP Taylor puts it:

> The Second World War was fought to liberate peoples from Nazi, and to a lesser extent Japanese, tyranny. In this it succeeded, at however high a price. No one can contemplate the present state of things, without acknowledging that people everywhere are happier, freer and more prosperous than they would have been if Germany and Japan had won … It was a war justified in its aims and successful in accomplishing them. Despite all the killing and destruction that accompanied it, the Second World War was a good war.[67]

In summary, attacking enemy aviators is a fact of war. Whether they are armed or not is not a legal consideration; nor, for most people, is it an ethical dilemma. Romantic notions of 'knights of the skies' are foolish and ill-considered, although it might be admitted they were useful propaganda. Killing the enemy is unpleasant, psychologically damaging and stressful, but it is what warfare revolves around.

Many examples given here have centred around aviators, but the same arguments are relevant to all in tactical combat. The reality of the necessities of battle must not be confused with the niceties of human endeavour in other activities. Battle is unique, and has its own dynamics and requirements. German paratroopers in the Battle of the Bulge were aware that speed was of great necessity in the Reich's attempt to halt the Allied invasion and attack its supply ports. Did this mean that prisoners should not be taken? A German sergeant

---

5   Following arguments generally attributed to St Augustine and other early Christian thinkers: the war must be fought for a just cause; made with the right intention; made by a legitimate authority; with a formal declaration; with a reasonable hope of success; as a last resort; and be conducted with proportionality. For a fuller explanation, see Richard Norman's *Ethics, Killing and War*, p. 118.

whose squad had captured a detachment of Americans was 'adamant that the prisoners should be shot', according to an American officer who understood German, but then a captain arrived and prevented it.[68]

The Americans were more savage than normal: one armoured infantry lieutenant pointed out to the somewhat-shocked Sergeant Forrest Pogue that, being tankers, they couldn't handle prisoners. Pogue also heard of prisoners being shot on the point of surrendering so there would be no need to shoot them later.[69] Similarly, Vietnam veteran Ed Treratola (not his real name) told Terry Lane that the assumption that 'Marines don't take prisoners' was routinely understood in his time in Vietnam: 'Every time before we went out on a patrol, Colonel Rogers used to … shake our hands and they'd tell us, if they wanted a prisoner, you know, bring one or two, but if they're going to slow you down, kill them.'[70]

Taking no chances

If a prisoner acts as if he is still a combatant, can he justifiably be shot? US soldier EB Sledge's unit took a Japanese prisoner on Okinawa towards the end of that campaign. Their prize was wearing nothing but a G-string, and weighed about 90 pounds. He was docile, and the unit was sitting around on their helmets, having called their corpsman over to check out the prisoner. Suddenly, out of his G-string, the prisoner produced a grenade, and pulled the pin, but not quickly enough to prevent one of the Americans shooting him with his pistol.[71] Another US soldier in the same campaign, Dick Thom, an operations officer for the 96th Infantry Division, said: 'My regiment took only one prisoner. We never turned any others in. We had another exit for them, particularly since quite a few of them held their hands up to surrender while carrying a grenade.'[72]

In guerilla warfare, matters can descend to the level where it is so difficult to tell who combatants actually are that prisoners are routinely not taken – because all who look suspicious are identified as enemy. In Vietnam, Marine Kenneth Campbell noted that his battalion had been given an order which related to how they should tell if surrendering personnel were genuine or not. They were told

> … not to take POWs if they came up to us and their hands, it looked like their fingers were curled, we were supposed to shoot them on sight. If their fingers were extended, their hands open, we were supposed to take them, and the rationale for this was given that they might have a grenade in their hands, so don't take chances. A lot of guys never even

bothered to see whether the fingers were uncurled or what, they just shot them, said it looked like they might have had something in their hand. Besides, the distance, maybe 3-400 metres away, walking toward us, you could not tell whether the hands were curled or not, and the guys just shot them anyway.[73]

The problem of identifying combatants is treated at length in another chapter.

13
The killing of enemy wounded – an excusable necessity?

We found and shot their wounded ...

Australian officer Cam Bennett, fighting in New Guinea in World War II.

Killing wounded enemy is sometimes a military necessity. This need ranges from ensuring one's own safety to ensuring the safety of one's troops. A related issue is the self-requested dispatch of the enemy ('mercy killing'), the following examples of which illustrate the reality of battle as opposed to the rules. Indeed, from 1949 and with modification in 1977, the Geneva Conventions mention attacking wounded and defenceless soldiers quite specifically. The Convention of 1949 describes the killing of a wounded soldier as a breach. Article 41 of the First Additional Protocol of 1977 says, among other provisions, that anyone who 'has been rendered unconscious or is otherwise incapacitated by wounds or sickness, and therefore is incapable of defending himself' shall not be attacked. Common Article 3 of the Geneva Conventions says that 'persons taking no active part in the hostilities, including members of armed forces who have laid down their arms and those placed hors de combat by sickness, wounds, detention, or any other cause, shall in all circumstances be treated humanely.' Nevertheless, the Conventions do not take account of reality; they are routinely disregarded, and for good reason.

Certainly, wounded are sometimes dispatched when they should not be. Sometimes this is quite routine, as one World War I British soldier observed: 'If it was just a wounded chap trying to help himself, that was just his bad luck – it was like they had us on the Somme.'[1] This may well refer to the apparent practice, in the first days of that battle, when the Germans shot at any Allied wounded who stirred in No Man's Land after the failed assaults of the first day. Certainly British soldier George Coppard, a machine-gunner in the attack, describes wounded soldiers brought in at night telling of such attacks.[2] ANZAC Albert Jones noted, of the first landings at Gallipoli: 'Although the Turk is supposed to be a fair fighter, he lost no opportunity in bayoneting and mutilating our wounded.'[3] It was sometimes the same in the European theatre: Captain Ambrose Cull of the Australian Army was told by a fellow captive officer of the Germans killing wounded Australians with their rifle butts after a failed attack, sparing only the officers for intelligence purposes.[4]

Infantry Officer Robert Graves said, of the Germans on patrolling duties, that if they ' ... found a wounded man, they were as likely as not to cut his throat'.[5] In some situations, it was easier to finish the enemy wounded off rather than flush them out one by one. A World War I British soldier was captured and told a German soldier ' ... about the wounded down one of the dug-outs. He took a stick grenade out, pulled the pin out and threw it down the dug-out. We heard the shrieks and were nauseated, but we were completely powerless.'[6]

Ensuring personal safety

It is important to draw a distinction between wounded enemy and enemy who have surrendered. Soldiers in close infantry combat routinely presume the enemy is dangerous unless obeying *all* of the rules of surrender. Some battlefield killing of wounded enemy is done as a precaution: the wounded soldier is still a danger. So, as Sergeant Audie Murphy relates, he shot enemy wounded after taking a position: 'I step around him and examine other foxholes. Each contains a body or two. One stirs, and I give it a burst as a precaution.'[7] Failure to ensure that the dead are indeed dispatched can result in capture, as two Germans who approached an apparently 'departed' Allied officer, found out in 1944 France. Feigning death, the officer was turned over by a German, who failed to verify his death or take the 'corpse's' revolver. As soon as they had turned their backs, the officer jumped to his feet and took them both prisoner.[8]

A German soldier came across three US paratroopers landing in D-Day. He shot one, who was on the ground, in the stomach, and then turned to finish the other two, who were hanging in their harnesses on the side of a church: they had come down on its roof and slid off. But the trooper on the ground fished out his .45 pistol and shot the German.[9] US infantryman Bruce Zorns was wounded in a fight against an SS unit in early 1945. He fell to the snow-covered ground and, as the battle withdrew from his position, he eventually saw two SS troops come forward to the dead and wounded Americans and begin bayoneting them. But the two became alarmed at something out of Zorn's vision, and fled before they got to him.[10] Ironically, he was later picked up from the battlefield by two other Germans soldiers, who carried him in a wheelbarrow for some time to a field hospital.

Wounded enemy who still fight draw a variety of responses. After a battle in North Africa, Major Robert Daniell and a party investigated the forward positions and found many German wounded in an anti-tank trench. They started giving them water, and a medical doctor with them began tending one of them, when 'I saw a German rise up on his feet and have a shot at him with a revolver'. The Major told the wounded they could tend to themselves, and the British withdrew.[11]

Allied flying personnel in New Guinea in 1944 with a Japanese soldier's helmet and a skull. The secret world of close quarter soldiers – perhaps? While all soldiers seem to souvenir, some take more personal trophies. But these can also be prized by rear-echelon soldiers, wanting to appear more important in the eyes of an idolized group. AWM P02875.459

Marine William Manchester quotes communications to the Marine Corps Commander about the Guadalcanal fighting: 'General, I have never heard or read of this kind of fighting. These people refuse to surrender. The wounded will wait until men come up to examine them ... and blow themselves and the other fellow to death with a hand grenade'.[12] Just because a Japanese was badly wounded did not mean he was not a willing combatant. Marine Major Frank O. Hough described a final Japanese charge where, behind the enemy forward formation, followed 'bandage-swathed men, amputees, men on crutches, walking wounded helping each other along. Some were armed, some carried only a bayonet lashed to a long pole or a few grenades, many had no weapons at all ... The carnage was ghastly beyond belief.'[13]

Some Marines on Okinawa, in their foxholes after a hard day's fighting and ready for night attacks, heard a dragging noise out in front of them. Eventually they made out, and then shot, a moving form – a Japanese soldier. Closer examination revealed he'd been shot in one leg previously; it was bandaged up. He'd also been wounded in an eye previously; that was bandaged too. One arm was in a sling, where he'd been carrying grenades. And he was *still* on the attack.[14] Some Japanese infantry, trying a quiet night attack, met up with Sergeant Iolo Evans in his foxhole. He shot the five near him: all five were hit and knocked down, but then all went for their hand grenades, and were hit again with rifle fire.[15]

Australian soldiers in New Guinea in World War II found out the hard way that wounded enemy were still very dangerous. Private Bert Treschman saw Captain Geoff Swan, leading a patrol, come across a Japanese who was wounded – and then Swan saw the grenade the soldier was holding. Swan told his men to stand back and fired his rifle, but the enemy soldier released the grenade at the same moment, badly wounding the captain.[16] The Allied troops learnt quickly. Marine Henry Lopez tells of the sign on the jungle-training course he completed in Hawaii. It read: 'IF THEY DON'T STINK, STICK THEM.'[17] Australians speedily adopted an attitude of testing any enemy fallen bodies to see if they were indeed dead: 'A man saw an apparently dead Jap move and shot him. Others came to life and were shot.' Private Frank Rolleston said: ' ... we were instructed not to take prisoners, and were to make sure that every Jap, whether wounded or apparently dead, was REALLY DEAD before we went past them.'[18] Colonel Clement Cummings, the Commanding Officer of 2/9th Battalion, paraded his men and told them: ' ... there will be no wounded Japs – they will all be DEAD! You make bloody sure that they are dead too.'[19] One just did not take chances. It became, really, quite an everyday matter. As a retired infantryman commented, without any hint of triumph: 'If we came across one who was wounded we shot him ... we helped them die for their Emperor.'[20]

The deaths of a force's wounded at the hands of the enemy arouses hatred for the other side. A sign on Guadalcanal announced:

Kill the Bastards!
Down this road marched one of the regiments
Of the United States Army
Knights serving the Queen of Battles.
Twenty of their wounded in litters were
Bayoneted, shot and clubbed
By the Yellow Bellies
Kill the Bastards![21]

More recent wars are no different. In the Vietnam War, James Adams – an alias – told his interviewer, Mark Lane, that killing wounded as you advanced on an assault in the Marines was the norm. 'If you should pass an enemy soldier wounded, lying on the deck, you never leave any wounded that you know about, laying around alive'.[22] The Vietcong routinely killed enemy wounded: one Long-Range Reconnaissance Patroller stayed hidden under other bodies 'while the VC walked all around them with knives, making sure'.[23] A wounded North Vietnamese soldier kept moving even after he was hit several times in the battle of Ia Drang – he refused to surrender and kept trying to bring his weapon up. 'A brave and determined soldier', was one American's comment.[24] Another was shamming death in what was thought to be a group of enemy machine-gunners; he suddenly moved and fired his gun, narrowly missing a US officer, who doubtless learnt from the experience at the same time as throwing a grenade in return.[25] The North Vietnamese, by some accounts, killed wounded Americans they found at Ia Drang: two were shot in the head by pistol at close range but survived, and crawled to American positions to tell their stories.[26]

The Battle of Long Tan saw a fierce fight between perhaps a company of Australians and an overwhelming number – some say 2500 – of attacking enemy Vietnamese. The action, fought out in a plantation, eventually saw the Vietnamese retreat as Armoured Personnel Carriers came to the Australians' aid at the same time as the infantry broke the contact. As the Australians went forward again some hours later to rescue their wounded, they were unsure of whether their enemy was still there, concealed. Sergeant Bob Buick notes that this was the reason why four wounded soldiers were shot when they were found: ' ... these two particular enemy were holding their weapons in the ready to fire position. We trained extensively to expect suicidal wounded enemy soldiers to shoot or throw grenades. If they had had their hands over their heads they would not have been killed.[27] There is a dispute over this Long Tan incident, however, which Buick addresses later in his book.[28]

In the Falklands War, an NCO from the advancing British Army spotted a wounded Argentine, who was being treated for leg injuries, produce a weapon. Even as the medical team worked on the Argentine's lower half, the NCO shot him in the upper body.[29] In another case from the Falklands, a British combat team showed remarkable restraint when they came across a body lying under a blanket. Suspecting a trap, they nevertheless carefully pulled the blanket away while keeping their weapons trained: the wounded Argentine was clutching a phosphorous grenade with the pin pulled, so he was killed with a burst of automatic fire. An officer remonstrated with the soldier who had fired, but was put in his place with the question of what would have happened to the ten or so British if the grenade had been thrown.[30]

If no visible surrender is exhibited, the experienced soldier presumes any enemy is dangerous. And sometimes they are. Sudden movement by enemy wounded is treated as dangerous behaviour by soldiers on hair-trigger reactions. Going forward in the fight for Longdon in the Falklands War, Lance Corporal Vincent Bramley's leg was grabbed by a wounded Argentine soldier: the sergeant who was with him immediately shot the man twice.[31]

The speed at which many a combat action takes place means that those wounded in the first few seconds of an assault are still deemed combatants. This typical account from the Falklands illustrates the point very well:

> Just across the bowl from us was an enemy position that looked quite strong. We thought there must be about four or five enemy in it. We looked at each other and agreed to take it out. Some of the lads withdrew a bit to cover us and I got out a light 66mm anti-tank rocket. I blasted the position with it, then Lieutenant Cox and I threw some grenades into it. As soon as the explosion went off we leapt in and thrust our bayonets into the enemy, firing quick double-tap rounds into them. All were dead. It had taken only seconds.[32]

Examined against the literal instructions of the Geneva Conventions, one could argue that the initial assault with the 66mm rocket was enough. Then, some might argue, the British could, and should, have called upon their enemy to surrender. If no response was forthcoming, must that therefore mean the enemy soldiers are 'hors de combat' and should be accorded the status of wounded soldiers? In reality, of course, by taking such actions, the British would be abandoning the element of surprise, and signalling their own direction to any enemy who might like to retaliate, perhaps with a thrown grenade.

One could also take the argument along the lines of having the British abandon their attack after the grenades were thrown. But again, wounded enemy are dangerous, and who knows what sort of last-ditch suicide action they might mount. No, for infantry in such combat, they pursue the action until, in the judgement of at least the squad commander, if not the individual soldier, their opponents are no longer a threat. Two journalists assert that they heard an instructor advise troops on the journey south not to bayonet enemy wounded in captured trenches – and to shoot them instead, but not if there was a TV crew nearby. The remark was probably made for the benefit of the journalists.[33]

The trouble often is that such a judgement is a matter of degree, and purely subjective. Soldiers with differing levels of experience judge the danger which an opponent presents differently. Experienced soldiers know they have to be quick to shoot, and such eagerness can often lead outsiders to draw the wrong conclusion: that the soldier is killing when he should not; that he is killing non-combatants, and so on. At least one such case seems to have occurred in the Iraq War in 2003–04, with a US marine 'withdrawn' from the battlefield because a media team saw him shoot a wounded enemy combatant: ' … the man who was killed didn't appear to be armed or threatening in any way, with no weapons visible in the mosque. The slain man was among a group of men wounded in fighting a day earlier at the mosque and left there.'[34] The Marine may have been acting in self-defence, however – there were reportedly incidents of some wounded faking death and then firing.[35]

The tone of many of the headlines surrounding the Iraqi incident illustrates one of the themes of this work: that the true nature of battle is routinely misunderstood by civilians, and even by some in the military. Wounded enemy soldiers are still combatants. A wounded soldier is still a very dangerous threat: we can call up the ghosts of those Japanese who lay in field hospitals in World War II, clutching a grenade, to see such an example. But this Marine's actions drew instant negative responses. Newspapers used terms such as 'Marine filmed killing Iraqi'[36] and 'Marine captured in cold-blooded murder'.[37] Even when an investigation cleared the soldier the tone persisted: 'US Marine escapes justice despite video of murder in cold-blood'[38], for example.

Mercy killing

Killing enemy wounded who are not going to live, as an act of mercy, is technically a crime, but supports the theme of this work: it occurs, it is understandable, but it is said to be wrong.

Prized possessions: Japanese skulls collected by US troops in New Guinea in 1944. Having "respect" for the enemy, and seeing them as fellow humans is abandoned as a concept by many soldiers. AWM 072100

Mercy killing is indeed sometimes to be found in one's own side: Robert Graves tells of the dispatching of mortally wounded British soldiers in the trench warfare of World War I, noting that 'We always carried morphia for emergencies like that.'[39] It seems, from the matter-of-fact account of one of the medical orderlies of the South Nottingham Hussars, that it was routine then, too: 'The actual decision about giving these men a lethal dose of morphine rested entirely with the Doctor who was completely justified. That included Captain Slinn and Lieutenant Timms – they would never have been normal human beings again. It was a relief for them … '[40] The alternative is often much worse than the taking of the life of one of your own. A Marine fighting in the battle for Okinawa was hit by a phosphorous grenade, hitting him 'with molten phosphorous. He burned, screaming, begging, 'Somebody kill me!' No one could bring himself to do it, and the youngster soon died in agony.'[41] The Japanese also practised it. One soldier's account describes a military hospital which was about to be overrun by the enemy: 'A barefoot army nurse came into a section of the field hospital, took a syringe from his rucksack and gave injections to those who were on the verge of death. They would all be dead in about seven seconds.'[42]

As far as the enemy is concerned, it occurs too. Stephen Ambrose interviewed one World War II officer, a Captain Leinbaugh, who, after a fierce street fight, came across a German major who was propped against a tree, missing his right leg, which had been cut off at mid-thigh. The major requested, in good English, that Leinbaugh shoot him. However, the captain refused, and later was talking with one of his sergeants, who also had had the request made to him and who in this case obliged the enemy officer.[43] US soldier EB Sledge was part of a unit that broke through Japanese lines in Okinawa. They searched a small hut and found a civilian, a badly wounded Japanese woman. The woman grasped Sledge's tommy gun and moved it to her forehead. Sledge pulled it away and called their corpsman, who dressed her wound and called up another soldier to take her to the rear. Instead he shot her, saying, 'She wanted to be put out of her misery and join her ancestors. So I obliged her'. Sledge was angry and told their sergeant, but nothing was done.[44] Captain Tadashi Suzuki of the Japanese Army led an attack against British positions fighting to defend Singapore, and came across a wounded Lieutenant-Colonel who 'signed to us to shoot him', which was done. Suzuki commented that it was an honourable military death and he respected the way his enemy had died.[45]

On the retreat from Russia, Wehrmacht infantryman Guy Sajer was part of several divisions pinned against the Dnieper River when some Russian tanks attacked them, inflicting many casualties. The next morning, Sajer says 'We shot a great many men to put them out of their misery, although mercy killings were strictly forbidden.'[46] But what were the Germans to do otherwise: they were exhausted; out of supplies including fuel, and had no hope of aid reaching the wounded. Experienced soldiers knew that in fact they were being kind. Australian infantryman Roland Griffiths-Marsh dispatched a wounded Japanese in Java, reflecting that 'I should have done the same to the mortally wounded Italian in Tobruk; I had lived with that failure ever since.'[47]

In Vietnam, Marine Johnnie Clark's platoon was involved in a fight which they won, and they found a Vietnamese woman soldier who had been wounded badly by being shot in the stomach.

Doc moved forward. He bent over her and shook his head. 'She'll never make it. I don't know why she's alive now. Look at all the blood coming out of her ears.'

'Did you hear that?' Striker said. 'Her stomach just made an awful sound, like a drain opening. She's really suffering.'

After a bit more debate, one of the soldiers shot her.[48] Australian infantryman Bob Buick had a very badly wounded enemy soldier lying in front of his position after the battle of Long Tan in Vietnam: he shot the man twice through the heart, reflecting that 'I hope I gave him the peace that he deserved.'[49]

Indeed, what might a judgemental critic of infantrymen make of a refusal to inflict a mercy killing when it was clearly the kinder thing to do? A Japanese soldier, taunting Americans, was eventually shot during the battle for Okinawa, and began screaming in his ditch. Out of sight in the small hills, caves and gullies of the torturous terrain, another US soldier shouted, ' "Hey Sarge, shoot him again!" And somebody else shouted back, "No, don't shoot him again. Let that son-of-a-bitch squeal. It's good morale for us up here." ' The wounded soldier took around half an hour to die.[50]

An Australian private in New Guinea in 1942 recalled:

> In the kunai grass I found a Jap flat on his back with dysentery. He was covered in flies and shit in the muddy water. He had no pants and was just crapping himself. I pointed the Thompson at him and (then) thought, well mate, you're gonna die, why waste one slug. So I turned and walked away from him. Ernie said later 'did you shoot the bastard?' I said no, I hope he suffers like I am. I'm afraid I retain a helluva hatred for the Japs, they started the bastard thing. They gave us the biggest tragedy and drama of our lives so why should you be kind to the bastards.[51]

In Vietnam, Marine Jeff Kelly came across a NVA soldier who had been injured in a napalm attack and who,

> with eyes runny from pain, silently pleaded for a bullet. I thought about helping him out; then I thought about them laughing as they ran through us last night and them spraying Willoughby and Myers for no reason. 'Keep moving, asshole,' I said. I put my boot in the small of his back and shoved him towards our lines.[52]

Kelly also recalled capturing a Vietnamese who was badly wounded – so badly that the unit's corpsman said he would surely die. However, the enemy soldier did not, and when the Marines were ready to move out, they had the dilemma of what to do with the prisoner: a sergeant shot him, saying that the shot was an 'AD' – Accidental Discharge.[53]

In the Falklands, Argentine prisoners were moving ammunition, with the permission of their captors, to make their prison safer. An unstable grenade went off, severely wounding one of them. A British medic shot him, and ' ... the other prisoners thanked him for putting the man out of his misery'.[54] Paratrooper Ken Lukowiak was present when an overrun position was found to contain a badly wounded Argentine soldier who had been shot in the head, just above one eye. Two of the British soldiers automatically began to attempt first aid, Lukowiak pushing 'pieces of brain back into the hole from which they came', when a sergeant intervened, told them to stand back, and dispatched the wounded soldier with a burst of bullets from his machine-gun.[55] Clearly, the Argentine was most likely going to die.

But the line between mercy killing and the dispatching of a potential prisoner is a fine one. In Iraq operations during May 2004, US tank commander Captain Rogelio Maynulet was part of a team that chased down a car with suspects in it. There was firing, and when one of the suspects was taken out of the car, it was clear he had suffered serious injuries to the head. Captain Rogelio shot him as an act of mercy, but another soldier disagreed and the matter ended up in court.[56]

Ensuring unit safety

In some situations, a wounded enemy cannot be assisted, cannot be taken prisoner, and necessarily must be dispatched. For example, Robert Graves describes the process of 'patrolling for the enemy' in World War I; that is, carrying out a surreptitious reconnaissance mission to find out who the enemy are, what their strength is, and where they are. A patrol of one or two or three men might come across a wounded German. Brought back to the British lines, he could provide intelligence. However, if wounded, he might not survive the trip, and therefore the usual practice was to remove any badges from his uniform. If the wounded man resisted, or struggled, the patrol would inevitably draw down fire on itself. So, as Graves says in his weary way, 'to do that quickly and silently, it might be necessary first to cut his throat or beat in his skull.[57] Again, how does this contrast with the so-called rules of war? Any soldier today on such a mission would do just what was done in this instance, and if it was found out, doubtless quite a few people would make trouble for that soldier. So the act is kept quiet, but still routinely carried out – and technically that soldier must conceal a so-called criminal act.

Sometimes wounded enemy can imperil a unit's safety, in a variety of ways. On the first day of the Battle of the Somme in 1916, wounded prisoners were scarce, according to Lyn Macdonald. She notes that this may well have been due to an order issued by General Headquarters on the eve of the battle. This stated that soldiers were to use their weapons 'until it is beyond all doubt' that the enemy combatants 'have definitely and finally abandoned all hope or intention of resisting further.'[58] However, as she goes on to note, the knowledge that the British were not taking prisoners would lead to an attitude in the German lines that they were not either, so 'Privately, individually the Tommies made up their own minds …'

An Australian section was attacking a part of the German line after being heavily shelled. When they came across a large detachment of the enemy, they attacked with bayonet to such effect that some Germans shammed being dead or wounded to escape attack. Then, as the attack passed on, some of the Germans came 'back to life', so to speak. WJ Harris of the 2/24th Battalion of the AIF commented that: ' … a number of these Huns rose up and started firing on us from the rear. That, naturally enough, made the boys see red. Their deaths were real enough after that.'[59]

In the Battle of the Bulge, two American soldiers managed to disable a tank with a bazooka; the surviving crew member got out wounded. The two Americans started to carry him into a nearby house, but the German began to revive and shout 'loudly and seemingly irrationally'. Deciding he would give their position away, the Americans killed him.[60]

Consolidating a new position in New Guinea routinely saw any Japanese wounded in front of the Line dispatched, according to Australian officer Cam Bennett. Logically enough, to give the Japanese wounded medical attention was very difficult, and why would you leave a combatant alive to keep fighting against you?

> We went out and made sure there was no enemy near us and maintained a small force forward of our position to ensure that this remained so while we reorganised. We found and shot their wounded, and if necessary, disposed of their dead.[61]

The same actions were taken by the Japanese, but a war correspondent who saw the bodies of wounded Americans who had been clubbed to death assessed the action as 'depraved'.[62]

To give away one's position by calling in transport for the wounded can be seen as dangerous. Vietnam veteran Ed Treratola (not his real name) told Terry Lane that it was routine to shoot wounded enemy. ' ... we don't have time to take any wounded, and we can't call in helicopters because they endanger the pilot's life, so they kill them ... you take an M-16 and you go around and, you know, look for them, look at the wounded, and you shoot them ...'[63]

Attacking medical units

Deliberate targeting of hospitals or vehicles carrying wounded enemy would seem to be less acceptable than attacking an injured soldier because he is still dangerous. However, it happens often enough. Stephen Westman of the German Army in World War I noted that, 'as a rule', their red-crossed trains full of wounded were attacked by French fliers. The French were unusually vindictive compared to the British when it came to using red crosses and white flags. The appearance of a white flag preceded by a red cross in the trenches meant that firing at that area ceased. Robert Graves, fighting in 1916, noted after one fierce battle, as they recovered wounded from 'No Man's Land': 'The Germans behaved generously. I do not remember hearing a shot fired that night, although we kept on until it was nearly dawn; then they fired a few warning shots, and we gave it up'.[64] George Coppard describes repulsing a night attack by the Germans in France in 1916; afterwards, noise was heard in No Man's Land, but 'being reasonably certain that German stretcher bearers were at work we stayed our hand'.[65] Steven Westman observed that such breaks in combat were practised between the British and Germans, but again not the French.[66] Australian soldier Albert Jones noted, in the Gallipoli campaign, the arranged 'armistice' of 24 May, when the Turks and Australians ceased fighting so the dead could be buried: the sides sent forward their parties under the Red Crescent and the Red Cross, respectively.[67]

In World War II, Max Hastings notes, truces often took place between the Germans and the British or Americans fighting each other so that wounded could be removed. Captain Walter Schaefer-Kuhnert saw, during one of these, a German soldier carry a wounded American back to his own lines, and he returned loaded with chocolate and cigarettes. The captain, who had fought on the Eastern Front, noted that this would never have happened there.[68] It didn't happen in the war against the Japanese, either. Battle surgeon Charles Veatch abandoned his issue medical case with its red cross because it was too tempting a target for Japanese snipers. He carried his equipment in a gas-mask case instead.[69] Japanese snipers had no respect for stretcher bearers, recalled US Marine EB Sledge, and constantly shot at them if they could: they 'were merciless in this, as in everything else in combat'.[70] He describes an incident where four Marines carrying a wounded man got hit by deliberate fire – the two in the rear were wounded, but eventually all five made it through the gauntlet.[71]

After D-Day, the advancing Canadians noted at least two occasions when the Red Cross flag was displayed and both sides broke off fighting to collect their wounded.[72] Royal Marine Edward Hill was wounded in the battle for Crete, and pinned down under machine-gun fire for a whole day. Eventually an Australian calling for wounded made his way to him, and carried Hill out on his shoulder – the German machine-gunners ceased firing.[73]

However, such stays in the fighting were not a set rule, nor universally accepted. During the crossings of the Moselle, Captain Jack Gerrie saw the Germans shooting down American medics; enraged, Gerrie sent out German prisoners to do the removals, and they were shot down too, so in reprisal all of the prisoners were shot.[74] Battle Surgeon Brendan Phibbs cites an example where an SS infantryman used a wounded US soldier's cries for help out in the open as bait to get a corpsman to rescue him. Then he machine-gunned them both, ignoring the medic's red crossed helmet and the similarly-adorned flag he carried.[75] One Canadian soldier observed a medic put a red cross on the end of a bayonet and hold it up during some fighting in 1945; there was no firing so he went forward. There was still no firing, so he crawled out – and was then shot at and hit in the leg.[76] US infantryman Bruce Zorns was wounded in a fight against an SS unit in early 1945 and called for a medic; one came forward with several red crosses on his helmet and on his sleeves, but a German machine-gun killed him the moment he got to Zorn.[77]

There are scores of incidents involving hospital ships being fired upon in World War II. The US vessel *Comfort* was hit by a kamikaze in the campaign to take Okinawa.[78] In the surprise raids on Darwin in 1942, the hospital ship *Manunda* was at anchor, her sides emblazoned with large red crosses. But she was indeed hit, leaving 58 personnel wounded and 12 killed. Some controversy surrounds this: there have been suggestions it was accidental, but other opinions are that it was deliberate. Australian Navy sailor Colin Price, in a letter written on 24 February to his mother, said he saw 'the hospital ship *Manunda* attacked repeatedly by dive bombers, she was hit and also machine-gunned...'[79] Lieutenant (E) Frederick Purves, RANR(S), later to become a Rear-Admiral, had a clear view of *Manunda* from the deck of *Platypus* and witnessed the attack by a group of dive bombers. He is certain that this group acted in concert, and that the attack was deliberate. For him, the only uncertainty is why the Japanese did not sink, rather than merely disable, the hospital ship.[80] Then again, the *Manunda* survived Japanese air attacks in Milne Bay later that year.

Parachutist Daniel Webster's unit of the 101st Airborne, advancing after D-Day, was engaged against some German positions when a jeep emerged from the enemy area and drove straight down the road. It had two stretchers on board and was flying a Red Cross flag. The soldiers, bemused by the unexpected sight, let it go until it was stopped by an officer. The driver was wearing a pistol, so he was ordered to be summarily shot. The two wounded were left by the side of the road to die.[81] Guards Officer Philip Brutton noted in his diary during their advance through Italy, 'Exchange of fire with Kraut ambulance' – obviously an unusual event, and one caused by its occupants opening fire on the British.[82]

Again, how many of the actions described here would result in criticism for the soldier acting out of necessity to cope with the realities of war? However, the cold-blooded shooting of wounded enemy for no military reason is an extension of the cases cited above, and is less acceptable. It occurs, though, and sometimes enemy are found dead for no apparent reason. Sergeant Martin of the Canadian Army was part of an advancing infantry force in 1944 when they came across some of their soldiers who had, Martin guessed, been retreating when they were overwhelmed and disarmed. All were wounded, but all had been 'pistol-shot in the temple'. Martin analysed his own feelings on this, and concluded that he knew what he would do when eventually he had the chance to take revenge. However, when that possibility later came up, he found he couldn't go through with it.[83] And then there are executions of obviously harmless wounded enemy, as a New Zealand doctor saw when the Russian Army took a hospital in their advance during 1944. A stretcher carrying a wounded German officer was being carried down some steps. 'As I looked, a young Cossack officer hurried after the stretcher, drew his revolver, and shot the German through the head.'[84] In more recent times, Paratrooper Jerry Phillips was leading a night patrol in the Falklands when, using his scout telescope, he saw a large Argentine ship 'smothered in red crosses' in Port Stanley unloading 'hundreds of Argie troops'. He tried to get an airstrike called down on it, but was unable to get a satisfactory response through the crowded radio network.[85]

In many circumstances, combat requires wounded enemy to be largely treated still as combatants. As we have seen, wounded enemy are extremely dangerous, and there is no second chance for any bold trooper. If he wants to become an old trooper, he needs to treat enemy wounded as still fighting unless they are exhibiting very clear signs of surrender. Even then, as we have seen, some enemy simply use that as an incentive to get their target to approach. There is a lesson here, too, for all armies: discourage such behaviour if you want your own wounded to survive. In summary, only the naive civilian thinks that once a soldier is wounded, he is no longer a fighter.

'14
Executions

Putting your hands up isn't going to save you.

Sergeant Nikolai Timoshenko of the Russian Army, World War II.

The illogicality of executing prisoners has been commented upon previously, and it is illustrated in no better way than by comparing, albeit briefly, the behaviour of the German and Russian armies in World War II towards each other. The German invasion of Russia had gone comparatively well in the early days of Operation Barbarossa, and the Germans took not thousands, but millions of prisoners. Shirer tells us that in the last six months of 1941, some 3,800,000 were captured. They were routinely kept in exposed conditions in freezing winters, denied rations, and marched through poor weather – and of course many thousands died. Wehrmacht infantryman Guy Sajer noted that those forced to work near him were given meagre, 'absurd' rations: one three-quart mess tin of weak soup between four prisoners every 24 hours, for example.[1] In 1943, Himmler commented that they 'died in tens and hundreds of thousands of exhaustion and hunger', dispassionately noting that this policy had been foolish in that they could have been used as slave labour instead. Indeed, those who survived were eventually put to work.[2]

In general, however, prisoners were not simply executed; indeed, German soldiers were indignant if it happened, at least early on in the Russian campaign. Wehrmacht Panzer driver Henry Metelmann saw a group of their own officers get drunk in the field. One of them summoned a Russian colonel from a nearby work gang and began interrogating and insulting him. The Russian was contemptuous of his treatment; the drunken officer pulled out his pistol and shot him dead. The German soldiers protested loudly, and demanded the major be charged.[3] Guy Sajer noted that prisoners robbing the German dead they were made to bury were indeed executed, but he deplored the sadism of the 'toughs' who did this: one tied three prisoners to a gate, then put a released grenade in one's pocket. Significantly, those who dismissed such treatment had returned from fighting the Russians, and argument ensued.[4] Sajer, who possessed a philosophical and thoughtful attitude towards the war, thought that 'Russian excesses did not in any way excuse us for the excesses by our own side.'[5]

When the Russians got the upper hand in latter stages of the war, their attitude towards their enemy was more savage. They routinely refused to take prisoners during their advance to Germany:

> At Dr Nikolai Senkevich's field hospital, a group of captured Germans refused to answer questions from their interrogators: 'We simply took them 100 metres off and they were shot.' Sergeant Nikolai Timoshenko said: 'The rule of war is that you go into battle, you see the enemy, and that enemy is not a human being. Putting your hands up isn't going to save you.'

> Only a minority of Germans who attempted to surrender reached PoW camps. 'We killed prisoners just like that,' said Captain Vasily Krylov, snapping his fingers. 'If soldiers were told to escort them to the rear, more often than not they were 'shot while trying to escape'.'[6]

However, as outlined above, such attitudes are foolish militarily, for they encourage the side that thinks it will receive wholesale execution if captured to fight all the harder. A report to Beria complained:

> There are many places where they do not take captured German officers and soldiers to the assembly points, but simply shoot them on the road. For instance [in one place] 80 German officers and men were captured, but only two were brought to the PoW assembly point. The rest were shot. The regimental commander interrogated these two, then released them to the Deputy Chief of Reconnaissance, who shot these men also. The deputy political officer of 4th Infantry Division, Lieutenant Colonel Urbanovich, shot nine prisoners who had deserted to our side, in the presence of a divisional intelligence officer.[7]

Charles B. MacDonald commanded a US infantry company in World War II. He noted some instances where prisoners were executed, quite informally, by their captors:

> … one of his sergeants told MacDonald over the radio that he had captured three prisoners but could not withdraw with them. 'Roger,' answered

MacDonald, 'do what you can.' The platoon returned without its prisoners. 'Today Company G committed a war crime,' wrote MacDonald. 'They are going to win the war, however, so I don't suppose it matters.'[8]

And:

The two men who had taken the prisoner to the rear returned. They had made a quick trip.

'Did you get him back OK?' I asked.

'Yessir,' they answered and turned quickly back toward their platoons.

'Wait a minute,' I said. 'Did you find A Company? What did Lieutenant Smith say?'

The men hesitated. One spoke out suddenly. 'To tell you the truth Cap'n, we didn't get to A Company. The sonofabitch tried to make a run for it. Know what I mean?'

'Oh, I see,' I said slowly, nodding my head. 'I see.'[9]

MacDonald noted another occasion when the company he was commanding was crossing the Weser River against German opposition. A sergeant told him over the radio that his platoon had captured three prisoners, and then changed that to two. MacDonald himself had seen at least three prisoners and heard about more, but accepted this as the reality of combat.[10]

US paratrooper and officer Richard Winters was present when his unit took some prisoners; he turned them over to a soldier who had a bad reputation with captives. The soldier's enthusiastic reception of his charges and the words 'Oh Boy! I'll take care of them' was the warning: Winters made him surrender all of his ammunition, except one round, to take the prisoners to the rear.[11] In the Battle of Alamein, Sergeant Carnduff of the 5th Seaforth Highlanders was approached by one of his men, who advised that there were some enemy hiding in trenches. 'Well, the boys had been moaning about having to carry the big anti-tank grenades. So we got rid of them.'[12]

Similar instances routinely occurred in other wars. A slightly wounded soldier of the Welch Fusiliers was given four German prisoners to take to the rear during the Battle of the Somme's first day. He explained to a friend later that he thought ' ... they were going to slip him, so he shot them'.[13] Soldiers can be careless with enemy lives. Keegan quotes one World War I account where an officer had to stop his men shooting prisoners being escorted to the rear: 'At his command, they stopped, but reluctantly. "After all," I heard a youngster say, "they are only Germans." '[14] Australian Army Private Fred Robson and some mates at Gallipoli took a Turkish prisoner, tied him to a tree, and then shot him 30 times.[15] The official Australian Army historian Captain Bean describes two executions on the Western Front during a raid at Fleurbaix in 1916.[16] After the war, the leader of that raid annotated a copy of Bean's work: a wounded German prisoner would not stop struggling while his captors were attempting to search him, so the order was given to kill him with a knobkerry club. On another occasion an Australian unit was about to take surrender from 'about 150' Germans when another battalion's machine-gunners opened up on the potential prisoners.[17] Lieutenant Aitkeen wrote to his mother that surrendering Germans who had dropped their weapons and ' … shove their hands up & yell for "Mercy, Kamarade" – they get it too sometimes.'[18]

The US Civil War soldiers had an expression: "Going to see the Elephant". Like a circus, warfare was a rare and strange event. Souvenirs of any event prove to yourself and others you were actually there. War, as one of the ultimate human experiences, provokes enthusiastic souvenir hunting from its participants. Here in Tobruk, Libya, with his rifle close by in case of alarm, Jerry Kerr of Australia polishes his collection. AWM 020912

Bizarre circumstances can also provoke execution. The Canadian forces advancing after D-Day were startled by a German soldier riding down the road towards them on a bicycle, 'gloriously drunk'. He was captured, but nothing could be got out of him for intelligence purposes; he was wheeled away on a wheelbarrow and then shot.[19]

RJ Berry of the Australian Army saw a Japanese prisoner brought in by some members of an infantry battalion at Finschhafen in October 1943. Tied up and with his trousers removed, he reminded Berry of a 'small, terrified animal'. The prisoner was to have been brought off by barge, but when that was cancelled:

The two infanteers moved off the beach and into the jungle with their prisoner. Shortly afterwards I heard the unmistakeable crack of a .303 rifle. Later I passed one of those men and asked, 'What happened to the little Jap?' He looked at me steadily for some seconds ... [20]

In the battles of the Far East in World War II, an detachment of Indian soldiers was guarding a section of Japanese prisoners, and one night all those prisoners were executed. No-one reported it. George MacDonald Fraser, nearby with a British detachment, did not think for a moment of taking action; if he had ' ... I'd have been regarded as eccentric. I'd have regarded myself as eccentric ...' As he put it, '... the notion of crying for redress against the perpetrators (my own comrades-in-arms, Indian soldiers who had gone the mile for us, and we for them), on behalf of a pack of Japs, would have been obnoxious, dishonourable even.'[21]

Some German prisoners were treated differently from others. The notorious[1] SS (Waffen-Schutzstaffel), related Glen McBride in the early weeks after D-Day, were separated from the others; they received a more rigorous search, and in general were given none of the sympathy that some Germans got from Allied troops. McBride notes that this was partly due to the SS having 'wantonly shot a number of Canadians' previously.[22] For that matter, German soldier Kurt Meyer saw the bodies of a group of Germans who had been lined up and shot through the head by Canadians.[23] Parachutist Daniel Webster witnessed a French tankman, advancing with the US forces in 1945, deal with three SS soldiers who had been caught: they were all shot at close range, to the dismay of several new

---

1 The Schutzstaffel, abbreviated to 'SS', was the section of the Nazi government responsible for 'racial purity, police control of local affairs, and Nazi control of the state', according to Patrick Brode. (17) The Waffen-Schutzstaffel was the army of this organisation.

replacements, who had been looking forward to action. ' "There's your goddamn war!" I said. "How do you like it?" '[24]

Some forces were preferable to surrender to than others. The partisans of Yugoslavia dealt harshly with Germans they caught in the final days of the war: in Pola, for example, groups of officers were rounded up and shot with machine-guns.[25]

As investigations started into the fate of various prisoners towards the end of the war, the investigations revealed more and more incidents. One Canadian court found that ' ... at least twenty-eight Canadian prisoners had been murdered in thirteen separate incidents' by the Waffen-SS.[26] As time and investigations went on, scores of incidents involving hundreds of Canadians were uncovered. Sixty-four Canadian and British prisoners, many of them wounded, were executed by the Waffen-SS within 10 days of the D-Day landings. Their leader, 'Panzer' Meyer, was tried and condemned to death for this after the war, but the sentence was commuted and he was eventually released in 1954.[27]

Treatment of Japanese prisoners, once captured, was often harsh but not always lethal. British Commando Peter Young noted that one Japanese prisoner refused to eat any rice because 'you will then pour water down my throat and jump on my stomach'.[28]

Lethal treatment meted out to prisoners was not confined to execution at the hands of those who had fought and captured the prisoner. For various reasons, rear-echelon troops could be homicidal. Gunner William Harding tells of several occasions when British and French prisoners, taken by the Germans, were shot on their forced marches for not keeping up, for trying to escape, or for disobeying orders.[29] In New Guinea, Australian soldiers who captured a downed Japanese pilot and brought him into their section were indignant when a cook – 'practically a non-combatant', one of the captors complained – seized a rifle and shot the prisoner dead.[30]

A desperation to be one of the 'real' soldiers led to incidents such as this:

> We were trying to take a Japanese prisoner in Leyte – this young lad and I were deciding to go into this cave, and while we were thinking, a Japanese soldier came out. He only had on a pair of trousers, but he was carrying a bayonet with his hands up. He came toward us and, while we were thinking of how to take him prisoner – we had heard so many stories about them hiding grenades and such like – two Americans from

the barge crowd came running up, saying, 'Let me shoot him, let me shoot him.' The lad had an Owen gun – they were very touchy on the trigger – and he just lowered it and filled this Japanese chap with bullets. I've often thought about that lad. He's probably dead, but I bet he never forgot that because while it was an understandable reaction – we were on a knife-edge nerves-wise – it was like murder ... [31]

An Australian soldier at Tobruk, who had been a troublemaker – with a history of what was apparently the wrong sort of violence – shot a prisoner his unit had captured. He was supposed to be guarding the captive for intelligence reasons, but he may have taken the action in revenge against his comrades, who had refused to take him out on patrol.[32] Australian infantryman Roland Griffiths-Marsh had a problem getting a captured Japanese back for interrogation in 1945:

At 0500 hours, I took the prisoner to the boat. The Australian crew kept muttering 'Chuck the bastard overboard', and similar comments. I stressed the importance of getting him to intelligence for questioning; it could save Australian lives ... [33]

But he heard later that the crew had indeed rolled the Japanese soldier over the side. A Japanese major, surviving the crash of his plane after the end of fighting on a Pacific island, was found asleep and was shot by two American soldiers. They were court-martialled, mainly because of the loss of the intelligence value he would have provided – his briefcase was full of maps.[34]

George MacDonald Fraser recounts an instance where fleeing Japanese prisoners – including wounded – were shot down by Allied troops in World War II. He concluded: 'There are many grey areas around the Geneva convention ...'[35] Discussing the horrors of what was discovered in Belsen in 1945, MacDonald Fraser noted that the term 'war crime' was new then, and that no such concept had been applied in World War I. Furthermore, the concept, when it was thought about, was only applied to the Germans and Japanese: few thought it could, or would, be applied to the Allied side, who – after all – were the winners.

Just because an enemy is running away does not mean he has surrendered: Guy Sajer's detachment of the Wehrmacht got into a desperate struggle with a strong partisan force, which they eventually broke. Then, 'The last of the partisans were running towards the mountains. For a moment, they were directly exposed to our fire, and we shot down twenty of them ...'[36]

Mariners in the water after their ship had been sunk were often strafed in World War II, particularly in the Pacific War. Some of these cases doubtless occurred when aircraft came back to attack ships which were sinking, with some personnel getting into lifeboats while others on the ship were still fighting. But often it was just sheer determination to kill the enemy in the water. The crew of the Australian corvette *Armidale* had largely abandoned their stricken vessel as it succumbed to the attentions of several aircraft in the Timor Sea in 1942. They were strafed enough to cause one of their gunners, Teddy Sheean, to return to his AA gun and engage the aircraft. He was killed at his post (a submarine is named after him). For that matter, Sub-Lieutenant Sakae Kogono survived the sinking of the giant battleship *Yamato* in the closing stages of the war, and he and his shipmates were strafed in the water by American aircraft.[37]

The Battle of the Bulge, where the German Army 'broke out' in 1944, saw a series of desperate actions on both sides as the Germans sought to go on the offensive and the Allies strove to contain the breakout, roll it back, and continue their advance to the east. There were several instances of prisoner massacres. The best known is probably the 'Malmedy massacre', where 86 captured Americans were shot – although, in the confusion, with some injured faking death under bodies, or looking too bloody to need a coup-de-grace, 43 escaped.[38] Prior to that, in a village on the road to Bullingen, groups of Americans were shot down: one group of eight who had been found asleep in a house, and two groups of five and four, respectively, who had tried to surrender under a white flag.[39] An SS detachment of three tanks and 40 infantry took fire from a house where American infantry were holed up; they stormed the building, and shot one wounded soldier who was still inside. They dragged the others out; killed three with automatic fire, and then shot the remaining three, who all fell wounded and feigned death while the Germans left. In fact, one died, but the other two escaped.[40] Such incidents aroused, as Max Hastings points out, among the Americans 'a hatred of the enemy that was conspicuously absent for much of the north-west Europe campaign.'[41] An American lieutenant shot a German prisoner in the back of the head on 24 December 1944 – reason unknown.[42] Private Donald Schoo noted that it was the only time he saw American troops shoot those trying to surrender, adding that it applied to those who wore black uniforms, which he thought were SS. Unfortunately for these Germans, this would also have included tank crews.

Death can be the penalty for not playing by the generally agreed rules in prisoner treatment. Here WWII German General Anton Dostler is tied to a stake before his execution by a firing squad. Dostler was convicted and sentenced to death by an American military tribunal in 1945 after the war. He had ordered, against protestations from his own men, the execution of 15 captured American soldiers during hostilities the previous year. NNSP 111-SC-225295

Phillip D. Chinnery compiled a depressing and appalling list of atrocities against prisoners committed by the Chinese and North Korean (NK) forces in the Korean War. Both forces routinely executed prisoners. In August 1950, 26 captured American soldiers were machine-gunned by their NK captors; one was wounded three times, but fell underneath his comrades' bodies and survived to make it to safety.[43] In November, 15 out of a group of 16 captured Allied personnel were shot after capture and mistreatment. PFC Edward Gregory Jr. was captured by the North Koreans and placed in a long column of prisoners. Their captors 'told us if the wounded held them up or slowed them down, they'd kill them.'[44] British infantryman Lofty Large was part of a large party of prisoners, many with serious wounds: Large himself still had two bullets in him. Despite this, they were made to march around 30 km a night.[45] In December, five US airmen were executed after being captured from a truck convoy; in the same month, 30 wounded US prisoners were shot and bayoneted to death.[46] Such treatment was routine. It became such standard behaviour that the NK leader Kim Il-Sung issued an order: 'Some of us are still slaughtering enemy troops that come to surrender. Therefore, the responsibility of teaching the soldiers to take prisoners of war and to treat them kindly rests on the political section of each unit.'[47]

Ten Marines were executed by the North Koreans in a planned operation in February 1951. Two officers took part in it and, when captured, gave the same confession. The Marines had been held for a week and then, their hands bound with wire, bayoneted to death and buried.[48] One researcher notes that 'at least six death marches' took place in the first year of the Korean War, with summary shootings of prisoners who couldn't keep pace.[49] Investigations in 1952 that there were 57,559 atrocity victims reported, with over 29,000 the probable accurate figure.[50]

Colonel David Hackworth saw his sergeant dispatch four prisoners who had not been able to be sent back to the rear. Company Intelligence had said they had no value, and advised, 'Just shoot them'. The section had to keep the prisoners overnight in hostile country. The sergeant had the men dig foxholes, as the Americans routinely did every night, but then shot the prisoners in these by-now graves. Hackworth noted his own annoyance, but did not do anything official; rather, he had the man transferred, commenting, 'What is war anyway but one big, raging atrocity?'[51] The Company Intelligence advice, of course, suggests such actions were routine.

Second Lieutenant Frank Muetzel noted matter-of-factly: 'We also picked up several North Korean stragglers who I sent to the rear with one of my walking wounded. He took them around a bend and shot them.'[52]

However, large numbers of prisoners were also routinely taken. In the landings at Inchon, a lieutenant-colonel's message in relation to his progress read: 'Captured forty-five prisoners ... meeting light resistance.'[53] However, treatment was still merciless to many. First Lieutenant Ed Jaworski noted that many North Koreans who had not been hit by the naval bombardment ' ... began to swim for Inch'on. Hell, we had guys lined up like it was a rifle range, shooting at those bobbing heads.'[54] Is that a war crime? It was not then, but probably would be seen as such by many now. There was a similar incident in the Falklands War, when a British helicopter was shot down into the sea and the surviving aircrew were shot at by an Argentine patrol as they struggled to shore. The British Intelligence apparatus found out the name of the platoon commander involved and unsuccessfully pursued him through the confusion of prisoner-handling after hostilities ceased.[55]

Vietnam

The Vietnam War was characterised by the taking of comparatively few prisoners by the North, as compared to the Allies fighting for South Vietnam. Marine Officer William Van Zanten observed 'Neither Charlie nor the ARVN bothered taking the other prisoner,'[56] and Marine Officer Philip Caputo noted that most of the interrogated prisoners they turned over to the South Vietnamese Army were shot.[57] An American VC sympathiser wrote in 1970 that it was a guerilla war which ' ... takes few prisoners by the very nature of its operations'.[58] Paratrooper Ian Kemp noted: 'The North Vietnamese didn't make a habit of taking prisoners ...'[59] When the North did take prisoners, they generally treated them very badly – far worse than the treatment meted out to those captured by their opposition. Lewy provides a figure of 20 per cent of American prisoners dying in North Vietnamese charge, with the deaths attributable to starvation and disease, with maltreatment rife.[60] The later-Admiral William Lawrence was shot down while piloting his F-4 Phantom over Vietnam, and spent almost six years in captivity, much of it in isolation, often interrogated and tortured, and generally very badly treated.[61]

The wounded were often killed when they could have instead been evacuated. In Vietnam, Second Lieutenant McDonough had an incident where he saw four enemy bodies and noticed that two of them had large wounds to the head, not characteristically the shape of the usual wound inflicted by an M-16. They were instead the size and shape inflicted by the .45 pistol, carried for self-defence only by the medic of the platoon. He asked the medic about this, but was told that all of them were 'dead by the time I got to them'.[62] On another occasion, he and his troops went out to find the bodies of the VC who had attacked them in their night. They found five dead, and one seriously wounded. 'We stared at him for a few seconds, then someone gave him a burst of three ...'[63]

PFC Louis E Willett was involved in a firefight on 17 November 1966 which saw 300 US troops pitted against a regiment of NVA. The fighting was very heavy indeed. One soldier recalled: 'We shot all their wounded [the] next day.'[64] Rifleman Thomas Bird's position was overrun by a Vietcong attack – he said, 'When they made the rush there was a lot of shooting. They shot all our wounded, killed them.' Bird and many others were taken prisoner.[65]

Wounded enemy were often dispatched on a whim. Lieutenant Bradford was sweeping the wire outside their encampment the morning after a firefight, when one of the bodies they encountered moved, so ' … a grunt gave it a magazine, full-auto, eighteen rounds. But we wanted prisoners. "Why'd you shoot that man?" "Cuz it's fun." '[66] No charges were laid.

(As an aside, in the Falklands, Paratrooper Ken Lukowiak gives an honest account of shooting an Argentine who probably should have been taken prisoner. The paratroopers had taken an Argentine position: prisoners had been taken and the area was quiet. Lokowiak decided to get out of the foxhole he had occupied and look for another. He then saw an Argentine soldier in another trench; the man had a rifle, but Lukowiak moved first and shot him. He spent many years afterwards replaying the scene in his head, with different endings.[67])

Cherokee Paul McDonald was a Second Lieutenant artillery observer in Vietnam. He was on the ground when he saw a Vietcong prisoner being thrown out of a helicopter to his death.[68] Marine Chuck Onan told an interviewer that this was outlined to him in training as a way to get information out of prisoners: ' … you throw the first one or two out to make the others talk. There are special ways to do it – you know, with precautions – so you don't fall out yourself. We were shown how.'[69] Lieutenant Bradford was in a helicopter with a suspect. 'Let's pitch this sucker out,' someone said.'[70] They didn't, but the statement was obviously not unusual. Kenneth B. Osborn, an Intelligence officer, testified in 1971 before the House Government Operations Committee that he had indeed told an earlier, informal civilian inquiry that he knew of an incident where a prisoner had been pushed out of a helicopter, but he refused to name the officer.[71] Lewy describes one such incident where an investigation confirmed that a dead body had been used for effect – the story appeared in the *Chicago Sun-Times* and the *Washington Post*. Captain Robert B Johnson stated to a war crimes investigation: ' … a major who had returned from Vietnam … told us a good way to get POWs to talk was to take 2 up in a helicopter and throw 1 out, and the other talked immediately. He said it in a very serious vein.'[72]

This treatment contrasts with another proven method of getting information: treating the enemy wounded with compassion. Battle Surgeon Brendan Phibbs noted that when enemy wounded came out of sedation and found themselves being well treated, they 'became babblers ... we could name their regiments and battalions ... together with assorted and often accurate observations about tanks, guns, minefields, and intact bridges.'[73]

Infantryman Charles Locke advised an investigation:

> ... they called down from the mountaintop and said they found 4 dinks moving ... at which time we lit out of there and went after them. When we caught up to them we fired at them. 1 was killed – he wasn't really killed, he was shot through the shoulder and through the jaw. He was wounded. We stopped and called the Col and told him we had 1 wounded dink, you know, and that we wanted him to send a chopper. The Col says, 'Is that what I heard you say? Wounded?' and the Sgt said, 'No.' and they blew his head off.
>
> Before we left on this mission the Capt of the company had told us definitely do not take any POWs. He didn't want to hear about any POWs. He wanted a body-count. He said he needed 7 more bodies before he could get his promotion to major.[74]

The training may also have reinforced the message that 'We never take prisoners'.[75] Army Sergeant Richard Dow said that, on more than one occasion, he went on missions where the order was given to not take prisoners, and so 'We killed everyone we caught', including those wounded.[76] Army Officer Alfred S. Bradford recalled one conversation where four enemy were reported killed and one captured wounded. The report of 'four victor charlie kilo, one victor charlie whiskey' was dubbed by the Operations receiver a 'transmission error', and was then 'corrected' to 'five victor charlie kilo', which was affirmed.[77]

Prisoners could also be killed accidentally. David Donovan, an infantry lieutenant, was present when his captain began interrogating two captured VC. The captain fired his rifle at them and, by accident, hit a propane gas cylinder, which began leaking and then exploded, killing both VC. Donovan reflected later that the captain was ' ... guilty of homicide'.[78]

Donovan also relates a later experience when he and some Special Forces members were interrogating prisoners, and Donovan himself 'played the game' of taking one out and letting off a round so the others would hear, and then continuing the questions. He relented, though, deciding the prisoners were not VC, and released them. Six weeks later, one of them was killed in action against the Americans.[79] Confirming the status of a captured person as an enemy is often difficult. Marine Jeff Kelly was in a squad that came across a Vietnamese in the jungle after a firefight; he was only wearing undershorts and proclaimed that he was a civilian. Kelly noted that, after 'one kick in his stomach', they got the truth: he had fled the battle. The Marines took him captive.[80]

Infantryman John Essex-Clark noted, of his experiences in Vietnam: 'We continue to shoot at small groups of dazed VC who seem to be totally disorganised and thoroughly beaten.'[81] He and his fellow soldiers then heard ox carts being brought up to carry away wounded VC. Essex-Clark wanted to pursue them but, not knowing enough about the situation, they did not.

Different forces had different attitudes to the concept of taking prisoners. The hill people of Vietnam – the Montagnards – were recruited into the Special Forces teams the US Army had developed for deep insertions and special anti-personnel work in the war. Soldier Franklin Miller led many Montagnards as an integral part of his team. He noted their propensity not to take prisoners, which presented a problem in a mission specifically tasked with obtaining one for intelligence purposes.[82] Miller also thought it was difficult to take prisoners because you didn't try to wound people – you tried to kill them. The weaponry in use by the US troops was extremely lethal, and the enemy was usually severely wounded or died in combat, rather than taking light wounds.[83]

Barry Petersen served with the Australian Special Air Service in Vietnam, and was employed in the early years of the war to train and lead the Montagnards. He too noted their propensity to not take prisoners; on an early patrol, he commented that: ' … I know my presence on those larger combat operations prevented indiscriminate killing by the Truong Son Force. They had little love for the Vietnamese …' Away in Saigon when another operation set out, he was delighted when they came back with 130 assorted weapons. He ' … asked how many prisoners were captured. "Sir," I was told, "none were captured. They all fought until they were killed." After that, I made certain that I didn't miss another major fight.'[84] Rifleman John Muir routinely saw the ARVN interpreters interrogate captives by asking, 'You VC?' If the answer was no, they would hit them in the head, and then progress to firing a round into one of the captive's feet. Of course, soon enough the answer to 'You VC?' would become 'Yes', and the prisoner was then shot because he was VC.[85]

Tiger Force – a special roving army unit under independent command in Vietnam – routinely executed prisoners, according to *The Toledo Blade*, an American newspaper which carried out an investigation into the command during 2003:

> During a morning patrol on May 8, the soldiers spotted two suspected Viet Cong – the local militia opposed to U.S. intervention – along the Song Tra Cau River. One jumped into the water and escaped through an underwater tunnel, but the other was captured.
>
> Taller and more muscular than most Vietnamese, the soldier was believed to be Chinese. Over the next two days, he was repeatedly beaten and tortured. At one point, his captors debated whether to blow him up with explosives, according to sworn witness statements.
>
> One former soldier, Spec. William Carpenter, told *The Blade* he tried to keep the prisoner alive, 'but I knew his time was up.' After he was ordered to run – and told he was free – he was shot by several unidentified soldiers.[86]

The *Toledo Blade* also said that its investigations showed another prisoner was ordered to dig bunkers, then beaten with a shovel before he was shot to death. However, this was probably not routine: Ian Kemp, who served with the Force in 1967, observed – after a particularly lengthy fire-fight – two prisoners having their wounds treated before departing for interrogation.[87]

The taking of prisoners in Vietnam, given that it seemed to be often only for intelligence purposes, also meant that they were not very well cared for. Major Gordon Livingston, working as a surgeon, had arguments about whether prisoners should be given medical care:

> … it was only by the flat statement that the POW was likely to die in front of him that I was able to achieve evacuation. I took this problem with one badly wounded POW directly to Col Patton in the hopes that his intercession would allow me to evacuate this man who I felt very badly that he needed surgery. Patton's reply was a flat statement, which I remember very well, that my job was just to keep that man alive for a few moments so he could be questioned, and after that he could die, it didn't matter to him.[88]

Prisoners in Vietnam may also have been routinely dispatched when their usefulness was over. Captain Robert B Johnson noted: 'When it became time to remove the POW to a regimental command post, I had to take him across the river. In the middle of the river, he was thrown out and shot to death.' The reaction of those others present suggests it was routine:

> The reaction of the people there on the base camp was, … this thing happens all the time, and after all, Asians know how to treat Asians. Another occasion, about 2 weeks later on a combat operation, about 20 miles south of Danang, we took a number of POWs again, and 1 of the POWs we took was wounded. Before we left, the Bn commander, Vietnamese Bn Commander in my presence, took out a .45 and shot to death the wounded POW.[89]

However, it was not the case that this was official procedure; indeed, many such cases were investigated and prosecuted. But there were deliberate kidnappings, rapes and murders, as in the late-1966 case detailed in the book, *Incident on Hill 192*. There, four soldiers out of five on an extended patrol took part in these crimes, with the fifth going to a chaplain and an officer about it some days after the squad's return. The site of the murder was found, evidence collected, the four protagonists tried, and all dishonourably discharged, reduced in rank, deprived of pay, and sentenced to hard-labour terms in prison.

The *US Army Combat Stress Control Handbook* notes six reasons for taking prisoners, and also that killing soldiers who are trying to surrender must be reported. Overlooking such incidents is 'understandable but unacceptable'.[90]

The concept of duty is also worth considering in this debate. That lethality is necessary is a concept central to this work, but a professional soldier might well consider that he is 'fighting himself' in the form of an enemy professional soldier. Glenn Gray thought: ' … many a professional soldier cherishes human sympathy for his opponent even before the decisive battle, but he dare not give it rein lest it incapacitate him for his destructive mission.'[91] Therefore, as professionals together, soldiers share much of the same warrior code. While dealing out violence is part of that, if there is no military point to killing prisoners, then one should not do it. So, while there is a military point to not letting 20 captured infantry loose into the country behind you – they may well re-group and attack your forces with whatever they can – there **is** a military point to taking captives if you safely can – they will do the same for our forces.

In essence, firstly, potential prisoners are routinely killed in the heat of combat. The laws and conventions of warfare should reflect that, and not visit sanctions upon warriors who are doing what anyone in their position would do.

Second, military necessity often dictates prisoners who are taken in tactical situations cannot be retained. Their presence compromises the safety of a mission, or its operations, and therefore they must be killed. The laws and conventions of warfare should reflect that, and not visit sanctions upon warriors who are doing what they must.

Third, warfare often sees revenge as part of everyday life. The laws and conventions of warfare should reflect that, and not visit sanctions upon warriors who are doing what anyone in their position would do.

Fourth, cold-blooded, wanton executions do take place. They should not, and the perpetrators should be brought to justice.

"How to Spot a Jap" was included in the *Pocket Guide to China*, a 7 page publication from the US War Department in 1942. The Guide was distributed to field troops in various sectors of the Pacific.

The explanatory pages on taking Japanese prisoners shows well how the US forces had learnt the hard way how dangerous Japanese troops could be, even if captured.

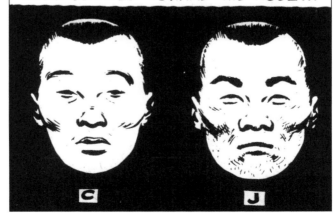

THE CHINESE HAS A SMOOTH FACE...THE JAP RUNS TO HAIR....LOOK AT THEIR PROFILES AND TEETH...C USUALLY HAS EVENLY SET CHOPPERS — J HAS BUCK TEETH...THE CHINESE SMILES EASILY — THE JAP USUALLY EXPECTS TO BE SHOT... AND IS VERY UNHAPPY ABOUT THE WHOLE THING...ESPECIALLY IF HE IS AN OFFICER!

YOU MAY FIND JAPS AMONG ANY ORIENTAL CIVILIAN GROUP... THAT IS A FAVORITE INFILTRATION TRICK...MAKE YOUR MAN WALK...THE CHINESE STRIDES...THE JAP SHUFFLES (BUT HE MAY BE CLEVER ENOUGH TO FAKE THE STRIDE)...MAKE HIM REMOVE HIS SOCKS AND SHOES, IF ANY...

THE CHINESE AND OTHER ASIATICS HAVE FAIRLY NORMAL FEET... THE JAP WORE A WOODEN SANDAL ("GETA") BEFORE HE WAS ISSUED ARMY SHOES... HE WILL USUALLY HAVE A WIDE SPACE BETWEEN THE FIRST AND SECOND TOES... OFTEN CALLOUSED FROM THE LEATHER STRAP THAT HELD THE "GETA" TO HIS FOOT...

SOMETIMES THE JAP OFFICERS HAVE NONE OF THESE CHARACTERISTICS — MANY OF THEM SPEAK ENGLISH, SOME KNOW OUR AMERICAN SLANG... BUT MOST JAPANESE HISS WHEN THEY PRONOUNCE THE LETTER "S" ... HAVE THE TWO MEN REPEAT A SENTENCE LIKE "SMITH LEFT THE FORTRESS" (OR A SIMILAR LINE)

SMITH LEFT THE FAULTLESS

SS-S-SMIT REFT THE FORTRESS-S-S

—OR TRY LALAPALOOZA ON THEM! —THAT'S A PANIC!

THE JAP SUCKS IN ON ANY "S" SOUND — AND HE CAN'T PRONOUNCE THE LETTER "L"

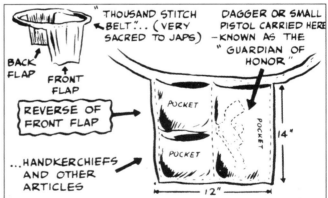

IF YOU JUST SLAP A JAP'S CLOTHING TO LOCATE CONCEALED WEAPONS YOU MAY LOSE A PRISONER — AND YOUR OWN LIFE... DON'T UNSCREW FOUNTAIN PENS OR TINKER WITH ANY OBJECT THAT COULD CONTAIN ACID OR AN EXPLOSIVE. WATCH OUT FOR SLEEVE GUNS AND OTHER COMIC STRIP GADGETS... THE JAPS ARE EXPERTS AT SUCH STUFF...

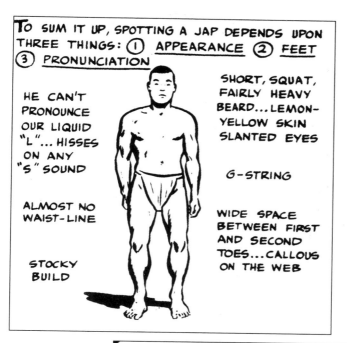

PART THREE

Targeting Civilians –
Who is the Enemy?

15
Verification of the enemy

Give me a hand grenade ... I know
where the Germans are. Let me kill them.

Dutch civilian in World War II to an advancing American soldier.

Civilians can be targeted in two main ways in war: as misidentified targets, or clearly as civilians from the enemy country who one force has decided to deliberately target. The first is clearly part of the tragedy of war, and the second is more contentious – but, as I argue here, it is also understandable and unavoidable. The problem in this latter area lies with decisions at high-command level that place the infantryman in situations where he cannot avoid carrying out such actions.

It is immediately noticeable in the examples below that the targeting of civilians occurs more in some conflicts than others. The presence of civilians in some conflicts and not others shows immediately where part of the problem lies. What exactly is a combatant? In most conflicts they are, in the main, identifiable because of their uniforms. It is where such easy identification is not possible that the problem begins.

The Boer War was characterised by respectful treatment of civilians at first. Indeed, on both sides there was a tacit acknowledgment of the opponents' soldiering qualities. However, eventually the British forces withdrew prisoners' soldier-status if they wore British khaki uniforms: such prisoners were not deemed combatants, and were shot. JFC Fuller thought this was 'enforcing a rule of war which is universally recognised.'[1] In some respects, under various rules of war this seems understandable. However, the Boers were down to such desperate measures as far as their resources went that they were using British uniforms in lieu of anything else. Deneys Reitz's account tells of him using a grain sack as a greatcoat, a practice for which he was derided but which was quickly followed by others. Reitz also spent eight months, mainly in the open, wearing nothing on his feet but a pair of handmade rawhide shoes; the taking of boots from prisoners, who were then usually let go, was common. Reitz's account also shows that, in the main and for a time, the Boers were unaware of the policy of death being meted out for appearing in khaki.[2]

In World War I, Steven Westman, then an infantryman with the German Army, was with his unit when they took fire from a French village they had overrun. They stormed the relevant houses, and found only civilians, with rifles still hot from firing. These civilians were marched away, and then the Germans sighted a column of about 30 men on bicycles, including the local mayor, who had assured them there were no troops in the village. However, each of the cyclists had a military tunic under his coat and was carrying a rifle. Westman observed that they were marched off to be court-martialled and probably executed, for 'this is the rule of war'.[3] So any civilian who picks up arms and uses them against uniformed military personnel instantly undergoes an identity change: they are now combatants themselves, and are instant targets.

This proves to be the case time and again in different theatres and in different types of war. What constitutes a warship? The sinking of the *Lusitania* in World War I is a case in point: was the presence of ammunition and weapon cargoes aboard her enough to justify her sinking? Was the use of 'Q-ships' – armed vessels disguised as unarmed to draw in the U-boats – a legitimate ruse of war?[4] In the case of these vessels of subterfuge – the Germans called them 'trap-ships' – the distinction between combatant and non-combatant is blurred; and the slide down into the abyss of open targeting soon follows.

In the Falklands War, the British fighting their way to Port Stanley eventually overran Argentine positions; the retreating occupying forces left behind the local civilians, who had mostly been imprisoned. These civilians gave active help to the British, supplying tractors and trailers, and helping to transport goods; at times this help even involved their children.[5] Had they become combatants? What was their status in a bombing raid, where the Argentine Air Force could have killed them – would the pilots have been killing non-combatants or soldiers?

Sometimes civilian-soldiers get away with it. Parachutist David Webster, fighting across Europe a few days after D-Day, was part of a unit storming some buildings when a young Dutchman ran up. 'Give me a hand grenade,' he pleaded. 'I know where the Germans are. Let me kill them.' Webster agreed.[6] But the civilian who becomes a combatant gets treated according to the same set of rules as soldiers do – if not more harshly, for breaking the almost-universally observed conventions of fighters wearing uniforms, and so on. Canadian troops advancing after D-Day took several casualties from a sniper who was deliberately targeting tank commanders. Eventually the building where the fire was coming from was stormed: the sniper was a girl of about 19, and she was cut down in a hail of gunfire from a Sten gun. Other civilians in the building said that she had become enraged at the death of her fiancée, killed by a Canadian tank.[7] In August 1944, advancing Canadian forces were shown the position of land mines by some members of a French village; they had watched the Germans lay the mines, then gone out after the retreating troops had left, and marked each spot with paper.[8]

Henry Metelmann, fighting in the German Army, saw several of the Panzers in his unit blown up by tellermines – a plate mine concealed in the soil – and eventually the soldiers found out who had been planting these in the roads at night: a Russian civilian woman of around sixty. She was summarily condemned to death, and the sentence was carried out by the Germans the next morning.[9] Metelmann had noted, on arrival in Russia, that several German units had a policy of executing those merely suspected of being partisans, and was of the opinion that the practice was stopped immediately by General Paulus.[10] But Guy Sajer, fighting on the same front in the Wehrmacht, had his first experience of combat in a small action which saw one partisan wounded and another killed. When he tried to get the wounded man onto a passing train full of wounded being taken to the rear, the lieutenant in charge was incredulous: 'Do you really think I'm going to saddle myself with one of those bastards who'll shoot you in the back any time …' He ordered two soldiers to shoot the partisan immediately.[11]

In Sajer's experience, in later years it became the norm. In a typical example, when partisans had shot up a German outpost, killing and wounding its soldiers, his detachment, which had come to its aid, pursued the Russians and opened fire. 'A few wounded partisans were trying to crawl into the forest. No order could have stopped our men. They fired at the Russians … ' Others captured were shot after interrogation.[12] On another occasion he infers execution, when about half of the partisans got away: 'Those who couldn't added to the numbers of the dead.'[13]

Spies are routinely executed, and often without trial. Robert Graves describes the execution of two spies in the early part of World War I in France: one a civilian sending information to the enemy, and the other a German in a British corporal's uniform, interfering with telephone wires.[14] Australian soldier Albert Jones noted, five days after the Gallipoli landings, that some German and Turkish officers had been caught 'wearing our uniforms: they were quickly dealt with.'[15] In fact, those found wearing the uniform of the enemy are routinely dispatched. Some advancing Canadians near Caen in World War II found two Germans of the SS, one in the uniform of a British captain, the other in a soldier's. Both fought to the death to avoid capture, doubtless knowing there was no alternative.[16]

Suspicion could be enough to warrant the quick execution of a civilian who might be a spy: Brigadier-General FP Crozier related such an incident in his 1937 account of World War I. A farm labourer was thought by a British officer to be passing on information on troop strengths and locations, for usually, after he left the farm for the day, the British positions would be shelled. The officer mentioned it to a French interpreter, and the labourer was quickly shot.[17] Is this a war crime?

Cam Bennett, an officer in the Australian Army, was too dazed and confused in the Allied retreat in Greece to wonder why a supposed naval officer in civilian clothes was wandering around asking the soldiers who they were, and the numbers of men present. His sergeant was more suspicious, and arrested the man at pistol-point. He asked Bennett to accompany him around and behind a building. The would-be spy was given the opportunity to say any final words: he gave the Nazi salute and cried, 'Heil Hitler!', and was shot.[18]

An old male civilian probably marked a British gun, concealed in a hedge, a few days after D-Day: he walked up to where it was, stopped, and then walked back again, while the British soldiers debated whether to shoot him. They didn't, but in the weeks that followed such niceties disappeared. In the words of historian Alexander Mackee: 'Elementary decency still prevailed over the instinct of self-preservation, in the same way that butter takes a few seconds before it melts on top of a red-hot stove'.[19] In a European prison camp of Australian soldiers, a spy who had been planted among them was detected, and the 10 NCOs in the compound drew lots to see who would have the job of dispatching him. His body was then disposed of 'so cunningly' that, despite searches and reprisals, it was never found.[20] British Army Corporal Edgar Rabbets, a sniper with the 5th Battalion, Northamptonshire Regiment, personally shot two Belgians who had ploughed their fields in such a way that they pointed to the British headquarters.[21]

Presuming that civilians had become combatants – and treating them as such – may well have been the cause behind the deaths of civilians after the famous St Nazaire raid. This assault saw the British destroyer *Campbeltown* ram into the dock of the French port. Unbeknown to the defending Germans, she was loaded with concealed explosives, which went off well after the initial assault. Some time later, a planted torpedo went off, and then an hour later another; this second explosion causing local French workers to try to flee the docks area. Germans soldiers began to assume an uprising, and the French civilians became, in the soldiers' minds, combatants. Inevitably, they were shot at, and as the panic spread, others were targeted, with the result that a total of 16 men, women and children, aged from five to 76, were killed, and another 26 wounded.[22]

Once civilians as a group take up arms, the enemy routinely assumes all are possible combatants, and they are treated like any other army. This, of course, means that movement – any movement – draws fire. Henry Metelmann's Panzer squadron was attacked by partisans as they entered a Russian village, and a tankman was badly injured. So, 'from then on they had shot at everything that moved …'[23] On 1 August 1944, the Polish Resistance launched its effort to dislodge its German occupier: 2500 of its fighters died on that day, and 35,000 civilians died in the first week. Max Hastings tells us of the savagery of the fighting: ' … wounded were machine-gunned. Prisoners were hurled from the windows of apartment buildings. Polish women and children were used as human shields for the advance of German troops.'[24] The struggle was eventually defeated, at immense cost.

As will be seen later in the Vietnam War, where there is a possibility of fire being taken from what is purportedly a civilian infrastructure, the oncoming commanders will resort to their instinctive reactions when under assault by the enemy. Response in as massive a form as can be arranged is poured onto the target. The surviving population is usually well aware that they had better not be identified as combatants, or sheltering combatants, in any way. Accidents take place because attacking fire is poured into possible shelters for the enemy. Henry Metelmann's crew in his Panzer did just that when advancing towards a Russian village, and then found they had killed a 12-year-old girl who was out collecting apples.[25] On another occasion, a group of teenage girls came running out of buildings ahead of Metalmann's advancing soldiers. The sudden movement attracted machine-gun fire – 'had they walked, none of us would have taken the slightest notice', commented the young Germans soldier – and two were killed.[26] Guy Sajer's section of the German Army in the Ukraine found that partisans were infiltrating crowds of refugees. 'At a given moment, they would shoot some of our men in the back, sowing general confusion. These maneuvers were supposed to crack our self-control, and provoke us to acts of reprisal, which would then turn the refugees against us.'[27] The only civilians killed in the Falklands campaign were hit by British artillery firing against Argentine artillery which had been positioned among houses – dwellings which the British thought had been evacuated.[28]

Any civilian in such a situation, observing how troops react against fire, would be sensibly advised to take precautions. Often white sheets or towels can signal civilian acceptance, and rejection of any idea of aiding retreating troops or 'left-behind' units, such as the Wehrwolf teams formed by the Germans in the last months of the war. As HR Trevor-Roper points out, the nature of these teams is often misunderstood: in fact, they did little damage and formed no credible resistance, in part because they had expected to fight in uniform, and did not.[29] They were primarily supposed to fight behind enemy lines as an arm of the German forces. But considerable resistance was expected, and so the oncoming Allied armies of WWII took village after village, and town after town, with fierce determination. As James Lucas puts it:

> God help any village if a shot was fired at the US troops, or if a rocket flare indicated a Panzerfaust team in action. In such cases the American commander on the ground called down an airstrike and anything that survived the fury of the aircraft was smashed in the systematic and prolonged bombardment of tank guns.[30]

Any research of World War II combat in the European theatre can readily find first-hand accounts of savage reprisals against civilians, well outside the systemic treatment of various groups by the German extermination machine. Accounts such as *Hitler's Willing Executioners* certainly exhibit much of this sort of behaviour: cold-blooded executions of civilians carried out by soldiers for no military reason – dishonourable and unforgivable.

The Japanese often carried out such actions in the territories they overran. Eighteen nurses, fleeing Singapore in the ship *Siang Wo*, were captured when the ship ran aground and were shot down by automatic weapons fire, with only the to-be-famous Nurse Bullwinkel surviving: although wounded, she was presumed dead by the executioners. The men from the ship were killed as well. [31]

Best not to be a civilian near the modern confusion of war. Modern combat has moved well beyond the orderly lines of the days of Napoleon. Warfare now is usually controlled chaos. Here, smashed by Japanese mortar and shellfire, trapped by Iwo Jima's treacherous sands, vehicles of war lie knocked out on the volcanic fortress. NNSP 26-G-4474

The use of submarines to target civilian shipping is an interesting variation on the targeting of civilians. It was routine in World War I and World War II to attack civilian shipping because of its strategic supply importance, and it became an accepted part of war: submarine commanders who had destroyed thousands of tons of freighters and tankers were not charged as war criminals after the conflicts ended. The von Ludendorff concept of total war saw such targeting in the same way as civilian cities being struck by enemy bombers of both sides. That aside, a variation on these actions probably would be regarded by some as outside the norms of combat. For example, US submarine commanders routinely carried out sinkings of sampans in the Pacific War, largely on the premise that they were supplying the islands they were sailing between, and those supplies would end up in Japanese hands. And so the *Flasher* is on record as sinking sampans by gunfire; the *Barb* 'trawlers, luggers and sampans'; and Mush Morton's famous submarine *USS Wahoo* surfaced in the middle of entire fishing-boat fleets, with his crew using their 20-millimetre gun and 'Molotov cocktails' to kill the fishermen. Morton reasoned that this was cutting down the Japanese supply of food, and would therefore shorten the war.[32]

Combatants disguised as civilians

What is a force to do when civilians may be unwillingly used as combatants, or when a side suspects that combatants are disguised as civilians? In Okinawa, the Japanese military drove civilians, including children, towards the front lines of the American Marines. Supposing them to be troops, the US soldiers opened fire.[33] One of the soldiers involved thought the Japanese did it for two reasons: to get the Americans to expend ammunition, and to lower their morale when they found out what they had done. And in fact it did have a devastating effect on many of the men when dawn broke and they saw the results of their actions.[34] In another incident, Japanese soldiers disguised as civilians were coming through the American lines and, as Rifleman Herman Buffington says, ' ... we were ordered to shoot some of these people'.[35]

Peter Young, fighting in a Commando unit in World War II, was present when ' ... a farmer fired his shotgun at 6 Troop. This act proved fatal to him ...'[36] And so it should: picking up a weapon turns a civilian into a combatant. The retreating British fired at what looked like civilians on their retreat in France in 1940; when Gunner William Harding questioned the shooting of an old woman, he was told: 'Orders mate, we are to shoot anyone dressed in cloaks, etc., looking like priests, as many are infiltrating fifth columnists carrying tommy-guns and some of our blokes have been killed.'[37] On another occasion he was present when the rifleman next to him shot a woman running out of a house, and when Harding protested, the soldier said, 'Five of my company have been shot by Germans dressed as nuns.'[38] Lieutenant-Commander Alexander Stanier, commanding the 1st Battalion of the Welsh Guards, was presented with a priest whose Bible had suspicious notes in it, according to Stanier's Intelligence Officer. The priest was thrown into a river, and he presumably drowned.[39]

The Korean War saw many instances of confusion as to the true nature of combatants and civilians. As is the norm in such cases, civilian casualties inevitably took place. US Army Sergeant CW Menninger noted that many of the civilians 'were actually enemy soldiers. Once they got behind us, weapons would appear and we'd have another roadblock to fight our way through.'[40] On other occasions, the identification was not as certain. PFC Leonard Korgie:

'People dressed in white – civilians being driven in front of the enemy or North Koreans dressed as civilians – appeared on the opposite hill, hundreds of them. They came down the hill and into the valley heading straight for us.' They were shot down.[41]

Almost 50 years after the suspension of the Korean War, allegations emerged in an Associated Press story that the mass killing of civilians took place in July 1950 at Nogun Ri in Korea.[42] Although untruths were found as the story made headlines around the world and developed further, it was suggested that hundreds of civilians had been rounded up and executed by US soldiers, and that many more had been herded into a tunnel and shot at for a number of days.

A US Army Review, however, found differently. It cited instances of fire coming from where civilians were, and US soldiers firing back. In essence, the review concluded:

> Korean civilians were caught between withdrawing U.S. forces and attacking enemy forces. As a result of U.S. actions during the Korean War in the last week of July 1950, Korean civilians were killed and injured in the vicinity of No Gun Ri. The U.S. Review Team did not find that the Korean deaths and injuries occurred exactly as described in the Korean account.[43]

Significantly, the Report also noted:

> Early on in the war, U.S. forces encountered the NKPA practice of infiltrating soldiers dressed as civilians among large refugee concentrations. Once behind American lines, these infiltrated soldiers would then conduct guerilla-style combat operations against American rear-area units and activities.[44]

In April 1951, 'Lofty' Large was deployed with his unit of the Gloucestershire Infantry in Korea. He witnessed a US Air Force Shooting Star ground-attack fighter kill 'a lot of Korean civilians'. He commented adversely on it and was advised by an 'old hand' that the North Koreans had infiltrated their lines dressed as civilians, so now no chances were being taken.[45]

On another occasion, the correct nature of the foe could not be identified. Fighting in Seoul, PFC Francis Killeen's company 'spotted a small party of soldiers … the rest we took for guerillas', who they shot at. They turned out to be civilian villagers and Korean Home Guard equivalents.[46] A British war correspondent may have witnessed part of this. Alan Winnington, passing through hordes of refugees, ' ... had seen a Mustang rake the people with its guns'.[47]

Misidentified targets

When a soldier thinks he is under attack, he will usually shoot first and ask questions later. This may be because of fear, but also because experience teaches the soldier that not to shoot can often have fatal results. So mistakes are made with mis-identified targets, often with tragic results. John Garcia was fighting in Okinawa when he shot at movement in the dark, and found – as light dawned – that he had killed a Japanese civilian and her baby. The Americans had distributed leaflets among the civilians they had found, warning them not to move at night as the island was still seeing fighting.[48]

It is worth noting that much of what has been written on Vietnam inaccurately portrays the American side of the war effort – in particular, as being based on the indiscriminate use of overwhelming firepower. It was most certainly not the usual case. Soldiers were given instruction on how they were to engage in combat, ranging from lectures to Rules of Engagement cards. Captain Greg Hayward recalled:

> ... every soldier who goes to Vietnam is issued a little pocket-sized card, and in many units he is fined if it isn't on his person at all times. Should an inspection come up, he is fined if he doesn't have this card. Listed on the card is the manner in which we are to treat civilians, the manner in which we are to treat POW's.

However, US soldier Peter Hefron noted that most people didn't keep these, and they certainly didn't look at them before going into battle.[49] Second Lieutenant (Marine) Philip Caputo observed, on his first night in Vietnam, with his unit dug in and already experiencing sniper fire, that they could not return fire except on the orders of a staff NCO or an officer.[50] There were also rules as to how attacks should be made, and there is evidence that these were adhered to. Indeed, the selective use of airpower and artillery was sometimes the cause for complaint in that it was too late in its application. One British observer thought that the precautions against the wrong result were almost too strict, and that 'The idea that air ordnance is scattered on hapless friend and foe alike is simply not true – good newspaper copy though it often seems to be.'[51]

A major problem, especially in the early days of the war, was actually finding the enemy. Marine Officer William Van Zanten found them 'ever-elusive', disappearing into tunnels with their wounded and dead (who they buried in the field).[52] 'We searched and searched for Charlie. He didn't show up very often …'

Civilians can easily get caught in the massive firepower of modern armies. A proportionate response is difficult if you think you or your troops will easily die. Here veteran field artillery of the US Army lay down a murderous barrage on troublesome Japanese gun positions in the Philippines, April, 1945. NNSP 111-SC-205918

James R. McDonough noted, of his US Army Vietnam experience, that it was very easy to open fire on what was supposed to be enemy movement, only to find that one would have targeted civilians. He related[53] an incident where he was about to open fire when a more experienced soldier, a private in the platoon, cautioned against it, investigated, and found that the targets were indeed Vietnamese civilians. Australian soldier Bob Buick was part of a patrol moving through a plantation when they saw a black-clad figure ahead moving quietly and suspiciously. They opened fire, but discovered they had fired on a civilian women; despite their first aid, she died.[54] The war, as it was postulated – with an amorphous, unidentifiable enemy melded with civilians, with the Western forces mired often in defensive positions – was, within these parameters, probably unwinnable. This book is not an analysis of the strategic military situation of Vietnam, although it is tempting to brood over what might have been the situation if the Allies had fought from behind a line where only their own forces operated, with search and destroy missions into the enemy's heartlands … Marine Officer William Van Zanten thought, of the efforts to help South Vietnam, that ' … our strategic plans to help them were extremely flawed. Our tactics may have been worse … For one thing, we never had a strategy for winning.'[55]

Lieutenant Bradford's company fired 'interdicting missions' at a location a prisoner had given under interrogation as being NVA or VC. After three nights of this, villagers reached them with the bodies of some children. The information was wrong: they had fired against friendly targets.[56] Guenter Lewy identified a study which attributed 23.7 per cent of US deaths from January 1967 to September 1968 to mines and booby traps.[57]

If the target is amorphous, the surrounding civilian population is in danger. If the soldiers are told, 'Do your job, but ensure the target is legitimate first', then those orders are on dubious ground.

If civilians – especially civilians who may be combatants – are present, then inevitably they may be targeted. The essence of the problem in Vietnam was that the Vietcong usually had no uniform, were Vietnamese, and therefore looked just like any villager. And just as inevitably, the infantry acknowledged the situation, and the civilian non-combatant 'became VC'. What do we expect? If we place people in a situation where it is a case of shoot first and survive, then that's what they will do.

This is the nature of the psychology of the infantry, and the nature of war. Do not blame the poor common soldier: he is doing what all soldiers have always done – fighting firstly for himself, secondly for his friends, and thirdly for whatever reason his country committed them. His survival depends on his reactions, or the lack of them.

Most soldiers probably reflect on the possibility of killing civilians by mistake, but until the time comes when one has to make that decision, it is probably not easily understood. In any war, against an enemy who can become a combatant simply by taking up arms, there will be inevitable confusion, mistakes, mayhem and death. If one side breaks the rules, the other side will soon follow. For civilians seeing conflict on their TV screens, they will inevitably rail against the seemingly savage and morally wrong dimensions of the conflict. Yet not being there and seeing only a fragment of the picture leads to a distortion of the reality of what is often self-defence. A US Army sergeant in Vietnam related:

> Yesterday I shot and killed a little 8- or 9-year-old girl, with the sweetest, most innocent little face, and the nastiest grenade in her hand, that you ever saw. Myself and six others were walking along, when she ran out to throw that grenade at us. Of course there is always the old argument that it was either us or her, but what in hell right did I have to kill a little child?[58]

Another soldier was shot at by a 13-year-old girl with a rifle. He killed her.[59] Marine John A. Daube recalled:

> One day a Vietnamese boy about eight years old approached our group wearing a knapsack. It looked like the bookbags kids use today. It was in the middle of the summer, so we were pretty certain there was no school. A reflection of the sun highlighted a wire that ran over the kid's shoulder and down his arm. One of the Marines shot him. As the child fell, he pulled the wire and blew himself up, This may sound barbaric to some, but it was common for the VC to sacrifice their children just to kill a few Marines.[60]

Private John O'Halloran was on patrol on his second day in Vietnam when:

> We were walking down a road, and coming from the opposite direction was a woman and a little baby in her arms. The Sergeant told us to watch out for a trap, because the V.C. use women all the time. We were maybe fifteen feet from her and she started crying like a baby. I didn't know what was going on, and the next thing I know the Sergeant shot the hell out of the both of them. She had a grenade under the baby's blanket which was noticeable, but she was afraid to sacrifice her kid to kill us, so she started crying. The Sergeant said it's a dirty war, but it's kill or be killed.[61]

The 'rear echelons' were never too safe, either: Saigon itself was the target of sapper groups who blew up restaurants and embassies; US officers were targeted by motorcycle-riding assassins, including a 'beautiful Tiger Lady'; and offices were barricaded with sandbags and heavily guarded.[62] A US colonel ruefully noted: 'Over there, we never knew who was the enemy, really. A little old twelve-year-old would come up, take your chewing gum, and the next minute drop a grenade.'[63]

Second Lieutenant James R. McDonough of the US Army's 173rd Airborne Brigade had the same experience. With villages close by, he observed the often close relationship of the young boys with the local US troops, but also that that 'did not prevent them setting booby traps against us.'[64] SSG (a sergeant) John Norwood, Jr, wrote that the Vietcong included ' ... the little flower girl who hands you her flowers with a smile on her face, hangs a grenade or explosive on your jeep, pulls the pin, and walks off into the crowd ...'[65]

Civilians who consorted with the enemy could often provide a useful source of information – and at the same time prove themselves not to be the innocent parties they proclaimed. In World War II, some Canadians who had taken many prisoners at D-Day were still being sniped at by the enemy. They solved the problem by surrounding themselves with a screen of prisoners as they took them to the rear.[66] In Vietnam, US Army combat adviser Martin Dockery saw the ARVN use this technique: they would drive villagers on paths ahead of them to reveal where the mines were laid. It was a two-edged sword for the villagers: if they came to a spot and baulked, they were showing they knew where the mine was and were thus concerting with the VC – and it was the worse for them. If they were killed in a mine explosion, that proved they weren't; if they were wounded, that also proved they were not a sympathiser. At least in the latter case, Dockery observed, the ARVN treated them well.[67] Sometimes they were sympathisers, or indeed VC, and sometimes they weren't – Dockery saw both scenarios. Australian soldier Bob Buick was on a patrol when they observed an old Vietnamese woman acting suspiciously: she was stopping every few metres on the path, and then reversed her direction. As Buick surmised, she knew there was a mine nearby, and as he yelled the order to spread out, the mine was detonated, killing the old woman and one of the patrol, and injuring ten.[68]

Suspicion that a civilian is not what he or she seems also leads to mistakes. Martin Dockery noted, of his patrols with the South Vietnamese Army, that 'any farmer who ran from us was shot'.[69] Infantryman Charles Gadd's unit took bad casualties from booby traps; one day, an old man – a local civilian – was seen contemplating their indecision as to whether to cross a bridge barricaded with brush. Someone suggested they use the old man to clear away the obstacle, as it was thought the locals always knew which areas to avoid. They forced the old man to do this, and the resulting explosion killed him.[70] Nearly 40 years later, a Marine lieutenant forced two Iraqis to search their own car. They began to do so, but then advanced towards him, ignoring commands to stop. Fearing they were booby-trapped bombers, the officer shot both – and was charged with murder ...[71]

SAS Captain Barry Petersen, serving in the early years of the Vietnam War, recalled Ngoc, an orphan who made his living by polishing shoes, one evening entering a bar packed with Vietnamese and American servicemen. He had a grenade in each hand with the pins removed, and made his way to the centre of the dance floor, where he let them off. The blast killed many, including a local bar girl. Petersen pondered: ' … surely he was too young to have a sufficiently strong political ideology to voluntarily carry out such a deed'.[72]

Lance Corporal Paul Hernandez was in a position which was regularly attacked by VC at night. The US force eventually noticed that they were always hit following the visit of a local woman, who sold them Cokes and then sat with them at their day haven until dark. Then she left, and they would be attacked a little while later – the location having been transmitted to the enemy. 'Well, needless to say, she was done away with. Not a very pretty sight, I can assure you.'[73] Similarly, Infantryman Charles Gadd, serving with the 101st Airborne, was part of a detachment that eventually figured out how they were accurately mortared every evening: a 'buffalo boy' tended his animals nearby through the day, and every evening left the US soldiers to report their position to the local VC. One night they captured him, and their Kit Carson scout questioned him, only to learn that his family would be endangered if he did not do this. The boy was kept overnight – and for the first time, the detachment was not mortared.[74]

Verifying the target

The Allied forces in Vietnam took care from the outset to engage the right targets, but confusion was quick and probably inevitable. Marine Officer Philip Caputo noted that they were instructed in early 1965, following an incident in which a civilian was shot due to mis-identification, that no fire was to be directed against Vietnamese unless they were running, a direction which left the soldiers confused. Upon discussion, this was interpreted as ' … if he's dead and Vietnamese, he's VC'.[75]

Lieutenant Donovan remembered the aftermath of the My Lai massacre, with warnings that:

> We were to take no chance that Vietnamese civilians would be endangered. The colonel knew he was asking the impossible, but I don't think that was even the point. He wanted to cover his ass … in a guerilla war there is no such thing as being one hundred percent sure about anything. The only way to make certain that a group of men passing by in the dark were really Viet Cong was to go up and ask them. We dammed sure weren't going to be doing that.[76]

Medic David Ross noted that the VC was actually 'the farmer you waved to from your jeep in the day who would be the guy with the gun out looking for you at night'. He painted a picture of these soldiers coming out of their civilian homes at night, getting together to 'drop a few mortar rounds and go home and call it a night.'[77]

Determining whether a building from where a soldier has been fired upon contains legitimate targets can be most difficult, as these photographs show. Soldiers of the US 55th Armored Infantry Battalion and a tank of the 22nd Tank Battalion move through a smoke filled street in Wernberg, Germany, 1945. NNSP 111-SC-205298

An unnamed soldier asserted that during the Tet Offensive, when he was involved in street fighting, it was customary – if you took fire from a house – to storm it, and usually find that any weapons used were hidden inside double walls. If they found them, the soldier said, it was customary to shoot the people in the house.[78] Another combat mission assaulted houses from where a US patrol had received fire in the unusual form of crossbow bolts. They fired through the walls of the huts, but only found dead and wounded women and children when they entered, so they presumed the VC combatants had escaped.[79] They evacuated one wounded child.

In this chapter, we have established that civilians in a combat zone are in an extremely dangerous position. If there is a possibility or a precedent of those civilians becoming combatants, their positions are more dangerous still. Similarly, for his part, the soldier and his comrades are placed in a situation that is often more hazardous physically, legally and ethically.

'16
Targeting civilians for military necessity

Die SS: das sind keine Leute mehr. (The SS aren't human).

Captured German soldiers' comments on the SS's habit of targeting civilians.

Targeting civilians in World War II

After World War I, the field of battle spread to include what the German General von Ludendorff called 'total war'. This meant that, while von Clausewitz saw war as an extension of politics, Ludendorff argued for war to be total: the political had to be subordinated to the military. War was to be waged politically, economically, culturally and with propaganda, and all society should become a war machine. This meant that war spread to include strikes against identified civilian targets, including strategic bombing, and – in the ultimate extension of that – with atomic weapons against civilian cities. In such a war as this, civilians become caught up in the desperate struggle of one society against another, both struggling to survive. In such combat, general strikes against civilians are the norm. And so the Zeppelin raids against London in World War I became the attacks by V1 and V2 rockets in World War II; strategic bombing raids by thousands of aircraft over Germany became, as mentioned, the atomic strikes of 1945. Germane to this work's overall themes is that, as this new reality sinks home, the perpetrators of war become more savage. As previously discussed, Bomber Harris becomes a national hero, while people like Curtis Le May, who planned the air attacks on Japan, ponder the oddities of such lethality:

> Killing Japanese didn't bother me very much at the time … I suppose if I had lost the war, I would have been tried as a war criminal … every soldier thinks something of the moral aspects of what he is doing. But all war is immoral and if you let that bother you, you're not a good soldier.[1]

Sometimes civilians are targeted for military necessity to cause panic and a general breakdown of civilian infrastructure, which can aid the enemy. During the retreat in France in 1940, British gunner William Harding saw German aircraft diving and strafing civilians on the packed roads.[2] Cam Bennett was part of the Australian force landing in Greece in World War II. He witnessed Greek civilians – old men and women, and children – being low-level bombed by the German Air Force, in an attempt 'to inflict casualties, to create panic, to do as much harm as possible against those who could not hit back, so that the will to resist would be shattered'.[3] Australian Infantryman Roland Griffiths-Marsh was also there, and indeed took prisoner a downed Stuka pilot, who discussed the practice with him. The Germans, he was told, justified it on the grounds that it led to panic and a rapid disintegration of the will to fight on the other side, thus shortening the war.[4]

The town of Caen's civilian infrastructure was targeted after D-Day to prevent it being used by the Germans. Leaflets were dropped by aircraft, warning that the railway station, electrical depot and other centres would be attacked. The buildings would be blown into the streets to delay German tank movements. But many civilians had nowhere to go, and were killed as a result. In a well-known incident, infantry operations were conducted between the opposing sides with the escaped residents of a local lunatic asylum wandering between the soldiers. The retreating German tanks were targeted on the roads by RAF Spitfires and, inevitably, civilians on the roads were also hit. [5] What became known as 'collateral damage' in later years is simply a spill-over effect: unfortunate but inevitable. When the German forces in World War II called on the Dutch to surrender Rotterdam and no surrender was forthcoming, the German Air Force attacked the city, bringing the charge that 30,000 civilians had been killed; in fact, the number was under 1000. Even so, despite care being taken to avoid unnecessary bloodshed, civilian loss of life was inevitable.[6] The nature of much of the weaponry used does not allow for too much discrimination in targeting. As one World War II soldier put it: 'When you're an artillery man and you help to fire shells – at that time I guess at nine or ten miles away – you're not really conscious of what destruction you're creating.' This soldier also mused that warfare was perhaps more civilised in older times, when the firepower wasn't available to kill so indiscriminately: 'Many soldiers, particularly artillerymen and fliers, had to kill innocent women and children – non-combatants. Seems to me in a moral sense there's been a great deterioration in modern war.'[7]

Fired upon by civilians? Infantrymen of the US 255th Infantry Regiment move down a street in Waldenburg to hunt out the enemy after a raid. NNSP 111-SC-205778

Jacques Raboud saw German aircraft, in 1940, strafing a train full of retreating civilians and, three days later, Italian aircraft shooting up civilians on the road.[8] But not all civilians killed were the result of deliberate targeting of non-combatants. In the last months of the war, with the Luftwaffe largely banished from the skies, Allied fighters roamed above the roads of Europe, looking for targets. Anything that moved could be shot up, noted Typhoon pilot Richard Hough, as only the military had petrol. But sometimes military units were deliberately placed amid civilian columns, so 'of course we killed civilians – we couldn't help it', said Hough.[9]

Civilians can be targeted for information. Incoming Japanese forces, landing to strengthen their presence on Guadalcanal, found the Chief of Police, Jacob Vouza, and demanded information about where the American forces' strong points were. He refused to tell them, so they tied him to a tree and bayoneted him until they thought he was dead. But Vouza was later able to release himself and crawl 5 km to the American positions – and, quite understandably, he joined the Marines.[10]

This situation shows there is little time to ensure a moving person in the wreckage is not a civilian: one of the most dangerous operations for infantry – house to house fighting with all of the risks of surprise and desperate action. In such situations two shots to make sure is the norm. (Italy, 1944). AWM 128656

Less excusable are actions carried out against civilians for no apparent reason. Max Hastings has noted the ferocity and vindictiveness of the Russian campaign against Germany in the final years of World War II. The advancing Russians exacted a terrible revenge for the German savagery during their invasion of the previous years: 'When the Russian troops caught up with the refugees, they would rake the columns with artillery and machine-guns. This owed nothing to military necessity, everything to vengeance.'[11] Guy Sajer, part of the fleeing but still-fighting Wehrmacht, noted that the Russians, ' … when they were not fighting our troops, pushed the tide of civilians along in front of them, firing at them and driving tanks through the terrified mob.'[12]

Similar behaviour occurred in campaigns such as the Battle of the Bulge, where German forces were attempting to go on the offensive against the Allies. On 18 December 1944, the killing of civilians by the German Army began in isolated hamlets in Belgium: 138 people were executed, probably in the main by SS troops.[13] No reasons were identified for the slayings, but it might be surmised that these soldiers – generally more vindictive than regular German soldiers – were taking 'reprisals'. Their target was the villagers who, until comparatively recently, had been under German rule, and who – in the eyes of the SS – might not have shown sufficient hostility to their new occupiers, the Allies. US battle surgeon Brendan Phibbs, who spoke German, noted that many captured soldiers commented to him, in what was a popular slogan of the time: '*Die SS: das sind keine Leute mehr.*' ('The SS aren't human.')[14] Revenge for a sniper firing at them was the apparent reason for a company of soldiers of the Der Fuhrer Regiment of the Waffen-SS, led by Sturmbannfuhrer Dickmann, killing 642 men, women and children at Oradour-sur-Glane in 1944.[15]

In the village of Bande on 24 December 1944, 32 civilian men were executed by soldiers of the SD – the *Sicherheitsdienst*, or Security Police of the SS. The villagers there recalled that the departing Germans had, back in September, made threats of 'We'll be back' as they were driven out by the advancing Allied forces.[16] Then again, reprisals were taken against Nazi civilian leaders at the end of the war by those they had subjugated – and not just aggrieved villagers, but soldiers, too. A detachment of the 101st Airborne were detailed off after hostilities had ended to find a local Nazi who had bossed several slave labour camps – and eliminate him. The soldiers did as they were told: they interrogated the civilian until they were sure they had the right man, and then prepared to shoot him. One soldier refused to participate, but the Nazi leader was executed just the same.[17] It would be interesting to see how this might have been treated in a courtroom …

In the final days of taking Okinawa, the American forces used loudspeakers to broadcast calls, in Japanese, to surrender, and they leafleted the areas where the enemy was still holed up. Some of the civilians on the island began to surrender, but unfortunately this meant they were targeted by Japanese soldiers –

presumably, as one American commented wryly, 'to save them from a fate worse than death': surrendering to the enemy. Estimates as to how many civilians died on Okinawa range from 75,000 to 140,000.[18]

Targeting civilians in the Vietnam War

It is worth noting that the targeting of civilians in the Vietnam War was not confined to the US Army. The Vietcong routinely executed many of the Vietnamese who they suspected of collaborating with their enemy. Lieutenant McDonough's patrol found an old woman who had been severely tortured and then shot, with a note left attached to her body. It read:

> Tuan Cao Ky has been found guilty by the People's Court of aiding the American imperialists in their suppression of the Vietnamese people. As an enemy of the people, she had been made to pay for her crimes. This is the justice that will be brought to all who consort with the Americans and aid them in the villainous suppression of our land.[19]

It should be noted here – boarding the boat of morality for just a moment – that it was never the **policy** of the US Forces and its allies to target civilians, whereas it seems it was indeed the policy of the NVA and the Vietcong. Such a distinction makes a world of difference. McDonough was in his own guarded position when a nearby village was targeted by the VC, who had ' … penetrated the eastern end of the village and were moving from thatch hut to thatch hut, throwing satchel charges inside and shooting anything that moved'.[20] On another occasion, the VC attacked one of their own villages because a US platoon was quartered there, and McDonough concluded: ' … we had fought a limited military war with constrained objectives; the enemy had fought a total political war with no preordained restrictions. We were doomed from the outset.'[21] US helicopter pilot Robert Mason's Huey took fire from what looked like a group of civilians. Upon examination, it proved to be a machine-gun firing from within a crowd of villagers. The helicopter's gunners tried to fire back near the group to make them run, but when they didn't – terrified they would be targeted by the machine-gunner, it was thought later – the helicopter narrowed its fire to target the gunner, causing many civilian casualties in the process.[22]

Bruce Lawlor, a case officer with the CIA for two years in the early 1970s, agreed, and thought that the American strategy was generally one of 'Expose yourself and draw fire'. He saw this as guaranteeing failure, because it gave the enemy the initiative and allowed them to manipulate the situation so that there would be 'more body bags leaving', which would raise political pressure on the US.[23] Rifleman Jonathen Polansky was with the 101st Airborne from November 1968 for a year. He was stationed near the village of Lang Co, on the Gulf of Tonkin. The village was eventually razed, he says, ' ... by VC destruction ... completely burned because all the people were American sympathisers'.[24]

The war produced much bitterness for the soldiers of America and its allies upon return to their own country. William Van Zanten thought the enemy ' ... indescribably barbaric, cruel and devastating, to their own people, and their neighbours. We were branded "baby killers". I was called that by anti-war activists on the campus of Arizona State University the first day I arrived ... I never saw one of our guys kill a baby. I saw the North Vietnamese do it day in and day out ... '[25] Marine Johnnie Clark noted with bitterness that 'Jane Fonda was telling the world we kill women and kids. Do you think for one second that rich witch mentioned the thousands of civilians the NVA butchered in Hue.'[26] Marine Officer Nicholas Warr commented bitterly that MACV (Military Assistance Command, Vietnam) reports indicated that as many as 3000 civilians had been killed by the NVA and buried in mass graves in that battle.[27]

International conventions meant little to the North, and this disadvantaged the forces fighting for the South. Ian Kemp, a British soldier who fought with the 101st Airborne, flew in medical-evacuation helicopters for some time. He noted that, out of 11 missions, they received hits on eight: ' ... our Red Cross markings appeared positively to attract Vietcong fire ... '[28] Charles Gadd saw a red-crossed helicopter hit by a mortar shell while taking out wounded. As the crippled aircraft was trying to land, it was targeted with several more rounds.[29] Artillery Observer, Second Lieutenant Cherokee Paul McDonald witnessed a targeted attack on a bus filled with Vietnamese civilians. The buried shell was detonated by a Vietcong observer, who chose the bus over any military target. Questioned by one of his men as to why, McDonald surmised that it was to show the population that the VC controlled the road.[30] In the final invasion of Saigon, Navy Hospital Corpsman Stephen Klinkhammer saw the incoming VC and NVA forces 'dropping the rockets right into the crowds of fleeing people' and, at one point, hitting a C-130 plane full of people upon take-off.[31]

Lieutenant David Donovan was embedded in a Vietnamese province to protect local villagers and assist their military efforts to resist the North Vietnamese Army. (The teams were given the designation 'MAT' – Military Assistance Team – and were commanded by MACV.) He dealt with one incident where scores of injured children were assisted by the villagers and the Army personnel – they had been targeted by the local Vietcong in reprisals. 'On two later occasions the local Cong unit booby-trapped schools in my district. There was no question that it was done intentionally.'[32] Infantryman Charles Gadd was present when their Kit Carson scout translated a story from a group of distressed villagers. They had been visited by some North Vietnamese soldiers, who had berated them for the village's lack of support. The oldest man and the youngest baby were picked and made to walk into a field, where the soldiers then shot them down. The same thing would happen every day from then on if support was not forthcoming.[33] First Lieutenant James Simmen came up with an interesting (illegal but effective) solution to booby traps. He wrote in a letter to his brother that, 'I'd always have civilians walk point for me. They ranged from 14-year-olds to men with canes, but they never hit a booby trap … '[34]

It was common for a Vietcong group to kill two village chiefs ; the third, noted US Army combat adviser Martin Dockery, was 'either sympathetic … or so petrified that he would do what they wanted'. Having captured the wives of four South Vietnamese farmers who were gathering wood, the local Vietcong turned up outside a fort where an ARVN patrol was quartered, and threatened to kill them unless their husbands joined them. Three did, but the fourth – a Catholic – said he could not. His wife was tortured and killed, and he was set free to spread the tale.[35]

The confused and amorphous nature of the target changed many of the soldiers fighting for the South into quick and vehement haters of the North, and doubtless led to them breaking the rules. Second Lieutenant Robert C. Ransom Jr. described his feelings about the Vietnamese in a letter home in 1968. In one month, his company lost four men killed and 30 wounded, without sighting a single enemy soldier. 'I've developed hate for the Vietnamese,' he wrote, because they would sell drinks to the soldiers, and then tell the VC ' … how many we are, where our positions are, and where the leaders position themselves … I felt like turning my machine-guns on the village to kill every man, woman and child in it.'[36] Infantryman Charles Gadd witnessed a sergeant of the 101st Airborne interrogate a mentally-retarded Vietnamese man found in a village. Gadd noted that 'past experience had taught us to stay out of another GI's business when he was venting his anger and frustrations.' But this time the matter went further: the sergeant got nowhere, and eventually fired his rifle on automatic at the Vietnamese. Gadd thought incidents like this were rare, but of note is the lack of reference to whether the matter went further officially.[37]

Binh Tuy Province, Vietnam, 1965. Allied soldiers close in on a known Viet Cong house. The raid netted two Viet Cong: the leader of the local women's auxiliary responsible for making booby traps, and the head of the local Viet Cong cadre. Both Viet Cong were later identified by local villagers. AWM SHA/65/0302/VN

Marine Jack Broz was present when the South Vietnamese forces attacked a village suspected of 'being VC'. They broke down a door, beat up two of the locals, and then there was a general firing of weapons, in which one American joined. Then the South's forces killed a woman coming out of a hut with machine-gun fire, fired a LAW (a light anti-tank weapon) at a hut, then finished by burning down the entire village and wounding many of the other villagers.[38]

Then again, it is not hard to understand why a Vietnamese village aided the VC. Marine Officer Nicholas Warr understood the frustration and rage of his own troops as they took casualties to mines that the villagers doubtless knew about, but he also realised that ' … these people either had to help the enemy or at least look the other way, or they were dead.'[39]

As Major HG Duncan saw it:

> ... the majority of Vietnamese would not cooperate with us by telling
> where the VC were located and when they had last been in the village.
> We failed to realise that the rural Vietnamese were also victims of the
> VC, and the VC were much more pointed in their dealings with them.
> They threatened to kill any village chief or villager who cooperated with
> the Americans, and they often punctuated their demands by inflicting
> mayhem.[40]

Often villagers knew of VC activity and chose not to say anything to the
foreign forces. Marine Art Falco remembers following some Vietnamese out of
the village one morning to work the fields; he noticed that they stepped off the
dike at a certain point and then back onto it a little later. There was a booby-
trapped 105-mm round there. He thought, however, that 'I can't blame them.
If they'd told us, they would've had to deal with the VC. By not telling us, they
had to deal with us. And we were the better choice.'[41]

Sometimes the violence was casual, and casually accepted:

> ... a little old man, who only wanted to avoid trouble, jumped on his
> bike and pedalled furiously away. The code states: Don't flee unless you
> wicked! Speedy, a platoon leader, yelled at him to stop. He pedalled faster,
> but not fast enough to outrun Speedy's bullet ... After the death of Lt.
> Artman ... after what I had been through, I wanted the old man to die,
> and everyone in the hamlet with him ... [42]

In March 1968, Marine Jeff Kelly's executive officer (XO) had problems with
local villagers, who were often deliberately moving into a free-fire zone to get to
a hill and gather wild vegetables and fruits from it. They had been warned several
times not to do this, and eventually, in frustration one day when the villagers
moved across the zone, the XO ordered white-phosphorous rounds to be fired in
front of them – and again when they chose a different route. When the villagers
would not withdraw, the XO ordered four rounds of high explosive to be fired
from the unit's mortars; they killed probably two and wounded several, and
the survivors ' ... limped home'.[43] US troops could often be casually cruel to
the South Vietnamese. Jeff Kelly recalled that in the trucks making runs along
roads in the South, some drivers made a habit of driving at high speed through
puddles, to splash muddy water over any nearby Vietnamese. Kelly remembered
looking into the face of the daughter of a woman who his truck had done

that – her look 'pierced the callus that had grown on my heart'. One of Kelly's friends commented: 'If she wasn't VC before, she is now', and Kelly vehemently agreed.[44] Journalist Peter Scholl-Latour thought that the US recreation areas in Saigon were a 'Sodom and Gomorrah set up by the descendents of the pious Pilgrim Fathers' – enough to make any Vietnamese, Communist or not, become anti-American.[45]

It is worth noting the activities of the International War Crimes Tribunal in the Vietnam War. Opening in May 1967, it examined reported crimes from Vietnam, but it examined possible crimes from only one side: the South (and its Western allies).[46] The media reports of the tribunal's findings, and the lack of reports about the other side's actions, have doubtless helped create the impression that war crimes were one-sided. It is obvious that they were not. Further, as author Guenter Lewy points out, it is equally clear that 'most soldiers' did not commit war crimes. Nevertheless, there was casual killing. Military surgeon Major Gordon Livingston's account is a most graphic example:

> An example of the distinction drawn between American and Vietnamese life, for example, just before I joined the unit … helicopter pilots flying what was euphemistically described as a low-level reconnaissance ran down and killed with his helicopter skids 2 Vietnamese women who were riding bicycles on the roads, to give some idea of how low-level that reconnaissance was. He was temporarily grounded and I had the opportunity to speak with him about that as the surgeon, and there was complete absence of any feeling other than regret that he was not drawing his flight pay, and interesting in terms of the official action taken was the fact that he was totally exonerated by a board of inquiry and returned to active flight duty … It was routine for the pilots flying north across the Danang River, as the phrase goes, to 'flat hat' the Vietnamese who were pulling their sampans along the river.[47]

We have seen that the targeting of civilians ranges across a spectrum in warfare. Some civilians are legitimate targets by their actions. Others are targets by their locations; they are mixed in with troops and are targeted by nature of the inaccuracy of weapons. Others still are targets of a dubious ethical and legal nature because of their actions as collaborators. Whatever the situation, the difficulties for tactical warriors are immense.

17

Is that village friendly?

> *… the VC only had to press the detonator and*
> *then blend in with the civilians.*
>
> **Marine Philip Caputo, commenting on his Vietnam experience.**

The situation in a scenario like Vietnam, or any other where civilians are enmeshed in the picture, is almost impossible for soldiers. As one writer put it:

> You approach a village and receive rifle fire. You take casualties. You know that air [strikes] and art[iller]y can wipe out the village. You also know there are women and children in the village. What do you do? There was no solid answer, and no rule in the book to go by. Most infantry officers, if asked about it, would reply that their first duty was to the safety of the men under their command.[1]

Many villages would therefore be targeted by artillery fire …

Marine Tom Harvey noted, on one of his first patrols, being told to 'shoot anything that moved' and, a while later, seeing a 'Vietnamese man in black trousers, a white shirt, and a khaki rain hat, riding a bike … I hesitated to shoot him because he wasn't a soldier.' A little while later, they took some fire from the area he'd gone into, and two members of the patrol were hit.[2]

And indeed, what was one to do about civilians aiding the enemy? Lieutenant McDonough noticed[3] that when a patrol went out, a light would go on in a certain hut in a nearby village. If the patrol went north, a local radio, playing loudly, would be tuned to a certain station. A nearby monastery would see these signals, and broadcast, by its own light and sound, telltale signals from its tower. What to do? McDonough had finally had enough of this: he had his men silence all broadcasts, and ambush the VC who came to investigate the failure of their intelligence source. Correspondent Michael Herr talked to one soldier who was on his second tour: in his first they had destroyed villages; in his second, they had orders not to return fire if they received it from inside a village – symptomatic of the military authorities trying to deal with the problem.[4]

Rifleman John Muir saw a search carried out in a village where there was no-one left but a family of four, who declared that everyone else had gone away. However, they had been cooking rice – enough for 50 people. The patrol concluded they were preparing food for the VC, burnt their house down, and sent the four off to a re-location camp.[5]

Lieutenant David Donovan noted that, eventually, 'We learned to trust no one, not even children … We wore our weapons constantly, even to a friend's house. We never went anywhere alone …'[6]

The destruction of a village could be part of an attempt to win a particular battle. Lieutenant Alfred S. Bradford related:

He ran to the chopper. The chopper rose. The AKs fired. The first platoon disengaged and swept back through the village, bombing all suspect hootches (and all hootches were suspect). Smoke billowed into the sky.

'CO's on the horn,' the RTO said.

We could all hear his voice through the handset.

'Who fired those hootches? I ordered you not to set fire to any hootches. Who did it? I want his name. I want the burning stopped. Do you read me? Over.'

Another hootch went up.

'Uh, Six, be advised,' Captain Ervin said, 'the fire was set by tracers coming from inside the hootches. Over.'

'I don't care … uh … inside? Over.'

'Affirmative.'

'Out.'[7]

Inexperience and fear led tactical leaders to sometimes use more force than necessary. Captain Greg Hayward noted an incident in November 1968 where a village was targeted because of movement at night. He questioned the platoon leader, who had not received any incoming fire, but he'd called in a white-phosphorous mortar round because he'd seen movement in the village. The village burnt down. As Hayward put it, 'People get up out of their homes at night just to go to the bathroom.' He reported it for administrative action, but nothing was done.[8]

About to encounter civilians – or Vietcong without uniforms? In Vietnam 1966, American helicopters fly overhead after landing Australian troops. The soldiers are moving through paddy fields during a search and destroy operation. Despite lacking the upper hand in technology, the North Vietnamese won this difficult war. AWM SHA/66/0007/VN

Revenge or frustration might cause a village to be shot at. Philip Caputo's Marine platoon took nine casualties from a homemade mine, which was detonated by wire from a nearby village: ' ... the VC only had to press the detonator and then blend in with the civilians, if indeed there were any true civilians in the village'. They fired four white-phosphorous rockets into the village in retaliation.[9] Frustrated and probably psychologically disturbed, one of Caputo's fellow officers was interrogating a Vietnamese woman in the field when she spat some betel-nut juice – by accident – on him. He took out his pistol and shot her through the chest, then told the Marine corpsman to tend to her.[10]

The Calley massacre

US Army Second Lieutenant William Calley, who was held responsible for the My Lai massacre, told of his experience in his own words after his trial. The account is significant.

Calley's troops were sniped at from Vietnamese villages, but they hardly made any contact with the enemy. They searched hamlets, found friendly villagers, but then found Vietcong flags. Calley was constantly asked what his unit's body count[1] was. They took reprisals for being sniped at, burning villages down. He interrogated civilians for the locations of the VC, and got nowhere.

Calley took a VC prisoner and sent him to the military police (MPs), who got nothing out of him. Calley took the same man prisoner again three weeks later. He queried this with the MPs. 'So why didn't you go and shoot him? I can't,' an MP said. 'I'm at headquarters with the Geneva people on me.'[11] The MP complained about having to house and feed prisoners, and accept their word that they were not VC. He finished up by advising Calley to shoot his prisoners if he didn't want to see them released.

This frustration was also commented upon by Second Lieutenant Robert Ransom Jr, an infantry platoon commander in Vietnam. He noted that:

> … more than once we have captured or killed people with weapons whom we recognized as one of those smiling faces we had picked up and released earlier. It's maddening because we know damn well that they're dinks but we can't do anything to them until we catch them with a weapon or actually shooting at us.[12]

Despite these sorts of difficult situations for himself and his men, Calley

---

1 A much-criticised method of assessing a combat unit's effectiveness in Vietnam. Often portrayed as prone to exaggeration or lying to show a unit's performance to be better than it was, the body-count methodology, as carried out in 1965, is outlined in detail in Philip Caputo's *A Rumor of War*, from which account it seems to have been carefully carried out in terms of accuracy.

did not execute civilians or 'suspected VC' in the field. He says, however, that: 'Everyone said eliminate them. I never met someone who didn't say it.' Then his troops lost a squad leader to a booby trap set in a village, killed an injured Vietnamese woman in reprisal, and then planned their response. According to the court-martial record, (Calley's superior) Captain Medina told the preliminary briefing that the women and children would be out of the hamlet, and all they could expect to encounter would be the opposition. The soldiers were to explode brick homes, set fire to thatch homes, shoot livestock, poison wells, and destroy the enemy. The soldiers, approximately 75 in number, would be supported in their assault by helicopter gunships.

Medina later said that he did not give any instructions as to what to do with the women and children in the village. Some soldiers agreed with that recollection; others thought that he had ordered them to kill every person in the village. It does seem that Medina intentionally gave the impression that everyone in My Lai would be their enemy.[13] As we have seen, women, children and old people in Vietnam sometimes could be just that.

On 16 March 1968, when landing from helicopters, the troops took ground fire. They began killing civilians; at first one by one in different ways, and in different areas; then more, and then many together in a ravine. Several soldiers testified that they killed the civilians: in one case, the witness said he regarded them as Vietcong, and added during testimony that he still did.[14] Calley was in tactical command on the spot, and it seems he took part in the shooting of around 500 civilians, executed by single shots and bursts of automatic gunfire. By lunchtime, there was no-one left alive.

With the operation over, Calley and his men returned to normal operations. In Calley's account, there was an increasingly casual attitude towards death, and the general feeling was to

> ... kill every man, woman and child in South Vietnam. GIs said to use napalm, or low-yield atomic bombs ... or to line up along the China Sea and say, 'Prepare to shake hands with your ancestors. We are rolling through' ... A GI became a quick philosopher and would say, 'God, if I go and kill everyone here, I could leave'.[15]

Some time later, after two of the men present had complained about the actions, Calley was transported back to the United States and tried. He was found guilty, and served a period – less than three years – in an Army prison, and was then released. He is still alive, and works in his father's jewellry business.

During and after the trial, he received considerable support from around America, which included letters from numerous veterans. This was for a variety of reasons: perhaps partly because, in Richard Holmes's words, with television beaming the conflict into lounge-rooms, 'War has become moving wallpaper, and its familiar pattern no longer horrifies us'[16]; but also because, in summing up many arguments, such procedures were acknowledged as being the norm. In *His Own Story*, Calley stated that he had received around 5000 letters during the period of his trial, and he listed some of the statements that recounted events similar to the massacre:

I served in Korea from June 1953 to August 1954. I heard of many similar incidents.

I'm a retired marine. I spent twenty years in the service of God and Country. I was in two operations in Korea where women and children were killed.

In 1943, 1944, 1945, and 1946 I was a first lieutenant with 45th Infantry Division. I was witness to many incidents similar to the one you're being held for.

I served in combat in the German war. My fellow soldiers and I did on occasion kill enemy soldiers, civilians and children. Marquess of Queensbury rules do not prevail in war.

During my duty in Africa we were under orders to shoot the Arabs to keep them from taking our clothes.

I was given the order to seal a cave where a mother and her eleven or twelve children were holed up. This took place in 1944 on the island of Ie Shima.

On Okinawa, I saw men throw grenades on old men and women, figuring what the hell – they're the enemy ...

Many years ago I had a platoon, and we went through the villages as you and your people had to.[17]

Calley recounted that he was amazed that he had been charged, when it was common practice to target civilians:

I couldn't understand it. An investigation of Mylai. Why not Operation

Golden Fleece? Or Operation Norfolk? Or Operation Dragon Valley? Or why not Saigon itself? We had killed hundreds of men, women and children there in February and March, 1968: in Tet … simply read it in *Stars and Stripes*. Or *The New York Times*.[18]

His allegation that such massacres were carried out is supported by others. Cherokee Paul McDonald said of his Vietnam experience: 'Both sides had their My Lais – ours were rare and highly publicized, theirs were continuous throughout the war and after and largely dismissed, ignored, defended, or rationalised by brave intellectuals.'[19]

Action against civilians. Commander ACC Miers, VC DSO, Royal Navy, displaying a replica of his "skull and crossbones" pennant to newspaper men during a conference. The pennant commemorates the exploits of the Royal Navy submarine HMS Torbay in the Mediterranean. AWM 140175

David Hackworth, who commanded Tiger Force – although not in the period investigated by *The Toledo Blade* – supported this scenario:

'Vietnam was an atrocity from the get-go,' Hackworth said in a recent telephone interview. 'It was that kind of war, a frontless war of great frustration. It was out of hand very early. There were hundreds of My Lais. You got your card punched by the numbers of bodies you counted.[20]

The US Army today refers to these incidents as 'misconduct stress behaviour' and notes, without any irony, that: ' ... overstressed human beings with loaded weapons are inherently dangerous'.[21] Its Handbook gives examples of such frustration in the field, and states:

> Commission of murder and other atrocities against noncombatants must be reported as a war crime and punished if responsibility is established. This must be done even though we may pity the overstressed soldier as well as the victims.

A central point of this work though is that if infantry are placed in a situation where civilians may be identified as combatants, then those soldiers will doubtless make mistakes and kill civilians who are not combatants. The politicians – and, behind them, the people – who make the decisions to send warriors into such situations need to accept their part of this responsibility. The worst consequences of these situations may be seen below.

Tiger Force

Tiger Force was a small unit of around 45 men of the 101st Airborne Division who were recruited for their abilities and who, by some accounts, were particularly savage in their treatment of the enemy during the Vietnam War in 1967. In 2003, *The Toledo Blade*, an American newspaper, published a four-part account of their actions, and accused them of killing many civilians.

William Doyle, a former Tiger Force sergeant now living in Missouri, said he killed so many civilians he lost count:

> 'We were living day to day. We didn't expect to live. Nobody out there with any brains expected to live,' he said in a recent interview. 'So you did any goddamn thing you felt like doing – especially to stay alive. The way to live is to kill because you don't have to worry about anybody who's dead.'

The findings of the newspaper's four-part report included the following:

- On 28 July 1967, four farmers were killed, with four members of the force saying later: 'We knew the farmers were not armed to begin with, but we shot them anyway.'

- In June, an elderly man in black robes, believed to be a Buddhist monk, was shot to death after he complained to soldiers about the treatment of villagers. A grenade was placed on his body to disguise him as an enemy soldier ...

- A soldier shot and killed a 15-year-old boy near the village of Duc Pho. He later told soldiers he shot the youth because he wanted his tennis shoes.

- The shooting death on July 23 of an elderly carpenter.

- Two partially blind men found wandering in a valley were escorted to a bend in the Song Ve River and shot to death.

- Two villagers, one of them a teenager, were executed because they were not in relocation camps.

- To cover up the shootings, platoon leaders began counting dead civilians as enemy soldiers.

- For 10 days beginning 11 November, entries show that platoon members claimed to have killed a total of 49 Vietcong. But no weapons were found in 46 deaths, the records show.

- A 13-year-old girl's throat was slashed after she had been sexually assaulted.

- A young mother was shot to death after soldiers torched her hut.

- An unarmed teenager was shot in the back after a platoon sergeant ordered the youth to leave a village.

- A baby was decapitated so that a soldier could remove a necklace.

- A grenade attack was mounted against villagers in bunkers.

- Tiger Force reported its 327th kill on 19 November, to match its official force number.

- Two elderly men were killed during an unprovoked attack on a hamlet near Tam Ky. One was beheaded, and the other, who was wounded, was shot by the platoon medic in a 'mercy killing'.

- An elderly man was shot to death by a soldier wanting to test a new 38-calibre handgun.

- Numerous villagers were shot by Tiger Force members in a hamlet near Chu Lai. The villagers were waving leaflets at the troops, asking to be relocated, but when enemy forces fired on the soldiers from another direction, the troops opened fire on everyone.[22]

Former Tiger Force platoon sergeant William Doyle said: 'If you wanted to pull the trigger, you pulled the trigger. If you wanted to burn a village down, you burned it down. You [did] whatever you wanted to do. Who's going to say anything to you?'[23]

Other villages targeted

Was My Lai the first such massacre? Once the news began to come out, an Associated Press reporter told of an incident he had witnessed three years previously, when an American Marine unit went into a village 'south of Da Nang in 1965' and a squad killed a group 'hiding in a civilian air raid shelter'.[24]

An investigating team looking into My Lai found evidence of a 'second massacre' on the same day, 16 March 1968, apparently perpetrated by members of Bravo Company, 4th Battalion, 3rd Infantry, 3 km to the east of My Lai. In 1970, an infantry officer, Captain Thomas K Willingham, was charged with 'either killing or ordering' the killing of up to 20 Vietnamese,[25] although Lewy says between '80 and 90' were killed. These charges were dismissed before trial.[26]

The South Korean Army had forces in Vietnam, and it seemed they took a tough line with villages suspected of sheltering the enemy. This caused them to be much disliked by the Vietnamese:

The Korean Marines wiped out a hamlet just south of us called Phong Nhi, after they took some sniper fire from the hamlet. This was near our sister CAP Delta-2. The villagers in our area hated the Koreans.[27]

This is probably the village referred to in this report:

On the morning of February 12, 1968, 74 women, children and elderly citizens from the villages of Phong Nhut, Phong Nhi, and Giap Ba of Dien Ban District in Central Vietnam were rounded up and massacred by South Korean soldiers. It was the third civilian massacre by South Korean troops in the northern villages of Quang Nam Province during the Vietnam War. The massacres were all witnessed and reported by foreign and Korean journalists.[28]

Lewy refers to the Phong Nhi incident, and says that 'more than 80 civilians' were killed.[29] Another civilian massacre was first reported in a Seoul newspaper in May 1999 – it was alleged that 1004 civilians were killed in the village of Binh Dinh in Central Vietnam during a six-week operation in 1966. A monument has apparently been erected there to mark the event.[30]

Marine Johnnie Clark referred to an incident he was involved in where the truck convoy he was travelling in had the lead truck blown up by a mine, with the driver losing both legs. The road was swept for mines every day, and the VC laid more every night. Clark noted that the nearby village knew about this, and that perhaps the Americans should have followed Korean practice: 'If they got ambushed or caught sniper rounds from a village in Vietnam, they levelled the village. But then, they were fighting a war, and we were fighting a police action.'[31]

Army Sergeant Richard Dow said that he participated in an operation which wiped out the village of Bau-Tri, around 250 km northeast of Saigon. After being told to leave the village by the chief, who they suspected of being VC, the patrol left and called in ' … napalm, mortar attacks, heavy artillery' and killed 'around four hundred' people.[32]

It is worth noting that the source of this account, and other footnoted examples, are disputed in part by some: for example, Mark Sheehan vigorously disputes the accounts' accuracy and veracity.[33] The account of Terry Whitmore, who says he took part in the destruction of a village, is also contested by Sheehan. Lewy, too, outlines the various movements, conferences, reports and the like which took place at the time, and notes the use of false witnesses, exaggerations, political motivation, lies and so on. It is therefore advisable to question reports from individuals, or at least to reserve judgement about their veracity.

The story of Lieutenant-Colonel Anthony B. Herbert is a case in point of how distortion got into the stories of atrocities. Herbert brought actions, 18 months after being relieved of his command in 1969, alleging the killing of prisoners and civilians, and failure to investigate this. Over the next years, his case was investigated and gradually fell apart: it was revealed to be unsubstantiated and driven by other factors.[34]

But that other villages were targeted and destroyed does seem, on the weight of the evidence, to be true. Harry Plimpton was present when a village was mortared after his patrol took fire from it and three soldiers were killed. His company commander used his mortar platoon to fire against it, and the village, which Plimpton estimated had 'five hundred people' living in it, was destroyed, with no survivors.[35]

Tim O'Brien was serving with Alpha Company of the 4th Battalion of the 20th Infantry when they encountered problems coming to grips with the enemy. Eventually, he recounts, they attacked a hamlet in which VC were taking shelter, and called in jet fighters and napalm.[36] On another occasion, they were supported by a troop of armoured personnel carriers when they were attacked with rocket-propelled grenades from a village in the 'Pinkville' area. Once again, aircraft and napalm were called in.[37]

Jimmy Roberson participated in an operation which killed 'around fifteen or twenty … old people, and a few women'. Afterwards, the village was levelled with bulldozers, ' … like it was never there. I mean, there was a big hole dug, and all these bodies were thrown in it and then, pst, we moved on.'[38]

One former Army sergeant described, in a Vietnam veterans' counselling session, how he was present when VC tunnels were found. An air strike was called in to destroy them, and then a group of local woodcutters, now suspected of being VC sympathisers, was rounded up and shot at by a squad of soldiers, killing many of them.[39]

Two Marines were convicted in 1970 and sentenced to jail terms for killing five women and 11 children in the village of Son Thang. No fewer than 160,000 citizens of Oklahoma signed a petition which was sent to the commandant of the Marine Corps, calling for their release.[40]

Although feelings of aggression towards the Vietnamese were very strong, and it was easy to 'turn villagers into VC', this was often resisted. Infantry Platoon Commander David Kibbey of the 7th Battalion of the Royal Australian Regiment recalled his men taking fire, with three killed and others wounded; his men were 'quite prepared to take revenge on this bloody town'. To counter this, he briefed his men, and then thought 'it would help purge us of the experience by actually going down the main street …', which they did without incident.[41]

US Senator John Kerry admitted to Dan Rather on CBS television[42] that he had led a platoon/squad into a Vietnamese village. He says they killed five men there, rather than take them prisoner, because that would have compromised their mission, which was to capture a local VC chief. The soldiers then took fire from a riverbank, and returned it, and then found they had killed 'twelve to fifteen' women and children. His story was countered, however, by a 62-year-old local woman, who claimed that Kerry had in fact killed five non-combatants – an old couple and three children – and then he and his squad had rounded up and killed the rest of the village, with her escaping by hiding in a bunker. Admittedly, the woman was probably VC herself; however, her story was backed up on camera by one of Kerry's squad, who agreed with her version.

Da Nang, Vietnam. 1965. Blindfolded Viet Cong captured by the Vietnamese Army sit in the rear section of a US Army truck inside a large hangar. Eventually – fighting an army with no uniforms, often returned to civilian life if proof of VC membership could not be made – the war saw hostilities boiling over into atrocities such as the My Lai massacre. AWM P01975.025

In a US House of Representatives investigation (popularly known as the 'Winter Soldier' cases), Daniel Barnes testified that his unit was engaged in burning down a village '15 miles south of Duc Pho' which had been attacked with mortars the previous night, when movement was spotted. The villagers

> put up a big fight about the burning down of their houses and things. Well, they came and they started, you know, grabbing to try to grab the torches away from us, and crying and yelling, you know? Trying to grab the torches. At 1st it was just pushing, just pushing them away, and then it got to be pushing a little harder with the rifles and it progressed. It got to be where a couple people got killed. I did not see the people being killed but there were 4-5 bodies laying on the ground and myself, I was involved in burning these vills ... We went into this vill and an old man was sitting there, he was inside and he was about 70-80, and he was dressed in white clothes. He was the only man in the vill that I saw and I went in with another guy and this other guy started tearing the things down off the wall and things and naturally the old man protested. Now this other guy pushed the old man away and shot him in the head.[43]

Soldier Daniel Notley testified to the House of Representatives investigation that he was present when a village by the name of Truoung Khanh, in Quang Ngai Province, was searched. Thirty villagers were killed: at first 10 women and children, and then another group of twenty. Notley was told to fire his 'canister' weapon at them; he fired at the ground instead, so others killed them.[44]

Marine Kenneth Campbell related an incident 'in 8-68 in Con Thien' when he had called in artillery – he was a forward artillery observer on a village where there was no enemy troop movement spotted, but rather civilians working in the fields. The rationale for the strike was that the villagers were probably feeding the VC. An estimated 30 people were killed.[45]

This is the nature of war, and trying to educate troops that it is not so, or that such actions are not to be taken, is pointless. These days, senior commanders will try and get things done by political means, if they are so directed. If the politicians tell them to observe the rules of engagement and ensure their troops cannot kill at will, then they will post soldiers on guard with unloaded weapons:

> Even though the members of the security detail on the [USS] *Cole* were at their posts on high alert – in an extremely dangerous port where they'd already been warned that a terrorist attack was highly probable – not one of their weapons had a round in the chamber ... The Rules of Engagement had stated that our weapons were to have no rounds in the chamber.[46]

> When rank rules, people say 'Yes Sir' when they should say 'No fucking way'. I wanted to instil a particular sort of insubordination, but don't get me wrong – when I told the men to do something, I wanted it done. But I also wanted an atmosphere where no one would be afraid to sound off and speak the truth.[47]

The consequences of placing such constraints on the soldier are manifold. First, the cost to the soldier is often his life. That may be self-evident, but it is notable that in many cases soldiers in the lower ranks are easily manipulated and coerced. If the soldier sees it as self-evident that taking the legal or ethical course may cost him his life, he will inevitably have doubts. Then, in addition, his friends point out that he would be foolish to follow that course – so he ends up killing a suspected enemy.

Second, what of the cost to the morale of troops forced into firing at targets which most people would identify, until they knew the reality, as non-combatants?

The troops are damned if they don't fire – as the suspected combatant may fire upon them at any time – and damned if they do fire – because the suspected enemy may indeed be a civilian.

Third, what of the long-term psychological effect on the troops? Forced into legal and ethical dilemmas, condemned at home if they kill civilian non-combatants, yet forced, in the field, to question every shot they fire … these are ideal conditions for producing high levels of stress both at the time and later.

As mentioned, if infantrymen are placed in a situation where civilians may be identified as combatants, then those soldiers will doubtless make mistakes and kill civilians who are not combatants. And if these soldiers are classically-trained infantry, it is difficult for them not to react in the way they have been trained: by pouring massive firepower into their target.

If soldiers are placed in situations where they get shot at constantly and cannot effectively return fire, they will become frustrated, and as their friends are wounded and killed, they will naturally seek vengeance. These are, after all, human beings, not automatons.

It is easy and convenient to blame the soldier on the front line. However, in his situation, where his reaction time keeps him alive, his situation is difficult, and unique. It is important to remember that much training of infantry, and of armed forces in general, accepts that their role is to deliver maximum force – not minimum force, as police do. If less than the maximum is wanted, then soldiers must be equipped with the training and equipment to deliver that.

The politicians – and, behind them, the people of a country – who make the decisions to send warriors into such situations need to accept their part of this responsibility. My Lai was inevitable, and it was not alone.

'18
Conclusion

This work has cited many examples where the truth of battle contradicts the so-called rules of war.

We should encourage maximum lethality in training, so that the aggressive, enthusiastic soldier will best carry out our aim, and also minimise casualties on our side.

With prisoner-taking, it is sometimes necessary to ignore surrender on the grounds of military necessity. If prisoners are killed for legitimate military necessity, then those soldiers should not be charged with any offence.

Regarding prisoner-taking furthermore, it is sometimes understandable that soldiers take revenge rather than take prisoners. If the action the soldier takes is that which any person in that situation would take, then the legalities of that situation can, and perhaps should, be ignored.

Soldiers engaged in tactical combat survive on their reflexes and skills. Unless an enemy combatant is clearly unarmed or clearly not about to use his weapon, and is clearly surrendering, then he is a threat that must be negated. Enemy combatants who, in general, have a clear reputation for deception are a double threat, and one may reasonably expect proportionally more force from an attacker to ensure they are rendered *hors de combat*.

Where there is a possibility of civilians being, in fact, combatants, then again, reasonably enough, we may expect those civilians to be targeted.

This is not to say that war should not have rules agreed to by warring nations. And to prevent those nations descending into the abyss of unrestricted violence, participating nations should enforce those rules among their own forces. But the evidence this book presents shows clearly that sections of the Geneva Conventions are routinely breached, and they always will be breached. The Conventions needs revision.

If these scenarios represent the true reality of what goes on in combat, as against what we think goes on, and if such behaviour will emerge no matter what the training or rule-enforcement stipulates, then nations may as well recognise these factors, and configure their rules accordingly.

World War II battle surgeon Brendan Phibbs emphasised most effectively what is behind this work. Speaking to us from the Battle of the Bulge – with months of combat experience behind him, seeing the best of men and the worst, saving hundreds of lives and losing many others – he was in a unique situation to comment on the rights and wrongs and the reality of battle. He had just seen a German SS trooper deliberately kill a clearly-identified and unarmed medic by luring him out of cover, using a wounded US soldier as the bait.

> War's war and murder's murder, and the more I see of war the more I know there's a difference. You hear civilians, who've never seen blood, yapping about total war, how logical it is. Kill everybody. Well, total war's a crime and the guy who thought it up is a goddam criminal against the last definition of the word human …

> Seems bizarre to worry about people killing unarmed medics when bombers are blowing whole cities to pieces, but even at the bottom of the night some idea of a code of human behaviour, some sense of caring for sick and wounded and helpless, some feeling of man for man not dictated by utility or advantage or generals, is sacred, to be cherished, something to keep us from sinking into a fanged past.[1]

So, let us understand the true nature of combat, and configure our expectations and rules accordingly.

References

Sources in print

Abbott, J. H. M. (John Henry Macartney). *Tommy Cornstalk; Being some account of the less notable features of the South African war from the point of view of the Australian ranks.* London; New York and; Bombay: Longmans, Green, and Co., 1902.

ABC News website 'It's fun to shoot some people: US General'.

http://www.abc.net.au/news/newsitems/200502/s1295615.htm 4 February 2005.

Adkin, Mark. *Goose Green.* London: Leo Cooper, 1992.

Adler, Bill (Ed.) *Letters from Vietnam.* New York: EP Dutton and Co., 1967.

AFP. 'NZ military say soldier killed in Timor had throat cut, ears removed.' http://www/etan.org/et2000c/november/ 12-18/17nz.htm. 26 April 2005.

Ambrose, Stephen E. *Band of Brothers: E Company, 506th Regiment, 101st Airborne: from Normandy to Hitler's Eagle's Nest.* New York: Simon & Schuster, 1992.

Ambrose, Stephen E. *Citizen Soldiers: The U.S. Army from the Normandy beaches to the Bulge to the surrender of Germany, June 7, 1944–May 7, 1945.* New York, N.Y: Simon & Schuster, 1997.

Archer, Wesley D. *Death in the Air.* London: Greenhill Books, 1985.

Arthur, Max. *Forgotten Voices of the Second World War.* London: Ebury Press, 2005.

Astor, Gerald. *Operation Iceberg: The Invasion and Conquest of Okinawa in World War II.* New York: Donald I. Fine, 1995.

Australian Associated Press, 'Army admits mistakes in SAS investigation', 17 February 2004. http://www.asia-pacific-action.org/southeastasia/easttimor/netnews/2004/end_02v3.htm#Army%20admits%20mistakes%20in%20SAS%20investigation

Bairnsfather, Bruce. *Bullets and Billets.* London: Grant Richards Ltd, 1916.

Baker, Clive and Greg Knight. *Milne Bay 1942.* NSW: Baker-Knight Publications, 1991.

Baker, Mark. *Nam: The Vietnam War in the words of the men and women who fought there.* New York: Morrow, 1981

Barham, Sergeant Andrew, Australian Army soldier and veteran of the East Timor campaign. Notes to the author, May 2005.

Baring, Maurice. *Flying Corps Headquarters 1914–1918*. London: Faber, 2008.

Barrett, John. *We Were There*. NSW: Allen and Unwin, 1995.

Belenky, Gregory. *Contemporary Studies in Combat Psychiatry*. New York: Greenwood Press, 1987.

Bennett, Cam. *Rough Infantry*. Victoria: Warrnambool Institute Press, 1984.

Bergerud, Eric M. *Fire in the Sky: The Air War in the South Pacific*. Boulder, Colo.: Westview Press, 2000.

Bergerud, Eric. *Touched with Fire: The land warfare in the South Pacific*. New York: Viking, 1996.

Best, Geoffrey. *Humanity in Warfare: The modern history of the international law of armed conflicts*. London: Weidenfeld and Nicolson, 1980.

Bidwell, Shelford. *Modern Warfare: A study of men, weapons and theories*. London: Allen Lane, 1973.

Bishop, William Avery. *Winged Warfare*. Folkestone: Bailey Brothers and Swinfen, 1975.

Blair, Clay. *Silent Victory: The U.S. submarine war against Japan*. Philadelphia: Lippincott, 1975.

Blair, Dale. *Dinkum Diggers*. Victoria: Melbourne University Press. 2001.

Blandford, Edmund L. *Green Devils – Red Devils: Untold tales of the Airborne Forces in the Second World War*. London: Leo Cooper, 1993.

Bott, Captain Alan. *Cavalry of the Clouds*. New York: Arno Press, 1972.

Bourke, Joanna. *An Intimate History of Killing: Face-to-face killing in twentieth-century warfare*. London: Granta Books, 1999.

Bowen, Ezra. *Knights of the Air*. Time-Life Books, 1980

Bowyer, Chaz. *Albert Ball, VC*. London: William Kimber, 1977.

Bradford, Alfred S. *Some Even Volunteered*. Westport: Praeger, 1994.

Bramley, Vincent. *Two Sides of Hell*. Great Britain: Bloomsbury, 1994.

Bransby, Guy. *Her Majesty's Interrogator*. London: Leo Cooper, 1996.

Bridgland, Tony. *Waves of Hate*. Leo Cooper: South Yorkshire, 2002.

Brode, Patrick. *Casual Slaughters and Accidental Judgments: Canadian war crimes prosecutions, 1944–1948*. Toronto: University of Toronto Press, 1997.

Brown, Gary. *The Kokoda Trail: Myth and reality*. Newcastle, NSW, 1971.

Brownell, RJ *From Khaki to Blue*. Canberra: The Military Historical Society of Australia, 1978.

Brown, Malcolm. *The Imperial War Museum book of the western front*. London: Sidgwick & Jackson in association with the Imperial War Museum, 1993.

Brune, Peter. *A Bastard of a Place: The Australians in Papua*. Crows Nest, N.S.W: Allen & Unwin, 2003.

Brutton, Philip. *Ensign in Italy*. London: Leo Cooper, 1992.

Buick, Bob, with Gary McKay. *All Guts and No Glory*. NSW: Allen and Unwin, 2000.

Burstall, Terry. *The Soldiers' Story: The Battle at Xa Long Tan Vietnam, 18 August 1966*. St. Lucia, Qld: University of Queensland Press, 1986.

Cable, Boyd. *Airmen O'War*. London: John Murray, 1918.

Calley, William L. *His Own Story*. New York: The Viking Press, 1971.

Caputo, Philip. *A Rumor of War*. New York: Holt, Rinehart and Winston, 1977.

Chinnery, Philip D. *Korean Atrocity: Forgotten War Crimes 1950–1953.* Annapolis, MD: Naval Institute Press, 2000.

Christopher, John. *Balloons at War: Gasbags, Flying Bombs and Cold War Secrets.* Stroud [England]: Tempus, 2004.

Clark, Johnnie M. *Guns Up!* New York: Ballantine, 1984.

Clausewitz, Carl von. *On War.* Princeton, N.J: Princeton University Press, 1984.

Cobby, Group Captain AH. *High Adventure.* Melbourne: Robertson and Mullens, 1942.

Cochrane, James Aikman. *Charlie Company: In service with C Company, 2nd Queen's Own Cameron Highlanders, 1940–44.* London: Chatto and Windus, 1977.

Coles, Alan. *Slaughter at Sea.* London: Robert Hale, 1986.

Connelly, Owen. *On War and Leadership.* New Jersey: Princeton University Press, 2002.

Cooke, James J. *The U.S. Air Service in the Great War, 1917–1919.* Westport, Conn: Praeger, 1996.

Coppard, George. *With a Machine Gun to Cambrai: The tale of a young Tommy in Kitchener's army 1914–1918.* London: H.M.S.O, 1969.

Coughlin, Jack. *Shooter: The autobiography of the top-ranked Marine sniper.* New York: St. Martin's Press, 2005.

Crozier, Brigadier-General FP. *A Brass Hat in No Man's Land.* London: J. Cape, 1930.

Crozier, Brigadier-General FP. *The Men I Killed.* London: Michael Joseph, 1937.

Cull, W. Ambrose. *At All Costs.* Melbourne: Australasian Authors' Agency, 1919.

Davis, Russell. *Marine at War.* Boston: Little, Brown and Company, 1961.

De Houst, Major Walter F. 'Offensive Air Operations of the Falklands War'. Marine Corps Command and Staff College, Marine Corps Development and Education Command Quantico, Virginia. 2 April 1984. http://www.globalsecurity.org/military/library/report/1984/DWF.htm

Dellums (House Of Representatives) War Crimes Hearings, Washington, DC, 1971. http://members.aol.com/warlibrary/vwch1.htm

De Mulinen, Frederic. *Handbook on the Law of War for Armed Forces.* Geneva: International Committee of the Red Cross, 1987.

Denfeld, D. Colt. *Hold the Marianas.* Pennsylvania: White Mane Publishing Company, 1997.

Denton, Kit. *Closed File.* Adelaide: Rigby, 1983.

Department of the Army. *US Army Combat Stress Control Handbook.* USA: Lyons Press, 2003.

DeRose, James F. *Unrestricted Warfare: How a new breed of officers led the submarine force to victory in World War II.* New York: John Wiley, 2000.

Devlin, Sir Patrick. 'Morals and the Criminal Law'. *Philosophy and Contemporary Issues.* USA: Macmillan, 1976.

Dexter, David. *The New Guinea Offensives.* Canberra: Australian War Memorial, 1961.

Dixon, Chris and Luke Auton. (Eds.) *War, Society and Culture: Issues and Approaches.* Brawley, Sean. Hangkuk, Diahan, Korean: Korean Voices of the Wol-nam-jon.American War/Vietnam War. University of Newcastle: Research Group for War, Society and Culture, 2002.

Dixon, Norman. *On the Psychology of Military Incompetence*. London: Pimlico, 1976.

Dockery, Martin J. *Lost in Translation: Vietnam, a combat advisor's story*. New York: Presidio Press, 2003.

Donnelly, Christopher N. 'The Soviet Attitude towards Stress in Battle', in Belenky, Gregory. *Contemporary Studies in Combat Psychiatry*. New York: Greenwood Press, 1987. (233–252)

Donovan, David. *Once a Warrior King*. USA: McGraw Hill, 1985.

Donovan, Robert J. *PT109, John F. Kennedy in World War II*. New York: McGraw-Hill, 1961.

Dornan, Peter. *Nicky Barr, an Australian Air Ace*. NSW: Allen and Unwin, 2002.

Duncan, David Douglas. *War without Heroes*. London: Thames and Hudson, 1971.

Dunn, Captain JC. *The War the Infantry Knew*. Great Britain: Jane's Publishing Company, 1987.

Dunnigan, James. *How to Make War*. New York: William Morrow and Company, 1982.

Dunnigan, James F. and Albert A Nofi. *The Pacific War Encyclopedia*. New York: Checkmark Books, 1998.

Dupuy, Trevor N. *Numbers, Predictions and War: Using history to evaluate combat factors and predict the outcome of battles*. London: Macdonald and Jane's, 1979.

Dwights, Don. *Famous Flyers and the Ships They Flew*. Grossett & Dunlap, Inc., 1969.

Dwight D. Eisenhower Library, Joe Lawton Collins Papers, Box 2, 201 Files – Personal Letters 1943. Comment on Japanese surrenders by Major General J. Lawton Collins. Via Internet discussion group H-NET Military History Discussion List H-WAR@H-NET.MSU.EDU 9 October 2004. Courtesy member Joerg Muth.

Edelman, Bernard. (Ed.) *Dear America: Letters home from Vietnam*. New York: WW Norton and Company, 1985.

Ellis, John. *The Sharp End*. Great Britain: Windrow and Green, 1990.

Essex-Clark, John. *Maverick Warrior*. Victoria: Melbourne University Press, 1991.

Estep, James. *Comanche Six: Company Commander, Vietnam*. CA: Presidio, 1991.

Evans, Michael and Alan Ryan. (Eds.) *The Human Face of Warfare: Killing, fear and chaos in battle*. St. Leonards, NSW: Allen & Unwin, 2000.

Faas, Horst. *Requiem*. New York: Random House, 1997.

Ferguson, Niall. *The Pity Of War*. London: Allen Lane, 1998.

Ferguson N. 'Prisoner Taking and Prisoner Killing in the Age of Total War: Towards a Political Economy of Military Defeat'. War in History, 1 April 2004, vol. 11, no. 2, (pp. 148–192) http://docserver.ingentaselect.com/deliver/cw/arn/09683445/v11n2/s2/p148.pdf?fmt=dirpdf&tt=2023&cl=38&ini=&bini=&wis=&ac=0&acs=&expires=1100492588&checksum=EA202FF35CD74AEEC93C6F6C8BDC169E&cookie=1874255872

Fitz-Gibbon, Spencer. *Not Mentioned in Despatches*. Cambridge: The Lutterworth Press, 1995.

FitzSimons, Peter. *Kokoda*. Sydney: Hodder Headline Australia, 2004.

Fonck, René. *Ace of Aces*. New York: Doubleday, 1967.

Ford, Roger. *Steel from the Sky: The Jedburgh raiders, France 1944*. London: Weidenfeld & Nicolson, 2004.

Fuller, J. F. C. *The Last of the Gentlemen's Wars: A subaltern's journal of the war in South Africa, 1899–*

1902. London: Faber and Faber, 1937.

Fussell, Paul. *The Great War and Modern Memory*. New York: Oxford University Press, 1975.

Gadd, Charles. *Line Doggie*. California: Presidio Press, 1987.

Galen, Esther. 'Survivors of Korean War massacre by US soldiers seek investigation'. 17 November 1999. http://www.wsws.org/articles/1999/nov1999/kor-n17.shtml 8 September 2004.

Gallishaw, John. *Trenching at Gallipoli*. New York: A.L. Burt Company, 1916.

Geneva Convention. Additions of 12 August 1949, relating to the Protection of Victims of International Armed Conflicts, 8 June 1977. http://www.genevaconventions.org/ May 2005.

Genoves Tarazaga, Santiago. *Is Peace Inevitable? Aggression, evolution, and human destiny*. London: Allen and Unwin, 1972.

Ginzberg, Eli. *The Ineffective Soldier: Lessons for management and the nation*. Westport, Conn: Greenwood Press, 1975, c1959

Goldhagen, Daniel Jonah. *Hitler's Willing Executioners: Ordinary Germans and the Holocaust*. New York: Knopf, 1996.

Graham, Don. *No Name on the Bullet: A biography of Audie Murphy*. New York: Viking, 1989.

Graves, Robert. *Goodbye to All That*. London: Penguin, 1960.

Gray, J. Glenn. *The Warriors: Reflections on men in battle*. New York: Harper & Rowe, 1967.

Grider, John MacGavock. *Diary of an Unknown Aviator*. College Station: Texas A&M University Press, 1988.

Griffiths-Marsh, Roland. *The Sixpenny Soldier*. NSW: Angus and Robertson, 1990.

Groom, W. H. A. *Poor Bloody Infantry: A memoir of the First World War*. London: Kimber, 1976.

Grossman, Lieutenant Colonel Dave. *On Killing: The Psychological Cost of Learning to Kill in War and Society*. Boston: Little, Brown and Company. 1996.

Guardian Unlimited. 'Back into Battle'. http://www.guardian.co.uk/military/story/0,11816,1490057,00.html 24 May 2005.

Hackworth, Colonel David H. and Julie Sherman. *About Face*. Melbourne: Macmillan, 1989.

Hackworth, Colonel David H. and Eilhys England. *Steel my Soldiers' Hearts*. New York: Rugged Land, 2002.

Hall, Bert. *One Man's War*. London: John Hamilton, Publication date not given.

Hallas, James H. *Killing Ground on Okinawa*. Connecticut: Praeger, 1996.

Halpin, John. *Blood in the Mists*. Sydney: Macquarie Head Press, 1934.

Ham, Paul. *Kokoda*. Sydney: HarperCollins, 2004.

Hammel, Eric M. *Ambush Valley: I Corps, Vietnam 1967: The story of a Marine infantry battalion's battle for survival*. Novato, CA: Presidio Press, 1990.

Hanbury-Sparrow, A.A. *The Land-Locked Lake*. Sydney: Broderick, 1977.

Hanson, Victor Davis. *Why the West has Won*. London: Faber and Faber, 2001.

Harding, William. *A Cockney Soldier*. Devon: Merlin Books, 1989.

Hart, Peter. *To the Last Round: The South Notts Hussars, 1939–1942*. Barnsley, England: Pen & Sword

Books, 1996.

Hartney, Harold E. *Up and at 'em.* New York: Arno Press, 1940.

Hastings, Max. *Armageddon: The Battle for Germany 1944–1945.* USA: Macmillan, 2004.

Hayes, Mike. *Angry Skies: Recollections of Australian combat fliers.* Sydney: ABC Books, 2003.

Heard, Barry. *Well Done Those Men.* Victoria: Scribe Publications, 2005.

Heinemann, Larry. *Paco's Story.* London: Faber, 1987.

Helmer, John. *Bringing the War Home: The American soldier in Vietnam and after.* New York: Free Press, 1974.

Hemingway, Al. *Our War was Different.* Maryland: Naval Institute Press, 1994.

Henri, Raymond. *The U.S. Marines on Iwo Jima.* Tennessee: Battery Press, 1987.

Herr, Michael. *Dispatches.* New York: Knopf, 1977.

Herrington, Stuart A. *Stalking The Vietcong: Inside Operation Phoenix – A Personal Account.* Presidio Press, 2002.

Hersh, Seymour M. *My Lai 4.* New York: Random House, 1970.

Hitchcock, Francis Clere. *Stand To: A diary of the trenches, 1915–1918.* London: Hurst and Blackett, 1937.

Holm, Jeanne. *Women in the Military: An Unfinished Revolution.* Novato, CA: Presidio Press, 1992.

Holman, Gordon (British War Corrospondent). *Commando Attack.* London: Hodder and Stoughton, 1944.

Holmes, Richard. *Acts of War: The behavior of men in battle.* New York: Free Press, 1986.

Holmes, Richard. *Firing Line.* London: Cape, 1985.

Holmes, Richard. *The Western Front.* London: BBC, 1999.

Holmes, Robert Derby. *A Yankee in the Trenches.* Boston: Little, Brown, and company, 1918.

Hordern, Marsden. *A Merciful Journey.* The Miegunyah Press: Victoria, 2005.

Hurst, James. *Game to the Last.* Melbourne: Oxford University Press, 2005.

International Committee of the Red Cross. *The Geneva Conventions of August 12, 1949.* Geneva.

International Committee of the Red Cross. *International Law Concerning the Conduct of Hostilities.* 'Rules of Air Warfare'. Geneva: International Committee of the Red Cross, 1996.

In Their Own Words. http://www.worldwar1.com/dbc/ow_6.htm 8 September 2004.

Jablonski, Edward. *The Knighted Skies.* London: Thomas Nelson and Sons, 1964.

Jackson, Murray Cosby. *A Soldier's Diary: South Africa, 1899–1901.* London: Goschen, 1913.

Jennings, Christian, and Adrian Weale. *Green-eyed Boys: 3 Para and the battle for Mount Longdon.* London: HarperCollins, 1996.

Jones, Albert James. *Corporal Jones' War: The Diary of an ANZAC.* Perth, W.A.: Black Swan Press, 2005.

Junger, Ernst. *The Storm of Steel.* London: Chatto & Windus, 1930.

Just, Ward S. *To What End.* Boston: Houghton Mifflin Company, 1968.

Kellett, Anthony. *Combat Motivation: The behavior of soldiers in battle.* Boston: Kluwer-Nijhoff, 1982.

Kelly, Jeff. *DMZ Diary: A combat marine's Vietnam memoir.* Jefferson, N.C.: McFarland, 1991.

Kennedy, Ludovic Henry Coverley. *On my Way to the Club: The autobiography of Ludovic Kennedy.*

London: Fontana, 1989.

Kerr, Greg. *Private Wars*. Victoria: Oxford University Press, 2000.

Kemp, Ian. *British G.I. in Vietnam*. London: Robert Hale, 1969.

Kemp, Paul. *Underwater Warriors*. London: Arms and Armour Press, 1996.

Kilduff, Peter. *Over the Battlefronts: Amazing Air Action of World War One*. London: Orion, 1997.

Kilduff, Peter. *The Red Baron*. London: Cassell, 1994.

Kiley, Kevin F. *Artillery of the Napoleonic Wars 1792–1815*. London: Mechanicsburg, PA: Stackpole Books, 2004.

Korean War Educator. 'The Nogun-ri Controversy' http://www.koreanwar-educator.org/topics/nogunri/p_no_gunri.htm February 2005.

Lane, Mark. *Conversations with Americans*. New York: Simon and Schuster, 1970.

Lang, Daniel. *Incident on Hill 192*. London: Secker & Warburg, 1970.

Large, Lofty. *One Man's War in Korea*. Wellingborough: Kimber, 1988.

Leckie, Robert. *Helmet for my Pillow*. Garden City, N.Y: Doubleday, 1979.

Lee, Arthur Gould. *No Parachute*. London: Jarrolds, 1968.

LeShan, Lawrence L. *The Psychology of War: Comprehending its mystique and its madness*. Chicago: Noble Press, 1992.

Lewis, Cecil Day. *Sagittarius Rising*. Pennsylvania: Giniger, 1963.

Lewis, C. S. *Surprised by Joy: The shape of my early life*. London: Collins, 1959.

Lewy, Guenter. *America in Vietnam*. New York: Oxford University Press, 1978.

Lifton, Robert Jay. *Home from the War: Vietnam veterans: neither victims nor executioners*. New York: Simon and Schuster, 1973.

Linder, Doug. 'An Introduction to the My Lai Courts-Martial'. http://www.law.umkc.edu/faculty/projects/ftrials/mylai/mylai.htm August 2004.

Long, Gavin. *To Benghazi*. Canberra: Australian War Memorial, 1952.

Longford, Elizabeth. *Wellington – The Years of the Sword*. New York: Harper and Row, 1969.

Longstreet, Stephen. *The Canvas Falcons*. London: Leo Cooper, 1995.

Lucas, James. *Last Days of the Reich*. London: Cassell, 1986.

Lukowiak, Ken. *A Soldier's Song*. London: Secker and Warburg, 1993.

Luvaas, Jay. (Editor and translator) *Napoleon on the Art of War*. New York: Touchstone, 1999.

Macaulay, Thomas Babbington. Stanza XXVII. 'Horatius: A Lay Made About the Year Of The City CCCLX'. *Lays of Ancient Rome*. http://www.themediadrome.com/content/poetry/horatius.htm 6 August 2005.

MacDonald, Charles B. *Company Commander*. Washington: Infantry Journal Press, 1947.

MacDonald, Charles B. *A Time for Trumpets: The untold story of the Battle of the Bulge*. New York: Morrow, 1984.

Macdonald, Donald Alister. *How we Kept the Flag Flying: The story of the siege of Ladysmith*. London: Ward Lock, 1900.

Macdonald, Lyn. *Somme*. London: Penguin, 1993.

Macdonald, Lyn. *They Called it Passchendaele*. London: Penguin, 1993.

MacDonald Fraser, George. *Flashman and the Redskins*. London: Williams Collins, 1982.

MacDonald Fraser, George. *Quartered Safe Out Here*. London: Harper Collins, 1995.

Mackie, JL. *Ethics. Inventing Right and Wrong*. Middlesex: Penguin, 1978.

MacMillan, Wing Commander Norman, OBE, MC, AFC. *Into the Blue*. London: Jarrolds, 1969.

Manchester, William. *Goodbye, Darkness: A memoir of the Pacific war*. London: Joseph, 1981.

Mantell, David Mark. *True Americanism: Green Berets and war resisters: A study of commitment*. New York: Teachers College Press, 1974.

Marks, Thomas Penrose. *The Laughter goes from Life: In the trenches of the First World War*. London: Kimber, 1977.

Marshall, SLA. *Men Against Fire*. Norman: University of Oklahoma Press, 2000.

Martin, Charles Cromwell. *Battle Diary: From D-Day and Normandy to the Zuider Zee and VE*. Toronto: Dundurn Press, 1994.

Mason, Robert. *Chickenhawk*. Middlesex: Penguin, 1984.

Mauldin, William Henry. *Up Front*. New York: H. Holt, 1945.

McAulay, Lex. *The Battle of Long Tan*. Victoria: Hutchinson, 1986.

McBride, Glen. *D-Day on Queen's Beach Red: An Australian's war from the Burma Road retreat to the Normandy beaches*. Brisbane, Qld: Prof. G. McBride, 1994.

McCudden, James, VC. *Flying Fury*. Hertforshire and California: Greenhill and Aeolus Publishing, 1987.

McDonald, Cherokee Paul. *Into the Green*. New York: Penguin, 2001.

McDonough, James R. *Platoon Leader*. CA: Presidio, 1985.

McGowan, Robert, and Jeremy Hands. *Don't Cry for Me, Sergeant-Major*. London: Futara, 1983.

McKay, Gary. *Vietnam Fragments: An oral history of Australians at war*. North Sydney: Allen & Unwin, 1992.

McKee, Alexander. *Caen: Anvil of victory*. London: Souvenir Press, 1964.

Merritt, William E. *Where the Rivers ran Backward*. Athens [Ga.]: University of Georgia Press, 1989.

Metelmann, Henry. *Through Hell for Hitler: A dramatic first-hand account of fighting with the Wehrmacht*. Wellingborough: Stephens, 1990.

Middlebrook, Martin. *The First Day of the Somme*. Penguin: Middlesex, 1984.

Middlebrook, Martin. *The Kaiser's Battle*. Penguin: London, 2000.

Mill, JS. *Utilitarianism, On Liberty, and Considerations on Representative Government*. Great Britain: JM Dent, 1972.

Miller, David. *Commanding Officers*. London: John Murray, 2001.

Miller, Franklin, with Elwood JC Kureth. *Reflections of a Warrior*. California: Presidio, 1991.

Milner, Samuel, *US Army in World War II*. 'Chapter VII: The Advance on the Beachhead'. http://www.ibiblio.org/hyperwar/USA/USA-P-Papua/USA-P-Papua-7.html 5 August 2005.

Mitchell, G.D. *Soldier in Battle*. Sydney; London: Angus & Robertson, 1941.

Moore, Harold G, and Joseph L. Galloway. *We Were Soldiers Once and Young: Ia Drang: The battle that changed the war in Vietnam*. New York: Random House, 1992.

Moran, Lord. *The Anatomy of Courage*. London: Constable, 1945.

Murphy, Audie. *To Hell and Back*. New York: Holt, Rinehart and Winston. 1949.

Musgrave, George Clarke. *In South Africa with Buller*. Boston: Little, Brown and Company, 1900.

My Way. 'U.S. Military Investigating Marine Shooting'. http://apnews.myway.com/article/20041116/D86D337G0.html 16 November 2004.

New York Daily News. 'Pix of dead Iraqis may seal his fate'. http://www.nydailynews.com/03-27-2005/news/wn_report/story/293771p-251526c.html 30 March 2005.

Norman, Richard. *Ethics, Killing and War*. New York: Cambridge University Press, 1995.

O'Brien, Tim. *If I Should Die in a Combat Zone*. USA: Delacorte Press, 1973.

Padfield, Peter. *War Beneath the Sea: Submarine conflict 1939–1945*. London: John Murray, 1995.

Parrish, Lieutenant Robert D. *Combat Recon*. New York: St Martin's Press, 1991.

Peters, Ralph. 'The Truth About War'. http://www.nypost.com/postopinion/opedcolumnists/39390.htm 14 February 2005.

Petersen, Barry, with John Cribbin. *Tiger Men*. Melbourne: Sun Books, 1988.

Phibbs, Brendan *The Other Side of Time: A Combat Surgeon in World War II*. Boston: Little, Brown, 1987.

Phillips, C. E. Lucas. *The Greatest Raid of All*. London: Readers Book Club, 1958.

Pinker, Steven. *The Blank Slate*. New York: Viking, 2002.

Pinney, Peter. *The Barbarians: A Soldier's New Guinea Diary*. St. Lucia, Qld: University of Queensland Press, 1988.

Porter, R. Bruce, with Eric Hammel. *Ace! A Marine Night-Fighter Pilot in World War II*. San Francisco: Pacifica Press, 1985.

Quarrie, Bruce. *Hitler's Samurai: The Waffen-SS in Action*. New York: Arco Pub, 1983.

Reitz, Deneys. *Commando: A Boer journal of the Boer War*. London: Faber and Faber, 1931.

Richards, Frank. *Old Soldiers Never Die*. Sydney: Angus & Robertson, 1933.

Richardson, Frank M. *Fighting Spirit: A study of psychological factors in war*. London: Cooper, 1978.

Richey, Paul. *Fighter Pilot*. London: Cassell, 2001.

Rickenbacker, Edward V. *Fighting the Flying Circus*. New York: Frederick A Stokes Company, 1919.

Rivett, Rohan D. *Behind Bamboo*. Sydney: Angus and Robertson Ltd, 1947.

Robinson, Derek. *Goshawk Squadron*. London: Bantam Books, 1986.

Robinson, LCDR Robert, USN. *The Invincible Russell*. (135) Copy supplied by the Washington Navy Yard from a donation by LCDR Robinson in 1995.

Rommel, Erwin. *Infantry Attacks*. Great Britain: Wren's Park Publishing, 2002.

Rooney, Andrew A. *My War*. New York: Times Books, 1995.

Rule, EJ, M.C., M.M. *Jacka's Mob*. Sydney: Angus and Robertson, 1933.

Rush, Robert Sterling. *Hell in Hurtgen Forest.* Kansas: University Press of Kansas, 2001.

Russell, Lord, of Liverpool. *The Knights of Bushido: A short history of Japanese War Crimes.* Bath: Chivers Press, 1989.

Sajer, Guy. *The Forgotten Soldier.* London: Weidenfeld and Nicolson, 1971.

SALUT. Col. Des Barker, *Women Pilots in Operational Combat.* http://www.mil.za/Magazines/SALUT/Sept%6099/sep6womenpilots.htm July 2005.

Santoli, Al. (Ed.) *Everything we Had: An oral history of the Vietnam War.* New York: Random House, 1981.

Sassoon, Siegfried. *Memoirs of an Infantry Officer.* Kent: Faber and Faber, 2000.

Schneider, Carl J. *World War II.* New York: Checkmark Books, 2003.

Scholl-Latour, Peter. *Eyewitness Vietnam.* London: Orbis, 1985.

Shaw, Jon A. 'Psychodynamic Considerations in the Adaption to Combat', in Belenky, Gregory. *Contemporary Studies in Combat Psychiatry.* New York: Greenwood Press, 1987. (117–131)

Sheehan, Mark. 'Mark Lane: Smearing America's Soldiers in Vietnam'. http://mcadams.posc.mu.edu/smearing.htm 30 August 2004.

Shirer, William L. *The Rise and Fall of the Third Reich: A history of Nazi Germany.* London: Secker & Warburg, 1960.

Sledge, E. B. *With the Old Breed, at Peleliu and Okinawa.* Novato, Calif: Presidio Press, 1981.

Slim, William. *Defeat into Victory.* London: Cassell, 1956.

Smith, Gary R. *Death in the Jungle: Diary of a Navy SEAL.* Boulder, Colo: Paladin Press, 1994.

Speer, Albert. *Inside the Third Reich.* London: Weidenfeld and Nicolson. 1970.

Stewart, Nora Kinzer. *Mates and Muchachos: Unit Cohesion in the Falklands/Malvinas War.* USA: Brassey's, 1991.

Stouffer, Samuel A. (et al) *The American Soldier.* Princeton, N.J: Princeton University Press, 1949.

Strauss, Ulrich. *The Anguish of Surrender: Japanese POWs of World War II.* Seattle: University of Washington Press, 2003.

Strozzi Heckler, Richard. *In Search of the Warrior Spirit: Teaching awareness disciplines to the Green Berets.* Berkeley, Calif.: North Atlantic Books, 2003.

Sydney Morning Herald. Deborah Snow. 'Elite soldier charged for kicking dead enemy'. 22 February 2003. http://www.smh.com.au/articles/2003/02/21/1045638486088.html?oneclick=true

Sym, J. (Ed.) *Seaforth Highlanders.* Aldershot: Gale and Polden, 1962.

Tamayam, Kazuo, and John Nunneley. *Tales by Japanese Soldiers.* London: Cassell and Co., 1992.

Terkel, Louis. *The Good War: An oral history of World War Two.* New York: Pantheon Books, 1984.

Terraine, John. *Impacts of War 1914 & 1918.* London: Hutchinson, 1970.

Terraine, John. *The Smoke and the Fire.* London: Sidgwick and Jackson, 1980.

Terraine, John. *The U-Boat Wars.* 1916–1945. New York: Henry Holt and Company, 1989.

Thanhnien News 'Koreans penitent for South Korean war crimes in Quang Nam'. http://www.thanhniennews.com/society/?catid=3&newsid=1453 27 August 2004.

The Australian. 'Marine captured in cold-blooded murder'. 17 November 2004. (1) Microfilm copy from the Australian National Library, Canberra.

The Canberra Times. 'Marine filmed killing Iraqi'. 17 November 2004. (2)

The Canberra Times. 'Quotes of the Year'. 1 January 2005. (B4)

The Canberra Times. 'Normandy to Berlin: The Third Reich's death throes'. (Review of Barry Turner's *Countdown to Victory*. 1 January 2005. (14)

The Detroit News. 'The Execution of Pvt. Eddie Slovik'. http://info.detnews.com/history/story/index. cfm?id=103&category=people 26 June 2005.

The Insider. 'US Marine escapes justice despite video of murder in cold blood'. http://www.theinsider. org/mailing/article.asp?id=991 2 June 2005.

The New York Times. John Kifner. 'Ex-G.I.'s tell of Vietnam brutality'. 29 December, 2003. http://www. xs4all.nl/~stgvisie/VISIE/Vietnam-Criminals.html

The Sunday Times. 'Iraq battle stress worse than WWII'. http://www.timesonline.co.uk/ article/0,,2087-1859664,00.html 6 November, 2005.

The Sydney Morning Herald. Craig Skehan. 'Enemy skull photo seen as an affront'. 30 April, 2005. (13)

The Toledo Blade. 'Rogue GIs unleashed wave of terror in Central Highlands'. http://www.toledoblade. com/apps/pbcs.dll/article?AID=/20031022/SRTIGERFORCE/110190168 23 August 2004.

The Toledo Blade. 'Inquiry ended without justice'. http://www.toledoblade.com/apps/pbcs.dll/ article?AID=/20031022/SRTIGERFORCE/110190168 23 August 2004.

The Toledo Blade. 'Pain lingers 36 years after deadly rampage'. http://www.toledoblade.com/apps/pbcs. dll/article?AID=/20031022/SRTIGERFORCE/110190168 23 August 2004.

The Toledo Blade. 'Demons of past stalk Tiger Force veterans'. http://www.toledoblade.com/apps/pbcs. dll/article?AID=/20031022/SRTIGERFORCE/110190168 23 August 2004.

The Washington Post. 'U.S. Soldier pleads not guilty in Iraqi man's death.' http://www.washingtonpost. com/wp-dyn/articles/A7998-2005Mar28.html 30 March 2005.

Throssell, Ric. *My Father's Son*. Richmond, Vic: William Heinemann, 1989.

Todd, Pamela. (Ed.) *Private Tucker's Boer War diary: The Transvaal War of 1899, 1900, 1901 & 1902 with the Natal Field Forces*. London: Elm Tree Books, 1980.

Toland, John. *In Mortal Combat*. New York: Morrow, 1991.

Toliver, Raymond F, and Trevor J Constable. *Fighter Aces of the USA*. CA: Aero Publishers, 1979.

Torrent, Andrew, MM. *A 'Day' in the Army*. Western Australia: South West Printing and Publishing Company, no publishing date.

Trevor-Roper, HR. *The Last Days of Hitler*. London: Pan, 1972.

Ulanoff, Stanley M, Lt. Col., in Fonck, René. *Ace of Aces*. New York: Doubleday, 1967.

United States Army. Department of the Army Inspector General. *No Gun Ri Review*. January 2001. www.army.mil/nogunri/BookCoverJan01Summary.pdf

United States Marine Corps, 1940. *Small Wars Manual*. Kansas: Military Affairs/Aerospace Historian Publishing, 1972.

Van Creveld, Martin L. *Fighting Power: German and US Army performance*, 1939–1945. Westport,

Conn: Greenwood Press, 1982.

Van Creveld, Martin L. *Men, Women and War*. London: Cassell, 2001.

Van Creveld, Martin L. *The Art of War: War and military thought*. London: Cassell, 2002.

Walpole, Brian. *My War – An Australian Commando in New Guinea and Borneo 1943–1945*. Sydney: ABC Books, 2004.

Ward, Commander 'Sharkey', DSC, AFC, RN. *Sea Harrier over the Falklands*. London: Leo Cooper, 1992.

Warr, Nicholas. *Phase Line Green: The battle for Hue, 1968*. Annapolis, MD: Naval Institute Press, 1997.

Wartime Magazine. Villains or victims? http://www.awm.gov.au/wartime/18/article.asp Australian War Memorial. 8 December 2004.

Washington Times. 'Marine charged in killing of Iraqis'. http://www.washingtontimes.com/national/20050214-121803-1937r.htm 14 February 2005.

Webster, Daniel Kenyon. *Parachute Infantry*. USA: Louisiana State University Press, 1994.

Welch, Ronald. *Tank Commander*. London: Oxford University Press, 1972.

Westman, Stephen Kurt. *Surgeon with the Kaiser's Army*. London: Kimber, 1968.

Weston, Richard, Anti-Tank Gun Commander. Letter to the Editor. *Quadrant* magazine. May 2005. (7)

Weston, Richard. Anti-Tank Gun Commander. 'Nine Lives'. Unpublished manuscript provided to the author. 2005.

Wexler, Sanford. *The Vietnam War – An Eyewitness History*. New York: Facts on File, 1992.

Wikipedia Encyclopedia. Treaty for the Limitation and Reduction of Naval Armament http://en.wikipedia.org/wiki/London_Naval_Treaty. 14 November 2005.

White, Osmar. *Green Armour*. Sydney: Angus and Robertson, 1943.

Whitehouse, Arch. *Decisive Air Battles of the First World War*. New York: Duell, Sloan and Pierce, 1963.

Whitehouse, Arch. *Heroes of the Sunlit Sky*. Garden City, N.Y: Doubleday, 1967.

Whiting, Charles. *Werewolf: The Story of the Nazi Resistance Movement 1944–1945*. London: Leo Cooper, 1972.

Wilson, Trevor. *The Myriad Faces of War*. Cambridge: Polity Press, 1986.

Winter, Denis. *25 April 1915*. Queensland: University of Queensland Press, 1994.

Wood, WJ. *Leaders and Battles*. California: Presidio, 1990.

Wright, Derrick. *A Hell of a Way to Die: Tarawa Atoll, 20–23 November 1943*. London: Windrow & Greene, 1997.

Yeates, VM. *Winged Victory*. London: Johnathan Cape, 1962.

Young, Peter. *Storm from the Sea*. Great Britain: Wren's Park Publishing, 2002.

Zorns, Bruce C. *I Walk Through the Valley: A World War II infantryman's memoir of war, imprisonment, and love*. Jefferson, N.C: McFarland & Co., 1991.

Films

20th Century Fox. *Aliens*. (Dir: James Cameron) 1986.

20th Century Fox. *The Blue Max*. (Dir: John Guillermin) 1966.

Australian Broadcasting Corporation. *Warrior: Reflections of Men at War.* Courtesy Library of the Australian Defence Force Academy, Canberra. 2004. (21'– 22'30')

BBC Television. (Dir. Fisher, John Hayes) *Meet the Ancestors – Billy and the Boys.* 2004.

Hollywood Pictures Home Video. *G.I. Jane.* (Dir. Ridley Scott) Burbank, Calif.: 1998

CBS Television, USA. *Sixty Minutes.* Version shown on Channel 9's Australia *Sunday* program, 13 May 2001.

Dreamworks. *Saving Private Ryan.* (Dir. Steven Spielberg) 1998.

Eagle Rock Entertainment. *The Fury and the Flames.* 'WWII Fighter Aces of the Luftwaffe'. 1999.

RKO Pictures. *Hamburger Hill.* (Dir. John Irvin.) 1987.

Universal Studios. *Aces High.* (Dir. Jack Gold.) 1976.

Warner Brothers. *Lafayette Escadrille.* (Dir: William Wellman) 1958.

Warner Brothers. *Dawn Patrol.* (Dir: Edmund Goulding) 1938. VHS version, 1993.

Interviews, letters and emails

Barham, Sergeant Andrew. Australian Army soldier and veteran of the East Timor campaign. Conversations April 2005.

Bergerud, Eric. Comment on the H-War Internet discussion list. 23 September 2004.

De Heer, Derrill. Australian Vietnam veteran. Conversation with the author at The Vietnam War, Thirty Years On Conference. 14 April 2005.

Hefron, Peter. American Vietnam veteran. Conversation with the author at The Vietnam War, Thirty Years On Conference. 15 April 2005.

McKay, Gary. Australian Vietnam veteran. Conversation with the author at The Vietnam War, Thirty Years On Conference, Newcastle, Australia. 14 April 2005.

Oslin, Bob, Lieutenant Colonel, US Army. (Ret.) Emails to the author. May–June 2005.

Price, Colin C. Crew member – *HMAS Katoomba,* letter written on 24 February 1942 – in the possession of the author; letters to the author, December 1995 to February 1996.

Purves, Frederick, Rear Admiral (retd.) and RAN diver in Darwin, WWII. Letters and annexures, 15 March, May 5 1996. (Letters written by son Robert Purves with his observations also added)

Veteran 1X. Interview with the author. 24 March 2006.

Weston, Richard, Anti-Tank Gun Commander. Emails and telephone conversations. May 2005. (7)

Williams, Peter. Military Historian. Interview with a 2/2 Infantry Battalion member of the Australian Army, referring to his experience of the fighting from Sept. 1942 to Dec. 1942. December 2004.

Williams, Peter. Military Historian. Interview with Australian Army Private, 2/31 Infantry Battalion, Gona, Dec 1942. 12 February 2005.

Endnotes

Introduction

1. Bourke, Joanna. *An Intimate History of Killing: Face-to-face killing in twentieth-century warfare*. London: Granta Books, 1999. (2)

2. Marshall, SLA. *Men Against Fire*. Norman: University of Oklahoma Press, 2000.

3. See, for example, Seymour Hersh 'Overwhelming Force -- What happened in the final days of the Gulf War?' *The New Yorker*, 22 May 22 2000. http://www.agitprop.org.au/stopnato/20000627hershtnyus.php or William Blum 'Iraq 1990–1991: Desert Holocaust – How the US induced Iraq to attack Kuwait and then bombed and radiated the hell out of the Iraqi people.' http://cameron.org.au/alister/iraq.html

4. 'As Major General John Sewall of the Institute for National Strategic Studies at the National Defense University in Washington pointed out, the peacekeeping disasters of the 1990s occurred in large part because countries contributing forces to United Nations operations had 'grown comfortable with traditional peacekeeping doctrine, emphasizing low force levels, restrictive rules of engagement, use of force only in self defense, compromise and impartiality'. Ryan, Dr Alan. 'Multinational Forces and United Nations Operations'. ACT: Land Warfare Studies Centre.

5. Green Party of New Zealand. 'The saving will come from disbanding the offensive capacity of the Defence Force.' 'Greens to halve defence spending'. Keith Locke, Green Party Defence Spokesperson. 7 June 1999. http://www.greens.org.nz/searchdocs/PR3877.html

6. Deborah Snow. 'Elite soldier charged for kicking dead enemy', *Sydney Morning Herald*, 22 February 2003. http://www.smh.com.au/articles/2003/02/21/1045638486088.html?oneclick=true

7. Several are described in Chapter 13, 'The killing of enemy wounded: an excusable necessity?'.

8. *The Sunday Times*. 'Iraq battle stress worse than WWII'. http://www.timesonline.co.uk/article/0,,2087-1859664,00.html 6 November 2005.

9. *Julius Caesar*, Act 3, Scene 1.

On the veracity of sources

1. Heard, Barry. *Well Done Those Men*. Victoria: Scribe Publications, 2005. (154-155)

2. Ambrose, Stephen E. *Citizen Soldiers: The U.S. Army from the Normandy beaches to the Bulge to the surrender of Germany, June 7, 1944-May 7, 1945*. New York, N.Y: Simon & Schuster, 1997. (352)

3. Rommel, Erwin. *Infantry Attacks*. Great Britain: Wren's Park Publishing, 2002. (43 footnote) Rommel charged that French troops had attacked wounded Germans lying by the roadside. The second reference in on page 186.

4. Buick, Bob, with Gary McKay. *All Guts and No Glory*. NSW: Allen and Unwin, 2000. (76-77)
Coppard, George. *With a Machine Gun to Cambrai: The tale of a young Tommy in Kitchener's army 1914-1918*. London: H.M.S.O, 1969.

5. Crozier, Brigadier-General FP. *A Brass Hat in No Man's Land*. London: J. Cape, 1930. (209)

6. Clark, Johnnie M. *Guns Up!* New York: Ballantine, 1984. (137)

7. Clark, *Guns Up!* 287.

8. Gray, J. Glenn. *The Warriors: Reflections on men in battle*. New York: Harper & Rowe, 1967. (139)

9. Sassoon, Siegfried. *Memoirs of an Infantry Officer*. Kent: Faber and Faber, 2000. (66)

10. Barrett, John. *We Were There*. NSW: Allen and Unwin, 1995. (308)

11. Weston, Richard, Anti-Tank Gun Commander. Letter to the Editor, *Quadrant* magazine. May 2005. (7), and subsequent emails and telephone conversations.

12. Gadd, Charles. *Line Doggie*. California: Presidio Press, 1987. (104)

13. Wexler, Sanford. *The Vietnam War – an Eyewitness History*. New York: Facts on File, 1992. (115)

14. Dockery, Martin J. *Lost in Translation: Vietnam, a combat advisor's story*. New York: Presidio Press, 2003. (46)

Chapter 1

1. Murphy, Audie. *To Hell and Back*. New York: Holt, Rinehart and Winston. 1949. (174)

2. Murphy, *To Hell and Back*, 176-179.

3. Michael Evans, 'Close combat: lessons from the cases of Albert Jacka and Audie Murphy'. Evans Michael and Alan Ryan. (Eds.) *The Human Face of Warfare: Killing, fear and chaos in battle*. (St. Leonards, NSW: Allen & Unwin, 2000), 45. *No Name on the Bullet: A biography of Audie Murphy*, suggests approximately 240. (102)

4. Graham, Don. *No Name on the Bullet: A biography of Audie Murphy*. New York: Viking, 1989. (101-102)

5. Rule, EJ, M.C., M.M. *Jacka's Mob*. Sydney: Angus and Robertson, 1933. (277)

6. Schneider, Carl J. *World War II*. New York: Checkmark Books, 2003. (222)

7. Gray, J. Glenn. *The Warriors: Reflections on men in battle*. New York: Harper & Rowe, 1967. (57)

8. Sledge, E. B. *With the old Breed, at Peleliu and Okinawa*. Novato, Calif: Presidio Press, 1981. (228)

9. Jones, Albert James. *Corporal Jones' War: The Diary of an ANZAC*. Perth, W.A.: Black Swan Press, 2005. (98)

10. Reitz, Deneys. *Commando: A Boer journal of the Boer War*. London: Faber and Faber, 1931. (51-52)

11. Dunn, Captain JC. *The War the Infantry Knew*. Great Britain: Jane's Publishing Company, 1987. (101)

12. Richards, Frank. *Old Soldiers Never Die*. Sydney: Angus & Robertson, 1933. (53-54)

13. Bairnsfather, Bruce. *Bullets and Billets*. London: Grant Richards Ltd, 1916. (96)

14. Coppard, George. *With a Machine Gun to Cambrai: The tale of a young Tommy in Kitchener's army 1914-1918*. London: H.M.S.O, 1969. (59)

15. Graves, Robert. *Goodbye to All That*. London: Penguin, 1960. (116, 118)

16. Sassoon, Siegfried. *Memoirs of an Infantry Officer*. Kent: Faber and Faber, 2000. (18)

17. Cited in Holmes, Richard. *Firing Line*. London: Pimlico. 1985. (319)

18. Heard, Barry. *Well Done Those Men*. Victoria: Scribe Publications, 2005. (121)

19. Lewis, C. S. *Surprised by Joy: The shape of my early life*. London: Collins, 1959. (156)

20. Rickenbacker, Edward V. *Fighting the Flying Circus*. New York: Frederick A Stokes Company, 1919. (280)

21. Coppard, *With a Machine Gun to Cambrai*, 25.

22. Gould Lee, Arthur. *No Parachute*. London: Jarrolds, 1968.

23. Blair, Dale. *Dinkum Diggers*. Victoria: Melbourne University Press. 2001. (143)

24. Mauldin, William Henry. *Up front*. New York: H. Holt, 1945. (48-50, 97)

25. Astor, Gerald. *Operation Iceberg: The Invasion and Conquest of Okinawa in World War II*. New York: Donald I. Fine, 1995. (414)

26. Middlebrook, Martin. *The Kaiser's Battle*. Penguin: London, 2000. (231)

27. Middlebrook, *The Kaiser's Battle*, 233.

28. Graves, *Goodbye to All That,* 112.

29. Hallas, James H. *Killing Ground on Okinawa*. Connecticut: Praeger, 1996. (126)

30. Griffiths-Marsh, Roland. *The Sixpenny Soldier*. NSW: Angus and Robertson, 1990. (107)

31. Warr, Nicholas. *Phase Line Green: The battle for Hue, 1968*. Annapolis, MD: Naval Institute Press, 1997. (171)

32. Bramley, Vincent. *Two Sides of Hell*. Great Britain: Bloomsbury, 1994. (149)

33. MacDonald, Charles B. *A Time for Trumpets: The untold story of the Battle of the Bulge*. New York: Morrow, 1984. (318-319)

34. Large, Lofty. *One Man's War in Korea*. Wellingborough: Kimber, 1988. (58)

35. Cochrane, James Aikman. *Charlie Company: In service with C Company, 2nd Queen's Own Cameron Highlanders, 1940-44*. London: Chatto and Windus, 1977. (56)

36. Bramley, *Two Sides of Hell*, 153.

37. Sledge, E. B. *With the old Breed, at Peleliu and Okinawa*. Novato, Calif: Presidio Press, 1981. (115)

38. Large, Lofty. *One Man's War in Korea*. Wellingborough: Kimber, 1988. (77)

39. McGowan, Robert, and Jeremy Hands. *Don't Cry for Me, Sergeant-Major*. London: Futara, 1983. (90)

40. *Guardian Unlimited*. 'Back into Battle'. http://www.guardian.co.uk/military/story/0,11816,1490057,00.html 24 May 2005.

41. Slim, William. *Defeat into Victory*. London: Cassell, 1956. (337)

42. Hallas, James H. *Killing Ground on Okinawa*. Connecticut: Praeger, 1996. (127)

43. Hallas, *Killing Ground on Okinawa*, 123.

44. Astor, Gerald. *Operation Iceberg: the Invasion and Conquest of Okinawa in World War II*. New York: Donald I. Fine, 1995. (416)

45. Tamayama, Kazuo and John Nunneley. *Tales by Japanese Soldiers*. London: Cassell, 1992. (171)

46. Kelly, Jeff. *DMZ diary: A combat marine's Vietnam memoir*. Jefferson, N.C: McFarland, 1991. (21)

47. Clark, Johnnie M. *Guns Up!* New York: Ballantine, 1984. (79, 90)

48. Heard, *Well Done Those Men*, 119-120, 138.

49. Astor, Gerald. *Operation Iceberg: The Invasion and Conquest of Okinawa in World War II*. New York: Donald I. Fine, 1995. (78)

50. Cochrane, James Aikman. *Charlie Company: In service with C Company, 2nd Queen's Own Cameron Highlanders, 1940-44*. London: Chatto and Windus, 1977. (172)

51. Caputo, Philip. *A Rumor of War*. New York: Holt, Rinehart and Winston, 1977. (xvii)

52. Junger, Ernst. *The Storm of Steel*. London: Chatto and Windus, 1930. (123)

53. Westman, Stephen Kurt. *Surgeon with the Kaiser's Army*. London: Kimber, 1968. (58-59)

54. Middlebrook, Martin. *The First Day of the Somme*. Penguin: Middlesex, 1984. (168)

55. Macdonald, Lyn. *They Called it Passchendaele*. London: Penguin, 1993. (99)

56. Holmes, Richard. *Acts of War: The behavior of men in battle*. New York: Free Press, 1986. (286)

57. Moore, Harold G, and Joseph L. Galloway. *We Were Soldiers Once and Young: Ia Drang: the battle that changed the war in Vietnam*. New York: Random House, 1992. (155)

58. Middlebrook, *The Kaiser's Battle*, 199.

59. Crozier, Brigadier-General FP. *The Men I Killed*. London: Michael Joseph, 1937. (107)

60. Cochrane, James Aikman. *Charlie Company: In service with C Company, 2nd Queen's Own Cameron Highlanders, 1940-44*. London: Chatto and Windus, 1977. (65)

61. Coughlin, Jack. *Shooter: The autobiography of the top-ranked Marine sniper*. New York: St. Martin's Press, 2005. (25)

62. Warr, Nicholas. *Phase Line Green: The battle for Hue, 1968.* Annapolis, MD: Naval Institute Press, 1997. (127)

63. Oslin, Bob, Lieutenant Colonel, US Army. (Ret.) Emails to the author. May – June 2005.

Chapter 2

1. Holmes, Richard. *Firing Line.* London: Pimlico. 1985. (376)

2. Sassoon, Siegfried. *Memoirs of an Infantry Officer.* Kent: Faber and Faber, 2000. (62)

3. Phibbs, Brendan. *The Other Side of Time: A Combat Surgeon in World War II.* Boston: Little, Brown, 1987. (128)

4. Cochrane, James Aikman. *Charlie Company: In service with C Company, 2nd Queen's Own Cameron Highlanders, 1940-44.* London: Chatto and Windus, 1977. (58)

5. Australian Broadcasting Corporation. *Warrior: Reflections of Men at War.* Courtesy Library of the Australian Defence Force Academy, Canberra. 2004. (28'30')

6. Barham, Sergeant Andrew, Australian Army soldier and veteran of the East Timor campaign. Conversations, April 2005.

7. Stewart, Nora Kinzer. *Mates and Muchachos: Unit Cohesion in the Falklands/Malvinas War.* USA: Brassey's, 1991. (82-83)

8. Grossman, Lieutenant Colonel Dave. *On Killing: The Psychological Cost of Learning to Kill in War and Society.* Boston: Little, Brown and Company. 1996. (234-235)

9. Young, Peter. *Storm from the Sea.* Great Britain: Wren's Park Publishing, 2002. (159)

10. McKee, Alexander. *Caen: Anvil of victory.* London: Souvenir Press, 1964. (118)

11. Hastings, Max. *Armageddon: The Battle for Germany 1944-1945.* USA: Macmillan, 2004. (90)

12. Sajer, Guy. *The Forgotten Soldier.* London: Weidenfeld and Nicolson, 1971. (288)

13. Peters, Ralph. 'The Truth About War'. http://www.nypost.com/postopinion/opedcolumnists/39390.htm 14 February 2005.

14. ABC News website, 'It's fun to shoot some people: US General'. http://www.abc.net.au/news/newsitems/200502/s1295615.htm 4 February 2005.

15. Lewis, C. S. *Surprised by Joy: The shape of my early life.* London: Collins, 1959. (155)

16. Ambrose, Stephen E. *Band of Brothers: E Company, 506th Regiment, 101st Airborne: from Normandy to Hitler's Eagle's Nest.* New York: Simon & Schuster, 1992. (113)

17. Bennett, Cam. *Rough Infantry.* Victoria: Warrnambool Institute Press, 1984. (197)

18. Kennedy, Ludovic Henry Coverley. *On My Way to the Club: The autobiography of Ludovic Kennedy.* London: Fontana, 1990, 1989. (146)

19. Hurst, James. *Game to the Last.* Melbourne: Oxford University Press, 2005. (44)

20. Holmes, *Firing Line,* 376-377.

21. MacDonald Fraser, George. *Quartered Safe Out Here.* London: Harper Collins, 1995. (86)

22. MacDonald Fraser, *Quartered Safe Out Here,* 118.

23. Astor, Gerald. *Operation Iceberg: The Invasion and Conquest of Okinawa in World War II.* New York: Donald I. Fine, 1995. (217)

24. Astor, *Operation Iceberg*, 412.

25. Ambrose, Stephen E. *Band of Brothers: E Company, 506th Regiment, 101ˢᵗ Airborne: from Normandy to Hitler's Eagle's Nest*. New York: Simon & Schuster, 1992. (234)

26. Knox, Donald. *The Korean War: An Oral History*. San Diego: Harcourt Brace Jovanovich, 1985. (278)

27. Clark, Johnnie M. *Guns Up!* New York: Ballantine, 1984. (49)

28. Kelly, Jeff. *DMZ Diary: A combat marine's Vietnam memoir*. Jefferson, N.C: McFarland, 1991. (105-106)

29. Caputo, Philip. *A Rumor of War*. New York: Holt, Rinehart and Winston, 1977. (xiii, p. 81)

30. McKee, Alexander. *Caen: Anvil of victory*. London: Souvenir Press, 1964. (104)

31. McKee, *Caen: Anvil of victory*, 59.

32. McGowan, Robert, and Jeremy Hands. *Don't Cry for Me, Sergeant-Major*. London: Futara, 1983. (63-64)

33. McGowan and Hands, *Don't Cry for Me, Sergeant-Major*, 40.

34. Bourke, Joanna. *An Intimate History of Killing: Face-to-face killing in twentieth-century warfare*. London: Granta Books, 1999. (90)

35. Coughlin, Jack. *Shooter: The autobiography of the top-ranked Marine sniper*. New York: St. Martin's Press, 2005. (26)

36. Phibbs, Brendan. *The Other Side of Time: A Combat Surgeon in World War II*. Boston: Little, Brown, 1987. (228) Phibbs used the term 'tank' as opposed to 'track', which may indeed have been the type of platform.

37. Norman, Richard. *Ethics, Killing and War*. New York: Cambridge University Press, 1995. (119)

38. Bransby, Guy. *Her Majesty's Interrogator*. London: Leo Cooper, 1996. (13)

39. Bramley, Vincent. *Two Sides of Hell*. Great Britain: Bloomsbury, 1994. (250)

40. Stewart, Nora Kinzer. *Mates and Muchachos: Unit Cohesion in the Falklands/Malvinas War*. USA: Brassey's, 1991. (108-109), and McGowan, Robert, and Jeremy Hands. *Don't Cry for Me, Sergeant-Major*. London: Futara, 1983. (242, 247)

41. Crozier, Brigadier-General FP. *A Brass Hat in No Man's Land*. London: J. Cape, 1930. (37)

42. United States Marine Corps, 1940. *Small Wars Manual*. Kansas: Military Affairs/Aerospace Historian Publishing, 1972. (4-3-b)

43. SALUT, Col Des Barker, 'Women pilots in operational combat', http://www.mil.za/Magazines/SALUT/Sept%6099/sep6womenpilots.htm July 2005.

44. Coughlin, Jack. *Shooter: The autobiography of the top-ranked Marine sniper*. New York: St. Martin's Press, 2005. (32)

45. Junger, Ernst. *The Storm of Steel*. London: Chatto and Windus, 1930. (254-255)

46. Moran, Lord. *The Anatomy of Courage*. London: Constable, 1945. (56)

47. Martin, Charles Cromwell. *Battle Diary: From D-Day and Normandy to the Zuider Zee and VE*. Toronto: Dundurn Press, 1994. (46)

48. Martin, *Battle diary,* 123.

49. Dockery, Martin J. *Lost in Translation: Vietnam, a combat advisor's story.* New York: Presidio Press, 2003. (5)

50. Heard, Barry. *Well Done Those Men.* Victoria: Scribe Publications, 2005. (154-155)

51. Rommel, Erwin. *Infantry Attacks.* Great Britain: Wren's Park Publishing, 2002. (43 footnote)

52. Sassoon, Siegfried. *Memoirs of an Infantry Officer.* (165)

53. Contrast, for example, the accounts given centering around p.112 in Davis, and p.208 in Sledge.

54. Rule, EJ, M.C., M.M. *Jacka's Mob.* Sydney: Angus and Robertson, 1933. (219)

55. Middlebrook, Martin. *The First Day of the Somme.* Penguin: Middlesex, 1984. (184)

56. Bennett, Cam. *Rough Infantry.* Victoria: Warrnambool Institute Press, 1984. (84)

57. *The Canberra Times.* 'Quotes of the Year'. 1 January 2005. (B4)

58. Barrett, John. *We Were There.* NSW: Allen and Unwin, 1995. (279)

59. Graves, Robert. *Goodbye to All That.* London: Penguin, 1960. (226)

60. Griffiths-Marsh, Roland. *The Sixpenny Soldier.* NSW: Angus and Robertson, 1990. (336)

61. Manchester, William. *Goodbye, Darkness: A memoir of the Pacific war.* London: Joseph, 1981. (123)

62. Manchester, *Goodbye, darkness,* 173.

63. Hastings, *Armageddon,* 211.

64. Stouffer, Samuel A. (et al) *The American Soldier.* Princeton, N.J: Princeton University Press, 1949. (164)

65. The reader might note that disquiet over Marshall's methodologies and findings arose in the late 1990s. The following provides discussion: Roger Spiller 'SLA Marshall and the Ratio of Fire,' *RUSI Journal,* 1988, 133 (4): 63-71.

66. Marshall, SLA. *Men Against Fire.* Norman: University of Oklahoma Press, 2000. (183)

67. Phibbs, Brendan. *The Other Side of Time: A Combat Surgeon in World War II.* Boston: Little, Brown, 1987. (155)

68. Mauldin, William Henry. *Up front.* New York: H. Holt, 1945. (43, 45)

69. Young, Peter. *Storm from the Sea.* Great Britain: Wren's Park Publishing, 2002. (175)

70. Phillips, C. E. Lucas. *The Greatest Raid of All.* London: Readers Book Club, in association with the Companion Book Club, 1958. (174)

71. Hastings, *Armageddon,* 18.

72. Sledge, E. B. *With the Old Breed, at Peleliu and Okinawa.* Novato, Calif: Presidio Press, 1981. (52)

73. Barham, Sergeant Andrew, Australian Army soldier and veteran of the East Timor campaign. Notes to the author, May 2005.

74. Stewart, Nora Kinzer. *Mates and Muchachos: Unit Cohesion in the Falklands/Malvinas War.* USA: Brassey's, 1991. (86)

75. Barrett, John. *We Were There*. NSW: Allen and Unwin, 1995. (227-228)

76. DeRose, James F. *Unrestricted Warfare: How a new breed of officers led the submarine force to victory in World War II*. New York: John Wiley, 2000. (81)

77. DeRose, *Unrestricted Warfare,*11.

78. Graham, Don. *No Name on the Bullet: A biography of Audie Murphy*. New York: Viking, 1989. (78, and 89-90) Murphy, according to Don Graham, was capable of both rage in combat and also 'a deadly calm'.

79. Hastings, *Armageddon*, 75.

80. Hackworth, Colonel David H. and Julie Sherman. *About Face*. Melbourne: Macmillan, 1989. (70)

81. Arthur, Max. *Forgotten Voices of the Second World War*. London: Ebury Press, 2005. (255-256)

82. Arthur, *Forgotten Voices*, 147.

83. Weston, Richard, Anti-Tank Gun Commander. Letter to the Editor, *Quadrant* magazine. May 2005. (7), and subsequent emails and telephone conversations.

Chapter 3

1. Donovan, Robert J. *PT109, John F. Kennedy in World War II*. New York: McGraw-Hill, 1961. (30)

2. Phibbs, Brendan. *The Other Side of Time: A Combat Surgeon in World War II*. Boston: Little, Brown, 1987. (213)

3. Hart, Peter. *To the Last Round: The South Notts Hussars, 1939-1942*. Barnsley, England: Pen & Sword Books, 1996. (163)

4. Hastings, Max. *Armageddon: The Battle for Germany 1944-1945*. USA: Macmillan, 2004. (56)

5. Ambrose, Stephen E. *Band of Brothers: E Company, 506th Regiment, 101st Airborne: from Normandy to Hitler's Eagle's Nest*. New York: Simon & Schuster, 1992. (94-102)

6. Ambrose, *Band of Brothers*, 155.

7. Young, Peter. *Storm from the Sea*. Great Britain: Wren's Park Publishing, 2002. (216)

8. Astor, Gerald. *Operation Iceberg: The Invasion and Conquest of Okinawa in World War II*. New York: Donald I. Fine, 1995. (407)

9. Phillips, C. E. Lucas. *The Greatest Raid of All*. London: Readers Book Club, 1958. (212)

10. Lukowiak, Ken. *A Soldier's Song*. London: Secker and Warburg, 1993. (53)

11. McKee, Alexander. *Caen: Anvil of victory*. London: Souvenir Press, 1964. (324)

12. Caputo, Philip. *A Rumor of War*. New York: Holt, Rinehart and Winston, 1977. (122)

13. Caputo, *A Rumor of War*, 267-268.

14. Caputo, *A Rumor of War*, 304.

15. Quoted in Moore, Harold G, and Joseph L. Galloway. *We Were Soldiers Once and Young: Ia Drang: the battle that changed the war in Vietnam*. New York: Random House, 1992. (292)

16. Phibbs, *The Other Side of Time*, 231.

17. Griffiths-Marsh, Roland. *The Sixpenny Soldier*. NSW: Angus and Robertson, 1990. (163)

18. Jennings, Christian, and Adrian Weale. *Green-eyed Boys: 3 Para and the battle for Mount Longdon*. London: HarperCollins, 1996. (142)

19. Brune, Peter. *A Bastard of a Place: The Australians in Papua*. Crows Nest, N.S.W: Allen & Unwin, 2003. (473)

20. Brune, *A Bastard of a Place,* 473.

21. Manchester, William. *Goodbye, Darkness: A memoir of the Pacific war*. London: Joseph, 1981. (240)

22. Wood, WJ. *Leaders and Battles*. California: Presidio, 1990. (32)

23. Wood, *Leaders and Battles*, 59.

24. Connelly, Owen. *On War and Leadership*. New Jersey: Princeton University Press, 2002. (91)

25. Welch, Ronald. *Tank Commander*. London: Oxford University Press, 1972. (135)

26. Macdonald, Donald Alister. *How We Kept the Flag Flying: The story of the siege of Ladysmith*. London: Ward Lock, 1900. (179)

27. Holmes, Richard. *Acts of War: The behavior of men in battle*. New York: Free Press, 1986. (349-351)

28. Sledge, E. B. *With the Old Breed, at Peleliu and Okinawa*. Novato, Calif: Presidio Press, 1981. (217)

29. Westman, Stephen Kurt. *Surgeon with the Kaiser's Army*. London: Kimber, 1968. (70)

30. Caputo, *A Rumor of War,* 193-194.

31. Manchester, *Goodbye, Darkness,* 237.

32. Rule, EJ, M.C., M.M. *Jacka's Mob*. Sydney: Angus and Robertson, 1933. (190)

33. Rule, *Jacka's Mob*, 71-72.

34. Graham, Don. *No Name on the Bullet:A biography of Audie Murphy*. New York: Viking, 1989. (59)

35. McDonough, James R. *Platoon Leader*. CA: Presidio, 1985. (18)

36. McDonough, *Platoon Leader*, 66.

37. De Heer, Derrill, Australian Vietnam veteran. Conversation with the author at The Vietnam War, Thirty Years On Conference. 14 April 2005.

38. Graves, Robert. *Goodbye to All That*. London: Penguin, 1960. (80)

39. Hemingway, Al. *Our War was Different*. Maryland: Naval Institute Press, 1994. (117)

40. Edelman, Bernard. (Ed.) *Dear America: Letters home from Vietnam*. New York: WW Norton and Company, 1985. (94-95)

41. Herr, Michael. *Dispatches*. New York: Knopf, 1977. (171)

42. Herr, *Dispatches,* 179.

43. Lane, Mark. *Conversations with Americans*. New York: Simon and Schuster, 1970. (36)

44. Just, Ward S. *To What End*. Boston: Houghton Mifflin Company, 1968. (171)

45. Just, *To What End,* 169.

46. Gray, J. Glenn. *The Warriors: Reflections on men in battle*. New York: Harper & Rowe, 1967. (26)

47. Gray, *The warriors*, 27.

48. Caputo, *A Rumor of War*, 230.

49. Kelly, Jeff. *DMZ Diary: A combat marine's Vietnam memoir*. Jefferson, N.C: McFarland, 1991. (189-190)

50. Australian Broadcasting Corporation. *Warrior: Reflections of Men at War*. Courtesy Library of the Australian Defence Force Academy, Canberra. 2004. (21'- 22'30')

51. Astor, Gerald. *Operation Iceberg: The Invasion and Conquest of Okinawa in World War II*. New York: Donald I. Fine, 1995. (258)

52. Moore, Harold G, and Joseph L. Galloway. *We Were Soldiers Once and Young: Ia Drang: the battle that changed the war in Vietnam*. New York: Random House, 1992. (199-203)

53. Burstall, Terry. *The Soldiers' Story: The Battle at Xa Long Tan Vietnam, 18 August 1966*. St. Lucia, Qld: University of Queensland Press, 1986. (98)

54. Warr, Nicholas. *Phase Line Green: The battle for Hue, 1968*. Annapolis, MD: Naval Institute Press, 1997. (91)

55. Warr, *Phase Line Green*, 124.

56. Webster, Daniel Kenyon. *Parachute Infantry*. USA: Louisiana State University Press, 1994. (74)

57. Adlin, Mark. *Goose Green*. London: Leo Cooper, 1992. (223)

58. Miller, Franklin, with Elwood JC Kureth. *Reflections of a Warrior*. California: Presidio, 1991. (94)

59. Miller and Kureth, *Reflections of a Warrior*, 197.

60. Dellums (House Of Representatives) War Crimes Hearings, Washington, DC, 1971 http://members.aol.com/warlibrary/vwch1.htm September 2004.

61. Gadd, Charles. *Line Doggie*. California: Presidio Press, 1987. (161)

62. Dockery, Martin J. *Lost in Translation: Vietnam, a combat advisor's story*. New York: Presidio Press, 2003. (58-59)

Chapter 4

1. Reitz, Deneys. *Commando: A Boer journal of the Boer War*. London: Faber and Faber, 1931. (149)

2. Todd, Pamela. (Ed.) *Private Tucker's Boer War Diary: The Transvaal War of 1899, 1900, 1901 & 1902 with the Natal Field Forces*. London: Elm Tree Books, 1980. (39)

3. Macdonald, Donald Alister. *How We Kept the Flag Flying: The story of the siege of Ladysmith*. London: Ward Lock, 1900. (107)

4. Macdonald, *How We Kept the Flag Flying*, 182.

5. Abbott, J. H. M. (John Henry Macartney). *Tommy Cornstalk; Being some account of the less notable features of the South African war from the point of view of the Australian ranks*. London; New York and; Bombay: Longmans, Green, and Co., 1902. (246)

6. See *In South Africa with Buller* (pp: 203-205, and 346); *Tommy Cornstalk* (pp: 244-245); *How we kept the flag flying* (p. 182).

7. Coppard, George. *With a Machine Gun to Cambrai: The tale of a young Tommy in Kitchener's army 1914-1918.* London: H.M.S.O, 1969. (85)

8. Richards, Frank. *Old Soldiers Never Die.* Sydney: Angus & Robertson, 1933. (65)

9. McGowan, Robert, and Jeremy Hands. *Don't Cry for Me, Sergeant-Major.* London: Futara, 1983. (246)

10. Marks, Thomas Penrose. *The Laughter goes from Life: In the trenches of the First World War.* London: Kimber, 1977. (175)

11. McKee, Alexander. *Caen: Anvil of victory.* London: Souvenir Press, 1964. (117)

12. Groom, W. H. A. *Poor Bloody Infantry: a memoir of the First World War.* London: Kimber, 1976. (133)

13. Gray, J. Glenn. *The Warriors: Reflections on men in battle.* New York: Harper & Rowe, 1967. (139)

14. Barrett, John. *We Were There.* NSW: Allen and Unwin, 1995. (308)

15. Australian Broadcasting Corporation. *Warrior: Reflections of Men at War.* Courtesy Library of the Australian Defence Force Academy, Canberra. 2004. (48'50')

16. Sassoon, Siegfried. *Memoirs of an Infantry Officer.* Kent: Faber and Faber, 2000. (66)

17. Richards, Frank. *Old Soldiers Never Die.* Sydney: Angus & Robertson, 1933. (65)

18. Wilson, Trevor. *The Myriad Faces of War.* Cambridge: Polity Press, 1986. (64)

19. Webster, Daniel Kenyon. *Parachute Infantry.* USA: Louisiana State University Press, 1994. (29, 31)

20. Ambrose, Stephen E. *Band of Brothers: E Company, 506th Regiment, 101st Airborne: from Normandy to Hitler's Eagle's Nest.* New York: Simon & Schuster, 1992. (112)

21. Zorns, Bruce C. *I Walk Through the Valley: A World War II infantryman's memoir of war, imprisonment, and love.* Jefferson, N.C: McFarland & Co., 1991. (107)

22. Hallas, James H. *Killing Ground on Okinawa.* Connecticut: Praeger, 1996. (199)

23. Hallas, *Killing Ground on Okinawa,* 151.

24. Sledge, E. B. *With the Old Breed, at Peleliu and Okinawa.* Novato, Calif: Presidio Press, 1981. (33-34, 155-156)

25. Manchester, William. *Goodbye, Darkness: A memoir of the Pacific war.* London: Joseph, 1981. (183)

26. Tamayama, Kazuo and John Nunneley. *Tales by Japanese Soldiers.* London: Cassell, 1992. (162)

27. Hastings, Max. *Armageddon: The Battle for Germany 1944-1945.* USA: Macmillan, 2004. (115)

28. Hastings, *Armageddon,* 268.

29. Metelmann, Henry. *Through Hell for Hitler: A dramatic first-hand account of fighting with the Wehrmacht.* Wellingborough: Stephens, 1990. (162-165)

30. Adler, Bill (Ed.) *Letters from Vietnam.* New York: EP Dutton and Co., 1967. (21-22)

31. Warr, Nicholas. *Phase Line Green: The battle for Hue, 1968.* Annapolis, MD: Naval Institute Press, 1997. (57-58)

32. Warr, *Phase Line Green,* 173.

33. Oslin, Bob, Lieutenant Colonel, US Army. (Ret.) Email to the author. 26 May 2005.

34. Mason, Robert. *Chickenhawk.* Middlesex: Penguin, 1984. (434-435)

35. Cochrane, James Aikman. *Charlie Company: In service with C Company, 2nd Queen's Own Cameron Highlanders, 1940-44.* London: Chatto and Windus, 1977. (71)

36. Stouffer, Samuel A. (et al) *The American Soldier.* Princeton, N.J: Princeton University Press, 1949. (159)

37. McKee, Alexander. *Caen: Anvil of victory.* London: Souvenir Press, 1964. (93-95)

38. McKee, *Caen: Anvil of victory,* 95.

39. Macdonald, *How We Kept the Flag Flying,* 210.

40. Sledge, E. B. *With the Old Breed, at Peleliu and Okinawa.* Novato, Calif: Presidio Press, 1981. (148)

41. Sledge, *With the Old Breed,* 307.

42. Merritt, William E. *Where the Rivers Ran Backward.* Athens [Ga.]: University of Georgia Press, 1989. (86)

43. Caputo, Philip. *A Rumor of War.* New York: Holt, Rinehart and Winston, 1977. (231)

44. Clark, Johnnie M. *Guns Up!* New York: Ballantine, 1984. (116)

45. Bramley, Vincent. *Two Sides of Hell.* Great Britain: Bloomsbury, 1994. (129)

Chapter 5

1. Grider, John MacGavock. *Diary of an Unknown Aviator.* College Station: Texas A&M University Press, 1988. (267)

2. Longstreet, Stephen. *The Canvas Falcons.* London: Leo Cooper, 1995. (51)

3. Rickenbacker, Edward V. *Fighting the Flying Circus.* New York: Frederick A Stokes Company, 1919. (239)

4. Rickenbacker, *Fighting the Flying Circus,* 262.

5. Lee, Arthur Gould. *No Parachute.* London: Jarrolds, 1968. (188)

6. *The Fury and the Flames.* 'WWII Fighter Aces of the Luftwaffe'. Eagle Rock Entertainment. 1999. (Approx 20' into film.)

7. Arthur, Max. *Forgotten Voices of the Second World War.* London: Ebury Press, 2005. (167)

8. *The Fury and the Flames.* (Approx 4' into film.)

9. Toliver, Raymond F, and Trevor J Constable. *Fighter Aces of the USA.* CA: Aero Publishers, 1979. (80)

10. Barrett, John. *We Were There.* NSW: Allen and Unwin, 1995. (426)

11. Whitehouse, Arch. *Decisive Air Battles of the First World War.* New York: Duell, Sloan and Pierce, 1963. (86)

12. Jablonski, Edward. *The Knighted Skies*. London: Thomas Nelson and Sons, 1964. (79)

13. Jablonski, *The Knighted Skies*, see opening pages.

14. Lewis, Cecil Day. *Sagittarius Rising*. Pennsylvania: Giniger, 1963. (136-137)

15. Jablonski, *The Knighted Skies*, 103-104.

16. Cobby, Group Captain AH. *High Adventure*. Melbourne: Robertson and Mullens, 1942. (154)

17. Johns, Captain W.E. *The Camels are Coming*. London: Random House, 1993. (150-151)

18. Longstreet, *The Canvas Falcons*, 70.

19. Jablonski, *The Knighted Skies*, 179.

20. Longstreet, *The Canvas Falcons*, 172-173.

21. Longstreet, *The Canvas Falcons*, 313.

22. MacMillan, Wing Commander Norman, OBE, MC, AFC. *Into the Blue*. London: Jarrolds, 1969. (102)

23. Rickenbacker, *Fighting the Flying Circus*, 125.

24. Lee, Arthur Gould. *No Parachute*. London: Jarrolds, 1968. (135)

25. Richey, Paul. *Fighter Pilot*. London: Cassell, 2001. (90)

26. *The Fury and the Flames*. (Approx 18' into film.)

27. Richey, *Fighter Pilot*, 38.

28. *The Fury and the Flames*. (Approx 12' into film.)

29. Arthur, *Forgotten Voices,* 88.

30. Grossman, Lieutenant Colonel Dave. *On Killing: The Psychological Cost of Learning to Kill in War and Society*. Boston: Little, Brown and Company. 1996. (59-60)

31. Cobby, Group Captain AH. *High Adventure*. Melbourne: Robertson and Mullens, 1942. (62)

32. Bowyer, Chaz. *Albert Ball, VC*. London: William Kimber, 1977. (86)

33. Longstreet, *The Canvas Falcons*, 320.

34. Lee, *No Parachute*, 72.

35. McCudden, James, VC. *Flying Fury*. Hertforshire and California: Greenhill and Aeolus Publishing, 1987. (125)

36. Grider, John MacGavock. *Diary of an Unknown Aviator*. College Station: Texas A&M University Press, 1988. (234)

37. Canadian Air Aces and Heroes http://www.constable.ca/caah/bbishop.htm Accessed July 2007.

38. Lee, *No Parachute*, 36.

39. Bott, Captain Alan. *Cavalry of the Clouds*. New York: Arno Press, 1972. (163)

40. Rickenbacker, *Fighting the Flying Circus*, 163.

41. Rickenbacker, *Fighting the Flying Circus*, 170.

42. Ulanoff, Stanley M, Lt. Col., in Fonck, René. *Ace of Aces*. New York: Doubleday, 1967. (XXIII)

43. Fonck, René. *Ace of Aces*. New York: Doubleday, 1967. (16)

44. Fonck, René. *Ace of Aces*. (48, 51, 65)

45. Fonck, René. *Ace of Aces*. (72)

Chapter 6

1. Mauldin, William Henry. *Up Front*. New York: H. Holt, 1945. (13-14)

2. Grossman, Lieutenant Colonel Dave. *On Killing: The Psychological Cost of Learning to Kill in War and Society*. Boston: Little, Brown and Company. 1996. (250)

3. Australian Broadcasting Corporation. *Warrior: Reflections of Men at War*. Courtesy Library of the Australian Defence Force Academy, Canberra. 2004. (37'10')

4. Australian Broadcasting Corporation, *Warrior: Reflections of Men at War*. 26'.

5. Graves, Robert. *Goodbye to All That*. London: Penguin, 1960. (100)

6. Marks, Thomas Penrose. *The Laughter Goes From Life: In the trenches of the First World War*. London: Kimber, 1977. (137)

7. Richards, Frank. *Old Soldiers Never Die*. Sydney: Angus & Robertson, 1933. (30)

8. Griffiths-Marsh, Roland. *The Sixpenny Soldier*. NSW: Angus and Robertson, 1990. (200)

9. Hanson, Victor Davis. *Why the West has Won*. London: Faber and Faber, 2001. (283) Hanson further estimates (298) that in the eight hours of fighting at Rorke's Drift, each rifleman had fired an average of 200 .45 cartridges.

10. Sledge, E. B. *With the Old Breed, at Peleliu and Okinawa*. Novato, Calif: Presidio Press, 1981. (12)

11. Ambrose, Stephen E. *Band of Brothers: E Company, 506th Regiment, 101stt Airborne: from Normandy to Hitler's Eagle's Nest*. New York: Simon & Schuster, 1992. (235)

12. Arthur, Max. *Forgotten Voices of the Second World War*. London: Ebury Press, 2005. (146)

13. Brune, Peter. *A Bastard of a Place: The Australians in Papua*. Crows Nest, N.S.W: Allen & Unwin, 2003. (562)

14. Large, Lofty. *One Man's War in Korea*. Wellingborough: Kimber, 1988. (56)

15. Arthur, *Forgotten Voices*, 196.

16. Gadd, Charles. *Line Doggie*. California: Presidio Press, 1987. (65)

17. Gadd, *Line Doggie*, 151-152.

18. Ellis, John. *The Sharp End*. Great Britain: Windrow and Green, 1990. (92)

19. Caputo, Philip. *A Rumor of War*. New York: Holt, Rinehart and Winston, 1977. (103)

20. McKee, Alexander. *Caen: Anvil of victory*. London: Souvenir Press, 1964. (313)

21. Moore, Harold G, and Joseph L. Galloway. *We Were Soldiers Once and Young: Ia Drang: the battle that changed the war in Vietnam*. New York: Random House, 1992. (148)

22. Dockery, Martin J. *Lost in Translation: Vietnam, a combat advisor's story*. New York: Presidio Press, 2003. (79)

23. Bairnsfather, Bruce. *Bullets and Billets*. London: Grant Richards Ltd, 1916. (56)

24. Gadd, *Line Doggie*, 158.

25. Marks, Thomas Penrose. *The Laughter Goes From Life: In the trenches of the First World War*. London: Kimber, 1977. (137)

26. MacDonald, Charles B. *A Time for Trumpets: The untold story of the Battle of the Bulge*. New York: Morrow, 1984. (169)

27. Santoli, Al. (Ed.) *Everything we Had: An oral history of the Vietnam War*. New York: Random House, 1981. (210)

28. Caputo, Philip. *A Rumor of War*. New York: Holt, Rinehart and Winston, 1977. (86)

29. Moore, Harold G, and Joseph L. Galloway. *We Were Soldiers Once and Young: Ia Drang: the battle that changed the war in Vietnam*. New York: Random House, 1992. (191)

30. Hastings, Max. *Armageddon: The Battle for Germany 1944-1945*. USA: Macmillan, 2004. (148)

31. McKee, Alexander. *Caen: Anvil of victory*. London: Souvenir Press, 1964. (313)

32. Astor, Gerald. *Operation Iceberg: the Invasion and Conquest of Okinawa in World War II*. New York: Donald I. Fine, 1995. (337)

33. Mitchell, G.D. *Soldier in Battle*. Sydney; London: Angus & Robertson, 1941. (134-135)

34. Marks, *The Laughter Goes From Life,* 137.

35. Coppard, George. *With a Machine Gun to Cambrai: The tale of a young Tommy in Kitchener's army 1914-1918*. London: H.M.S.O, 1969. (53)

36. Sajer, Guy. *The Forgotten Soldier*. London: Weidenfeld and Nicolson, 1971. (316)

37. MacDonald, *A Time for Trumpets,* 109.

38. Grossman, Lieutenant Colonel Dave. *On Killing: the Psychological Cost of Learning to Kill in War and Society*. Boston: Little, Brown and Company. 1996. (250-261)

39. Hanson, Victor Davis. *Why the West has Won*. London: Faber and Faber, 2001. (298) Hanson proposes an even higher figure for Isandhlwana on the same day – around five to seven per British – a Pyrrhic victory indeed for King Cetshwayo, who had wiped out a small British force for the loss of one tenth of his army.

40. Shaw, Jon A. 'Psychodynamic Considerations in the Adaption to Combat', in Belenky, Gregory. *Contemporary Studies in Combat Psychiatry*. New York: Greenwood Press, 1987. (117)

41. Genoves Tarazaga, Santiago. *Is Peace Inevitable?: Aggression, evolution, and human destiny*. London: Allen and Unwin, 1972. (19)

42. Genoves Tarazaga. *Is Peace Inevitable?* 21.

43. Crozier, Brigadier-General FP. *The Men I Killed*. London: Michael Joseph, 1937. (94-95)

44. Bramley, Vincent. *Two Sides of Hell*. Great Britain: Bloomsbury, 1994. (231)

45. Bramley, *Two Sides of Hell*, 239.

46. Bramley, *Two Sides of Hell*, 248-249.

47. Bramley, *Two Sides of Hell*, 218.

48. Coles, Alan. *Slaughter at Sea*. London: Robert Hale, 1986. (151)

49. Richards, Frank. *Old Soldiers Never Die*. Sydney: Angus & Robertson, 1933. (38)
50. Graves, *Goodbye to All That*, 195.
51. Bourke, Joanna. *An Intimate History of Killing: Face-to-face killing in twentieth-century warfare*. London: Granta Books, 1999. (8)
52. Macaulay, Thomas Babbington. Stanza XXVII. 'Horatius: A Lay Made About the Year Of The City CCCLX'. *Lays of Ancient Rome*. http://www.themediadrome.com/content/poetry/horatius.htm 6 August 2005.

Chapter 7

1. Sassoon, Siegfried. *Memoirs of an Infantry Officer*. Kent: Faber and Faber, 2000. (121)
2. Graves, Robert. *Goodbye to All That*. London: Penguin, 1960. (198)
3. Coppard, George. *With a Machine Gun to Cambrai: The tale of a young Tommy in Kitchener's army 1914-1918*. London: H.M.S.O, 1969. (VIII)
4. Coppard, *With a Machine Gun to Cambrai*, 19.
5. Coppard, *With a Machine Gun to Cambrai*, 77.
6. Crozier, Brigadier-General FP. *The Men I Killed*. London: Michael Joseph, 1937. (74)
7. Holmes, Richard. *Acts of War: The behavior of men in battle*. New York: Free Press, 1986. (339)
8. Fussell, Paul. *The Great War and Modern Memory*. New York: Oxford University Press, 1975. (178)
9. Halpin, John. *Blood in the Mists*. Sydney: Macquarie Head Press, 1934. (92)
10. Sassoon, Siegfried. *Memoirs of an Infantry Officer*. Kent: Faber and Faber, 2000. (59)
11. Graves, *Goodbye to All That*, 155.
12. Blair, Dale. *Dinkum Diggers*. Victoria: Melbourne University Press. 2001. (127)
13. Crozier, *The Men I Killed*, 60.
14. Westman, Stephen Kurt. *Surgeon with the Kaiser's Army*. London: Kimber, 1968. (127)
15. Crozier, *The Men I Killed*, 65.
16. Coppard, *With a Machine Gun to Cambrai*, 120.
17. Richards, Frank. *Old Soldiers Never Die*. Sydney: Angus & Robertson, 1933. (29)
18. Holmes, *Acts of War: The behavior of men in battle*, 227.
19. Richards, *Old Soldiers Never Die*, 139.
20. Mitchell, G.D. *Soldier in Battle*. Sydney; London: Angus & Robertson, 1941. (166, 51)
21. Sledge, E. B. *With the Old Breed, at Peleliu and Okinawa*. Novato, Calif: Presidio Press, 1981. (101)
22. Phibbs, Brendan. *The Other Side of Time: A combat surgeon in World War II*. Boston: Little, Brown, 1987. (136)
23. *The Detroit News*. 'The Execution of Pvt. Eddie Slovik'. http://info.detnews.com/history/story/index.cfm?id=103&category=people 26 June 2005.

24. Hastings, Max. *Armageddon: The Battle for Germany 1944-1945*. USA: Macmillan, 2004. (184)

25. Metelmann, Henry. *Through Hell for Hitler: a dramatic first-hand account of fighting with the Wehrmacht*. Wellingborough: Stephens, 1990. (152)

26. Hastings, Max. *Armageddon: The Battle for Germany 1944-1945*. USA: Macmillan, 2004. (289)

27. MacDonald, Charles B. *Company Commander*. Washington: Infantry Journal Press, 1947. (199)

28. Hastings, Max. *Armageddon: The Battle for Germany 1944-1945*. USA: Macmillan, 2004. (130)

29. Donnelly, Christopher N. 'The Soviet Attitude towards Stress in Battle', in Belenky, Gregory. *Contemporary Studies in Combat Psychiatry*. New York: Greenwood Press, 1987. (233)

30. Hastings, Max. *Armageddon: The Battle for Germany 1944-1945*. USA: Macmillan, 2004. (130)

31. Graves, *Goodbye to All That*, 94.

32. Crozier, *The Men I Killed*, 72.

33. Metelmann, *Through Hell for Hitler*, 94-97.

34. Barrett, John. *We Were There*. NSW: Allen and Unwin, 1995. (200)

35. Metelmann, *Through Hell for Hitler*, 172-175.

36. Sajer, Guy. *The Forgotten Soldier*. London: Weidenfeld and Nicolson, 1971. (390)

37. Arthur, Max. *Forgotten Voices of the Second World War*. London: Ebury Press, 2005. (154)

38. Arthur, *Forgotten Voices*, 65, 66.

39. Astor, Gerald. *Operation Iceberg: The Invasion and Conquest of Okinawa in World War II*. New York: Donald I. Fine, 1995. (264)

40. Ambrose, Stephen E. *Band of Brothers: E Company, 506th Regiment, 101st Airborne: from Normandy to Hitler's Eagle's Nest*. New York: Simon & Schuster, 1992. (210-211)

41. Graves, *Goodbye to All That*, 128. Frank Richards describes the same incident in *Old Soldiers Never Die* (p. 109)

42. Brutton, Philip. *Ensign in Italy*. London: Leo Cooper, 1992. (81)

43. Murphy, Audie. *To Hell and Back*. New York: Holt, Rinehart and Winston. 1949. (162)

44. McDonough, James R. *Platoon Leader*. CA: Presidio, 1985. (75)

45. Rush, Robert Sterling. *Hell in Hurtgen Forest*. Kansas: University Press of Kansas, 2001. (ff. 317)

46. Hemingway, Al. *Our War was Different*. Maryland: Naval Institute Press, 1994. (98)

47. McKay, Gary. *Vietnam Fragments: An oral history of Australians at war*. North Sydney: Allen & Unwin, 1992. (128)

48. Bramley, Vincent. *Two Sides of Hell*. Great Britain: Bloomsbury, 1994. (132)

49. McGowan, Robert, and Jeremy Hands. *Don't Cry for Me, Sergeant-Major*. London: Futara, 1983. (249)

Chapter 8

1. See Book 24 of *The Iliad*.

2. Walpole, Brian. *My War – An Australian Commando in New Guinea and Borneo 1943-1945*. Sydney: ABC Books, 2004. Another such incident is related in *We Were There*, p. 440-441.

3. Department of the Army. *US Army Combat Stress Control Handbook*. USA: Lyons Press, 2003. (60)

4. Moore, Harold G, and Joseph L. Galloway. *We Were Soldiers Once and Young: Ia Drang: the battle that changed the war in Vietnam*. New York: Random House, 1992. (158)

5. Clark, Johnnie M. *Guns Up!* New York: Ballantine, 1984. (137)

6. Clark, *Guns Up!* 287.

7. *Sydney Morning Herald*. Deborah Snow. 'Elite soldier charged for kicking dead enemy'. 22 February 2003. http://www.smh.com.au/articles/2003/02/21/1045638486088. html?oneclick=true

8. 'Army admits mistakes in SAS investigation' Australian Associated Press – February 17, 2004. http://www.asia-pacific-action.org/southeastasia/easttimor/netnews/2004/end_02v3. htm#Army%20admits%20mistakes%20in%20SAS%20investigation

9. Sassoon, Siegfried. *Memoirs of an Infantry Officer*. Kent: Faber and Faber, 2000. (152)

10. Ambrose, Stephen E. *Band of Brothers: E Company, 506th Regiment, 101st Airborne: from Normandy to Hitler's Eagle's Nest*. New York: Simon & Schuster, 1992. (25)

11. Astor, Gerald. *Operation Iceberg: The Invasion and Conquest of Okinawa in World War II*. New York: Donald I. Fine, 1995. (199)

12. Sajer, Guy. *The Forgotten Soldier*. London: Weidenfeld and Nicolson, 1971. (187)

13. McKay, Gary, Australian Vietnam veteran. Conversation with the author at The Vietnam War, Thirty Years On Conference. 14 April 2005.

14. Clark, *Guns Up!* 65.

15. Mason, Robert. *Chickenhawk*. Middlesex: Penguin, 1984. (387)

16. Baker, Mark. *Nam: The Vietnam War in the words of the men and women who fought there*. New York: Morrow, 1981. (78)

17. Herr, Michael. *Dispatches*. New York: Knopf, 1977. (19)

18. Gadd, Charles. *Line Doggie*. California: Presidio Press, 1987. (153)

19. Coughlin, Jack. *Shooter: The autobiography of the top-ranked Marine sniper*. New York: St. Martin's Press, 2005. (2)

20. Caputo, Philip. *A Rumor of War*. New York: Holt, Rinehart and Winston, 1977. See the chapters entitled 'The Officer in Charge of the Dead'.

21. Holmes, Robert Derby. *A Yankee in the Trenches*. Boston: Little, Brown, and company, 1918. (170)

22. Graves, Robert. *Goodbye to All That*. London: Penguin, 1960. (97)

23. Cull, W. Ambrose. *At All Costs*. Melbourne: Australasian Authors' Agency, 1919. (53)

24. Richards, Frank. *Old Soldiers Never Die*. Sydney: Angus & Robertson, 1933. (149)

25. Hitchcock, Francis Clere. *Stand To: A diary of the trenches, 1915-1918*. London: Hurst and Blackett, 1937. (77)

26. Buick, Bob, with Gary McKay. *All Guts and No Glory*. NSW: Allen and Unwin, 2000. (119)

27. McAulay, Lex. *The Battle of Long Tan*. Victoria: Hutchinson, 1986. (129)

28. *The Sydney Morning Herald*. Craig Skehan. 'Enemy skull photo seen as an affront'. 30 April, 2005. (13)

29. McGowan, Robert, and Jeremy Hands. *Don't Cry for Me, Sergeant-Major*. London: Futara, 1983. (156)

30. From the war souvenir collection of Sergeant Andrew Barham of the Australian Army – viewed by the author.

31. Kelly, Jeff. *DMZ Diary: A combat marine's Vietnam memoir*. Jefferson, N.C: McFarland, 1991. (42)

32. Herr, *Dispatches,* 34, 57 and 198-199.

33. Lukowiak, Ken. *A Soldier's Song*. London: Secker and Warburg, 1993. (99-101, 154)

34. *New York Daily News*. 'Pix of dead Iraqis may seal his fate'. http://www.nydailynews.com/03-27-2005/news/wn_report/story/293771p-251526c.html 30 March 2005.

35. Clark, *Guns Up!* 55-56.

36. Clark, *Guns Up!* 143.

37. Dockery, Martin J. *Lost in Translation: Vietnam, a combat advisor's story*. New York: Presidio Press, 2003. (81)

38. Kerr, Greg. *Private Wars*. Victoria: Oxford University Press, 2000. (151)

39. Sajer, Guy. *The Forgotten Soldier*. London: Weidenfeld and Nicolson, 1971. (208)

40. Schneider, Carl J. *World War II*. New York: Checkmark Books, 2003. (225)

41. Warr, Nicholas. *Phase Line Green: The battle for Hue, 1968*. Annapolis, MD: Naval Institute Press, 1997. (167-168)

42. Hackworth, Colonel David H. and Eilhys England. *Steel my Soldier's Hearts*. New York: Rugged Land, 2002. (133)

43. Herr, *Dispatches,*174.

44. Mason, Robert. *Chickenhawk*. Middlesex: Penguin, 1984. (434-435)

45. Barham, Sergeant Andrew. Australian Army soldier and veteran of the East Timor campaign. Conversations April 2005.

46. Kilduff, Peter. *The Red Baron*. London: Cassell, 1994. (53)

47. This was the well-known Major Hawker, who von Richthofen bested on 23 November 1916. The German ace was particularly elated about the prowess of his victim, referring to him in his diary as the 'English Immelmann.' See *Richthofen: The Red Fighter Pilot*. http://www.richthofen.com/arcdocs/richt_08.htm

48. Coles, Alan. *Slaughter at Sea*. London: Robert Hale, 1986. (76)

49. Jones, Albert James. *Corporal Jones' War: The Diary of an ANZAC*. Perth, W.A.: Black Swan Press, 2005. (60)

50. Halpin, John. *Blood in the Mists.* Sydney: Macquarie Head Press, 1934. (90)

51. Veteran 1X. Interview with the author. 24 March 2006.

52. Coppard, George. *With a Machine Gun to Cambrai: The tale of a young Tommy in Kitchener's army 1914-1918.* London: H.M.S.O, 1969. (62, 89)

53. Bairnsfather, Bruce. *Bullets and Billets.* London: Grant Richards Ltd, 1916. (192)

54. Webster, Daniel Kenyon. *Parachute Infantry.* USA: Louisiana State University Press, 1994. (XVIII)

55. Graves, Robert. *Goodbye to All That.* London: Penguin, 1960. (178)

56. Hart, Peter. *To the Last Round: The South Notts Hussars, 1939-1942.* Barnsley, England: Pen & Sword Books, 1996.

57. Ambrose, *Band of Brothers,* 90, 107.

58. Sledge, E. B. *With the Old Breed, at Peleliu and Okinawa.* Novato, Calif: Presidio Press, 1981. (64, 123)

59. Astor, Gerald. *Operation Iceberg: The Invasion and Conquest of Okinawa in World War II.* New York: Donald I. Fine, 1995. (405)

60. Hordern, Marsden. *A Merciful Journey.* The Miegunyah Press: Victoria, 2005. (163)

61. Gadd, Charles. *Line Doggie.* California: Presidio Press, 1987. (172)

62. Heard, Barry. *Well Done Those Men.* Victoria: Scribe Publications, 2005. (120-121)

63. McGowan, Robert, and Jeremy Hands. *Don't Cry for Me, Sergeant-Major.* London: Futara, 1983. (229)

64. Barham, Sergeant Andrew, Australian Army soldier and veteran of the East Timor campaign. Conversations April 2005.

65. Dunn, Captain JC. *The War the Infantry Knew.* Great Britain: Jane's Publishing Company, 1987. (216)

66. Richards, Frank. *Old Soldiers Never Die.* Sydney: Angus & Robertson, 1933. (33)

67. Richards, *Old Soldiers Never Die*, 77.

68. Arthur, Max. *Forgotten Voices of the Second World War.* London: Ebury Press, 2005. (240)

69. Sledge, *With the Old Breed ...*, 134.

70. Sassoon, Siegfried. *Memoirs of an Infantry Officer.* Kent: Faber and Faber, 2000. (61, and for another example p. 53)

71. Sledge, *With the Old Breed ...*, 248.

72. Terkel, Louis. *The Good War: An oral history of World War Two.* New York: Pantheon Books, 1984. (50-51)

73. Webster, Daniel Kenyon. *Parachute Infantry.* USA: Louisiana State University Press, 1994. (177, 182)

74. Clark, *Guns Up!* 55.

75. Griffiths-Marsh, Roland. *The Sixpenny Soldier.* NSW: Angus and Robertson, 1990. (319)

76. Bennett, Cam. *Rough Infantry.* Victoria: Warrnambool Institute Press, 1984. (187)

77. Davis, Russell. *Marine at War.* Boston: Little, Brown and Company, 1961. (181)

78. Bramley, Vincent. *Two Sides of Hell.* Great Britain: Bloomsbury, 1994. (201)

79. MacDonald Fraser, George. *Quartered Safe Out Here.* London: Harper Collins, 1995. (37)

80. Hordern, *A Merciful Journey,* 233.

81. Griffiths-Marsh, Roland. *The Sixpenny Soldier.* NSW: Angus and Robertson, 1990. (292)

82. Bergerud, Eric. *Touched with Fire: The land warfare in the South Pacific.* New York: Viking, 1996. (407)

83. Astor, Gerald. *Operation Iceberg: The Invasion and Conquest of Okinawa in World War II.* New York: Donald I. Fine, 1995. (448-449)

84. O'Brien, Tim. *If I Should Die in a Combat Zone.* USA: Delacorte Press, 1973. (79)

85. Caputo, Philip. *A Rumor of War.* New York: Holt, Rinehart and Winston, 1977. (67)

86. Lane, Mark. *Conversations with Americans.* New York: Simon and Schuster, 1970. (67)

87. Lewy, Guenter. *America in Vietnam.* New York: Oxford University Press, 1978. (322)

88. Vietnam War Crimes Hearings. http://members.aol.com/warlibrary/vwch1d.htm

89. Heinemann, Larry. *Paco's Story.* London: Faber, 1987. (8)

90. Mason, Robert. *Chickenhawk.* Middlesex: Penguin, 1984. (454)

91. Sledge, *With the Old Breed …,* 152.

92. Clark, *Guns Up!* 18.

93. Dellums (House Of Representatives) War Crimes Hearings, Washington, DC, 1971. http://members.aol.com/warlibrary/vwch10.htm September 2004.

94. Hersh, Seymour M. *My Lai 4.* New York: Random House, 1970. (24)

95. Baker, Mark. *Nam: The Vietnam War in the words of the men and women who fought there.* New York: Morrow, 1981. (84)

96. Hefron, Peter, American Vietnam veteran. Conversation with the author at The Vietnam War, Thirty Years On Conference. 15 April 2005.

97. Van Zanten, William. *Don't Bunch Up.* Connecticut, Archon, 1993. (202)

98. McGowan, Robert, and Jeremy Hands. *Don't Cry for Me, Sergeant-Major.* London: Futara, 1983. (112)

99. Musgrave, George Clarke. *In South Africa with Buller.* Boston: Little, Brown and Company, 1900. (311)

100. Dunn, Captain JC. *The War the Infantry Knew.* Great Britain: Jane's Publishing Company, 1987. (159)

101. Ambrose, *Band of Brothers,* 91.

102. Leckie, Robert. *Helmet for my Pillow.* Garden City, N.Y: Doubleday, 1979. (76, 106, 212, 259)

103. Terkel, Louis. *The Good War: An oral history of World War Two.* New York: Pantheon Books, 1984. (62)

104. Sledge, *With the Old Breed …,* 64, 123.

105. Sledge, *With the Old Breed ...*, 119-120.

106. Hallas, James H. *Killing Ground on Okinawa*. Connecticut: Praeger, 1996. (126)

107. Sajer, Guy. *The Forgotten Soldier*. London: Weidenfeld and Nicolson, 1971. (373)

108. Lukowiak, Ken. *A Soldier's Song*. London: Secker and Warburg, 1993. (39)

109. Abbott, J. H. M. (John Henry Macartney). *Tommy Cornstalk; being some account of the less notable features of the South African war from the point of view of the Australian ranks*. London; New York and; Bombay: Longmans, Green, and Co., 1902. (172)

110. Bennett, Cam. *Rough Infantry*. Victoria: Warrnambool Institute Press, 1984. (200)

111. Dellums (House Of Representatives) War Crimes Hearings, Washington, DC, 1971. http://members.aol.com/warlibrary/vwch1.htm September 2004.

112. Santoli, Al. (Ed.) *Everything We Had: An oral history of the Vietnam War*. New York: Random House, 1981. (204)

113. Parrish, Lieutenant Robert D. *Combat Recon*. New York: St Martin's Press, 1991. (89)

114. Bourke, Joanna. *An Intimate History of Killing: Face-to-face killing in twentieth-century warfare*. London: Granta Books, 1999. (38-41)

115. LeShan, Lawrence L. *The Psychology of War: Comprehending its mystique and its madness*. Chicago: Noble Press, 1992. (84-85)

116. Webster, Daniel Kenyon. *Parachute Infantry*. USA: Louisiana State University Press, 1994. (XV)

117. Barrett, John. *We Were There*. NSW: Allen and Unwin, 1995. (189)

118. Ambrose, *Band of Brothers*, 20.

119. Ambrose, *Band of Brothers*, 227-228.

120. Graves, Robert. *Goodbye to All That*. London: Penguin, 1960. (225)

121. Sledge, *With the Old Breed ...*, 267.

122. Moore, Harold G, and Joseph L. Galloway. *We Were Soldiers Once and Young: Ia Drang: the battle that changed the war in Vietnam*. New York: Random House, 1992. (191)

123. Sajer, Guy. *The Forgotten Soldier*. London: Weidenfeld and Nicolson, 1971. (113)

124. Ambrose, *Band of Brothers*, 173.

125. Caputo, Philip. *A Rumor of War*. New York: Holt, Rinehart and Winston, 1977. (247)

126. Coppard, George. *With a Machine Gun to Cambrai: The tale of a young Tommy in Kitchener's army 1914-1918*. London: H.M.S.O, 1969. (107)

127. Baker, Clive and Greg Knight. *Milne Bay 1942*. NSW: Baker-Knight Publications, 1991. (271)

128. Phibbs, Brendan. *The Other Side of Time: A Combat Surgeon in World War II*. Boston: Little, Brown, 1987. (128)

129. Holmes, Richard. *Acts of War: The behavior of men in battle*. New York: Free Press, 1986. (361)

130. Terkel, Louis 'Studs'. *The Good War: An oral history of World War Two*. New York: Pantheon Books, 1984. (63)

131. Gray, J. Glenn. *The Warriors: Reflections on men in battle*. New York: Harper & Rowe, 1967. (133)

132. Jennings, Christian, and Adrian Weale. *Green-eyed Boys: 3 Para and the battle for Mount Longdon*. London: HarperCollins, 1996. (160)

Chapter 9

1. See Grossman p. 204.

2. Hastings, Max. *Armageddon: The Battle For Germany 1944-1945*. Macmillan, 2004. Macmillan, 2004. Abridged extract courtesy Peter Williams.

3. International Committee of the Red Cross. *The Geneva Conventions of August 12, 1949*. Geneva. Article III.

4. Caputo, Philip. *A Rumor of War*. New York: Holt, Rinehart and Winston, 1977. (325)

5. Sajer, Guy. *The Forgotten Soldier*. London: Weidenfeld and Nicolson, 1971. (239-241)

6. Metelmann, Henry. *Through Hell for Hitler: a dramatic first-hand account of fighting with the Wehrmacht*. Wellingborough: Stephens, 1990. (60)

7. Macdonald, Lyn. *They called it Passchendaele*. London: Penguin, 1993. (106)

8. Macdonald, *They called it Passchendaele*, 114.

9. Middlebrook, Martin. *The First Day of the Somme*. Penguin: Middlesex, 1984. (192)

10. Bramley, Vincent. *Two Sides of Hell*. Great Britain: Bloomsbury, 1994. (178)

11. Adlin, Mark. *Goose Green*. London: Leo Cooper, 1992. (125)

12. Gray, J. Glenn. *The warriors: reflections on men in battle*. New York: Harper & Rowe, 1967. (137-138)

13. McKee, Alexander. *Caen: anvil of victory*. London: Souvenir Press, 1964. (51)

14. Todd, Pamela. (Ed.) *Private Tucker's Boer War diary: the Transvaal War of 1899, 1900, 1901 & 1902 with the Natal Field Forces*. London: Elm Tree Books, 1980. (117)

15. Musgrave, George Clarke. *In South Africa with Buller*. Boston: Little, Brown and Company, 1900. (113-114)

16. Musgrave, George Clarke. *In South Africa with Buller*. Boston: Little, Brown and Company, 1900. (100, 250, 281, 317)

17. Macdonald, Donald Alister. *How we kept the flag flying: the story of the siege of Ladysmith*. London: Ward Lock, 1900. (21-22)

18. Abbott, J. H. M. (John Henry Macartney). *Tommy Cornstalk; being some account of the less notable features of the South African war from the point of view of the Australian ranks*. London; New York and; Bombay: Longmans, Green, and Co., 1902. (81)

19. Winter, Denis. *25 April 1915*. Queensland: University of Queensland Press, 1994. (174)

20. Keegan, John. *The Face of Battle*. London: Pimlico, 2000. (49)

21. Coppard, George. *With a machine gun to Cambrai: the tale of a young Tommy in Kitchener's army 1914-1918*. London: H.M.S.O, 1969. (71)

22. Cull, W. Ambrose. *At All Costs*. Melbourne: Australasian Authors' Agency, 1919. (29)

23. Mitchell, G.D. *Soldier in Battle*. Sydney; London: Angus & Robertson, 1941. (136-137)

24. Long, Gavin. *To Benghazi*. Canberra: Australian War Memorial, 1952. (171)

25. Ambrose, Stephen E. *Band of Brothers: E Company, 506th Regiment, 101ˢᵗ Airborne: from Normandy to Hitler's Eagle's Nest*. New York: Simon & Schuster, 1992. (76)

26. Halpin, John. *Blood in the Mists*. Sydney: Macquarie Head Press, 1934. (101)

27. Weston, Richard, Anti-Tank Gun Commander. Letter to the Editor. *Quadrant* magazine. May 2005. (7), and subsequent emails and telephone conversations.

28. Holmes, Robert Derby. *A Yankee in the trenches*. Boston: Little, Brown, and company, 1918. (141)

29. Fitz-Gibbon, Spencer. *Not Mentioned in Despatches*. Cambridge: The Lutterworth Press, 1995. (49)

30. Sledge, E. B. *With the old breed, at Peleliu and Okinawa*. Novato, Calif: Presidio Press, 1981. (65-66)

31. Sledge, *With the old breed*, 116.

32. Ambrose,. *Band of Brothers*, 80.

33. Young, Peter. *Storm from the Sea*. Great Britain: Wren's Park Publishing, 2002. (91)

34. Hastings, Max. *Armageddon: The Battle for Germany 1944-1945*. USA: Macmillan, 2004. (88)

35. McKee, *Caen: anvil of victory*, 79.

36. McKee, *Caen: anvil of victory*, 200.

37. Schneider, Carl J. *World War II*. New York: Checkmark Books, 2003. (172)

38. Ambrose, *Band of Brothers*, 212.

39. Fitz-Gibbon, Spencer. *Not Mentioned in Despatches*. Cambridge: The Lutterworth Press, 1995. (35)

40. Jennings, Christian, and Adrian Weale. *Green-eyed boys: 3 Para and the battle for Mount Longdon*. London: HarperCollins, 1996. (104-105)

41. Adlin, Mark. *Goose Green*. London: Leo Cooper, 1992. (234-237)

42. Reitz, Deneys. *Commando: a Boer journal of the Boer War*. London: Faber and Faber, 1931. (169, 135)

43. Rule, EJ, M.C., M.M. *Jacka's Mob*. Sydney: Angus and Robertson, 1933. (277)

44. Crozier, Brigadier-General FP. *A Brass Hat in No Man's Land*. London: J. Cape, 1930. (184)

45. Middlebrook, Martin. *The Kaiser's Battle*. Penguin: London, 2000. (213)

46. Keegan, *The Face of Battle*, 50.

47. McKee, *Caen: anvil of victory*, 58.

48. Weston, Richard. Anti-Tank Gun Commander. "Nine Lives". Unpublished manuscript provided to the author. 2005.

49. Long, *To Benghazi*, 178.

50. Long, *To Benghazi*, 229.

51. Griffiths-Marsh, Roland. *The Sixpenny Soldier*. NSW: Angus and Robertson, 1990. (107-108, and for another such incident, see p. 129)

52. Dockery, Martin J. *Lost in translation: Vietnam, a combat advisor's story*. New York: Presidio Press, 2003. (80)

53. Coles, Alan. *Slaughter at Sea*. London: Robert Hale, 1986. (114)

54. Graves, Robert. *Goodbye to All That*. London: Penguin, 1960. (161)

55. MacDonald, Charles B. *A Time for Trumpets: the untold story of the Battle of the Bulge*. New York: Morrow, 1984. (226)

56. McBride, Glen. *D-Day on Queen's Beach Red: an Australian's war from the Burma Road retreat to the Normandy beaches*. Brisbane, Qld: Prof. G. McBride, 1994. 9147)

57. Dunn, Captain JC. *The War the Infantry Knew*. Great Britain: Jane's Publishing Company, 1987. (84)

58. Hastings, Max. *Armageddon: The Battle for Germany 1944-1945*. USA: Macmillan, 2004. (88)

59. Griffiths-Marsh, *The Sixpenny Soldier*, 210.

60. Hallas, James H. *Killing Ground on Okinawa*. Connecticut: Praeger, 1996. (125)

61. Ford, Roger. *Steel from the sky: the Jedburgh raiders, France 1944*. London: Weidenfeld & Nicolson, 2004. (67)

62. Ford, *Steel from the sky*, 9.

63. Ford, *Steel from the sky*, 246.

64. Terkel, Louis. *The Good War: an oral history of World War Two*. New York: Pantheon Books, 1984. (488)

65. Mitchell, G.D. *Soldier in Battle*. Sydney; London: Angus & Robertson, 1941. (136)

66. Metelmann, Henry. *Through Hell for Hitler: a dramatic first-hand account of fighting with the Wehrmacht*. Wellingborough: Stephens, 1990. (77)

67. Shirer, William L. *The rise and fall of the Third Reich: a history of Nazi Germany*. London: Secker & Warburg, 1960. (955)

68. Webster, Daniel Kenyon. *Parachute Infantry*. USA: Louisiana State University Press, 1994. (10)

Chapter 10

1. Holmes, Richard. *Firing Line*. London: Pimlico. 1985. (389)

2. Winter, Denis. *25 April 1915*. Queensland: University of Queensland Press, 1994. (158-159)

3. Bourke, Joanna. *An Intimate History of Killing: Face-to-face killing in twentieth-century warfare*. London: Granta Books, 1999. (182)

4. Gallishaw, John. *Trenching at Gallipoli*. New York: A.L. Burt Company, 1916. (162)

5. Rule, EJ, M.C., M.M. *Jacka's Mob*. Sydney: Angus and Robertson, 1933. (25)

6. Holmes, Robert Derby. *A Yankee in the Trenches*. Boston: Little, Brown, and company, 1918. (142)

7.   Rommel, Erwin. *Infantry Attacks*. Great Britain: Wren's Park Publishing, 2002. (12)

8.   Groom, W. H. A. *Poor Bloody Infantry: A memoir of the First World War*. London: Kimber, 1976. (118)

9.   Rule, EJ, M.C., M.M. *Jacka's Mob*. Sydney: Angus and Robertson, 1933. (96)

10. Junger, Ernst. *The Storm of Steel*. London: Chatto and Windus, 1930. (262-263)

11. Junger, *The Storm of Steel*, 311.

12. Caputo, Philip. *A Rumor of War*. New York: Holt, Rinehart and Winston, 1977. (117)

13. Longstreet, Stephen. *The Canvas Falcons*. London: Leo Cooper, 1995. (103-104, and 210)

14. Grider, John MacGavock. *Diary of an Unknown Aviator*. College Station: Texas A&M University Press, 1988. (172)

15. Johns, Captain W.E. Biggles: *The Camels are Coming*. London: Random House, 1993. (150-151)

16. Whitehouse, Arch. *Decisive Air Battles of the First World War*. New York: Duell, Sloan and Pierce, 1963. (86)

17. Jablonski, Edward. *The Knighted Skies*. London: Thomas Nelson and Sons, 1964. (79)

18. Jablonski, Edward. (See opening pages)

19. Cobby, Group Captain AH. *High Adventure*. Melbourne: Robertson and Mullens, 1942. (154)

20. Grider, John MacGavock. *Diary of an Unknown Aviator*. College Station: Texas A&M University Press, 1988. (261)

21. Cobby, *High Adventure*, 119-120.

22. Yeates, VM. *Winged Victory*. London: Jonathan Cape, 1962. (8)

23. Yeates, *Winged Victory*, 202.

24. Yeates, *Winged Victory*, 100.

25. McBride, Glen. *D-Day on Queen's Beach Red: An Australian's war from the Burma Road retreat to the Normandy beaches*. Brisbane, Qld: Prof. G. McBride, 1994. (139)

26. Toliver, Raymond F, and Trevor J Constable. *Fighter Aces of the USA*. CA: Aero Publishers, 1979. (173)

27. BBC Television. Fisher, John Hayes (Dir.) *Meet the Ancestors – Billy and the Boys*. 2004

28. Dornan, Peter. *Nicky Barr, an Australian Air Ace*. NSW: Allen and Unwin, 2002. (83)

29. Dornan, *Nicky Barr*, 124.

30. Harding, William. *A Cockney Soldier*. Devon: Merlin Books, 1989. (128)

31. Porter, R. Bruce, with Eric Hammel. *Ace! A Marine Night-Fighter Pilot in World War II*. San Francisco: Pacifica Press, 1985. (121-123)

32. Bergerud, Eric M. *Fire in the Sky: The Air War in the South Pacific*. Boulder, Colo.: Westview Press, 2000. (451)

33. Bergerud, *Fire in the Sky*, 527.

34. Robinson, LCDR Robert, USN. *The Invincible Russell*. (135) Copy supplied by the Washington Navy Yard from a donation by LCDR Robinson in 1995.

35. Adlin, Mark. *Goose Green*. London: Leo Cooper, 1992. (66)

36. Adlin, *Goose Green*, 249.

37. Murphy, Audie. *To Hell and Back*. New York: Holt, Rinehart and Winston. 1949. (126-127)

38. Martin, Charles Cromwell. *Battle Diary: From D-Day and Normandy to the Zuider Zee and VE*. Toronto: Dundurn Press, 1994. (84)

39. Rush, Robert Sterling. *Hell in Hurtgen Forest*. Kansas: University Press of Kansas, 2001. (238)

40. Cochrane, James Aikman. *Charlie Company: In service with C Company, 2nd Queen's Own Cameron Highlanders, 1940-44*. London: Chatto and Windus, 1977. (72)

41. Ambrose, Stephen E. *Citizen Soldiers: The U.S. Army from the Normandy beaches to the Bulge to the surrender of Germany, June 7, 1944-May 7, 1945*. New York, N.Y: Simon & Schuster, 1997. (352)

42. Ambrose, *Citizen Soldiers*, 354.

43. Terkel, Louis. *The Good War: An oral history of World War Two*. New York: Pantheon Books, 1984. (381)

44. Ferguson N. 'Prisoner Taking and Prisoner Killing in the Age of Total War: Towards a Political Economy of Military Defeat'. War in History, 1 April 2004, vol. 11, no. 2. (177)

45. Dwight D. Eisenhower Library, Joe Lawton Collins Papers, Box 2, 201 Files – Personal Letters 1943. Via Internet discussion group H-NET Military History Discussion List H-WAR@H-NET.MSU.EDU, 9 October 2004. Courtesy of member Joerg Muth.

46. Bergerud, Eric. *Touched with Fire: The land warfare in the South Pacific*. New York: Viking, 1996. (Photographs in-between pages 166 and 167)

47. Young, Peter. *Storm from the Sea*. Great Britain: Wren's Park Publishing, 2002. (216)

48. Slim, William. *Defeat into Victory*. London: Cassell, 1956. (418)

49. Tamayama, Kazuo and John Nunneley. *Tales by Japanese Soldiers*. London: Cassell, 1992. (202)

50. Schneider, Carl J. *World War II*. New York: Checkmark Books, 2003. (187)

51. Hallas, James H. *Killing Ground on Okinawa*. Connecticut: Praeger, 1996. (127)

52. Hallas, *Killing Ground on Okinawa*, 194.

53. Astor, Gerald. *Operation Iceberg: The Invasion and Conquest of Okinawa in World War II*. New York: Donald I. Fine, 1995. (439, 451)

54. Baker, Clive and Greg Knight. *Milne Bay 1942*. NSW: Baker-Knight Publications, 1991. (260)

55. Baker and Knight, *Milne Bay 1942*, 299.

56. Baker and Knight, *Milne Bay 1942*, 140.

57. Baker and Knight, *Milne Bay 1942*, 217.

58. Baker and Knight, *Milne Bay 1942*, Appendix 9: pp: 435-438.

59. Manchester, William. *Goodbye, Darkness: A memoir of the Pacific war*. London: Joseph, 1981. (166)

60. Schneider, Carl J. *World War II*. New York: Checkmark Books, 2003. (205)

61. Bergerud, *Touched with Fire,* 407.

62. Bergerud, *Touched with Fire,* 405-406.

63. Stouffer, Samuel A. (et al) *The American Soldier.* Princeton, N.J: Princeton University Press, 1949. (162)

64. Bergerud, *Touched with Fire,* 371.

65. Young, Peter. *Storm from the Sea.* Great Britain: Wren's Park Publishing, 2002. (208)

66. Baker and Knight, *Milne Bay 1942* , (29)

67. Sledge, E. B. *With the Old Breed, at Peleliu and Okinawa.* Novato, Calif: Presidio Press, 1981. (18)

68. Moore, Harold G, and Joseph L. Galloway. *We Were Soldiers Once and Young: Ia Drang: the battle that changed the war in Vietnam.* New York: Random House, 1992. (190)

69. Russell, Lord, of Liverpool. *The Knights of Bushido: A short history of Japanese War Crimes.* Bath: Chivers Press, 1989. (172)

70. Russell, *The Knights of Bushido,* 173.

71. DeRose, James F. *Unrestricted Warfare: How a new breed of officers led the submarine force to victory in World War II.* New York: John Wiley, 2000. (84)

72. DeRose, *Unrestricted warfare,* 245.

73. Bridgland, Tony. *Waves of Hate.* Leo Cooper: South Yorkshire, 2002. (28, 85-112)

74. Kennedy, Ludovic Henry Coverley. *On my Way to the Club: The autobiography of Ludovic Kennedy.* London: Fontana, 1989. (340-342)

75. Santoli, Al. (Ed.) *Everything we Had: An oral history of the Vietnam War.* New York: Random House, 1981. (25)

76. Adler, Bill (Ed.) *Letters from Vietnam.* New York: EP Dutton and Co., 1967. (29)

77. Bergerud, *Touched with Fire,* 374.

78. Gadd, Charles. *Line Doggie.* Califonia: Presidio Press, 1987. (90)

79. Bergerud, *Touched with Fire,* 421.

80. Denfeld, D. Colt. *Hold the Marianas.* Pennsylvania: White Mane Publishing Company, 1997. (127)

81. Brune, Peter. *A Bastard of a Place: The Australians in Papua.* Crows Nest, N.S.W: Allen & Unwin, 2003. (548)

82. Brune, *A Bastard of a Place,* 408, and reporting cannibalism, 241 and 587.

83. Ham, Paul. *Kokoda.* Sydney: HarperCollins, 2004. (344-348)

84. Strauss, Ulrich. *The Anguish of Surrender: Japanese POWs of World War II.* Seattle: University of Washington Press, 2003. (46)

85. Barrett, John. *We Were There.* NSW: Allen and Unwin, 1995. (222)

86. Hordern, Marsden. *A Merciful Journey.* The Miegunyah Press: Victoria, 2005. (229, 279)

87. Terkel, Louis. *The Good War: An oral history of World War Two.* New York: Pantheon Books, 1984. (80)

88. Barrett, *We Were There,* 251.

89. Ham, Paul. *Kokoda*. Sydney: HarperCollins, 2004. (529)

90. Young, *Storm from the Sea*, 205, 219.

91. Bergerud, *Touched with Fire*, 413.

92. Wright, Derrick. *A Hell of a Way to Die: Tarawa Atoll, 20-23 November 1943*. London: Windrow & Greene, 1997. (123)

93. DeRose, James F. *Unrestricted Warfare*, (248)

94. DeRose, *Unrestricted Warfare*, 251.

95. Henri, Raymond. *The U.S. Marines on Iwo Jima*. Tennessee: Battery Press, 1987. (230)

96. Brune, *A Bastard of a Place*, 551.

97. Brune, *A Bastard of a Place*, 484.

98. Barrett, John. *We Were There* , (309)

99. Bennett, Cam. *Rough Infantry*. Victoria: Warrnambool Institute Press, 1984. (196)

100. Ham, *Kokoda* , (393); and see *US Army in WWII*. Samuel Milner, 'Chapter VII The Advance on the Beachhead'. http://www.ibiblio.org/hyperwar/USA/USA-P-Papua/USA-P-Papua-7. html 5 August 2005.

101. Ham, *Kokoda*, 430.

102. Ham, *Kokoda*, 434.

103. Wright, *A Hell of a Way to Die*, 131.

104. Wright, *A Hell of a Way to Die*, 156.

105. Holmes, *Firing Line*, 323.

106. Leckie, Robert. *Helmet for my Pillow*. Garden City, N.Y: Doubleday, 1979. (271)

107. Denfeld, *Hold the Marianas*, 97.

108. Ham, *Kokoda*, (517)

109. Denfeld, *Hold the Marianas*, 206.

110. Schneider, Carl J. *World War II*. New York: Checkmark Books, 2003. (205)

111. Bergerud, *Touched with Fire*, 422.

112. Dexter, David. *The New Guinea Offensives*. Canberra: Australian War Memorial, 1961. (407-408)

113. Bergerud, Eric. Comment on the H-War Internet discussion list. 23 September 2004.

114. Dunnigan, James F. and Albert A Nofi. *The Pacific War Encyclopedia*. New York: Checkmark Books, 1998. (513)

115. Wright, *A Hell of a Way to Die*, 105.

116. Leckie, *Helmet for my Pillow*, 225.

117. MacDonald Fraser, George. *Quartered Safe Out Here*. London: Harper Collins, 1995. (xx)

118. Dexter, *The New Guinea Offensives*, (520)

119. Young, *Storm from the Sea*, 206.

Chapter 11

1. Todd, Pamela. (Ed.) *Private Tucker's Boer War Diary: The Transvaal War of 1899, 1900, 1901 & 1902 with the Natal Field Forces*. London: Elm Tree Books, 1980. (78; Buller's reference p. 43)

2. Jackson, Murray Cosby. *A Soldier's Diary: South Africa, 1899-1901*. London: Goschen, 1913. (215, 229, 285)

3. Fuller, J. F. C. *The Last of the Gentlemen's Wars: A subaltern's journal of the war in South Africa, 1899-1902*. London: Faber and Faber, 1937. (252)

4. Generally summarised from Denton, Kit. *Closed File*. Adelaide: Rigby, 1983.

5. *Wartime* Magazine. 'Villains or victims?' http://www.awm.gov.au/wartime/18/article.asp. Australian War Memorial. 8 December 2004.

6. Groom, W. H. A. *Poor Bloody Infantry: A memoir of the First World War*. London: Kimber, 1976. (141)

7. Bourke, Joanna. *An Intimate History of Killing: Face-to-face killing in twentieth-century warfare*. London: Granta Books, 1999. (183)

8. Richards, Frank. *Old Soldiers Never Die*. Sydney: Angus & Roberston, 1933. (228)

9. Coles, Alan. *Slaughter at Sea*. London: Robert Hale, 1986. (50,)

10. Rule, EJ, M.C., M.M. *Jacka's Mob*. Sydney: Angus and Robertson, 1933. (161)

11. Graves, Robert. *Goodbye to All That*. London: Penguin, 1960. (153)

12. Holmes, Richard. *Firing Line*. London: Pimlico. 1985. (386)

13. McKee, Alexander. *Caen: Anvil of Victory*. London: Souvenir Press, 1964. (200)

14. McKee, Alexander. *Caen: Anvil of Victory*, in Ellis, John. *The Sharp End*. Great Britain: Windrow and Green, 1990. (318)

15. Barrett, John. *We Were There*. NSW: Allen and Unwin, 1995. (439)

16. Sajer, Guy. *The Forgotten Soldier*. London: Weidenfeld and Nicolson, 1971. (105)

17. Warr, Nicholas. *Phase Line Green: The battle for Hue, 1968*. Annapolis, MD: Naval Institute Press, 1997. (202-203)

18. Dockery, Martin J. *Lost in Translation: Vietnam, a combat advisor's story*. New York: Presidio Press, 2003. (83)

19. Adlin, Mark. *Goose Green*. London: Leo Cooper, 1992. (231)

20. Rush, Robert Sterling. *Hell in Hurtgen Forest*. Kansas: University Press of Kansas, 2001. (249)

21. Phillips, C. E. Lucas. *The Greatest Raid of All*. London: Readers Book Club, 1958. (227)

22. Griffiths-Marsh, Roland. *The Sixpenny Soldier*. NSW: Angus and Robertson, 1990. (172-175)

23. Hastings, Max. *Armageddon: The Battle for Germany 1944-1945*. USA: Macmillan, 2004. (53)

24. Young, Peter. *Storm from the Sea*. Great Britain: Wren's Park Publishing, 2002. (52)

25. MacDonald, *A Time for Trumpets: The untold story of the Battle of the Bulge*. New York: Morrow, 1984. 229.

26. Hackworth, Colonel David H. and Julie Sherman. *About Face*. Melbourne: Macmillan, 1989. (55)

27. Hackworth and Sherman, *About Face*, 66.

28. Hackworth and Sherman, *About Face*, 105-106.

29. Knox, Donald. *The Korean War: An Oral History*. San Diego: Harcourt Brace Jovanovich, 1985. (98)

30. Knox, *The Korean War*, 117-188.

31. Kelly, Jeff. *DMZ Diary: A combat marine's Vietnam memoir*. (131)

32. Caputo, Philip. *A Rumor of War*. New York: Holt, Rinehart and Winston, 1977. (118-119)

33. Caputo, *A Rumor of War*, 228-229.

34. Dao, Quynh. 'Vietnam protesters fall silent'. *The Australian*. http://www.theaustralian.news.com.au/common/story_page/0,5744,15116942%255E7583,00.html 29 April 2005.

35. Sajer, Guy. *The Forgotten Soldier*. London: Weidenfeld and Nicolson, 1971. (119)

Chapter 12

1. Longford, Elizabeth. *Wellington – the Years of the Sword*. New York: Harper and Row, 1969. (481)

2. Holmes, Richard. *Acts of War: The behavior of men in battle*. New York: Free Press, 1986. (306)

3. Young, Peter. *Storm from the Sea*. Great Britain: Wren's Park Publishing, 2002. (132)

4. Arthur, Max. *Forgotten Voices of the Second World War*. London: Ebury Press, 2005. (181)

5. Sledge, E. B. *With the Old Breed, at Peleliu and Okinawa*. Novato, Calif: Presidio Press, 1981. (304)

6. Astor, Gerald. *Operation Iceberg: The Invasion and Conquest of Okinawa in World War II*. New York: Donald I. Fine, 1995. (36)

7. Strauss, Ulrich. *The Anguish of Surrender: Japanese POWs of World War II*. Seattle: University of Washington Press, 2003. (38-39)

8. Strauss, *The Anguish of Surrender*, 22.

9. Slim, William. *Defeat into Victory*. London: Cassell, 1956. (538)

10. Metelmann, Henry. *Through Hell for Hitler: A dramatic first-hand account of fighting with the Wehrmacht*. Wellingborough: Stephens, 1990. (65)

11. Sajer, Guy. *The Forgotten Soldier*. London: Weidenfeld and Nicolson, 1971. (301)

12. Sajer, *The Forgotten Soldier*, 410.

13. McKee, Alexander. *Caen: Anvil of victory*. London: Souvenir Press, 1964. (47)

14. *The Canberra Times*. 'Normandy to Berlin: The Third Reich's death throes'. (Review of Barry Turner's *Countdown to Victory*. 1 January 2005. (14)

15. Shirer, William L. *The Rise and Fall of the Third Reich: A history of Nazi Germany*. London: Secker & Warburg, 1960. (227)

16. Ambrose, Stephen E. *Band of Brothers: E Company, 506th Regiment, 101st Airborne: from Normandy to Hitler's Eagle's Nest*. New York: Simon & Schuster, 1992. (223)

17. Shirer, *The Rise and Fall of the Third Reich,* 1088.

18. Metelmann, *Through Hell for Hitler,* 166.

19. Trevor-Roper, HR. *The Last Days of Hitler.* London: Pan, 1972. (92)

20. Webster, Daniel Kenyon. *Parachute Infantry.* USA: Louisiana State University Press, 1994. (178)

21. Speer, Albert. *Inside the Third Reich.* London: Weidenfeld and Nicolson. 1970. (423)

22. Hastings, Max. *Armageddon: The Battle for Germany 1944-1945.* USA: Macmillan, 2004. (160)

23. Metelmann, *Through Hell for Hitler,* 183.

24. Holmes, *Acts of War,* 268.

25. Gadd, Charles. *Line Doggie.* California: Presidio Press, 1987. (104)

26. Rule, E. J. MC, MM. *Jacka's Mob.* Sydney: Angus & Robertson, 1933. (71)

27. Rule, *Jacka's Mob,* 72.

28. Coles, Alan. *Slaughter at Sea.* London: Robert Hale, 1986. (151)

29. Barrett, John. *We Were There.* NSW: Allen and Unwin, 1995. (251)

30. Bourke, Joanna. *An Intimate History of Killing: Face-to-face killing in twentieth-century warfare.* London: Granta Books, 1999. (189)

31. Marks, Thomas Penrose. *The laughter goes from life: in the trenches of the First World War.* London: Kimber, 1977. (124-131)

32. Sajer, Guy. *The Forgotten Soldier.* London: Weidenfeld and Nicolson, 1971. (176)

33. Jennings, Christian, and Adrian Weale. *Green-eyed boys: 3 Para and the battle for Mount Longdon.* London: HarperCollins, 1996. (149-150)

34. Jennings and Weale. *Green-eyed boys,* 135.

35. Sajer, Guy. *The Forgotten Soldier.* London: Weidenfeld and Nicolson, 1971. (186)

36. Gray, J. Glenn. *The Warriors: Reflections on men in battle.* New York: Harper & Rowe, 1967. (139)

37. Rush, Robert Sterling. *Hell in Hurtgen Forest.* Kansas: University Press of Kansas, 2001. (258)

38. Rush, *Hell in Hurtgen Forest,* 317.

39. Webster, Daniel Kenyon. *Parachute Infantry.* USA: Louisiana State University Press, 1994. (162-166)

40. Crozier, Brigadier-General FP. *A Brass Hat in No Man's Land.* London: J. Cape, 1930. (111)

41. Webster, *Parachute Infantry,* 14.

42. Ambrose, *Band of Brothers.* (63, 65)

43. Grider, John MacGavock. *Diary of an Unknown Aviator.* College Station: Texas A&M University Press, 1988. (See page 199) Cobby's *High Adventure* also refers to this practice – p. 107.

44. Robinson, Derek. *Goshawk Squadron.* Great Britain: Sphere, 1981. (155-156)

45. Brownell, RJ *From Khaki to Blue.* Canberra: The Military Historical Society of Australia, 1978. (174)

46. *In Their Own Words.* http://www.worldwar1.com/dbc/ow_6.htm 8 September 2004.

47. Rule, *Jacka's Mob*, 200.

48. Marks, *The Laughter goes from Life*, 76.

49. Christopher, John. *Balloons at War: Gasbags, Flying Bombs and Cold War Secrets*. Stroud [England]: Tempus, 2004. (69-70)

50. Bishop, William Avery. *Winged Warfare*. Folkestone: Bailey Brothers and Swinfen, 1975. (113)

51. Cobby, Group Captain AH. *High Adventure*. Melbourne: Robertson and Mullens, 1942. (111)

52. Cable, Boyd. *Airmen O'War*. London: John Murray, 1918. (176-177)

53. Luvaas, Jay. (Editor and translator) *Napoleon on the Art of War*. New York: Touchstone, 1999. (56)

54. Kiley, Kevin F. *Artillery of the Napoleonic Wars 1792-1815*. London: Mechanicsburg, PA: Stackpole Books, 2004. (28)

55. Terraine, John. *The Smoke and the Fire*. London: Sidgwick and Jackson, 1980. (173 and 132)

56. Dunnigan, James. *How to Make War*. New York: William Morrow and Company, 1982. (65)

57. De Houst, Major Walter F. 'Offensive Air Operations of The Falklands War'. Marine Corps Command and Staff College, Marine Corps Development and Education Command Quantico, Virginia. 2 April 1984. http://www.globalsecurity.org/military/library/report/1984/DWF.htm Major De Houst cites as his source 'The Force of Our Force,' AEROSPACIO, September/ October 1982, p. 67.

58. Ward, Commander 'Sharkey', DSC, AFC, RN. *Sea Harrier over the Falklands*. London: Leo Cooper, 1992. (239-240)

59. See the opening pages of *The Geneva Conventions of August 12, 1949*, for an outline of how the rules of war were formalised.

60. International Committee of the Red Cross. *The Geneva Conventions of August 12, 1949*. Geneva. The Geneva Convention Relative to the Treatment of the Prisoners of War of August 12, 1949. Article 62. Working Pay. 'Prisoners of war shall be paid a fair working rate of pay by the detaining authorities direct. The rate shall be fixed by the said authorities, but shall at no time be less than one-fourth of one Swiss franc for a full working day'.

61. International Committee of the Red Cross. *International Law Concerning the Conduct of Hostilities*. 'Hostilities'. Geneva: International Committee of the Red Cross, 1996. (22)

62. International Committee of the Red Cross. *International Law Concerning the Conduct of Hostilities*. 'Rules of Air Warfare'. Drafted by a commission of jurists at The Hague. December 1922 – February 1923. Chapter IV, Article 20. Geneva: International Committee of the Red Cross, 1996.

63. Additional to the Geneva Conventions of 12 August 1949, and relating to the Protection of Victims of International Armed Conflicts, 8 June 1977. http://www.genevaconventions.org/ May 2005.

64. Largely paraphrased from Devlin, Sir Patrick. 'Morals and the Criminal Law'. *Philosophy and Contemporary Issues*. USA: Macmillan, 1976. (233- 245)

65. See 'The Subjectivity of Values', in Mackie, JL. *Ethics: Inventing Right and Wrong.* Middlesex: Penguin, 1978.

66. Norman, Richard. *Ethics, Killing and War.* New York: Cambridge University Press, 1995. (72)

67. Quoted in Norman. *Ethics, Killing and War.* (73)

68. MacDonald, Charles B. *A Time for Trumpets: The untold story of the Battle of the Bulge.* New York: Morrow, 1984. (304)

69. Hastings. *Armageddon.* (210)

70. Lane, Mark. *Conversations with Americans.* New York: Simon and Schuster, 1970. (92)

71. Terkel, Louis. *The Good War: An oral history of World War Two.* New York: Pantheon Books, 1984. (61)

72. Astor. *Operation Iceberg.* (451)

73. Dellums (House Of Representatives) War Crimes Hearings, Washington, DC, 1971. http://members.aol.com/warlibrary/vwch7.htm September 2004.

Chapter 13

1. Middlebrook, Martin. *The Kaiser's Battle.* Penguin: London, 2000. (188)

2. Coppard, George. *With a Machine Gun to Cambrai: The tale of a young Tommy in Kitchener's army 1914-1918.* London: H.M.S.O, 1969. (82)

3. Jones, Albert James. *Corporal Jones' War: The Diary of an ANZAC.* Perth, W.A.: Black Swan Press, 2005. (50)

4. Cull, W. Ambrose. *At All Costs.* Melbourne: Australasian Authors' Agency, 1919. (93)

5. Graves, Robert. *Goodbye to All That.* London: Penguin, 1960. (111)

6. Middlebrook, Martin. *The Kaiser's Battle.* (215)

7. Murphy, Audie. *To Hell and Back.* New York: Holt, Rinehart and Winston. 1949. (175)

8. McKee, Alexander. *Caen: Anvil of victory.* London: Souvenir Press, 1964. (217)

9. Schneider, Carl J. *World War II.* New York: Checkmark Books, 2003. (168)

10. Zorns, Bruce C. *I Walk Through the Valley: A World War II infantryman's memoir of war, imprisonment, and love.* Jefferson, N.C: McFarland & Co., 1991. (111)

11. Hart, Peter. *To the Last Round: The South Notts Hussars, 1939-1942.* Barnsley, England: Pen & Sword Books, 1996. (122)

12. Manchester, William. *Goodbye, Darkness: A memoir of the Pacific war.* London: Joseph, 1981. (183)

13. Schneider, Carl J. *World War II.* New York: Checkmark Books, 2003. (223-224)

14. Hallas, James H. *Killing Ground on Okinawa.* Connecticut: Praeger, 1996. (174)

15. Astor, Gerald. *Operation Iceberg: The Invasion and Conquest of Okinawa in World War II.* New York: Donald I. Fine, 1995. (214)

16. Baker, Clive and Greg Knight. *Milne Bay 1942.* NSW: Baker-Knight Publications, 1991. (232)

17. Astor, *Operation Iceberg*, 36.

18. Baker and Knight, *Milne Bay 1942*, 233.

19. Baker and Knight, *Milne Bay 1942*, 254.

20. Williams, Peter. Military Historian. Interview with a 2/2nd Infantry Battalion member of the Australian Army, referring to his experience of the fighting from Sept 1942 to Dec 1942. Interview conducted December 2004.

21. Schneider, Carl J. *World War II.* (218)

22. Lane, Mark. *Conversations with Americans.* New York: Simon and Schuster, 1970. (131)

23. Herr, Michael. *Dispatches.* New York: Knopf, 1977. (5)

24. Moore, Harold G, and Joseph L. Galloway. *We Were Soldiers Once and Young: Ia Drang: the battle that changed the war in Vietnam.* New York: Random House, 1992. (190)

25. Moore and Galloway, *We Were Soldiers Once and Young,* 193.

26. Moore and Galloway, *We Were Soldiers Once and Young,* 284-285.

27. Buick, Bob, with Gary McKay. *All Guts and No Glory.* NSW: Allen and Unwin, 2000. (113-114)

28. On pp. 217-218 Buick discusses this. Another veteran – Terry Burstall – is said to have been quoted in *The Age* newspaper in 1986 saying that 17 enemy were 'murdered', although this does not reconcile with the account in his own work, *The Soldiers' Story: The Battle at Xa Long Tan*, which roughly agrees with Buick.

29. Jennings, Christian, and Adrian Weale. *Green-eyed Boys: 3 Para and the battle for Mount Longdon.* London: HarperCollins, 1996. (168)

30. Jennings and Weale, *Green-eyed Boys,* 147.

31. Jennings and Weale, *Green-eyed Boys,* 154.

32. Bramley, Vincent. *Two Sides of Hell.* Great Britain: Bloomsbury, 1994. (152)

33. McGowan, Robert, and Jeremy Hands. *Don't Cry for Me, Sergeant-Major.* London: Futara, 1983. (74)

34. My Way. 'U.S. Military Investigating Marine Shooting'. http://apnews.myway.com/article/20041116/D86D337G0.html 16 November 2004.

35. *The Canberra Times.* 'Marine filmed killing Iraqi'. 17 November 2004. (2)

36. *The Canberra Times*, 'Marine filmed killing Iraqi', 2.

37. *The Australian.* 'Marine captured in cold-blooded murder'. 17 November 2004. (1) Microfilm copy from the Australian National Library, Canberra.

38. The Insider. http://www.theinsider.org/mailing/article.asp?id=991 2 June 2005.

39. Graves, Robert. *Goodbye to All That.* (134)

40. Hart, Peter. *To the Last Round.* (212)

41. Hallas, James H. *Killing Ground on Okinawa.* (89)

42. Tamayama, Kazuo and John Nunneley. *Tales by Japanese Soldiers.* London: Cassell, 1992. (209)

43. Ambrose, Stephen E. *Citizen Soldiers: The U.S. Army from the Normandy beaches to the Bulge to the surrender of Germany, June 7, 1944–May 7, 1945*. New York, N.Y: Simon & Schuster, 1997. (390)

44. Terkel, Louis. *The Good War: An oral history of World War Two*. New York: Pantheon Books, 1984. (63-64)

45. Tamayam, Kazuo, and John Nunneley. *Tales by Japanese Soldiers*. London: Cassell and Co., 1992. (34)

46. Sajer, Guy. *The Forgotten Soldier*. London: Weidenfeld and Nicolson, 1971. (262)

47. Griffiths-Marsh, Roland. *The Sixpenny Soldier*. NSW: Angus and Robertson, 1990. (318)

48. Clark, Johnnie M. *Guns Up!* New York: Ballantine, 1984. (187-188)

49. Buick, Bob, with Gary McKay. *All Guts and No Glory*. (113)

50. Hallas, *Killing Ground on Okinawa*, 76.

51. Williams, Peter. Military Historian. Interview with Private, 2/31st Infantry Battalion, Gona, Dec 1942. 12 February 2005.

52. Kelly, Jeff. *DMZ Diary: A combat marine's Vietnam memoir*. Jefferson, N.C: McFarland, 1991. (109)

53. Kelly, *DMZ Diary*, 65.

54. McGowan and Hands, *Don't Cry for Me, Sergeant-Major*, 159.

55. Lukowiak, Ken. *A Soldier's Song*. London: Secker and Warburg, 1993. (36-37)

56. *The Washington Post*. 'U.S. Soldier pleads not guilty in Iraqi man's death.' http://www.washingtonpost.com/wp-dyn/articles/A7998-2005Mar28.html 30 March 2005.

57. Graves, *Goodbye to All That*, 112.

58. Macdonald, Lyn. *Somme*. London: Penguin, 1993. (289)

59. Macdonald, Lyn. *They Called it Passchendaele*. London: Penguin, 1993. (192)

60. MacDonald, Charles B. *A Time for Trumpets: The untold story of the Battle of the Bulge*. New York: Morrow, 1984. (400)

61. Bennett, Cam. *Rough Infantry*. Victoria: Warrnambool Institute Press, 1984. (165)

62. White, Osmar. *Green Armour*. Sydney: Angus and Robertson, 1943. (245)

63. Lane, Mark. *Conversations with Americans*. (94-95)

64. Graves, *Goodbye to All That*, 134.

65. Coppard, George. *With a Machine Gun to Cambrai*. (61)

66. Westman, Stephen Kurt. *Surgeon with the Kaiser's Army*. London: Kimber, 1968. (72, 93)

67. Jones, Albert James. *Corporal Jones' War: The Diary of an ANZAC*. Perth, W.A.: Black Swan Press, 2005. (60)

68. Hastings, Max. *Armageddon: The Battle for Germany 1944-1945*. USA: Macmillan, 2004. (169)

69. Hallas, *Killing Ground on Okinawa*, 129.

70. Sledge, E. B. *With the Old Breed, at Peleliu and Okinawa*. Novato, Calif: Presidio Press, 1981. (128)

71.   Sledge, *With the Old Breed,* 216.

72.   McKee, *Caen: Anvil of victory*, 85, 92.

73.   Arthur, Max. *Forgotten Voices of the Second World War*. London: Ebury Press, 2005. (147)

74.   Hastings, *Armageddon,* 87-88.

75.   Phibbs, Brendan. *The Other Side of Time: A Combat Surgeon in World War II*. Boston: Little, Brown, 1987. (138)

76.   McKee, Alexander. *Caen: Anvil of victory*. (239)

77.   Zorns, Bruce C. *I Walk Through the Valley*. (110)

78.   Astor, *Operation Iceberg,* 293.

79.   Price, Colin C. Crewmember – *HMAS Katoomba*, letter written on 24 February 1942 – in the possession of the author; letters to the author December, 1995 to February 1996.

80.   Purves, Frederick, Rear Admiral (retd.) and RAN diver in Darwin, World War II. Letters and annexures, 15 March, May 5 1996. (Letters written by son Robert Purves with his observations also added)

81.   Webster, Daniel Kenyon. *Parachute Infantry*. USA: Louisiana State University Press, 1994. (41)

82.   Brutton, Philip. *Ensign in Italy*. London: Leo Cooper, 1992. (129)

83.   Martin, Charles Cromwell. *Battle Diary: from D-Day and Normandy to the Zuider Zee and VE*. Toronto: Dundurn Press, 1994. (23)

84.   Hastings, Max. *Armageddon*. (255)

85.   Bramley, Vincent. *Two Sides of Hell*. (124)

Chapter 14

1.   Sajer, Guy. *The Forgotten Soldier*. London: Weidenfeld and Nicolson, 1971. (118)

2.   Shirer, William L. *The Rise and Fall of the Third Reich: A history of Nazi Germany*. London: Secker & Warburg, 1960. (952-954)

3.   Metelmann, Henry. *Through Hell for Hitler: A dramatic first-hand account of fighting with the Wehrmacht*. Wellingborough: Stephens, 1990. (75-76)

4.   Sajer, *The Forgotten Soldier*, 119.

5.   Sajer, *The Forgotten Soldier*, 119.

6.   Hastings, Max. *Armageddon: The Battle for Germany 1944-1945*. USA: Macmillan, 2004. (109)

7.   Hastings, *Armageddon,* 249.

8.   Holmes, Richard. *Firing Line*. London: Pimlico. 1985. (385)

9.   MacDonald, Charles B. *Company Commander*. Washington: Infantry Journal Press, 1947. (126)

10.   MacDonald, *Company Commander*, 177-179.

11.   Ambrose, Stephen E. *Band of Brothers: E Company, 506th Regiment, 101st Airborne: from Normandy to Hitler's Eagle's Nest*. New York: Simon & Schuster, 1992. (152)

12. Sym, J. (Ed.) *Seaforth Highlanders*. Aldershot: Gale and Polden, 1962, in Ellis, John. *The Sharp End*. Great Britain: Windrow and Green, 1990. (318)

13. Dunn, Captain JC. *The War the Infantry Knew*. Great Britain: Jane's Publishing Company, 1987. (220)

14. Keegan, John. *The Face of Battle*. London: Pimlico, 2000. (277-278)

15. Kerr, Greg. *Private Wars*. Victoria: Oxford University Press, 2000. (91)

16. Kerr, *Private Wars*, 150.

17. Kerr, *Private Wars*, 153.

18. Kerr, *Private Wars*, 153.

19. McKee, Alexander. *Caen: Anvil of victory*. London: Souvenir Press, 1964. (59)

20. Barrett, John. *We Were There*. NSW: Allen and Unwin, 1995. (440)

21. MacDonald Fraser, George. *Quartered Safe Out Here*. London: Harper Collins, 1995. (190-191)

22. McBride, Glen. *D-Day on Queen's Beach Red: An Australian's war from the Burma Road retreat to the Normandy beaches*. Brisbane, Qld: Prof. G. McBride, 1994. (139)

23. McKee, Alexander. *Caen*. (85)

24. Webster, Daniel Kenyon. *Parachute Infantry*. USA: Louisiana State University Press, 1994. (186-187)

25. Lucas, James. *Last Days of the Reich*. London: Cassell, 1986. (128-129)

26. Brode, Patrick. *Casual Slaughters and Accidental Judgments: Canadian war crimes prosecutions, 1944-1948*. Toronto: University of Toronto Press, 1997. (15)

27. Quarrie, Bruce. *Hitler's Samurai: The Waffen-SS in Action*. New York: Arco Pub, 1983. (105)

28. Young, Peter. *Storm from the Sea*. Great Britain: Wren's Park Publishing, 2002. (206)

29. Harding, William. *A Cockney Soldier*. Devon: Merlin Books, 1989. (143, 146, 147, 210)

30. Barrett, John. *We Were There*. (251)

31. Corey, Private William Thomas. World War II Australian Army infantry soldier SX 5389. Interview with the author, April 2011.

32. Torrent, Andrew, MM. *A 'Day' in the Army*. Western Australia: South West Printing and Publishing Company, no publishing date. (24)

33. Griffiths-Marsh, Roland. *The Sixpenny Soldier*. NSW: Angus and Robertson, 1990. (309)

34. Astor, Gerald. *Operation Iceberg: The Invasion and Conquest of Okinawa in World War II*. New York: Donald I. Fine, 1995. (322)

35. MacDonald Fraser, *Quartered Safe Out Here*, 118.

36. Sajer, *The Forgotten Soldier*, 372.

37. Astor, Gerald. *Operation Iceberg*. (187)

38. MacDonald, Charles B. *A Time for Trumpets: The untold story of the Battle of the Bulge*. New York: Morrow, 1984.. (218-219)

39. MacDonald, *A Time for Trumpets*, 203.

40. MacDonald, *A Time for Trumpets,* 385.

41. Hastings, *Armageddon,* 210.

42. MacDonald, *A Time for Trumpets,* 554.

43. Toland, John. *In Mortal Combat.* New York: Morrow, 1991. (152-153)

44. Knox, Donald. *The Korean War: An Oral History.* San Diego: Harcourt Brace Jovanovich, 1985. (173)

45. Large, Lofty. *One Man's War in Korea.* Wellingborough: Kimber, 1988. (83)

46. Chinnery. (88-89)

47. Toland, *In Mortal Combat,* 129.

48. Chinnery, Philip D. *Korean Atrocity: Forgotten war crimes 1950-1953.* Annapolis, MD: Naval Institute Press, 2000. (129)

49. Chinnery, *Korean Atrocity,* 135.

50. Chinnery, *Korean Atrocity,* 206.

51. Hackworth, Colonel David H. and Julie Sherman. *About Face.* Melbourne: Macmillan, 1989. (136-137)

52. Knox, Donald. *The Korean War.* (185)

53. Knox, *The Korean War.* 229.

54. Knox, *The Korean War.*231.

55. Bransby, Guy. *Her Majesty's Interrogator.* London: Leo Cooper, 1996. (76)

56. Van Zanten, William. *Don't Bunch Up.* Connecticut, Archon, 1993. (160)

57. Caputo, Philip. *A Rumor of War.* New York: Holt, Rinehart and Winston, 1977. (205)

58. Lewy, Guenter. *America in Vietnam.* New York: Oxford University Press, 1978. (334)

59. Kemp, Ian. *British G.I. in Vietnam.* London: Robert Hale, 1969. (137)

60. Lewy, *America in Vietnam,* 333.

61. Santoli, Al. (Ed.) *Everything we Had: An oral history of the Vietnam War.* New York: Random House, 1981. (229-246)

62. McDonough, James R. *Platoon Leader.* CA: Presidio, 1985. (159)

63. McDonough, *Platoon Leader,* 164.

64. Edelman, Bernard. (Ed.) *Dear America: Letters home from Vietnam.* New York: WW Norton and Company, 1985. (74)

65. Santoli, *Everything we Had,* 39.

66. Bradford, Alfred S. *Some Even Volunteered.* Westport: Praeger, 1994. (109)

67. Lukowiak, Ken. *A Soldier's Song.* London: Secker and Warburg, 1993. (150-152)

68. McDonald, Cherokee Paul. *Into the Green.* New York: Penguin, 2001. (39-40)

69. Lane, Mark. *Conversations with Americans.* New York: Simon and Schuster, 1970. (29)

70. Bradford, *Some Even Volunteered,* 75.

71. Lewy, Guenter. *America in Vietnam.* New York: Oxford University Press, 1978. (318)

72. Dellums (House Of Representatives) War Crimes Hearings, Washington, DC, 1971. http://members.aol.com/warlibrary/vwch1d.htm September 2004.

73. Phibbs, Brendan. *The Other Side of Time: A Combat Surgeon in World War II.* Boston: Little, Brown, 1987. (224)

74. Dellums (House Of Representatives) War Crimes Hearings, Washington, DC, 1971. http://members.aol.com/warlibrary/vwch10.htm September 2004.

75. Lane, Mark. *Conversations with Americans.* (39)

76. Lane, *Conversations with Americans,* 53.

77. Bradford, *Some Even Volunteered,* 10-11.

78. Donovan, David. *Once a Warrior King.* USA: McGraw Hill, 1985. (75)

79. Donovan, *Once a Warrior King,* 218-222.

80. Kelly, Jeff. *DMZ diary: A combat marine's Vietnam memoir.* Jefferson, N.C: McFarland, 1991. (42)

81. Essex-Clark, John. *Maverick Warrior.* Victoria: Melbourne University Press, 1991. (152-13)

82. Miller, Franklin, with Elwood JC Kureth. *Reflections of a Warrior.* California: Presidio, 1991. (87)

83. Miller and Kureth. *Reflections of a Warrior,* 110-111.

84. Petersen, Barry, with John Cribbin. *Tiger Men.* Melbourne: Sun Books, 1988. (106)

85. Santoli, Al. (Ed.) *Everything we Hhad* (25)

86. *Toledo Blade* Website. http://www.toledoblade.com/apps/pbcs.dll/article?AID=/20031022/SRTIGERFORCE/110190168 August 2004.

87. Kemp, *British G.I. in Vietnam,* 143.

88. Dellums (House Of Representatives) War Crimes Hearings, Washington, DC, 1971. http://members.aol.com/warlibrary/vwch1d.htm September 2004.

89. Dellums (House Of Representatives) War Crimes Hearings, Washington, DC, 1971. http://members.aol.com/warlibrary/vwch1d.htm September 2004.

90. Department of the Army. *US Army Combat Stress Control Handbook.* USA: Lyons Press, 2003. (59)

91. Gray, J. Glenn. *The Warriors: Reflections on men in battle.* New York: Harper & Rowe, 1967. (145)

Chapter 15

1. Fuller, J. F. C. *The Last of the Gentlemen's Wars: A subaltern's journal of the war in South Africa, 1899-1902.* London: Faber and Faber, 1937. (217)

2. Reitz, Deneys. *Commando: A Boer journal of the Boer War.* London: Faber and Faber, 1931. (See pages 236, 245 and 250 for such examples)

3. Westman, Stephen Kurt. *Surgeon with the Kaiser's Army.* London: Kimber, 1968. (40)

4. Coles, Alan. *Slaughter at Sea.* London: Robert Hale, 1986. (see pp: 42-51 for some explanation)

5.   Bransby, Guy. *Her Majesty's Interrogator*. London: Leo Cooper, 1996. (99)

6.   Webster, Daniel Kenyon. *Parachute Infantry*. USA: Louisiana State University Press, 1994. (72)

7.   McKee, Alexander. *Caen: Anvil of victory*. London: Souvenir Press, 1964. (58)

8.   McKee, *Caen: Anvil of victory*, 315.

9.   Metelmann, Henry. *Through Hell for Hitler: A dramatic first-hand account of fighting with the Wehrmacht*. Wellingborough: Stephens, 1990. (83-84)

10. Metelmann, *Through Hell for Hitler*, 67.

11. Sajer, Guy. *The Forgotten Soldier*. London: Weidenfeld and Nicolson, 1971. (33)

12. Sajer, *The Forgotten Soldier*, 338-339.

13. Sajer, *The Forgotten Soldier*, 367.

14. Graves, Robert. *Goodbye to All That*. London: Penguin, 1960. (100)

15. Jones, Albert James. *Corporal Jones' War: The Diary of an ANZAC*. Perth, W.A.: Black Swan Press, 2005. (53)

16. McKee, *Caen: Anvil of victory*, 197.

17. Crozier, Brigadier-General FP. *The Men I Killed*. London: Michael Joseph, 1937. (57-58)

18. Bennett, Cam. *Rough Infantry*. Victoria: Warrnambool Institute Press, 1984. (90)

19. McKee, *Caen: Anvil of victory*, 57.

20. Barrett, John. *We Were There*. NSW: Allen and Unwin, 1995. (263-264)

21. Arthur, Max. *Forgotten Voices of the Second World War*. London: Ebury Press, 2005. (53)

22. Phillips, C. E. Lucas. *The Greatest Raid of All*. London: Readers Book Club, 1958. (252-263)

23. Metelmann, *Through Hell for Hitler*, 149.

24. Hastings, Max. *Armageddon: The Battle for Germany 1944–1945*. USA: Macmillan, 2004. (99-100)

25. Metelmann, *Through Hell for Hitler*, 70.

26. Metelmann, *Through Hell for Hitler*, 138.

27. Sajer, *The Forgotten Soldier*, 363.

28. McGowan, Robert, and Jeremy Hands. *Don't Cry for Me, Sergeant-Major*. London: Futara, 1983. (250)

29. Trevor-Roper, HR. *The Last Days of Hitler*. London: Pan, 1972. (92-97)

30. Lucas, James. *Last Days of the Reich*. London: Cassell, 1986. (79)

31. Rivett, Rohan D. *Behind Bamboo*. Sydney: Angus and Robertson Ltd, 1947. (41)

32. DeRose, James F. *Unrestricted warfare: how a new breed of officers led the submarine force to victory in World War II*. New York: John Wiley, 2000. (102, and for other examples 128, and 135, where the *Hokusei Maru* was sunk and her crew of 30 killed.)

33. Schneider, Carl J. *World War II*. New York: Checkmark Books, 2003. (228)

34. Astor, Gerald. *Operation Iceberg: The Invasion and Conquest of Okinawa in World War II*. New York: Donald I. Fine, 1995. (216)

35. Schneider, *World War II,* 237.

36. Young, Peter. *Storm from the Sea.* Great Britain: Wren's Park Publishing, 2002. (82)

37. Harding, William. *A Cockney Soldier.* Devon: Merlin Books, 1989. (134)

38. Arthur, *Forgotten Voices,* 51.

39. Arthur, *Forgotten Voices,* 53. Presumably the rank is an error – lieutenant-commander is a naval term.

40. Knox, Donald. *The Korean War: An Oral History.* San Diego: Harcourt Brace Jovanovich, 1985. (44)

41. Knox, *The Korean War: An Oral History,* 69.

42. Galen, Esther. 'Survivors of Korean War massacre by US soldiers seek investigation'. 17 November 1999. http://www.wsws.org/articles/1999/nov1999/kor-n17.shtml 8 September 2004. See also Korean War Educator. 'The Nogun-ri Controversy' http://www.koreanwar-educator.org/topics/nogunri/p_no_gunri.htm February 2005.

43. United States Army. Department of the Army Inspector General. *No Gun Ri Review.* January 2001. (XVI). www.army.mil/nogunri/BookCoverJan01Summary.pdf

44. United States Army. Department of the Army Inspector General. *No Gun Ri Review.* January 2001. (VI). www.army.mil/nogunri/BookCoverJan01Summary.pdf

45. Large, Lofty. *One Man's War in Korea.* Wellingborough: Kimber, 1988. (51)

46. Knox, *The Korean War: An Oral History,* 277.

47. Toland, John. *In Mortal Combat.* New York: Morrow, 1991. (127)

48. Terkel, Louis. *The Good War: An oral history of World War Two.* New York: Pantheon Books, 1984. (23)

49. Hefron, Peter, American Vietnam veteran. Conversation with the author at The Vietnam War, Thirty Years On Conference. 15 April 2005.

50. Caputo, Philip. *A Rumor of War.* New York: Holt, Rinehart and Winston, 1977. (57)

51. Lewy, Guenter. *America in Vietnam.* New York: Oxford University Press, 1978. (304)

52. Van Zanten, William. *Don't Bunch Up.* Connecticut, Archon, 1993. (22, and 118)

53. McDonough, James R. *Platoon Leader.* CA: Presidio, 1985. (110-111)

54. Buick, Bob, with Gary McKay. *All Guts and No Glory.* NSW: Allen and Unwin, 2000. (69)

55. Van Zanten, *Don't Bunch Up,* 206.

56. Bradford, Alfred S. *Some Even Volunteered.* Westport: Praeger, 1994. (122)

57. Lewy, Guenter. *America in Vietnam.* New York: Oxford University Press, 1978. (309)

58. Wexler, Sanford. *The Vietnam War – an Eyewitness History.* New York: Facts on File, 1992. (115)

59. Mantell, David Mark. *True Americanism: Green Berets and war resisters: a study of commitment.* New York: Teachers College Press, 1974. (157)

60. Hemingway, Al. *Our War was Different.* Maryland: Naval Institute Press, 1994. (120)

61. Adler, Bill (Ed.) *Letters from Vietnam.* New York: EP Dutton and Co., 1967. (15)

62. Herr, Michael. *Dispatches*. New York: Knopf, 1977. (40-41)

63. Calley, William L. *His Own Story*. New York: The Viking Press, 1971. (19)

64. McDonough, James R. *Platoon Leader*. CA: Presidio, 1985. (69)

65. Adler, Bill (Ed.) *Letters from Vietnam*. New York: EP Dutton and Co., 1967. (56))

66. McKee, *Caen: Anvil of victory*, 51.

67. Dockery, Martin J. *Lost in Translation: Vietnam, a combat advisor's story*. New York: Presidio Press, 2003. (88)

68. Buick and McKay, *All Guts and No Glory*, 150.

69. Dockery, Martin J. *Lost in Translation: Vietnam, a combat advisor's story*. (46)

70. Gadd, Charles. *Line Doggie*. California: Presidio Press, 1987. (111-112)

71. *Washington Times*. 'Marine charged in killing of Iraqis'. http://www.washingtontimes.com/national/20050214-121803-1937r.htm 14 February 2005.

72. Petersen, Barry, with John Cribbin. *Tiger Men*. Melbourne: Sun Books, 1988. (110)

73. Hemingway, Al. *Our War was Different*. (174)

74. Gadd, *Line Doggie*, 110.

75. Caputo, *A Rumor of War*, 74.

76. Donovan, David. *Once a Warrior King*. USA: McGraw Hill, 1985. (223)

77. Santoli, Al. (Ed.) *Everything we Had: An oral history of the Vietnam War*. New York: Random House, 1981. (49)

78. Baker, Mark. *Nam: The Vietnam War in the words of the men and women who fought there*. New York: Morrow, 1981. (83)

79. Mantell, David Mark. *True Americanism: Green Berets and war resisters: a study of commitment*. (158-159)

Chapter 16

1. http://www.historylearningsite.co.uk/curtis_lemay.htm

2. Harding, William. *A Cockney Soldier*. Devon: Merlin Books, 1989. (120)

3. Bennett, Cam. *Rough Infantry*. Victoria: Warrnambool Institute Press, 1984. (80)

4. Griffiths-Marsh, Roland. *The Sixpenny Soldier*. NSW: Angus and Robertson, 1990. (172-175)

5. McKee, Alexander. *Caen: Anvil of victory*. London: Souvenir Press, 1964. (65-67)

6. Blandford, Edmund L. *Green Devils – Red Devils: Untold tales of the Airborne Forces in the Second World War*. London: Leo Cooper, 1993. (43-45)

7. Australian Broadcasting Corporation. *Warrior: Reflections of Men at War*. Courtesy Library of the Australian Defence Force Academy, Canberra. 2004. (26'30')

8. Terkel, Louis. *The Good War: An oral history of World War Two*. New York: Pantheon Books, 1984. (417)

9. Hastings, Max. *Armageddon: The Battle for Germany 1944-1945*. USA: Macmillan, 2004. (323)

10. Manchester, William. *Goodbye, Darkness: A memoir of the Pacific war*. London: Joseph, 1981. (184)

11. Hastings, Max. *Armageddon: The Battle for Germany 1944-1945*. Abridged extract courtesy Peter Williams and Greg Blake.

12. Sajer, Guy. *The Forgotten Soldier*. London: Weidenfeld and Nicolson, 1971. (415)

13. MacDonald, Charles B. *A Time for Trumpets: The untold story of the Battle of the Bulge*. New York: Morrow, 1984. (438)

14. Phibbs, Brendan. *The Other Side of Time: A Combat Surgeon in World War II*. Boston: Little, Brown, 1987. (166)

15. Quarrie, Bruce. *Hitler's Samurai: The Waffen-SS in Action*. New York: Arco Pub, 1983. (105)

16. MacDonald, *A Time for Trumpets*, 574.

17. Ambrose, Stephen E. *Band of Brothers: E Company, 506th Regiment, 101st Airborne: from Normandy to Hitler's Eagle's Nest*. New York: Simon & Schuster, 1992. (284-285)

18. Astor, Gerald. *Operation Iceberg: The Invasion and Conquest of Okinawa in World War II*. New York: Donald I. Fine, 1995. (431, 439)

19. McDonough, James R. *Platoon Leader*. CA: Presidio, 1985. (77-78)

20. McDonough, *Platoon Leader*, 188.

21. McDonough, *Platoon Leader*, 190.

22. Mason, Robert. *Chickenhawk*. Middlesex: Penguin, 1984. (266-268)

23. Santoli, Al. (Ed.) *Everything we Had: An oral history of the Vietnam War*. New York: Random House, 1981. (177))

24. Santoli, *Everything we Had: An oral history of the Vietnam War*, 61.

25. Van Zanten, William. *Don't Bunch Up*. Connecticut, Archon, 1993. (205)

26. Clark, Johnnie M. *Guns Up!* New York: Ballantine, 1984. (147)

27. Warr, Nicholas. *Phase Line Green: The battle for Hue, 1968*. Annapolis, MD: Naval Institute Press, 1997. (135)

28. Kemp, Ian. *British G.I. in Vietnam*. London: Robert Hale, 1969. (58)

29. Gadd, Charles. *Line Doggie*. California: Presidio Press, 1987. (97)

30. McDonald, Cherokee Paul. *Into the Green*. New York: Penguin, 2001. (208-212)

31. Santoli, *Everything we Had: An oral history of the Vietnam War*, 253.

32. Donovan, David. *Once a Warrior King*. USA: McGraw Hill, 1985.

33. Gadd, *Line Doggie*, 166-167.

34. Edelman, Bernard. (Ed.) *Dear America: Letters home from Vietnam*. New York: WW Norton and Company, 1985. (96)

35. Dockery, Martin J. *Lost in Translation: Vietnam, a combat advisor's story*. New York: Presidio Press, 2003. (57-58)

36. Edelman, Bernard. (Ed.) *Dear America: Letters home from Vietnam*. (181)

37. Gadd, *Line Doggie*, 156-157.

38. Hemingway, Al. *Our War was Different*. Maryland: Naval Institute Press, 1994. (128-129)

39. Warr, Nicholas. *Phase Line Green: The battle for Hue, 1968*. (136)

40. Hemingway, *Our War was Different*, 156.

41. Hemingway, *Our War was Different*, 162.

42. Bradford, Alfred S. *Some Even Volunteered*. Westport: Praeger, 1994. (83)

43. Kelly, Jeff. *DMZ Diary: A combat marine's Vietnam memoir*. Jefferson, N.C: McFarland, 1991. (52)

44. Kelly, *DMZ Diary*, 164.

45. Scholl-Latour, Peter. *Eyewitness Vietnam*. London: Orbis, 1985. (117)

46. See Lewy, Guenter. *America in Vietnam*. New York: Oxford University Press, 1978. (311-313, and 315)

47. Dellums (House Of Representatives) War Crimes Hearings, Washington, DC, 1971. http://members.aol.com/warlibrary/vwch1c.htm September 2004.

Chapter 17

1. Just, Ward S. *To What End*. Boston: Houghton Mifflin Company, 1968. (147)

2. Hemingway, Al. *Our War was Different*. Maryland: Naval Institute Press, 1994. (74)

3. McDonough, James R. *Platoon Leader*. CA: Presidio, 1985. (134-141)

4. Herr, Michael. *Dispatches*. New York: Knopf, 1977. (29)

5. Santoli, Al. (Ed.) *Everything we Had: An oral history of the Vietnam War*. New York: Random House, 1981. (26)

6. Donovan, David. *Once a Warrior King*. USA: McGraw Hill, 1985. (101)

7. Bradford, Alfred S. *Some Even Volunteered*. Westport: Praeger, 1994. (72-73)

8. Dellums (House Of Representatives) War Crimes Hearings, Washington, DC, 1971. http://members.aol.com/warlibrary/vwch1f.htm September 2004.

9. Caputo, Philip. *A Rumor of War*. New York: Holt, Rinehart and Winston, 1977. (284)

10. Caputo, *A Rumor of War*, 313.

11. Calley, William L. *His Own Story*. New York: The Viking Press, 1971. (82-83)

12. Edelman, Bernard. (Ed.) *Dear America: Letters home from Vietnam*. New York: WW Norton and Company, 1985. (48)

13. Linder, Doug. 'An Introduction to the My Lai Courts-Martial'. http://www.law.umkc.edu/faculty/projects/ftrials/mylai/mylai.htm August 2004.

14. Linder, Doug. 'An Introduction to the My Lai Courts-Martial'. http://www.law.umkc.edu/faculty/projects/ftrials/mylai/mylai.htm August 2004. http://www.law.umkc.edu/faculty/projects/ftrials/mylai/Myl_tmead.htm

15. Calley, *His Own Story*, 124-125.

16. Holmes, Richard. *Firing Line*. London: Pimlico. 1985. (404)

17. Calley, *His Own Story*, 10-11.

18. Calley, *His Own Story*, 147-148.

19. McDonald, Cherokee Paul. *Into the Green*. New York: Penguin, 2001.

20. *The New York Times*. John Kifner. 'Ex-G.I.'s tell of Vietnam brutality'. 29 December, 2003. http://www.xs4all.nl/~stgvisie/VISIE/Vietnam-Criminals.html

21. Department of the Army. *US Army Combat Stress Control Handbook*. USA: Lyons Press, 2003. (65)

22. *The Toledo Blade*. 'Rogue GIs unleashed wave of terror in Central Highlands'. http://www.toledoblade.com/apps/pbcs.dll/article?AID=/20031022/SRTIGERFORCE/110190168 23 August 2004.

23. *The Toledo Blade*. 'Inquiry ended without justice' http://www.toledoblade.com/apps/pbcs.dll/article?AID=/20031022/SRTIGERFORCE/110190168 23 August 2004.

24. Hersh, Seymour M. *My Lai 4*. New York: Random House, 1970. (140-141)

25. Hersh, *My Lai 4*, 177-178.

26. Lewy, Guenter. *America in Vietnam*. New York: Oxford University Press, 1978. (362)

27. Hemingway, *Our War was Different*, 74.

28. Thanhnien News 'Koreans penitent for South Korean war crimes in Quang Nam'. http://www.thanhniennews.com/society/?catid=3&newsid=1453 27 August 2004.

29. Lewy, Guenter. *America in Vietnam*. (327)

30. Dixon, Chris and Luke Auton. (Eds.) *War, Society and Culture: Issues and Approaches*. Brawley, Sean. Hangkuk, Diahan, Korean: Korean Voices of the Wol-nam-jon.American War/Vietnam War. University of Newcastle: Research Group for War, Society and Culture, 2002. (84)

31. Clark, Johnnie M. *Guns Up!* New York: Ballantine, 1984. (227)

32. Lane, Mark. *Conversations with Americans*. New York: Simon and Schuster, 1970. (50)

33. Sheehan, Mark. 'Mark Lane: Smearing America's Soldiers in Vietnam'. http://mcadams.posc.mu.edu/smearing.htm 30 August 2004.

34. Lewy, Guenter. America in Vietnam. New York: Oxford University Press, 1978. (322-323)

35. Lane, Mark. *Conversations with Americans*. New York: Simon and Schuster, 1970. (106)

36. O'Brien, Tim. *If I Should Die in a Combat Zone*. USA: Delacorte Press, 1973. (116) O'Brien notes that names and physical descriptions have been changed.

37. O'Brien, *If I Should Die in a Combat Zone*, 146-147.

38. Lane, Mark. *Conversations with Americans*. New York: Simon and Schuster, 1970. (59)

39. Lifton, Robert Jay. *Home from the War: Vietnam veterans: neither victims nor executioners*. New York: Simon and Schuster, 1973. (118)

40. Lewy, *America in Vietnam*, 356.

41. McKay, Gary. *Vietnam Fragments: An oral history of Australians at war*. North Sydney: Allen & Unwin, 1992. (97)

42. *Sixty Minutes*. CBS Television, USA. Version shown on Channel 9's Australia 'Sunday Show', 13 May 2001.

43. Dellums (House Of Representatives) War Crimes Hearings, Washington, DC, 1971. http://members.aol.com/warlibrary/vwch2.htm September 2004. (Also see http://www.sirnosir.com/archives_and_resources/library/war_crimes/dellums/dellums_2.html) Accessed 2010.

44. Dellums (House Of Representatives) War Crimes Hearings, Washington, DC, 1971. http://members.aol.com/warlibrary/vwch4.htm September 2004.

45. Dellums (House Of Representatives) War Crimes Hearings, Washington, DC, 1971. http://members.aol.com/warlibrary/vwch7.htm September 2004.

46. Hackworth, Colonel David H. and Eilhys England. *Steel my Soldiers' Hearts*. New York: Rugged Land, 2002. (412)

47. Hackworth and England, *Steel my Soldiers' Hearts*, 419.

Chapter 18

1. Phibbs, Brendan. *The Other Side of Time: A combat surgeon in World War II*. Boston: Little, Brown, 1987. (139)

Index

A

A Bridge Too Far 41

Abbott, Corporal 140

Abbott, JHM 65

Aces High 81

Adams, James 205

aerial combat 74–85

   bombing 75, 259

   chivalry 76–81, 153

   killing in cold blood 191–5

   reality 83–5

   surrender and 152–7

Afghanistan 31

aggression 1–2, 16–17

   flying tactics, in 74–85

   training in 37, 58

   women 39

Ahrens, PFC John 43

air raids 259

Aitkeen, Lieutenant 220

Akins, PFC Floyd 180

al-Sahaf, Mohammed 35

Alien 39

Alvarez, Corporal 110

Ambrose, Stephen 5, 49, 130, 158, 209

Band of Brothers 108

Anderson, Lieutenant Colonel CGW 45

Annan, Lieutenant J 27

Archer, Wesley 154

Argentine Air Force 195

Argentine Special Forces 65

Argentine troops *90*, 110

Armidale 224

ARVN 28, 63, 92, 118, 146, 255

Ashworth, Tony

   Trench Warfare, 1914–18: the Live and Let Live System 19

Australia-Vietnam Human Rights Committee 181

Australian Flying Corps 78

Australian Military Handbook (1941) 105

B

Bader, Douglas 76

Bagby, Kenneth W 163

Bairnsfather, Bruce 18, 92, 120

   Bullets and Billets 41

Ball, Albert 80–1, 83

Ball, Royal Navy Stoker LH 44

balloon observers 74, 191–4

Barb 163, 248

Barham, Sergeant Andrew 30, 45, 119, 122

Barker, Signalman George 161

Barnes, Daniel 282

Barr, Nicky 156

Barreto, Felix 73

Barry, Lieutenant Jim 144

Batchelor, Corporal Charles *127*

battle discipline 102–11

Battle for Hurtgen Forest 158, 177–8, 190

Battle of Bardia 141, 146

Battle of Britain 81

Battle of El Alamein 188, 219

Battle of Elandslaagte 140

Battle of Gettysburg 86–7

Battle of Goose Green 62, 157, 177

Battle of Ia Drang 27, 61, 92, 93, 113, 131, 205

Battle of Long Tan 61, 110, 117, 205, 210

Battle of Milne Bay 165, 215

Battle of Muar 45

Battle of Pieter's Hill 172

Battle of Rabaul 165

Battle of the Bulge 23, 43, 147, 198, 212, 224, 263, 286

Battle of the Somme 26–7, 152, 212

Battles of Ypres 20, 27, 138, 151

bayonets, saw-back 66

Beamon, Mike 129

Bean, Captain Charles 220

Bennett, Cam 32, 42, 123, 129, 167, 212, 245, 260

Bergerud, Eric 156, 161, 168, 170

    Touched with Fire: The Land Warfare in the South Pacific 159

Berry, RJ 221

'Berserker', the 39–47

Bethune, Lieutenant Frank P 114

Bezich, Peter 165

Bicks, Captain Charles 161

Bishop, Billy 80, 83, 84, 193

Bishop, PFC John 33

Bleszynski, Nick

    Shoot Straight, You Bastards! 174

The Blue Max 79

body-part souveniring 123–8, *203, 208*

    group loyalty 130–3

    monetary gain, for 128–9

    proof of enemy death 129–3

Boelcke, Oswald 80

Boer War 11, 18, 53, 64, 65, 71, 128, 129, 140, 144, 172, *173*, 173–4

    civilian treatment 242–3

    illegal ammunition 65–6

Boston Transcript 78

Bourke, Joanna 35, 98

    An Intimate History of Killing 1, 2, 130, 170

Boyle, Leo 131

Bradbury, David

    Frontline 181

Bradford, Lieutenant Alfred S 228, 229, 253, 271

Bramley, Vincent 206

    Two Sides of Hell 96

Bransby, Guy 37

Braun, NCO Oberfeldwebel Hans Erich 34

Bridges, Major Tom 27

British Air Force 37

British SAS 24

Brownell, RJ 192–3

Broz, Jack 267

Brutton, Philip 109, 215

Buckner, General Simon 51, 94

Buffington, Herman 249

Buick, Sergeant Bob 7, 205, 210, 252, 255

Buller, Sir Redvers 172

Bullwinkel, Nurse 248

Burford, Private James 57–8

burial parties 116

Burt, Ted 44

C

Calley, Lieutenant William 2, 7, 273–7
   His Own Story 275
Cambronne, General 183
Camden, Alan 125
Campbell, Kenneth 199, 283
Campin, Private A 69
Caputo, Second Lieutenant (Marine) Philip 26, 34, 51–2, 59, 72, 92, 116, 125, 131, 136, 152, 180, 227, 251, 256, 272–3
Carey, Flight Lieutenant Frank 81
Carnduff, Sergeant 219
Carpenter, William 231
Carrizo, Oscar 139
Carver, Brigadier Michael 31
Cavalry of the Clouds 84
Centurion, Lieutenant Gomez 144
Chapman, Victor 78
Chicago Sun-Times 228
Chinnery, Phillip D 225
Churchill, Winston 147
civilians 10–11
   combatants disguised as 249–51
   misidentified targets 251–6
   shipping 248
   spies 245
   targeting for military necessity 259–69
   verification of enemy and 242–58
   verification of target and 256–8
   Vietnam War 264–9
   villages 270–84
   World War II 259–64
Clark, Johnnie 8–9, 25, 33, 73, 113, 115–16, 118, 123, 126, 209, 265, 280
Cobby, AH 83, 154, 193

Cochrane, Second Lieutenant Peter 24, 26, 28, 30, 71, 158
Collins, Major General J Lawton 158
combat behaviours 8–10
   cowardice 102–6
   discipline 102–11
   group loyalty 130–3
   killing enemy wounded 201–16
   killing in cold blood 183–200
   prevalence of lethal behaviour 86–101
   revenge as motivation 64–73, 172–82
combat euphoria 30–47
combat fatigue 105
combat fulfilment 21–9
combat personnel
   the 'Berserker' 39–47
   civilians, disguised as 249–51
   competency in firearms *see* firearms
   discipline 102–11
   enjoyment of combat 30–2
   fulfilment 32–8
   military leadership *see* military leadership
   peacetime, in 96–8
   personal accounts, validity 4–8, 11, 40–1
   rules, playing by 17–21, 285–6
   ultimate warriors 17–29
   women 38–9
Comfort 214
Congressional Medal of Honour 54
Connery, Kevin 24, 97, 189
Connick, Denzil 97
Coppard, George 18–19, 21, 66, 94, 102–3, 104, 120, 132, 140, 202, 213
Coughlin, Sergeant Jack 28, 35, 116
court martials 102, 107
Cousino, Michael 109
cowardice 102–6

Cox, Corporal Lofty 132

Cox, Lieutenant Mark 189

Crombie, John Eugene 189

Crozier, Brigadier-General FP 8, 28, 38, 96, 103, 107, 144, 191, 245

    The Men I Killed 96, 103–4

Cull, Captain Ambrose 117, 141, 202

Cummings, Colonel Clement 160, 204

D

Daniell, Major Robert 203

Darwin 214

Daube, John A 254

Davies, Ken 128

Davis, Neil 181

Davis, Russell 123

    Marine at War 41

Dawn Patrol 78, 81

Day, Corporal James 159

DeHaven, Robert 156

Derrick, TC 'Diver' 45

desecration of dead 112–33

    body-part souveniring 123–33

    cannibalism 164–5

    casual abuse and mockery 115–18

    humour 116–17

    mutilation 118–19, 161

    psychology of 113, 116–17

    rituals 112–13

    souveniring 119–23, *220*

Dickmann, Sturmbannfuhrer 263

Dietrich, Sepp 179

discipline 102–11

Distinguished Conduct Medal 45

Dockery, Martin 11, 40, 63, 118, 146, 177, 255, 266

Donitz Order 163

Donovan, Lieutenant David 229, 256, 265, 271

Dostler, General Anton *225*

Dougherty, Lieutenant Bob 53

Dow, Sergeant Richard 229, 280

Doyle, William 277, 279

Drake, Billy 156

Duncan, Major HG 268

Dunnigan, James

    How to Make War 194

Dyer, Forward Observer Lieutenant 180

E

Easley, General Claude 51

East Timor campaign 30, 45, 113, 119

Eck, Kapitanleutnant Heinz 163

Elliott, Warrant Officer Richard 70

enemy, treatment of 9–10, 66–7

    dehumanisation 116, 132

    desecration of corpses 112–33

Essex-Clark, John 230

Essex Regiment 51

Estes, Lance Corporal Ed 70–1

Evans, Sergeant Iolo 204

Ewart, Driver 118–19

executions

    military offences 102–3, 105, 107

    prisoners 217–33

F

Falco, Art 268

Falklands War 11, 22, 24, 30, 34–5, *36*, 37, 45, *50*, 51, *65*, 66, 96–7, 110, 117, 121–2, 144, 189, 195, 206, 211, 226–7, 243, 247

5th Battalion, Northamptonshire Regiment 246

5th Seaforth Highlanders 219

firearms 88–94

    Lee-Enfield .303 89, 91

    training 89–91

1st Battalion of the Welsh Guards 249

1st Cavalry Division 70

1st Royal Fusiliers 39

1st SS Panzer 45

Fitzpatrick, Sergeant J 22

589th Field Artillery Battalion 23

Flasher 167, 248

flying tactics 74–85

Flynn, Errol 78

Fonck, René 84–5

Ford, Roger 148

4/5th Royal Gurka Rifles 47

4th Dragoon Guards 27

fragging 107

Fraser, George MacDonald 33, 123, 170, 221, 223

fraternisation *138*

Fry, Lieutenant William 83

Fuller, JFC 173, 242

Fusco, 1st Sergeant Pasquale 92

G

Gadd, Charles 10, 62, 91, 92, 116, 121, 187, 255, 256, 265, 266

Gallipoli 32, 129, 150–1, 202, 220, 245

Gallishaw, Corporal John 151

Galloway, Joe 27–8

Garcia, John 251

Gariepy, Sergeant 34, 71, 185

Geneva Conventions 64, 157, 286

   attacking aviators under parachute 196

   killing wounded soldiers 201

   shortcomings 195–9

Genoves, Santiago 96

German Army 105, 185–7, *188*, *196*

   SS motto 185

Gerrie, Captain Jack 214

Gerth, Edwin 193

G.I. Jane 39

Gibbes, Bobby 155

Gloucestershire Infantry 250

Goettge patrol incident 68

Goode, Lieutenant 193

Graves, Robert 19, 22, 42, 57–8, 88, 98, 102, 103, 107, 109, 116–17, 129, 147, 175, 202, 208, 211, 213, 245

Gray, Dominic 22, 97

Gray, J Glenn 9, 17, 59, 66, 120, 132, 139, 190, 232

   The Warriors 59

Gregory, Tony 96

Gregory Jr, PFC Edward 225

Griffiths-Marsh, Roland 22, 43, 52, 89, 123, 124, 147, 148, 178, 209, 223, 260

Groom, Corporal WHA 66, 151, 174

Grossman, Dave 31, 83, 88, 95

   On Killing 86–7

Grossman, Sam 136

Guadacanal 43, 68

Guderian, General 186

Gurka soldiers 46–7

Guynemer, Georges

H

Hackworth, Major David 46, 59, 119, 179–80, 226, 276–7

Hagee, General Michael 32

Haggard, Lieutenant Commander HAV 46

Halpin, Sergeant John 103, 120, 142

Halsey, Admiral William F. 48

Ham, Paul 164

hand-to-hand combat 35

Handcock, Lieutenant Peter J 173–4

Harding, William 156, 222, 249, 260

Harris, Air Marshal 'Bomber' 97, 99, *100*, 259

Harris, WJ 212

Hartmann, Erich 76

Harvey, Tom 270

Hastings, Max 454, 105, 136, 148, 213, 224, 246, 262

Hawkings, Lieutenant William 53

Hayward, Captain Greg 251, 271–2

Heard, Barry 5, 19, 25–6, 40, 121

Heese, Daniel 174

Hefron, Peter 126

Henlye, Captain 190

Herbert, Lieutenant-Colonel Anthony B 280

Hernandez, Lance Corporal Paul 256

Heron, Captain 'Chips' 161

Herr, Michael 116, 118, 126, 271

Higinbotham, Captain Lewis 59

Hill, Royal Marine Edward 47, 91, 214

Himmler, Heinrich 185, 217

Hines, Private J 20

Hitler, Adolf 148, 185, 186

Hitlerjugend (Hitler Youth) 189

Hitler's Willing Executioners 247

HMS *Baralong* 120, 174

HMS *Campbeltown* 183, 246

HMS *Tartar* 32

Holman, Gordon
    Commando Attack 41

Holmes, R Derby 116, 142, 151

Holmes, Richard 132, 150, 175, 275
    Acts of War 53–4

Hoobler, Don 32

Hordern, Sub-Lieutenant Marsden 124, 164

Horta, José Ramos 113, 115

hospital ships 214

Hough, Major Frank O 204

Hough, Richard 261

Houston, Sam 175

Howard, Professor Sir Michael 93

Howard, Sergeant Leonard 108

Hue, battle for 61, 176

Hutchinson, Lieutenant Colonel Graham Seton 103

I

Immelmann, Max 76, 153

Imperial War Museum 102

Incident on Hill 191 232

infantry
    definition 11
    depictions in books and films 41–2
    house to house fighting *262*
    need for 35, 37–8
    prisoner-taking in World War II 157–8
    savagery in combat 16–17
    training 60–1

International War Crimes Tribunal 269

Iraq 2, 24, 31, 35, 122, 207, 211

Isaachsen, Lieutenant-Colonel Cedric 91

Israeli Army 38

Iwo Jima *248*

J

Jacka, Albert 16–17, 55, *56*, 98, 187

Jackson, Murray Cosby 173

Japanese Army *160*, 161
    cannibalism reports 164–5
    Field Service Code (*Senjinkun*) 184
    identification guide *234–9*
    refusal to surrender 158–62, 164–70, 184

Japanese carrier *110*

Japanese infantry 24–5, 68

Jaworski, First Lieutenant Ed 226

Jay, Rocky 58

Johns, Sergeant Robert 165

Johns, WE 153

Johnson, Captain Robert B 125, 228, 232

Jones, Albert 18, 202, 213, 245

Jones, Colonel H 51

Jones, Colonel Tim 24

Jones, Edgar 121

Jones, Private 125

Jordan, Flying Officer AT *169*

Junger, Ernst 39, 152

   The Storm of Steel 26

jus in bello 37

K

Kameyama, Captain Shosaku 68

Keegan, John 139

Keitel, Field Marshal 186

Kelly, Jeff 25, 34, 59–60, 118, 180, 210, 230, 268–9

Kemp, Ian 227, 231, 265

Kendle, Lance-Corporal 9, 30, 67

Kennedy, Ludovic 32, 163

Kerr, Jerry 220

Kerry, Senator John 281

Kibbey, Platoon Commander David 281

Killeen, PFC Francis 250

Killigan, Private 57

Kim Il-Sung 226

King Stephen 188

Klinkhammer, Navy Hospital Corpsman 265

Knowland, George 49, 51

Knowlton, Captain William 46

Kogono, Sub-Lieutenant Sakae 224

Korean War 11, 23–4, 33, 179, 225–6, 249–51

   civilian killings 250

Korgie, PFC Leonard 249–50

Krupinski, Walter 76

Krylov, Captain Vasily 218

Kuribayashi, General 167

L

Ladysmith, siege of 64

Lane, Mark

   Conversations with Americans 125, 295

Lane, Terry 199, 213

Large, Lofty 23–4, 91, 225, 250

Laughlin, Captain Fred 129

Lawlor, Bruce 264

Lawrence, Admiral William 227

Le May, Curtis 259

Lea, Roland 108

Lear, PFC Malcolm 67

Leckie, Robert 128, 168, 170

Lee, Arthur Gould 21, 80, 83, 84

Leinbaugh, Captain 209

LeShan, Lawrence 130

Lewis, Cecil 77

Lewis, CS 19, 32

Lewy, Guenter 253, 269, 279

Liebgott, Joseph 128

Little, Lieutenant Bill 33

Livingston, Major Gordon 231, 269

Lloyd George, Prime Minister 77, 153

Loan, Nguyen Ngoc 181

Locke, Charles 126, 229

Logan, Sam 156

Lopez, Henry 184, 204

Love, Ben 161

Lucas, James 247

Lucy, Corporal John 67

Lukowiak, Ken 118, 129, 211, 228

Lusitania 174, 243

M

MacArthur, Engineer Officer Bob 159

Macauley, Lord 99, 101

McBride, Glen 147, 155, 221

McClean, Lieutenant Doug 167

McCudden, James 83

MacDonald, Charles B 93, 218–19

Macdonald, Donald 53, 65, 71, 140

Macdonald, Lyn 212

McDonald, Paul 228, 265, 276

McDonough, Lieutenant James R 55, 57, 109, 227, 252, 254, 264, 270–1

McDowell, Malcolm 81

McGee, Private Bill 161

McKay, Gary 115

Mackee, Alexander 245

Mackie, JL 197

McLaughlin, Corporal Stewart 52–3, 133

MacMillan, Norman 80

MacNair, Jock 42

Malarkey, Don 131

'Malmedy massacre' 158, 224

Manchester, Sergeant William 43, 54–5, 68, 203

Mannock, Mick 83–4

Manunda 214–15

Maravelas, Louis 165

marine warfare 162, *178*, 224

Marks, Sergeant Thomas 66, 89, 92–3, 94, 189, 193

Marsh, Warrant Officer David 160

Marshall, Lieutenant Michael 47

Marshall, SLA 1–2, 43–4

   Men Against Fire 43–4

Martin, Sergeant Charles 40, 157, 215

Mason, Robert 116, 125, 264

Mattis, Lieutenant General James 31–2

Mauldin, Bill 21, 44, 86

Mavin, Corporal JJ *169*

Maynulet, Captain Rogelio 211

medical units, attacking 213–16

Medina, Captain 274

Menninger, Sergeant CW 249

mercy killing 207–11

Meredith, Sergeant John 177

Merritt, William 72

Metelmann, Henry 18, 70, 105, 107, 137, 149, 184, 185, 187, 217, 244, 246–7

Meyer, Kurt 221, 222

Middlebrook, Martin 27

Miers, Commander ACC *276*

Military Cross 55

military leadership 48–63

military necessity

   killing prisoners 183–200

military operations 17–19

Miller, Franklin 62, 230

Mofflin, Ted 32

Mollison, Lieutenant Colonel Charles 117

Monash, General 104

Montgomery, General 53

Moran, Lord 39–40

Morant, Lieutenant Harry 'Breaker' 173–4

Morgan Private W 138

Moris, A Ashurt 174

Morison, Samuel Eliot 61

Morton, Lieutenant Commander Dudley 'Mush' 45, 162, 248

Muetzel, Second Lieutenant Frank 226

Muir, John 163, 230, 271

Murphy, Audie 16, 17, 46, 55, *82*, 98, 109, 157, 202

Murray, Major Roy 122

Musgrave, George Clarke 140

MV *Behar* 162

MV *Sutley* 162

My Lai massacre 7, 126, 256, 273–7, 279

N

Neiman, Bob 25

New Guinea 45, 53, 91, 132, 164, 165, 168, 176, 204, 210, 212, 222

New Zealand troops *23*

   Maori soldiers 47, *57*

Newman, Lieutenant Colonel AC 51

Niland, Private First Class 22

Nishiji, Staff Sergeant Yasumasa 124

Norman, Richard 197–8

Norwood Jr, John 255

Notley, Daniel 283

Nungesser, Charles 80

O

O'Brien, Major Gilbert 76, 155

O'Brien, Tim 125, 280

O'Connor, Corporal 67–8

officers 48–55

    incompetent 54–5

O'Halloran, Private John 254

Okinawa 22, 24, 33, 67, 108, 115, 121, 128, 148, 159, 199, 204, 208, 209, 214, 249, 251, 263–4

Onan, Chuck 228

101st Airborne Brigade 59, 185, 190, 215, 263, 265, 266

173rd Airborne Brigade 55, 254

Operation Barbarossa 217

Operation Market Garden 49, 178

Opie, LM 167

Oradour-sur-Glane massacre 263

orders to maintain position *114*

Osborn, Kenneth B 228

Oslin, Second Lieutenant Bob 28–9, 71

P

Pacific War Encyclopedia 170

Pantano, Lieutenant Ilario 118

parachutes 74

Parkinson, Private J 139

Parrish, Lieutenant Robert D 129

Patton, General 17, 61, 93, 98, 158

Patton, Sergeant 105

Paulus, General 244

Pavlichenko, Lyudmila 38

Pearson, Lieutenant-Colonel JHC 51

Peiper, Jochen 158

Peleus 163

Peppard, George 79

Petersen, Captain Barry 230, 255–6

Phibbs, Brendan 30, 44, 48, 52, 132, 214, 228, 263, 286

Phillips, Jerry 215

Phong Nhi incident 279

Pinker, Stephen

    The Blank Slate 39

Platoon 2

Platypus 215

Plimpton, Harry 280

Plumley, Sergeant Major Basil 27–8

Pocket Guide to China 234

Pogue, Sergeant Forrest 199

Polanksy, Jonathen 265

Poore, Provost Marshal 174

Porter, R Bruce 156

Potts, Brigadier Arnold 165

Prendergast, Richard M 122

Price, Colin 214

prisoners 136–49

    commandos 148–9

    danger of 137

    executions 217–33

    German *145, 146*

    infantry in World War II 157–8

    Japanese in World War II 158–62, *166, 234–9*

    killing in cold blood 183–200

    logic 136–7

    'Malmedy massacre' 158, 224

    reality 137

    rules of surrender 138–41, 195–9

    snipers 148

    special forces 147–9

    status 141–7

submariners 147

torture 174

Vietnam War 227–33

Purves, Lieutenant Frederick 214

Q

Quynh Dao 181

R

Rabbets, Corporal Edgar 245–6

Raboud, Jacques 261

Ransom Jr, Second Lieutenant Robert C 266, 273

Rather, Dan 281

Reasoner, Frank 54

Reitz, Deneys 243

Rhodes, Captain Anthony 108

Richards, Frank 66, 67, 89, 98, 104, 117, 122, 174

Richey, Paul 81

Rickenbacker, Eddie 20, 75, 80, 83, 84

Roberson, Jimmy 281

Robinson, Derek

Goshawk Squadron 191–2

Robson, Private Fred 220

Rolleston, Private Frank 204

Rommel, Erwin 151

Infantry Attacks 5–6, 41

Rose, Lieutenant-Colonel Mike 24

Rosenblum, Walter 158

Ross, David 257

Royal Flying Corps 77

11th Squadron 83

16th Squadron 79

Royal Irish Fusiliers 38

Royal Irish Regiment 24

Royal Marine Commandos 50

Royal Navy 32

toast 21

Royal Welch Fusiliers 128

Rubitsky, David 17

Rule, EJ 42, 144, 151, 174, 193

Rules of Engagement 2, 17, 97, 177, 251

Rush, Robert Sterling

Military Leadership 109

Russell, Lord

The Knights of Bushido 162

Russian Army 70, 106

refusal to surrender 184

Ryakhovsky, Major Yury 106

S

St Nazaire raid 44, 51, 178, 183, 246

Sajer, Guy 31, 94–5, 107, 115, 119, 129, 131, 137, 176, 181, 184, 189, 190, 209, 217–18, 223, 244, 247, 263

Santa Anna, General 175

Sassoon, Siegfried 9, 19, 30, 41, 42, 67, 102, 103, 115, 122, 131

Saving Private Ryan 182

Scannell, Corporal Vernon 91

Scariano, Anthony 148

Schaefer-Kuhnert, Captain Walter 213

Scholl-Latour, Peter 269

Schoo, Private Donald 224

2nd Parachute Regiment 51

Selby, CJ 107

Senkevich, Dr Nikolai 218

September 11 2001 terrorist attacks 32

Setelin, Sergeant John 92, 131

Severn Leigh 163

Sexton, Martin 26

Sheehan, Mark 280

Sheean, Teddy 224

Sherman, General 26, 52

Siang Wo 247

Simmen, First Lieutenant James 58, 266

Sinclair, Lance Sergeant Ian 120

356

Skorzeny, Lieutenant Colonel Otto 147

Sledge, EB 18, 24, 45, 54, 68, 72, 105, 119, 121, 122, 126, 128, 131, 132, 142–3, 161, 184, 199, 209, 214

    With the Old Breed 41

Slim, General William 24, 30, 159, 184

Slovik, Willy 105

Smith, Corporal Harry Bloodworth 31, 66

SNAFU 6, 18

South Nottingham Hussars 49, 208

Speirs, Lieutenant 108

spies 245

SS *Ascot* 162

SS *British Chivalry* 162

SS *Daisy Moller* 162

SS *Jean Nicolet* 162

SS *John A Johnson* 162

SS *Nancy Moller* 162

SS *Tjisalak* 612

Stanier, Lieutenant-Commander Alexander 249

Steinhoff, Johannes 81

Stewart, Nora 30, 37

Stouffer, Samuel 43

Strauss, Ulrich 164

Strayer, Major Robert 115

submarine warfare 162–3

Sullivan, Corporal 144

surrender

    abuse of 146–7

    aerial combat and 152–7

    enemy refusal 183–91

    Japanese in World War II 158–62, 164–70, 184

    non-acceptance of 150–2

    rules of 138–41, 195–9

    Russians in World War II 184–5

    sea, at 162–3

    special forces 147–9

status of prisoners 141–7

Suzuki, Captain Tadashi 209

Swan, Captain Geoff 204

T

tactical fighting 8–9

Tames, Private Charles 151

Taylor, AJP 198

Taylor, General Maxwell 191

Telling, Edward 107

Terraine, John

    The Smoke and the Fire 194

Thom, Dick 168, 199

Thompson, Captain AAB 79

Timoshenko, Sergeant Nikolai 218

Tirpitz 32

The Toledo Blade 231, 276, 277

Treschman, Private Bert 204

Trevor-Roper, HR 186, 247

Truant 46

Tucker, Frederick 140, 172

12th SS Panzer 71

U

U-37 163

U-852 163

Udet, Ernst 79

United Nations 2

US Army 46, 51, 60–1, 143, *252, 257*

    Combat Stress Control Handbook 232

US Marine Corps, 22, 24, 35, 43, 51, *106,* 124, 161

    1st Tank Battalion 25

    Small Wars Manual 38

USS *Russell* 157

USS *Tinosa* 167

V

Van Zanten, William 126, 227, 252, 253, 265

Veatch, Charles 213

Victoria Cross 45, 51, 55

Viera, Arthur 113

Vietcong (VC) 28–9, 38, 51–2, 62, *73*, 205, 264–8, 271, *282*

    defectors 57

Vietnam War 2, 5, 6, 7, 10–11, 25, 26, 27, 34, 40, 51–2, 57, 58–9, 61–2, 72, 91, 113, 121, 126, 129, 205, 251–6, *267*, 270–82

    Australian Special Air Service 230

    execution of prisoners 227–33

    fragging 107

    Montagnards 230

    My Lai massacre 7, 126, 256, 273–7

    search and destroy operations *272*

    targeting civilians 264–9

    Tiger Force 59, 231, 276, 277–9

von Clausewitz, Carl 18, 53, 259

von Ludendorff, General 97, 259

von Richthofen, Baron Manfred 76, *77*, 119, 152–3

Vouza, Jacob 262

W

Wahoo 45, 162, 167, 248

Wake, Major H 143

Wake, Nancy 39, 42

Walker, Tom 168

war

    necessity, when 2

    outside attitudes 2, 95–6

Ward, Lieutenant Commander 'Sharkey' 195

warfare 95–101

    conventions and rules 3, 17–29, 195–9

    morals and ethics 197–8

    necessary efficiency 16–17

    psychology of defeat 87

Warr, Nicholas 22, 61, 70–1, 119, 176–7, 265, 267

Washington Post 228

Waters, CW 42

Wavell, General 53

We Were Soldiers 27

Webb, Sir William 161

Webster, Daniel 61, 67, 123, 131, 186, 190, 215, 221

Webster, David 32, 14, 191, 243–4

Weeks, Neil 110

Welch, Ronald 41, 53

Westman, Stephen 26, 54, 213, 243

Weston, RJ 9, 10, 47, 142, 145

Whitmore, Terry 280

Willett, PFC Louis 227

Willingham, Captain Thomas K 279

Winnington, Alan 251

'Winter Soldier' case 282–3

Winters, Paratrooper Richard 49

Winters, Richard 219

Witton, George R 173–4

    Scapegoats of the Empire 174

women in combat 38–9

Wood, Lieutenant 23

Wood, WJ

    Leaders and Battles 53

World War I 6, 10, 11, 18–21, 26, 39, 41, 42, 54, 55, 103–4, 140, 243

    flying tactics 75–6, 79

World War II 1, 9–10, 11, 16, 18, 21, *23*, 24, 30, 31, 42, 43–4, 52, 61, 105, 117, *261*

    flying tactics 76

    infantry prisoner-taking 157–8

    targeting civilians 259–64

Wortley, Flying Officer RS 75

wounded enemy, killing 201–16

    attacking medical units 213–16

    mercy killing 207–11

    personal safety 202–7

unit safety 211–13

Wright, Derrick 167

Y

Yamato 224

Yeates, VM

   Winged Victory 154–5

Yokoi, Sergeant Shoichi 168

Young, Peter 31, 44, 143, 159, 165, 170, 179, 183, 222, 249

Z

Zorns, Bruce 67, 202–3, 214

Zulu Wars 89